BORDER CROSSINGS

BORDER CROSSINGS

SECOND EDITION

CULTURAL WORKERS

AND THE POLITICS

OF EDUCATION

HENRY A. GIROUX

Routledge
Taylor & Francis Group

NEW YORK AND LONDON

Published in 2005 by
Routledge
Taylor & Francis Group
270 Madison Avenue
New York, NY 10016

Published in Great Britain by
Routledge
Taylor & Francis Group
2 Park Square
Milton Park, Abingdon
Oxon OX14 4RN

© 2005 by Taylor & Francis Group, LLC
Routledge is an imprint of Taylor & Francis Group

Printed in the United States of America on acid-free paper
10 9 8 7 6 5 4 3 2 1

International Standard Book Number-10: 0-415-95148-8 (Hardcover) 0-415-95149-6 (Softcover)
International Standard Book Number-13: 978-0-415-95148-7 (Hardcover) 978-0-415-95149-4 (Softcover)
Library of Congress Card Number 2004022353

Library of Congress Cataloging-in-Publication Data

Giroux, Henry A.
  Border crossings : cultural workers and the politics of education / Henry A. Giroux.-- 2nd ed.
    p. cm.
  Includes bibliographical references and index.
  ISBN 0-415-95148-8 (hardback : alk. paper) -- ISBN 0-415-95149-6 (pbk. : alk. paper)
  1. Education--United States--Philosophy. 2. Critical pedagogy--United States. 3. Politics and education--United States. I. Title.

  LB885.G47B67 2005
  370.11'5--dc22   2004022353

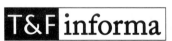

Taylor & Francis Group
is the Academic Division of T&F Informa plc.

Visit the Taylor & Francis Web site at
http://www.taylorandfrancis.com

and the Routledge Web site at
http://www.routledge-ny.com

For Susan, again and again

Contents

Acknowledgments   *ix*

Introduction   *1*

Part I. Schooling and Cultural Politics

1 *Postcolonial Ruptures/Democratic Possibilities*   *11*
2 *Crossing the Boundaries of Educational Discourse:*
   Modernism, Postmodernism, and Feminism   *31*
3 *Redefining the Boundaries of Race and Ethnicity:*   *83*
   Beyond the Politics of Pluralism

Part II. Cultural Workers and Cultural Pedagogy

4 *Critical Pedagogy and Cultural Power:*   *123*
   An Interview with Henry A. Giroux
5 *Cultural Studies, Resisting Difference and*   *137*
   the Return of Critical Pedagogy
6 *Popular Culture as a Pedagogy of Pleasure and*   *157*
   Meaning: Decolonizing the Body

Part III. Neoliberalism and the Militarization
of Public Space

7 *Interview: Politics of Radical Pedagogy*   *187*
8 *Challenging Neoliberalism's New World Order:*   *209*
   The Promise of Critical Pedagogy
9 *Education after Abu Ghraib: Revisiting*   *221*
   Adorno's Politics of Education

Index   *255*

Acknowledgments

In developing the second edition of this book, I received a great deal of support from my wife, Susan Searls Giroux, as well as from my graduate students Christopher Robbins, Jake Kennedy, and Grace Pollock. As I complete this work, I find myself writing from the perspective of someone who has become an immigrant, living in Canada and teaching at McMaster University. Given this experience, "border crossing" has become not just an intellectual metaphor, but also a deeply personal one for me. I am especially grateful to Nasrin Rahimieh, the dean of the faculty of humanities at McMaster, for providing me with such generous support while I was writing this book. I also want to thank Catherine Bernard, my editor at Routledge, for her support and encouragement in convincing me to write a second edition of *Border Crossings*.

Portions of this book have appeared elsewhere in different form. I extend my gratitude to the publishers for permission to make use of the following materials: versions of Chapter 2 first appeared in *College Literature* 17 (1990), © West Chester University; Chapter 3 was published in a shorter version in *Postmodernism, Feminism, and Cultural Politics* (1990), © State University of New York Press. The interview in Chapter 4 was published in *Afterimage* 18 (1990). A different version of Chapter 6 was published in *Cultural Studies*. Chapter 7 was published in *Education, Power, and Personal Biography: Dialogues with Critical Educators*, Carlos Alberto Torres, Ed., Routledge, 1998. Chapter 8 was largely published in *Tikkun*.

place in any viable social and educational theory. In an era of unprecedented global flows both real and virtual, the ethics and politics of border crossing appear more pressing to the current historical juncture than when I first engaged the concept over a decade ago. For me, the concept of borders provides a continuing and crucial referent for understanding the co-mingling—sometimes clash—of multiple cultures, languages, literacies, histories, sexualities, and identities. Thinking in terms of borders allows one to critically engage the struggle over those territories, spaces, and contact zones where power operates to either expand or to shrink the distance and connectedness among individuals, groups, and places. In the broader political sense, the concept of borders and border crossing serves to highlight that the goal of politics is transformative of both relations of power as well as public consciousness.

With the accelerated growth of global markets, borders, ironically, appear more constrained than ever before as the ever-widening gap between the rich and the poor leads to greater insecurity and instability. New forms of authoritarianism and militarism now attempt to contain oppressed groups, reduce citizenship to consumerism, and wage war on every conceivable sphere of public life. The porousness of borders in the afterglow of the toppled Berlin Wall became impervious fortresses in the new millennium, a militarized response to a world plunged into the Great War Against Terror. The proliferation of policed borders not only requires a new politics, but also a new political vocabulary and a strategy of resistance through which a public pedagogy can be forged capable of constructing what Chandra Mohanty calls forms of "transborder democratic citizenship."[1] The concept of a borderless world as used in this book, while seemingly utopian, speaks powerfully to both deconstructing the meaning of globalization and redefining it around democratic values rather than through the ideology of market fundamentalism and its ever-growing alliance with the forces of militarism.

I am convinced that the mutually related concepts of borders and border crossing are even more timely today in light of the growing need on the part of many educators, progressives, artists, and cultural workers to rethink the meaning of politics for the twenty-first century. As war, fear, and virulent contempt for social needs have become the dominant motifs shaping the domestic and foreign policies of the United States, borders have become the primary category for signifying spaces of confinement, internment, punishment, surveillance, and control. A militarization of public life has emerged under the combined power and influence of neoliberal zealots, religious fanatics, and far right-wing neo-conservatives who currently control the United States government. The primacy of a politics of constraining borders is seen also in the destruction of a liberal democratic political order and a growing culture of surveillance, inequality, and cynicism. As the United States increasingly imprisons more of its poor youth of color, rings the globe with military bases, transforms agencies for immigration into those of homeland security, and expands the imperatives of empire in a reckless invasion and occupation of Iraq, the signs of a highly militarized society become more visible than ever. In a post-September 11th world, American power is being restructured domestically around a growing culture of fear and a rapidly increasing militarization of public space and culture. As U.S. military action is spreading under the guise of an unlimited war against terrorism, public spaces on the domestic front are increasingly being organized around values supporting a highly militarized, patriarchal, and jingoistic culture that is undermining centuries of democratic gains. Borders increasingly appear more rigid, entrenched, and impassible as the United States moves inexorably toward a more closed and authoritarian society.

We are living in dangerous times in which a new type of post-democratic society is emerging, one that builds on ancient historical tendencies but is unlike anything we have seen in the past—a society in which concentrated economic and political power reinforce each other through a media consolidated in the hands of a few multinational corporations. Unlike any other time in American history, we are living in a period in which a culture of fear and concentrated wealth reinforce each other so as to drastically limit the possibilities of a democratic society. Not only are civil liberties being rolled back, and public resources gutted because of a massive $422 billion deficit, but power no longer appears to reside largely within the sphere of politics, controlled largely by nation states. Power is now set free from its political shackles and resides primarily with economic and military forces. Political power is being replaced by economic power just as state sovereignty is being replaced by corporate sovereignty.[2] Power has now become coercive, roaming the globe for new markets under the guise of American triumphalism and the quest for the rewards of empire. The United States is increasingly marked by a poverty of critical public discourse, making it more difficult for the American people to appropriate a critical language outside of the market that would allow them to link private problems to public concerns and issues. Within this utterly privatized discourse, politics conceived as public activity is replaced with a politics that is banal, reduced to the politics of lifestyle choices, tabloid spectacle, or "patriotic" conformism. One result is a social order that seems dangerously incapable of questioning itself, even as it wages a merciless, top-down war against the poor, the young, women, people of color, and the elderly.

The obsession with the private (even as the right to privacy evaporates) not only burdens politics and undermines critical forms of individual and social agency, it also negates any viable notion of the public good and the social contract. As the social contract is shredded, government relies more heavily on its policing and military functions, giving free reign to the principle of security and border patrols at the expense of an open, free society. A culture of fear now overshadows a commitment to public service, endorsing property rights over human rights. A spreading culture of fear in an age of automated surveillance and repressive legislation is creating a security state that gives people the false choice between being safe or being free. Even as surveillance cameras make their way into the nation's public schools and FBI agents hang out in libraries and bookstores in order to examine what people are reading, there is barely a protest from academics or the general public over the shredding of constitutional freedoms and civil liberties. It gets worse. The CIA and the Pentagon are now allowed to engage in domestic intelligence work; the Patriot Act allows people to be detained indefinitely in secret *without* access to either lawyers or family; children are not only held without legal representation as enemy combatants in possibly inhumane conditions at the military's infamous Camp Delta at Guantanamo Bay, but they are also subjected to abuse and torture by American soldiers at the infamous Abu Ghraib prison in Iraq.[3] The war against terrorism increasingly appears to be a war against immigrants, dissent, and democracy itself as the racial state extends the ugly reach of discrimination under the guise of Homeland Security.[4] Under such circumstances, the fundamental governing principles of democracy are not just being subverted but deliberately sabotaged. This kind of democracy is the problem, not the solution.

What all this suggests is that since *Border Crossings* was written, the American state has changed radically. No longer viewed as a force for the public good and social justice, it now operates largely as a legitimating force for corporate power, willingly disposed to serve the needs of concentrated wealth, racial disparity, corporate global-ization, and empire. Under the pressure of a relentless campaign of top-down class, racial, and ideological warfare, the state is being hollowed out and the public sector is being stripped not only of its positive social and democratic functions, but is increasingly reduced to its policing and repressive functions.

In the shadow of the tragic and horrible events of September 11th, a brute authoritarianism becomes increasingly more ominous as society is organized relentlessly around a culture of fear, cynicism, and unbridled self-interest. Within this post-9/11 space, matters of politics and pedagogy coincide to produce a new kind of authoritarianism, one in which consent is manufactured and the militarization of every-day life proceeds largely unchallenged. While critical pedagogy was a fundamental con-cept for expanding the possibility of democracy in the first edition of *Border Crossings*, my focus has now shifted to the broader concept of public pedagogy which, I argue, is essential to defining the nature of politics itself. At the dawn of the new millennium, an authoritarian regime proceeds within the parameters of what I call a new kind of public pedagogy, one in which the production, dissemination, and circulation of ideas emerges from the educational force of the entire culture. Public pedagogy in this sense refers to a powerful ensemble of ideological and institutional forces whose aim is to produce competitive, self-interested individuals vying for their own material and ideo-logical gain. Corporate public pedagogy now largely cancels out or devalues gender, class-specific, and racial injustices of the existing social order by absorbing the demo-cratic impulses and practices of civil society within narrow economic relations. This form of dominant public pedagogy has become an all-encompassing cultural horizon for producing market identities, values, and practices. The good life, in this discourse, "is construed in terms of our identities as consumers—we are what we buy."[5] For example, the Pentagon even considered, if only for a short time, turning the war on terror and security concerns over to futures markets, subject to online trading. Thus, non-commodified public spheres are replaced by commercial spheres as the substance of critical democracy is emptied out and replaced by a democracy of goods available to those with purchasing power and to the increasing expansion of the cultural and political power of corporations throughout the world.

Dominant public pedagogy with its narrow and imposed schemes of classification and limited modes of identification uses the educational force of the culture to negate the basic conditions for critical agency. As public space is increasingly commodified and the state is aligned more closely with capital, public pedagogy mobilizes power in the interest of a Darwinian world order marked by the increasing removal of autonomous spheres of cultural production such as journalism, publishing, and film; the destruction of collective structures capable of counteracting the widespread imposition of commercial values and effects of market forces; the creation of a global reserve army of the unemployed; and the subordination of nation-states to the real masters of the economy.

As I point out in the third section of *Border Crossings*, the new sites of public pedagogy which have become the organizing force of market fundamentalism are not restricted to instrumental curricula, blackboards, and test taking. They do not simply incorporate the limited forms of address found in schools. Such sites operate within a wide variety of social institutions and formats including sports and entertainment media, cable television networks, the Internet, churches, and channels of elite and popular culture such as advertising. Profound transformations have taken place in the public sphere, producing new sites of pedagogy marked by a distinctive confluence of new digital and media technologies, growing concentrations of corporate power, and unparalleled meaning-producing capacities. Unlike traditional forms of pedagogy, knowledge and desire are inextricably connected to modes of pedagogical address mediated through unprecedented electronic technologies that include high-speed computers, new types of digitized film and CD-ROMs. The result is a public pedagogy that plays a decisive role in producing a diverse cultural sphere that gives new meaning to education as a political force. What is surprising about the cultural politics of market fundamentalism is that many social theorists have either ignored or largely underestimated the symbolic and pedagogical dimensions of the struggle that neoliberal corporate power has put into place for the last twenty years, particularly under the ruthless administration of George W. Bush.

In the years since I have written *Border Crossings*, neoliberalism—with its unbridled support of the market as a template for all social and economic relations—has become the hegemonic ideology of our time. Much more than an economic theory, neoliberalism can also be defined as a cultural politics, one that created an array of institutions

used unmuzzled military police dogs "to make juveniles—as young as 15 years old—urinate on themselves as part of a competition." See Josh White and Thomas E. Ricks, "Iraqi
Teens Abused at Abu Ghraib, Report finds," *The Washington Post* (August 24, 2004), AO1.

4. I have taken up this issue extensively in Henry A. Giroux, *The Terror of Neoliberalism* (Boulder, CO: Paradigm Press, 2004).

5. Alan Bryman, *Disney and His Worlds* (New York: Routledge, 1995), 154.

6. Nick Couldry, "In the Place of a Common Culture, What?" *The Review of Education, Pedagogy, and Cultural Studies* 26: 1 (2004), 4.

I

Schooling and
Cultural Politics

Postcolonial Ruptures/
Democratic Possibilities

The choice of language and the use to which it is put is central to a people's definition of themselves in relation to their natural and social environment, indeed in relation to the entire universe.[1]

I begin this chapter with a quote from Ngugi Wa Thiong'o, an African writer who is in the forefront of postcolonial struggles to redefine meaning as a historical and social construction. At stake here is not merely the refusal to take language for granted but to understand how it is produced and rewritten within the ideological and material legacies of imperialism and colonialism. Hence, it is in the domain of language that the traces of a theoretical and political journey begin to emerge as part of a broader attempt to engage meaning as a form of social memory, social institutions as powerful carriers and legitimators of meaning, and social practices as sites in which meaning is re-invented in the body, desire, and in the relations between the self and others.

Language in all of its complexity becomes central not only in the production of meaning and social identities but also as a constitutive condition for human agency. For it is in language that human beings are inscribed and give form to those modes of address that constitute their sense of the political, ethical, economic, and social.

This book is about what is often called the crises in meaning and authority that have beset many of the Western democracies in the 1990s. Of course, any one crisis can be refigured to secure the authority of a specific ideological position. My interest is not to secure the authority of a totalizing narrative that enshrines truth as a science and agency as a universalizing category. Rather I attempt to challenge the authority and discourses of those practices wedded to the legacy of a colonialism that either directly constructs or is implicated in social relations that keep privilege and oppression alive as active constituting forces of daily life within the centers and margins of power. Within the currency of the language of cultural crisis and authority, postcolonial discourses have pushed against the politics of such crises by inserting the primacy of a politics of difference and struggle. They scan the surface language that constructs such crises and ask: which crisis, for whom is there a crisis, and who speaks in the name of such a crisis? "How do we construct a discourse, which displaces the effects of the colonizing gaze while we are still under its influence?"[2] Postcolonialism challenges how imperial centers of power construct themselves through the discourse of master narratives and totalizing systems; they contest monolithic authority wielded through representations of "brute institutional relations" and the claims of universality. Postcolonial theorists offer resistance to social practices that relegate otherness to the margins of power; they interrogate how centers of power and privilege are implicated in their own politics of location as forms of imperializing appropriation; and, of crucial importance, postcolonialism contests the dominant Eurocentric writing of politics, theory, and history. In effect, postcolonial discourses have not only redefined a new cultural politics of difference, they have also helped to create a new amalgam of cultural workers whose distinctive features are, according to Cornel West:

> to trash the monolithic and homogenous in the name of diversity, multiplicity, and heterogeneity; to reject the abstract, general, and universal in light of the concrete, specific, and particular; and to historicize, contextualize and pluralize by highlighting the contingent, provisional, variable, tentative, shifting, and changing . . . what makes these [gestures] novel—along with the cultural politics they produce—is how and what constitutes difference, the weight and gravity it is given in representation, and the way in which highlighting issues like exterminism, empire, class, race, gender, sexual orientation, age, nation, nature, and region at this historical moment acknowledges some of the discontinuity and disruption from previous forms of cultural critique.[3]

Postcolonial discourses have also made clear that the old legacies of the political left, center, and right can no longer be so easily defined. Indeed, postcolonial theorists have gone further and provided important insights into how such discourses either actively construct colonial relations or are implicated in their construction. From this perspective, Robert Young argues that postcolonialism is a dislocating discourse that raises theoretical questions regarding how dominant and radical theories "have themselves been implicated in the long history of European colonialism—and, above all, the extent to which [they] continue to determine both the institutional conditions of knowledge as well as the terms of contemporary institutional practices—practices which extend beyond the limits of the academic institution."[4] This is especially true for many of the new social movements that have taken up the language of difference and a concern with the politics of the other. Many theorists within these movements have addressed a number of pressing political and pedagogical issues through the construction of binary oppositions that represent both a new vanguardism while simultaneously falling into the trap of simply reversing the old colonial legacy and problematic of oppressed vs. oppressor. In doing so, they have often unwittingly imitated the colonial model of erasing the complexity, complicity, diverse agents, and multiple situations that constitute the enclaves of colonial/hegemonic discourse and practice.[5]

In this chapter, and throughout this book, I will argue that postcolonial theory, in its many varieties, provides the possibility of both challenging and transforming a cultural politics formed in binary oppositions that both silence and invite people to deskill themselves as educators and cultural workers. The challenge that postcolonialism presents to educators and cultural workers calls for new ideas, pedagogical strategies, and social movements capable of constructing a politics of difference within critical public cultures forged in the struggle to deepen and extend the promise of radical and cultural democracy. This suggests a politics and pedagogy developed around new languages capable of acknowledging the multiple, contradictory, and complex subject positions people occupy within different social, cultural, and economic locations. At issue here is a challenge to the growing anti-intellectualism and theoretical reductionism that have become characteristic of so much critical educational theory within the last decade.

Central to this book is the need to take up the relationship between language and the issues of knowledge and power on the one hand, and to retheorize language within a broader politics of democracy, culture, and pedagogy on the other. This suggests creating a new language that extends the meaning of pedagogy as a form of cultural production that takes place in a variety of sites and is produced by a diverse number of cultural workers. It also proposes appropriating some of the most insightful aspects of postcolonial discourse to further our understanding of the limits and possibilities of what it means to recognize that every new paradigm has to create its own language because the old paradigms, through their use of particular language forms, produce knowledge and social relations that often serve to legitimate specific relations of power. Oppositional paradigms provide new languages through which it becomes possible to deconstruct and challenge dominant relations of power and knowledge legitimated in traditional forms of discourse. These oppositional paradigms offer the possibility for producing constructive languages that provide the opportunity for educators to understand and engage the experiences of both the classroom and other cultural sites. This opposition often reflects major changes in thinking that are mediated and produced through related shifts in new ways of speaking and writing. Oppositional languages are generally unfamiliar, provoking questions and pointing to social relations that will often appear alien and strange to many educators (what Roger Simon calls the fear of theory). What is at stake here is whether such languages offer a vision and practice for new forms of understanding, social practice, and collective struggle.

In this book, I argue that the varied discourses of postmodernism, feminism, modernism and postcolonialism provide diverse but theoretically provocative and valuable insights for educators and cultural workers to construct an oppositional and transformative politics. A dialogical encounter between these discourses offers cultural workers the opportunity to reexamine the partiality of their respective views. Similarly, such an encounter points to new possibilities for sharing and integrating the best insights of these varied discourses as part of a broader radical democratic project. In effect, this is a call for educators and cultural workers to become border crossers engaged in an effort to create alternative public spheres. In my mind, alternative public spheres are central not only for creating the conditions for "the formation and enactment of social identities," but also for enabling the conditions "in which social equality and cultural diversity coexist with participatory democracy."[6] It is through the development of such public spheres that the discourses of democracy and freedom can address what it means to educate students for forms of citizenship forged in a politics of difference that educate people in the Gramscian sense of governing as agents who can locate themselves in history, while simultaneously shaping the present as part of a discourse and practice that allow people to imagine and desire beyond society's existing limitations and practices.

A caveat must be noted here. To appropriate the discourses of postcolonialism, modernism, postmodernism, and feminism is not another academic attempt to construct new topologies, nor is it meant to suggest a textual encounter based on a refusal of politics. On the contrary, I am taking a subject position, a point of view that argues that without a political project, there can be no ground on which to engage questions of power, domination, human suffering, and the possibilities of human struggle. In this case, I embrace a point of view rooted in a discourse of emancipation that recognizes that subjective and objective forms of domination need to be addressed as part of an educational project that is the starting point for political engagement. Hence, the varied theoretical positions critically appropriated in this book become important to the degree that they provide the categories and theoretical practice by which to engage in forms of transgression that challenge knowledge and social relations structured in dominance. This suggests a political project that goes beyond merely discursive struggles, one that also attempts to transform nondiscursive and institutional relations of power by connecting educational struggles with broader struggles for the democratization, pluralization, and reconstruction of public life.

In what follows, I want to briefly analyze some of the central theoretical assumptions that characterize the diverse work of a number of postcolonial theorists.[7] In doing so, I want to critically appropriate these assumptions as part of an effort to both enter into dialogue with this body of work and also engage its criticisms as part of an attempt to challenge some of the primary categories that construct current forms of radical educational theory and practice (including my own work). At the same time, I want to use some of the central insights of postcolonial theories to problematize and extend the possibilities that have emerged within the complex and sometimes contradictory discourses of modernism, feminism, and postmodernism. Finally, I want to define the central theoretical categories around which I develop the notions of border crossing and border pedagogy as forms of cultural politics.

Colonizing Language and the Politics of Reversals

Must we always polarize in order to polemicize? Are we trapped in a politics of struggle where the representation of social antagonisms and historical contradictions can take no other form than a binarism of theory vs. politics? Can the aim of freedom or knowledge be the simple inversion of the relation of oppressor and oppressed, margin and periphery, negative image and positive image? Is our only way out of such dualism the espousal of an implacable oppositionality or the invention of an originary counter-myth of radical purity? Must the project of our liberationist aesthetics be forever part of a totalizing, Utopian vision of Being and History that seeks to transcend the contradictions and ambivalences that constitute the very structure of human subjectivity and its systems of cultural representations?[8]

The logic of binary oppositions appears to have become an obsessive fatal attraction. More obviously, this is true for neoconservatives who consistently attempt to maintain imperial control over the Other through categories of discourse developed in repressive totalities and exclusions. For many neoconservatives, the issues of complexity, absence, difference, and specificity constitute a threat to monumentalism, cultural homogeneity, and master narratives that maintain the varied dimensions of Eurocentrism. This is evident in the current debates within the United States regarding the politics, content, and use of the academic canon. Neoconservatives such as members of the National Association of Scholars see these debates as less of an expression of academic freedom than as a threat to the very nature of Western civilization. The attack on a politics of cultural difference is also evident in the struggles being waged by the English First movement, which is indicative of the emerging new nativism that has gained credibility in the Reagan-Bush Era. The opposition to cultural democracy is further evident in the numerous attacks on radical approaches to multiculturalism that display a renewed interest in forms of democracy that challenge the violence of racism, bigotry, and cultural chauvinism.[9]

But the violence of master narratives formed in the language of binary oppositions is not simply characteristic of neoconservative discourse; it is also a major problem in the work of many critical cultural workers and educators. Women of color have made this quite clear in their criticism of those largely middle class, white feminist theorists who have developed theories of patriarchy and feminism that either excluded class and racial differences or simply reduced patriarchy to a struggle between men and women.[10]

More recently, some radical educational feminists have employed the language of binary oppositions to develop positions that may actually reproduce rather than challenge the assumptions and practices of Eurocentricism. For example, a case has been made for feminist pedagogy by defining it against what is alleged to be the unified discourse of critical pedagogy. Beyond the theoretical and political problem of refusing to deal with the differences, heterogeneity, and complexity of the varied discourses that constitute critical pedagogy, this view of feminist pedagogy is often constructed in terms of a violent opposition that reproduces the very problematic of center and margin that characterizes colonial discourses. Unfortunately, within such polarities there is little room for understanding the points of resistance, multiplicities, complicities, oppressions, and liberating elements that undermine all binary oppositions. Within this discourse, "heterogeneity is repressed in the monolithic figures and stereotypes of colonialist representation."[11]

What is at issue here is not simply the specifics of the arguments made by such theorists but the debilitating effects of a problematic encoded in the simple reversal of colonial binarisms that reproduce a reductionistic "us" against "them" discourse. Implicit in these oppositions is the assumption that feminist pedagogues have become the central bearers of knowledge and social practice while those educators who define themselves within the discourses of critical pedagogy have nothing to say or contribute. Such oppositions make it extremely difficult for critical educators to interrogate their own complicity with forms of domination that connect and refigure the centers and peripheries of power. Within this discourse of dualisms, there is little understanding of the other as multiple complex subjects who both reproduce and refuse systems of domination. Similarly, there is a refusal to acknowledge the multiple rather than monolithic forms of power exercised through various institutions and diverse forms of representation. Finally, there are, as Gayatri Spivak has noted, few attempts to call into question the binary opposition of colonizer/colonized (in its many expressions) in order to "examine the heterogeneity of 'colonized power' and to disclose the complicity of the two poles of that opposition as it constitutes the disciplinary enclave of the critique of imperialism."[12]

Another example of how binary oppositions have undermined critical educational theory can be seen in the debate over language that has been enjoined by a growing number of educational writers.[13] These authors have constructed a defense and critique of radical discourse through the binary opposition of clarity vs. complexity. The theoretically flawed nature of such an argument is quite extensive and includes a number of the following considerations: it often subscribes to a universal referent for clarity and linguistic unity that is elitist as well as anti-intellectual; it tends to simplify the politics of representation, reducing it to an unproblematic issue of clarity that is never deconstructed as perhaps complicitous with the construction of domination; and it reproduces a troublesome politics of erasure by claiming to represent a universal standard of literacy while failing to consider a plurality of audiences and constituencies. Hence, it eliminates the complexity and specificity of a readership that occupies multiple, diverse public cultures.

The clarity vs. complexity binarism is based on the presupposition that a simple invocation of clear language can by itself confer sense. This position ignores what Homi Bhabha calls a central feature of political maturity: "that there are many forms of political writing whose different effects are obscured when they are divided between the 'theoretical' and the 'activist' [whose corresponding correlates are complexity and clarity]."[14] Similarly, the clarity vs. complexity argument also disregards how language and power come together in complex ways to exclude diverse narratives that rupture dominant codes and open up new spaces and possibilities for reading, writing, and acting within rather than outside of a democratic politics of difference. Inherent in this call to clarity is an assumed rather than demonstrated consensus about what clarity actually is and why it can only be taken up in progressive terms. Implicitly, this position represents a politics of containment, one that is silent about its own role in legitimating universalizing referents that marginalize and exclude multiple narratives expressed through a variety of complex discursive forms.

By ignoring these concerns, many critical educators appeal to a universal standard of literacy and clarity that is never examined. Such an appeal suppresses questions of context such as who reads what, and under what conditions. It also strongly suggests that the power of language is defined through a stylized aesthetic of clarity, one that presupposes the commonsense assumption that language is a transparent medium merely expressing existing facts that need only be laid out in an agreed-upon fashion. As previously suggested, this position does more than deny the politics of representation by situating language outside of theory, politics, and struggle. It also refuses to explore the complex issue of how language that challenges traditional educational paradigms is obligated to create new categories in order to reclaim new spaces of resistance, to establish new identities, or to construct new knowledge/power relations. Most importantly, the binary opposition that constructs this view of language appears to reproduce a central criticism posed by postcolonial critics regarding how the legacy of colonialism continually reasserts itself in an Eurocentric discourse and practice forged in relations in which the Other is subsumed or erased in the violence of binary oppositions. At work here is a form of Eurocentrism that refuses to interrogate the grounds of its own narration, its own sense of location, and how it is inscribed in a politics of difference. By refusing to interrogate how Eurocentrism may be complicit with the formation of their own identity as it is constructed in the interplay of language and difference, critical educational theorists find it difficult to understand how language itself can be used to shut down partiality, possibilities, and a politics of representation that is central to the construction of multiple social identities, public cultures, and forms of political practice.[15]

The Politics of Location, Agency, and Struggle in Postcolonial Discourse

The first set of problems is concerned with . . . issues like who writes or studies [the Other], in what institutional or discursive setting, for what audience, and with what ends in mind, the second set of problems [focuses on] . . . how the production of knowledge best serves communal, as opposed to factional, ends, how knowledge that is nondominative and noncoercive can be produced in a setting that is deeply inscribed with the politics, the considerations, the positions, and the strategies of power.[16] As a radical standpoint, perspective, position, 'the politics of location' necessarily calls those of us who would participate in the formation of counter-hegemonic cultural practice to identify the spaces where we begin the process of revision. . . . [It] is that place which enables and promotes varied and everchanging perspectives, a place where one discovers new ways of seeing reality, frontiers of difference.[17]

Edward Said and bell hooks illuminate different aspects of the debate on the politics of location that have become fundamental to a number of theoretical paradigms, including various versions of feminism and postmodernism. Central to all of these positions is the importance of challenging, remapping, and renegotiating those boundaries of knowledge that claim the status of master narratives, fixed identities, and an objective representation of reality. Within feminist and postmodern discourses, this has expressed itself in recognizing the situated nature of knowledge, the partiality of all knowledge claims, the indeterminacy of history, and the shifting, multiple, and often contradictory nature of identity.[18] At question here is the issue of who speaks, under what conditions, for whom, and how knowledge is constructed and translated within and between different communities located within asymmetrical relations of power. In addition, there is the important issue of how identity itself is constituted and what the enabling conditions might be for human agency. What the various discourses on the politics of location have made clear is that the relationship between knowledge and power on the one hand and the self and others on the other is as much an issue of ethics and politics as it is one of epistemology.[19] The legacy of a politics of location has provided a new vocabulary for analyzing how we are situated differently in the interplay of power, history, and culture. It also engages issues about how our psyches, desires, and bodies provide a reference point "to be able to name our location, to politicize our space and to question where our particular experiences and practice fit within the articulations and representations that surround us."[20] In various feminist and postmodern discourses, the politics of location has fruitfully pointed to how social identities occupy contradictory and shifting locations in which it becomes possible to open up new spaces for conversations and forms of solidarity. Rejecting the discourse of universality and essentialism, feminist theorists in particular have argued that politics and epistemology must be connected, not in an empty relativism, but in forms of discourse that are always "interpretive, critical, and partial. . . . [Where there] is a ground for conversation, rationality, and objectivity, which is power-sensitive, not 'pluralist' conversation."[21] In this context, a politics of location provides both a form of address as well as a historically constituted site from which expression and action proceed.

Postcolonial discourse has extended the parameters of this debate in a number of ways. First, it has made it clear that the relationship of history and the politics of difference is often informed by a legacy of colonialism that must be called into question so as to make visible the exclusions and repressions that allow specific forms of privilege to remain unacknowledged in the language of Western educators and cultural workers. At stake here is deconstructing not only those forms of privilege that benefit males, whiteness, heterosexuality, and property holders, but also those conditions that have disabled others to speak in places where those who are privileged by virtue of the legacy of colonial power assume authority and the conditions for human agency. This suggests, as Spivak has pointed out, that more is at stake than problematizing discourse; more importantly, educators and cultural workers must be engaged in "the unlearning of one's own privilege. So that, not only does one become able to listen to that other constituency, but one learns to speak in such a way that one will be taken seriously by that other constituency."[22] In this instance, postcolonial discourse extends the radical implications of difference and location by making such concepts attentive to providing the grounds for forms of self-representation and collective knowledges in which the subject *and* object of European culture are problematized, though in ways radically different from those taken up by Western radicals and conservatives.

Second, postcolonial discourse rewrites the relationship between the margin and the center by deconstructing the colonialist and imperialist ideologies that structure Western knowledge, texts, and social practices. Here, there are attempts to demonstrate how European culture and colonialism "are deeply implicated in each other."[23] This suggests more than rewriting or recovering the repressed stories and social memories of the other; it means understanding and rendering visible how Western knowledge is encased in historical and institutional structures that both privilege and exclude particular readings, voices, aesthetics, authority, representations, and forms of sociality. The West and otherness relate not as polarities or binarisms in postcolonial discourse but in ways in which both are complicitous and resistant, victim and accomplice. While it cannot be forgotten that the legacy of colonialism has meant large-scale death and destruction as well as cultural imperialism for the other, the other is not merely the opposite of Western colonialism, nor is the West a homogeneous trope of imperialism.

This suggests a third insight provided by postcolonial discourses. The current concern with the "death of the subject" cannot be confused with the necessity of affirming the complex and contradictory character of human agency. Postcolonial discourse reminds us that it is ideologically convenient and politically suspect for Western intellectuals to talk about the disappearance of the speaking subject from within institutions of privilege and power. This is not to suggest that postcolonial theorists accept the humanist notion of the subject as a unified and fixed identity. On the contrary, postcolonial discourse agrees that the speaking subject must be decentered but does not mean that all notions of human agency and social change must be dismissed. Understood in these terms, the postmodernist notion of the subject must be accepted and modified in order to extend rather than erase the possibility for enabling human agency. At the very least, this would mean coming to understand the strengths and limits of practical reason, the importance of affective investments, the discourse of ethics as a resource for social vision, and the availability of multiple discourses and cultural resources that provide the very grounds and necessity for agency.

Postcolonial discourses represent a space in which to retheorize, locate, and address the possibilities for a new politics based on the construction of new identities, zones of cultural difference, and forms of ethical address that allow cultural workers and educators alike to transform the languages, social practices, and histories that are part of the colonial inheritance. This position offers new hope for expanding both the practice of cultural work and the liberatory possibilities of crossing borders that open up new political and pedagogical possibilities. It is to these issues that I will now turn.

Border Pedagogy: An Introduction

In what follows, I want to delineate what might be some useful and transformative aspects of border pedagogy by situating it within those broader cultural and political considerations that are beginning to redefine our traditional view of community, language, space, and possibility. Border pedagogy is attentive to developing a democratic public philosophy that respects the notion of difference as part of a common struggle to extend the quality of public life. It presupposes not merely an acknowledgment of the shifting borders that both undermine and reterritorialize different configurations of culture, power, and knowledge. It also links the notions of schooling and the broader category of education to a more substantive struggle for a radical democratic society.

What does this suggest for redefining radical educational theory and practice as a form of border pedagogy? There are a number of theoretical considerations that need to be unpacked in reference to this question. First, the category of border signals a recognition of those epistemological, political, cultural, and social margins that structure the language of history, power, and difference. The category of border also prefigures cultural criticism and pedagogical processes as a form of border crossing. That is, it signals forms of transgression in which existing borders forged in domination can be challenged and redefined. Second, it also speaks to the need to create pedagogical conditions in which students become border crossers in order to understand otherness in its own terms, and to further create borderlands in which diverse cultural resources allow for the fashioning of new identities within existing configurations of power.

Third, border pedagogy makes visible the historically and socially constructed strengths and limitations of those places and borders we inherit and that frame our discourses and social relations. Moreover, as part of a broader politics of difference, border pedagogy makes primary the language of the political and ethical. It stresses the political by examining how institutions, knowledge, and social relations are inscribed in power differently; it highlights the ethical by examining how the shifting relations of knowing, acting, and subjectivity are constructed in spaces and social relationships based on judgments that demand and frame "different modes of response to the other; that is, between those that transfigure and those that disfigure, those that care for the other in his/her otherness and those that do not."[24] As part of a radical pedagogical practice, border pedagogy points to the need for conditions that allow students to write, speak, and listen in a language in which meaning becomes multiaccentual and dispersed and resists permanent closure. This is a language in which one speaks *with* rather than exclusively *for* others. Border pedagogy necessitates combining the modernist emphasis on the capacity of individuals to use critical reason to address the issue of public life with a postmodernist concern with how we might experience agency in a world constituted in differences unsupported by transcendent phenomena or metaphysical guarantees. In that way, border pedagogy can reconstitute itself in terms that are both transformative and emancipatory.

Border Pedagogy and the Representation of Practice

Central to the notion of border pedagogy is an understanding of how the relationship between power and knowledge works as both the practice of representation and the representation of practice to secure particular forms of authority.[25] But challenging such representations and practices entails more than revealing the Eurocentric, patriarchal, racist, and class-specific interests that are both produced and legitimated by the canon at various levels of schooling. Although the borders of existing disciplinary knowledge do need to be challenged and refigured, it is also crucial to recognize that knowledge formation is, as Spivak has also pointed out, both "the conditions of institutions and the effects of institutions."[26] In this case, border pedagogy must take up the dual task of not only creating new objects of knowledge but also addressing how inequalities, power, and human suffering are rooted in basic institutional structures. I want to develop certain aspects of border pedagogy as they relate specifically to schooling, but at the same time I want to maintain that many of the practices at work here apply to other cultural sites as well (this is demonstrated in other chapters in this book).

As a pedagogical process intent on challenging existing boundaries of knowledge and creating new ones, border pedagogy offers the opportunity for students to engage the multiple references that constitute different cultural codes, experiences, and languages. This means educating students to both read these codes historically and critically while simultaneously learning the limits of such codes, including the ones they use to construct their own narratives and histories. In this case, partiality becomes the basis for recognizing the limits built into all discourses and necessitates taking a critical view of authority as it is used to secure all regimes of truth that deny gaps, limits, specificity, and counter-narratives. Within this discourse, students should engage knowledge as border-crossers, as people moving in and out of borders constructed around coordinates of difference and power.[27] These are not only physical borders, they are cultural borders historically constructed and socially organized within rules and regulations that limit and enable particular identities, individual capacities, and social forms. In this case, students cross over into realms of meaning, maps of knowledge, social relations, and values that are increasingly being negotiated and rewritten as the codes and regulations that organize them become destabilized and reshaped. Border pedagogy decenters as it remaps. The terrain of learning becomes inextricably linked to the shifting parameters of place, identity, history, and power. Border pedagogy shifts the emphasis of the knowledge/power relationship away from the limited emphasis on the mapping of domination toward the politically strategic issue of engaging the ways in which knowledge can be remapped, reterritorialized, and decentered in the wider interests of rewriting the borders and coordinates of an oppositional cultural politics. This is not an abandonment of critique as much as it is an extension of its possibilities.

In this sense, border pedagogy extends the meaning and importance of demystification as a central pedagogical task. Depending upon the level of schooling, students must be offered opportunities to read texts that both affirm and interrogate the complexity of their own histories. They must also be given the opportunity to engage and develop a counter discourse to the established boundaries of knowledge. For example, educators such as William Bigelow and Norman Diamond have created alternative curriculum materials dealing with the history of work and workers in the United States.[28] Roger Simon and his cohorts at The Ontario Institute for Studies in Education have produced curriculum materials as a student-based approach to work education.[29] Equally important is the need for students to be able to create their own texts. In this regard, Katie Singer has worked with students at South Boston High School in Massachusetts to conduct oral histories of their communities, family life, neighborhood, and other issues as part of a broader project to produce anthologies to be used in the writing and bilingual programs.[30] In these examples, not only are borders being challenged, crossed, and refigured, but borderlands are being created in which the very production and acquisition of knowledge is being used by students to rewrite their own histories, identities, and learning possibilities.

In addition to reading different texts and refiguring the grounds on which knowledge is produced, border pedagogy takes up the important task of establishing conditions for dominant and subordinate texts to be read differently. Texts must be decentered and understood as historical and social constructions marked by the weight of a range of inherited and specified reading. Hence, texts can be read by focusing on how different audiences might respond to them, thus highlighting the possibilities of reading against, within, and outside their established boundaries.[31] Texts must also be understood in terms of the principles that structure them. This suggests not only identifying precise ideological interests, whether they be racist, sexist, or class specific, but also understanding how distinctive practices actually frame such texts by looking at the elements that produce them within established circuits of power.[32] This implies analyzing the political economy of publishing companies, the forces outside of the schools that render certain texts legitimate objects of knowledge, particular forms of state legislation and assessment that privilege certain readings of texts, and how students from different social formations and locations might read texts differently and why. As such, border pedagogy reads against totalizing curriculum and pedagogical practices that marginalize diverse student cultures and histories by taking up issues of production, audience, address, and reception. Similarly, border pedagogy reads against the grain of transmission teaching or what Paulo Freire has called "banking education" by opposing learning premised on the voyeuristic consumption of texts.[33] By "interrupting" representational practices that make a claim to objectivity, universality, and consensus, critical educators can develop pedagogical conditions in which students can read and write within and against existing cultural codes while simultaneously having the opportunity to create new spaces for producing new forms of knowledge, subjectivity, and identity. Within such a discourse, important social and political realities would be engaged rather than excluded from the school curriculum and the process of reading differently and critically would be aimed not only at dominant texts but also inwardly upon itself.

More specific examples of border pedagogy can be found in some of the recent work being done on educational theory and popular culture.[34] Three important issues are being worked out within the parameters of this work. First, there is a central concern for understanding how the production of meaning is related to affective investments and the production of pleasure.[35] In this view, it is necessary for teachers to incorporate into their pedagogies a theoretical understanding of how the production of meaning and economies of pleasure become mutually constitutive of students' identities, how students view themselves, and how students construct a particular vision of their future. Second, the nature of how students are inscribed in and take up different affective economies needs to be rethought in light of a number of important pedagogical considerations. One such consideration is that the production and regulation of desire must be seen as a crucial aspect of how students mediate, relate, resist, and create particular cultural forms and forms of knowing. Another concern is that popular culture be seen as a legitimate aspect of the everyday lives of students and be analyzed as a primary force in shaping the various and often contradictory subject positions that students take up. Third, popular culture needs to become a serious object of study in the official curriculum. This can be done by treating popular culture either as a distinct object of study within particular academic discipline such as media studies or by drawing upon the resources it produces for engaging various aspects of the official curriculum. I take up this issue in more detail in another section of this book.

In all of these examples, important elements of a border pedagogy point to ways in which those master narratives based on white, patriarchal, and class-specific versions of the world can be challenged critically and effectively deterritorialized. That is, by offering a theoretical language for establishing new boundaries with respect to knowledge most often associated with the margins and periphery of the cultural dominant, border pedagogy opens up the possibility for incorporating into the curriculum cultural and social practices that no longer need be mapped or referenced solely on the basis of the dominant models of Western culture. In this case, knowledge forms emanating from the margins can be used to redefine the complex, multiple, heterogeneous realities that constitute those relations of difference that make up the experiences of students who often find it impossible to define their identities through the cultural and political codes that characterize the dominant culture.

Border Pedagogy and the Politics of Identity and Community

If the concept of border pedagogy is to be linked to the imperatives of a critical democracy, as it must be, educators must possess a theoretical grasp of the ways in which difference is constructed through various representations and practices that name, legitimate, marginalize, and exclude the voices of subordinate groups in American society. Two considerations need to frame this project. First, the liberal notion of multiculturalism that links difference within the horizon of a false equality and a depoliticized notion of consensus must be replaced by a radical notion of cultural difference and citizenship that recognizes the "essentially contested character of the signs and signifying material we use in the construction of our social identities."[36] Second, the central values of a democratic revolution–freedom, equality, liberty, and justice–must provide the principles by which differences are affirmed within rather than outside of a politics of solidarity forged through diverse public spheres.

Central to this task is the need for critical educators to take up culture as a vital source for developing a politics of identity, community, and pedagogy. In this perspective, culture is not viewed as monolithic or unchanging, but as a shifting sphere of multiple and heterogeneous borders where different histories, languages, experiences, and voices intermingle amid diverse relations of power and privilege. For example, within the pedagogical cultural borderland known as school, subordinate cultures push against and permeate the alleged unproblematic and homogeneous borders of dominant cultural forms and practices. Critical educators cannot be content to merely map how ideologies are inscribed in the various relations of schooling, whether they be the curriculum, forms of school organization, or in teacher-student relations. A more viable critical pedagogy needs to go beyond these concerns by analyzing how ideologies are actually taken up in the contradictory voices and lived experiences of students as they give meaning to the dreams, desires, and subject positions that they inhabit. Critical educators need to provide the conditions for students to speak differently so that their narratives can be affirmed and engaged critically along with the consistencies and

contradictions that characterize such experiences. They must not only hear the voices
of those students who have been traditionally silenced, they must take seriously what
all students say by engaging the implications of their discourse in broader historical
and relational terms. Equally important is the need to provide safe spaces for students
to critically engage teachers, other students, as well as the limits of their own positions
as border-crossers who do not have to put their identities on trial each time they address social and political issues that they do not experience directly. Put simply, students
must be encouraged to cross ideological and political borders as a way of furthering
the limits of their own understanding in a setting that is pedagogically safe and socially
nurturing rather than authoritarian and infused with the suffocating smugness of a
certain political correctness. More specifically, student experience has to be analyzed
as part of a broader democratic politics of voice and difference.

   As part of a project of voice and difference, a theory of border pedagogy needs to
address the question of how representations and practices that name, marginalize, and
define difference as the devalued other are actively learned, internalized, challenged, or
transformed. That is, it is imperative that such a pedagogy acknowledge and critically
interrogate how the colonizing of differences by dominant groups is expressed and
sustained through representations in which the humanity of the other is either ideologically disparaged or ruthlessly denied. In addition, such a pedagogy needs to address
how an understanding of these differences can be taken up in order to challenge the
prevailing relations of power that sustain them. Border pedagogy must provide the
conditions for students to engage in cultural remapping as a form of resistance. Students should be given the opportunity to engage in systematic analyses of the ways in
which the dominant culture creates borders saturated in terror, inequality, and forced
exclusions. Students need to analyze the conditions that have disabled others to speak
in the places where those who have power exercise authority. Thus, critical educators
must give more thought to how the experience of marginality at the level of everyday
life lends itself productively to forms of oppositional and transformative consciousness. Similarly, those designated as Other must both reclaim and remake their histories, voices, and visions as part of a wider struggle to change those material and social
relations that deny radical pluralism as the basis of democratic political community.
This suggests a pedagogy in which occurs a critical questioning of the omissions and
tensions that exist between the master narratives and hegemonic discourses that make
up the official curriculum and the self-representations of subordinated groups as they
might appear in "forgotten" or erased histories, texts, memories, experiences, and community narratives.

   At issue here is a pedagogical practice that is not concerned with simply marking
difference as a historical construct; rather, it is also attentive to inserting differences
within a cultural politics that attempts to create within schools, universities, and other
educational sites what Chandra Mohanty calls "public cultures of dissent." By this she
means:

creating spaces for epistemological standpoints that are grounded in the interests of people and which recognize the materiality of conflict, of privilege, and of domination. Thus, creating such cultures is fundamentally about making the axes of power transparent in the context of academic, disciplinary, and institutional structures as well as in interpersonal relationships (rather than individual relations in the academy).[37]

Furthermore, students must appropriate in a similarly critical fashion, when necessary, the codes and knowledges that constitute broader and less familiar historical and cultural traditions. Underlying this pedagogical practice is the importance of understanding how subjectivities are produced within those configurations of knowledge and power that exist outside of the immediacy of one's experience but are central to forms of self and social determination, the obligations of critical citizenship, and the construction of critical public cultures. Border pedagogy also points to the need to raise fundamental questions regarding how students make particular investments of meaning and affect, how they are inscribed within triad relations of knowledge, power, and pleasure, and why students might be indifferent to the forms of authority, knowledge, and values that are produced and legitimated within our classrooms and universities.

In addition, the concept of border pedagogy suggests more than simply opening diverse cultural histories and spaces to students. It also means understanding how fragile identity is as it moves into borderlands crisscrossed within a variety of languages, experiences, and voices. There are no unified subjects here, only students whose multilayered and often contradictory voices and experiences intermingle with the weight of particular histories that will not fit easily into the master narrative of a monolithic culture. Such borderlands should be seen as sites for both critical analysis and as a potential source of experimentation, creativity, and possibility. Moreover, these pedagogical borderlands where blacks, whites, latinos, and others meet demonstrate the importance of a multicentric perspective that allows students to recognize and analyze how the differences within and between various groups can expand the potential of human life and democratic possibilities.

Border Pedagogy and the Discourse of Teacher Location

Central to the notion of border pedagogy are a number of important pedagogical issues regarding the role that teachers might play at the interface of a number of concerns taken up in the discourses of postcolonialism introduced in the first part of this chapter.

Border pedagogy provides opportunities for teachers to deepen their own understanding of the discourse of various others in order to effect a more dialectical self-critical understanding of the limits, partiality, and particularity of their own politics, values, and pedagogy. By being able to listen critically to the voices of their students, teachers also become border-crossers through their ability both to make different narratives available to themselves and to legitimate difference as a basic condition for understanding the limits of one's own knowledge. What border pedagogy makes undeniable is the relational, constructed, and situated nature of one's own politics and personal investments. But at the same time, border pedagogy emphasizes the primacy of a politics in which teachers assert rather than retreat from the pedagogies they utilize in dealing with the various differences represented by the students who come into their classes.

At stake here is an important theoretical issue that is worth repeating. Knowledge and power come together not to merely reaffirm difference but to also interrogate it, to open up broader theoretical considerations, to tease out its limitations, and to engage a vision of community in which student voices define themselves in terms of their distinct social formations and their broader collective hopes. For critical educators, this entails speaking *to* important social, political, and cultural issues from a deep sense of the politics of their own location and the necessity to engage and often unlearn the habits of institutional (as well as forms of racial, gender, and class-specific) privilege that buttress their own power while sometimes preventing others from becoming questioning subjects. This does not suggest that as educators we should abandon our authority as much as we should transform it into an emancipatory practice that provides the conditions for us to speak and be taken seriously. Of course, as teachers we can never speak inclusively *as* the other, though we may be the other with respect to issues of race, class, or gender; but we can certainly work *with* diverse others to deepen both our own and their understanding of the complexity of the traditions, histories, knowledges, and politics that they bring to the schools. More specifically, while teachers may not speak as others whose experiences they do not share, they certainly can speak about and to the experiences of racism, sexism, class discrimination, and other concerns as historical and contingent issues that affect public life. In other words, as a heterosexual, white, middle/working class educator, I cannot, for example, speak as or for Afro-Americans or women, but I can speak self-reflectively from the politics of my own location about the issues of racism and sexism as ethical, political, and public issues, which implicate in their web of social relations all those who inhabit public life, though from different spheres of privilege and subordination. Extending the logic of such a position is to create conditions within particular institutions that allow both teachers and students to locate themselves and others in histories that mobilize rather than destroy their hopes for the future. Such a position reconstructs teachers as intellectuals whose own narratives must be situated and examined as discourses that are open, partial, and subject to ongoing debate and revision.

In conclusion, I think it is essential that educators and other cultural workers address the issues at stake in the new cultural politics of difference as pedagogical and political concerns. These concerns need to be taken up within broader mobilizing articulations such as public life, nationalism, and citizenship. The pedagogical issue at work here is to articulate difference as part of the construction of a new type of politics, language, and subject, which would be both multiple and democratic.

Notes

1. Ngugi Wa Thiong'o, *Decolonizing the Mind: The Politics of Language in African Literature* (London and Nairobi: Heinemann, 1986), 4.
2. Linda Hutcheon, "Circling the Downspout of Empire," in Ian Adam and Helen Tiffin, eds., *Past the Last Post* (Calgary: University of Calgary Press, 1990), 176.
3. Cornel West, "The New Cultural Politics of Difference," *October* 53 (Summer 1990), 93.
4. Robert Young, *White Mythologies: Writing History and the West* (London: Routledge, 1990), viii.
5. For an excellent discussion of these issues as they specifically relate to postcolonial theory, see Benita Parry, "Problems in Current Theories of Colonial Discourse," *The Oxford Literary Review* Vol. 9 (1987), 27–28; Abdul JanMohamed, *Manichean Aesthetics: The Politics of Literature in Colonial Africa* (Amherst: University of Massachusetts Press, 1983); Gayatri C. Spivak, *The Post-Colonial Critic: Interviews, Strategies, Dialogues*, Sarah Harasym, ed. (New York: Routledge, 1990).
6. Both quotes are taken from: Nancy Fraser, "Rethinking the Public Sphere: A Contribution to the Critique of Actually Existing Democracy," *Social Text* Nos. 25/26 (1990), 68, 69.
7. The literature on anticolonialism and postcolonialism is far too vast to cite here, but would include some of the following: Frantz Fanon, *The Wretched of the Earth* (New York: Grove Press, 1963); *Black Skin, White Masks* (New York: Grove Press, 1967); Kwame Nkrumah, *Consciencism* (New York: Monthly Review Press, 1964); Albert Memmi, *The Colonizer and the Colonized* (Boston: Beacon Press, 1965); Paulo Freire, *Pedagogy in Process: The Letters to Guinea-Bissau* (New York: Seabury Press, 1978); Ngugi Wa Thiong' o, *Decolonizing the Mind*; Jan Carew, *Fulcrums of Change* (Trenton, N.J.: Africa World Press, 1988); Edward W. Said, *Orientalism* (New York: Vintage Books, 1979); Rinajit Guha and Gayatri C. Spivak, eds., *Selected Subaltern Studies* (New York: Oxford University Press, 1988); Special Issue of *Inscriptions* on "Feminism and the Critique of Colonial Discourse," Nos. 3/4 (1988); James Clifford, *The Predicament of Culture* (Cambridge: Harvard University Press, 1988); Bill Ashcroft, Gareth Griffiths, and Helen Tiffin, *The Empire Writes Back: Theory and Practice in Post-Colonial Literatures* (London: Routledge, 1989); Howard Adams, *Prison of Grass: Canada From a Native Point of View* (Saskatoon: Fifth House Publishers, 1989); Homi K. Bhabha, ed., *Nation and Narration* (London: Routledge, 1990); Gayatri C. Spivak, *The Post-Colonial Critic*; Ian Adam and Helen Tiffin, eds., *Past the Last Post: Theorizing Post-Colonialism and Post-Modernism* (Calgary, Canada: University of Calgary Press, 1990); Marianna Torgovnick, *Gone Primitive: Savage Intellects, Modern Lives* (Chicago: University of Chicago Press, 1990); Robert Young, *White Mythologies*.
8. Homi Bhabha, "The Commitment to Theory," *New Formations* 5 (Summer 1988), 5. See also Tony Crowley, *Standard English and the Politics of Language* (Urbana: University of Illinois Press, 1989).
9. For an example of how these issues are taken up around the struggle over multiculturalism in the academy, see Gregory S. Jay, "The End of 'American' Literature: Toward a Multicultural Practice," *College English* 53:3 (March 1991), 264–281.
10. I take up this issue extensively in this book, see especially Chapters 3 and 5.
11. The most influential example of this position can be found in Elizabeth Ellsworth, "Why Doesn't This Feel Empowering? Working Through the Repressive Myths of Critical

Pedagogy," *Harvard Educational Review* 59:3 (1989), 297–324. Ellsworth isn't alone in constructing comfortable binary oppositions that simply reverse the violence of one hierarchical opposition for another. See Patti Lather, *Getting Smart: Feminist Research and Pedagogy with/in the Postmodern* (New York: Routledge, 1991); Jennifer M. Gore, "What Can We Do for You! What Can 'We' Do for 'You'?" *Educational Foundations* 4:2 (Summer 1990), 5–26. For a brilliant deconstruction of the debilitating effects of the binarisms inherent in Lather's position, see Peter McLaren, "Introduction: Postmodernism, Post-colonialism, and Pedagogy," in Peter McLaren, ed., *Postmodernism, Post-colonialism, and Pedagogy* (Albert Park, Australia: James Nicholas Publishers, 1995). Of course, women of color have consistently refused to construct binary oppositions between varied critical pedagogies and the discourses of race and feminism. See for example Chandra T. Mohanty, "On Race and Voice: Challenges for Liberal Education in the 1990s," *Cultural Critique* No. 14 (Winter 1990), 179–208. See also bell hooks, *Talking Back* (Boston: South End Press, 1989); *Yearning* (Boston: South End Press, 1990); Michele Wallace, *Invisibility Blues* (London: Verso Press, 1991). What is interesting in these works is how they both critically engage and selectively appropriate the various positions taken up in critical pedagogy. hooks, in particular, is deeply influenced by the work of Paulo Freire, but does not suggest that because he does not make race and gender central to his work that it should simply be dismissed.

12. Gayatri C. Spivak, quoted in Angela McRobbie, "Strategies of Vigilance: An Interview with Gayatri Chakravorty Spivak," *Block* 10 (1985), 9.

13. See for example Michael Apple, "Introduction" in Daniel P. Liston, *Capitalist Schools* (New York: Routledge, 1989); William Profriedt, "Review of *Capitalist Schools* and *Schooling and the Struggle for Public Life*" in *Socialism and Democracy* No. 9 (Fall/Winter 1989), 173–78; Jennifer M. Gore, "What Can We Do for You! What Can 'We' Do for 'You'? *Educational Foundations* 4:3 (Summer 1990), 5–26; Stan Karp, "A Review of Peter McLaren's *Life in Schools*," *Radical Teacher* No. 39 (Winter 1991), 32–34. See my extended response to the issue of clarity and languages in Henry A. Giroux, "Writing for the Masses and Other Liberal Simplicities," *Socialism and Democracy* No. 11 (September 1990), 163–71; Henry A. Giroux and Peter McLaren, "Language, Schooling, and Subjectivity: Beyond a Pedagogy of Reproduction and Resistance," in Kathryn Borman, Piyush Swami, and Lonnie Wagstaff, eds., *Contemporary Issues in U.S. Education* (Norwood, N.J.: Ablex Publishing, 1991), 1–59.

14. Bhabha, "The Commitment to Theory," 7.

15. Related to this argument around clarity is a broader issue. The political and strategic inadequacy of much of what constitutes critical and radical versions of educational theory is largely evident in its overall refusal to engage the theoretical gains that have come to characterize the fields of literary studies, Marxist studies, feminist theory, poststructuralism, postmodernism, and democratic theory. Theoretically isolated from the many innovations taking place in the larger world of social theory, many educational theorists have removed themselves from critically engaging the limitations of the political projects implicit in their own work and have resorted instead to preaching the importance of the accessibility of theoretical language and the privileging of practice over theory. The call to writing in an educational language that is touted as clear and familiar appears to have become the political and ideological equivalent of a moral and political vision that increasingly collapses under the weight of its own anti-intellectualism and self-referential elitism. Similarly, educational theory is increasingly dissolved into practice under the vote-catching call for the importance of focusing on the concrete as the all-embracing sphere of educational strategy and relevance. To argue against these concerns is not meant as a clever exercise intent on merely reversing the relevance of the categories so that theory is prioritized over practice, or abstract language over the language of popcorn imagery. Nor am I merely suggesting

that critical educators mount an equally reductionist argument against the use of clear language or the importance of practice. At issue here is the need to both question and reject the reductionism and exclusions that characterize the binary oppositions that inform these overly pragmatic tendencies.

16. Edward W. Said, "Orientalism Reconsidered," *Cultural Critique* No. 1 (Fall 1985), 91.

17. hooks, Chapter 15, *Yearning,* 145, 149.

18. One important reference for this position is Donna Haraway, "Situated Knowledges: The Science Question in Feminism and the Privilege of Partial Perspective," *Feminist Studies* 14:3 (Fall 1989), 575–599.

19. Ibid.

20. Joan Borsa, "Towards a Politics of Location," *Canadian Woman Studies* (Spring 1990), 36.

21. Donna Haraway, "Situated Knowledges," 589.

22. Gayatri C. Spivak, *The Post-Colonial Critic,* 42.

23. Robert Young, *White Mythologies,* 119.

24. Richard Kearney, *The Wake of Imagination* (Minneapolis: University of Minnesota Press, 1988), 369.

25. Gayatri C. Spivak, "The Making of Americans, the Teaching of English, and the Future of Cultural Studies," *New Literary History* 21:4 (1990), 781–798.

26. Ibid., 785.

27. For example, see Guillermo Gomez-Peña, "The Other Vanguard," in Ivan Kapp, Christine Kreamer, and Steven Lavine, eds., *Museums and Communists: The Politics of Public Culture* (Washington, DC: Smithsonian Institution Press, 1992), 65–75.

28. William Bigelow and Norman Diamond, *The Power in Our Hands* (New York: Monthly Review Press, 1988).

29. Roger I. Simon, Don Dippo, and Arleen Schenke, *Learning Work* (New York: Bergin and Garvey Press, 1991).

30. Katie Singer, *Mosaic: Coming of Age in Boston–Across the Generations* (South Boston: Mosaic, 1984).

31. Tony Bennett, *Outside Literature* (London: Routledge, 1990).

32. Richard Johnson, "What is Cultural Studies Anyway?" *Social Text* No. 16 (Winter 1986/87), 38–80.

33. Paulo Freire, *Pedagogy of the Oppressed* (New York: Seabury Press, 1973).

34. Henry A. Giroux and Roger I. Simon, eds., *Popular Culture, Schooling, and Everyday Life* (New York: Bergin and Garvey Press, 1988).

35. Lawrence Grossberg, "The Context of Audiences and the Politics of Difference," *Australian Journal of Communication* No. 16 (1989), 13–35.

36. Kobena Mercer, quoted in Lorraine Kenny, "Traveling Theory: The Cultural Politics of Race and Representation: An Interview with Kobena Mercer," *Afterimage* (September 1990), 8.

37. Chandra T. Mohanty, "On Race and Voice," *Cultural Critique* No. 14 (Winter 1989/90), 207.

2

Crossing the Boundaries
of Educational Discourse

Modernism, Postmodernism,
and Feminism

We have entered an age that is marked by a crisis of power, patriarchy, authority, identity, and ethics. This new age has been described, for better or worse, by many theorists in a variety of disciplines as the age of postmodernism.[1] It is a period torn between the ravages and benefits of modernism; it is an age in which the notions of science, technology, and reason are associated not only with social progress but also with the organization of Auschwitz and the scientific creativity that made Hiroshima possible.[2] It is a time in which the humanist subject seems to no longer be in control of his or her fate. It is an age in which the grand narratives of emancipation, whether from the political right or left, appear to share an affinity for terror and oppression. It is also a historical moment in which culture is no longer seen as a reserve of white men whose contributions to the arts, literature, and science constitute the domain of high culture. We live at a time in which a strong challenge is being waged against a modernist discourse in which knowledge is legitimized almost exclusively from a European model of culture and civilization. In part, the struggle for democracy can be seen in the context of a broader struggle against certain features of modernism that represent the worst legacies of the Enlightenment tradition. And it is against these features that a variety of oppositional movements have emerged in an attempt to rewrite the relationship between modernism and democracy. Two of the most important challenges to modernism have come from divergent theoretical discourses associated with postmodernism and feminism.

31

Postmodernism and feminism have challenged modernism on a variety of theoretical and political fronts, and I will take these up shortly, but there is another side to modernism that has expressed itself more recently in the ongoing struggles in Eastern Europe. Modernism is not merely about patriarchy parading as universal reason, the increasing intensification of human domination over nature in the name of historical development, or the imperiousness of grand narratives that stress control and mastery.[3] Nor is modernism simply synonymous with forms of modernization characterized by the ideologies and practices of the dominating relations of capitalist production. It exceeds this fundamental but limiting rationality by offering the ideological excesses of democratic possibility. By this I mean that, as Ernesto Laclau and Chantal Mouffe have pointed out, modernism becomes a decisive point of reference for advancing certain and crucial elements of the democratic revolution.[4]

Beyond its claims to certainty, foundationalism, and epistemological essentialism, modernism provides theoretical elements for analyzing both the limits of its own historical tradition and for developing a political standpoint in which the breadth and specificity of democratic struggles can be expanded through the modernist ideals of freedom, justice, and equality. As Mark Hannam points out, modernism does have a legacy of progressive ambitions, that have contributed to substantive social change, and these ambitions need to be remembered in order to be reinserted into any developing discourses on democracy. For Hannam, these include: "economic redistribution towards equality, the emancipation of women, the eradication of superstition and despotism, wider educational opportunities, the improvement of the sciences and the arts, and so forth. Democratization was one of these ambitions and frequently was perceived to be a suitable means towards the realization of other, distinct ambitions."[5] What is important to note is that the more progressive legacies of modernism have been unleashed not in the West, where they have been undermined by modernism's undemocratic tendencies, but in Eastern Europe where the full force of political modernism has erupted to redraw the political and cultural map of the region. What this suggests is neither the death of modernism nor the facile dismissal of the new oppositional discourses that have arisen within postmodernism and feminism, but a rethinking of how the most critical aspects of these discourses can be brought to bear to deepen the democratic possibilities within the modernist project itself. For what is at stake here is not simply the emergence of a new language in order to rethink the modernist tradition, but also the reconstruction of the political, cultural, and social preconditions for developing a radical conception of citizenship and pedagogy.

That we live in an age in which a new political subject is being constructed can be seen most vividly in the events that have recently taken place in Eastern Europe within the last few years: the Berlin Wall has fallen; the Stalinist communist parties of the Eastern bloc are, for all intents and purposes, in disarray; the Soviet Union is radically modifying an identity forged in the legacy of Leninism and Bolshevism; and the master narratives of Marxism are being refigured within the shifting identities, cultural practices, and imaginary possibilities unleashed in the nascent discourse of a radical democracy. In Eastern Europe, the theoretical and political preconditions for a postmodern citizen are being constructed, even if only at the present they exist as a faint glimmer. This is a political subject that rejects the authoritarianism of master narratives, that refuses traditions that allow only for a reverence of what already is, that denies those instrumental and universalized forms of rationality that eliminate the historical and the contingent, that opposes science as a universal foundation for truth and knowledge, and that discredits the Western notion of subjectivity as a stable, coherent self. What these shifting perspectives and emergent social relations have done is to radicalize the possibilities of freedom and affirm the capacity of human beings to shape their own destinies as part of a larger struggle for democracy.

In the Western industrial countries, the revolutions in Eastern Europe for freedom, equality, and justice appear in the dominant media as the valiant struggle of the other against enslavement through communism. But in the United States these are events that take place on the margins of civilization, related but not central to the political and cultural identity of the West except as mimesis. In the mass media, the struggles for equality and freedom in Eastern Europe have been analyzed through the lens of a modernist discourse that reproduces highly problematic notions of the Enlightenment tradition. For example, many Western theorists view the redrawing of the political and social borders of Eastern Europe in reductionist modernist terms as the "end of history," a metaphor for the already unquestionable triumph of capitalist liberal democracy. In this scenario, the ideological characteristics that define the center of civilization through the discourse of the Western democracies have now been extended to the culturally and politically "deprived" margins of civilization.

This is a curious position, because it fails to recognize that what the revolutions in Eastern Europe may be pointing to is not the "end of history" but to the exhaustion of those hierarchical and undemocratic features of modernism that produce state oppression, managerial domination, and social alienation in various countries in both the East and the West. It is curious because the "end of history" ideology, when applied to the Western democracies, is quite revealing; that is, it points to a political smugness that presupposes that democracy in the West has reached its culmination. Of course, beneath this smugness lies the indifference of Western-style democracy toward substantive political life; in effect, what has become increasingly visible in this argument is the failure of democracy itself. Hannam captures this point: "Formal democracy has failed because it has generated indifference towards many of the substantive goals of political activity. Western democracy believes itself to be at its own endpoint; it has given up the ambition of social change, of which it was once a central, but never an exclusive part."[6]

While Western ruling groups and their apologists may choose to see only the triumph of liberal ideology beneath the changes in Eastern Europe, there is more being called into question than they suspect. In fact, the revolutions in Eastern Europe call into question not only the master narrative of Marxism, but also all master narratives that make a totalizing claim to emancipation and freedom. In this case, the events taking place in Eastern Europe and in other places like South Africa represent part of a broader struggle of oppressed peoples against all totalizing forms of legitimation and cultural practice that deny human freedom and collective justice. What the West may be witnessing in Eastern Europe is the emergence of a new discourse, one that does not pit socialism against capitalism, but democracy against all forms of totalitarianism. In opposition to a limited modernist version of democracy, the struggles in Eastern Europe implicitly suggest the conditions for creating a radical democracy, one in which people control the social and economic forces that determine their existence. In this case, the struggle for democracy exceeds its modernist framework by extending the benefits of freedom and justice beyond the strictly formal mechanisms of democracy. What appears at work in these revolutions is a discourse that has the potential to deepen the radical implications of modernism through considerations of a rather profound set of questions: What set of conditions is necessary to create social relations for human liberation within historically specific formations? How might individual and social identities be reconstructed in the service of human imagination and democratic citizenship? How can the assertion of history and politics serve to deconstruct all essentialisms and totalizing rationalities? How can political and social identities be constructed within a politics of difference that is capable of struggling over and deepening the project of radical democracy while constantly asserting its historical and contingent character? Put another way, what can be done to strengthen and extend the oppositional tendencies of modernism?

I want to argue that modernism, postmodernism, and feminism represent three of the most important discourses for developing a cultural politics and pedagogical practice capable of extending and theoretically advancing a radical politics of democracy. While acknowledging that all three of these discourses are internally contradictory, ideologically diverse, and theoretically inadequate, I believe that when posited in terms of the interconnections between *both* their differences and the common ground they share for being mutually correcting, they offer critical educators a rich theoretical and political opportunity for rethinking the relationship between schooling and democracy. Each of these positions has much to learn from the theoretical strengths and weaknesses of the other two discourses. Not only does a dialogical encounter among these discourses offer them the opportunity to re-examine the partiality of their respective views. Such an encounter also points to new possibilities for sharing and integrating their best insights as part of a broader radical democratic project. Together these diverse discourses offer the possibility for illuminating how critical educators might work with other cultural workers in various movements to develop and advance a broader discourse of political and collective struggle. At stake here is an attempt to provide a political and theoretical discourse that can move beyond a postmodern aesthetic and a feminist separatism in order to develop a project in which a politics of difference can emerge within a shared discourse of democratic public life. Similarly, at issue is also the important question of how the discourses of modernism, postmodernism, and feminism might be pursued as part of a broader political effort to rethink the boundaries and most basic assumptions of a critical pedagogy consistent with a radical cultural politics.

I want to develop these issues through the following approach. First, I will analyze in schematic terms some of the central assumptions that characterize various modernist traditions, including Jürgen Habermas's spirited defense of social and political modernism. Second, I will analyze some of the central issues that postmodernism has made problematic in its encounter with modernism. Third, I will highlight the most progressive aspects of what can be loosely labeled postmodern feminist theory to be used in the service of advancing both its own critical tendencies and the most radical aspects of modernism and postmodernism. Finally, I will indicate how these three discourses might contribute to developing some important principles in the construction of a critical pedagogy for democratic struggle. It is to these issues that I will now turn.

Mapping the Politics of Modernism

To invoke the term "modernism" is to immediately place oneself in the precarious position of suggesting a definition that is itself open to enormous debate and little agreement.[7] Not only is there a disagreement regarding the periodisation of the term, there is enormous controversy regarding to what it actually refers. To some it has become synonymous with terroristic claims of reason, science, and totality.[8] To others it embodies, for better or worse, various movements in the arts.[9] And to some of its more ardent defenders, it represents the progressive rationality of communicative competence and support for the autonomous individual subject.[10] It is not possible within the context of this essay to provide a detailed history of the various historical and ideological discourses of modernism even though such an analysis is essential to provide a sense of the complexity of both the category and the debates that have emerged around modernism.[11] Instead, I want to focus on some of the central assumptions of modernism. The value of this approach is that it serves not only to highlight some of the more important arguments that have been made in the defense of modernism, but also to provide a theoretical and political backdrop for understanding some of the central features of various postmodernist and feminist discourses. This is particularly important with respect to postmodernism, which presupposes some idea of the modern and also various elements of feminist discourse, which have increasingly been forged largely in opposition to some of the major assumptions of modernism, particularly as these relate to notions such as rationality, truth, subjectivity, and progress.

The theoretical, ideological, and political complexity of modernism can be grasped by analyzing its diverse vocabularies with respect to three traditions: the social, the

aesthetic, and the political. The notion of social modernity corresponds with the tradition of the new, the process of economic and social organization carried out under the
growing relations of capitalist production. Social modernity approximates what Matei
Calinescu calls the bourgeois idea of modernity, which is characterized by:

> The doctrine of progress, the confidence in the beneficial possibilities of science and
> technology, the concern with time (a measurable time, a time that can be bought and
> sold and therefore has, like any other commodity, a calculable equivalent in money), the
> cult of reason, and the ideal of freedom defined within the framework of an abstract
> humanism, but also the orientation toward pragmatism and the cult of action and suc-
> cess.[12]

Within this notion of modernism, the unfolding of history is linked to the "continual progress of the sciences and of techniques, the rational division of industrial
work, which introduces into social life a dimension of permanent change, of destruction
of customs and traditional culture."[13] At issue here is a definition of modernity that
points to the progressive differentiation and rationalization of the social world through
the process of economic growth and administrative rationalization. Another characteristic of social modernism is the epistemological project of elevating reason to an ontological status. Modernism in this view becomes synonymous with civilization itself,
and reason is universalized in cognitive and instrumental terms as the basis for a model
of industrial, cultural, and social progress. At stake in this notion of modernity is a
view of individual and collective identity in which historical memory is devised as a
linear process, the human subject becomes the ultimate source of meaning and action,
and a notion of geographical and cultural territoriality is constructed in a hierarchy of
domination and subordination marked by a center and margin legitimated through
the civilizing knowledge/power of a privileged Eurocentric culture.[14]

The category of aesthetic modernity has a dual characterization that is best exemplified in its traditions of resistance and formal aestheticism. But it is in the tradition
of opposition, with its all consuming disgust with bourgeois values and its attempt
through various literary and avant-garde movements to define art as a representation
of criticism, rebellion, and resistance that aesthetic modernism first gained a sense of
notoriety. Fueling this aesthetic modernism of the nineteenth and early twentieth centuries was an alienation and negative passion whose novelty was perhaps best captured
in Bakunin's anarchist maxim, "To destroy is to create."[15] The cultural and political
lineaments of this branch of aesthetic modernism are best expressed in those avant-
garde movements that ranged from surrealism and futurism to the conceptualism of
the 1970s. Within this movement, with its diverse politics and expressions, there is an
underlying commonality and attempt to collapse the distinction between art and politics and to blur the boundaries between life and aesthetics. But in spite of its oppositional tendencies, aesthetic modernism has not fared well in the latter part of the

twentieth century. Its critical stance, its aesthetic dependency on the presence of bourgeois norms, and its apocalyptic tone became increasingly recognized as artistically fashionable by the very class it attacked.[16]

The central elements that bring these two traditions of modernism together constitute a powerful force not only for shaping the academic disciplines and the discourse of educational theory and practice, but also for providing a number of points where various ideological positions share a common ground. These elements can be recognized in modernism's claim for the superiority of high culture over and against popular culture, its affirmation of a centered if not unified subject, its faith in the power of the highly rational, conscious mind, and its belief in the unequivocal ability of human beings to shape the future in the interest of a better world. There is a long tradition of support for modernism and some of its best representatives are as diverse as Marx, Baudelaire, and Dostoevsky. This notion of the unified self based on the universalization of reason and the totalizing discourses of emancipation have provided a cultural and political script for celebrating Western culture as synonymous with civilization itself and progress as a terrain that only needed to be mastered as part of the inexorable march of science and history. Marshall Berman exemplifies the dizzying heights of ecstasy made possible by the script of modernism in his own rendition of the modernist sensibility:[17]

> Modernists, as I portray them, are simultaneously at home in this world and at odds with it. They celebrate and identify with the triumphs of modern science, art, technology, communications, economics, politics—in short, with all the activities, techniques, and sensibilities that enable mankind to do what the Bible said God could do to "make all things new." At the same time, however, they oppose modernization's betrayal of its own human promise and potential. Modernists demand more profound and radical renewals: modern men and women must become the subjects as well as the objects of modernization; they must learn to change the world that is changing them and to make it their own. The modernist knows this is possible: the fact that the world has changed so much is proof that it can change still more. The modernist can, in Hegel's phrase, "look at the negative in the face and live with it." The fact that "all that is solid melts into air" is a source not of despair, but of strength and affirmation. If everything must go, then let it go: modern people have the power to create a better world than the world they have lost.[18]

Of course, for many critics, the coupling of social and aesthetic modernism reveals itself quite differently. Modernist art is criticized for becoming nothing more than a commercial market for the museums and the corporate boardrooms and a depoliticized discourse institutionalized within the universities. In addition, many critics have argued that under the banner of modernism, reason and aesthetics often come together in a technology of self and culture that combines a notion of beauty that is white, male, and European with a notion of mastery that legitimates modern industrial technologies and the exploitation of vast pools of labor from the "margins" of Second and Third World economies. Robert Merrill gives this argument a special twist in claiming that the modernist ego with its pretensions to infallibility and unending progress has actually come to doubt its own promises. For example, he argues that many proponents of modernism increasingly recognize that what has been developed by the West in the name of mastery actually indicates the failure of modernism to produce a technology of self and power that can deliver on the promises of providing freedom through science, technology, and control. He writes:

> [A loss of faith in the promises of modernism] . . . is no less true for corporate and governmental culture in the United States which displays a . . . desperate quest for aestheticization of the self as modernist construct—white, male, Christian, industrialist—through monumentally styled office buildings, the Brooks Brothers suit (for male and female), designer food, business practices which amount only to the exercise of symbolic power, and most of all, the Mercedes Benz which as the unification in design of the good (here functional) and the beautiful and in production of industrial coordination and exploitation of human labor is preeminently the sign that one has finally achieved liberation and mastery, 'made it to the top' (even if its stylistic lines thematize what can only be called a fascist aesthetics).[19]

It is against the claims of social and aesthetic modernism that the diverse discourses of postmodernism and feminism have delivered some of their strongest theoretical and political criticisms, and these will be taken up shortly. But there is a third tradition of modernism that has been engaged by feminism but generally ignored by postmodernism. This is the tradition of political modernism, which, unlike its related aesthetic and social traditions, does not focus on epistemological and cultural issues as much as it develops a project of possibility out of a number of Enlightenment ideals.[20] It should be noted that political modernism constructs a project that rests on a distinction between political liberalism and economic liberalism. With the latter, freedom is conflated with the dynamics of the capitalist marketplace, whereas with the former, freedom is associated with the principles and rights embodied in the democratic revolution that has progressed in the West over the last three centuries. The ideals that have emerged out of this revolution include "the notion that human beings ought to use their reason to decide on courses of action, control their futures, enter into reciprocal agreements, and be responsible for what they do and who they are."[21] In general terms, the political project of modernism is rooted in the capacity of individuals to be moved by human suffering so as to remove its causes, to give meaning to the principles of equality, liberty, and justice; and to increase those social forms that enable human beings to develop those capacities needed to overcome ideologies and material forms that legitimate and are embedded in relations of domination.

The tradition of political modernism has largely been taken up and defended in opposition to and against the discourse of postmodernism. Consequently, when postmodernism is defined in relation to the discourse of democracy it is pitted against the Enlightenment project and seen as reactionary in its political tendencies, [22] grafted onto a notion of economic liberalism that converts it into an apology for rich Western democracies, [23] or portrayed in opposition to the emancipatory project of Marxism [24] and feminism. [25.] I want to examine next some of the challenges that Jürgen Habermas presents to various versions of postmodernism and feminism through his defense of modernity as an unfinished emancipatory project.

Habermas and the Challenge of Modernism

Habermas has been one of the most vigorous defenders of the legacy of modernism. Habermas's work is important because in forging his defense of modernism as part of a critique of the postmodernist and poststructuralist discourses that have emerged in France since 1968, he has opened up a debate between these seemingly opposing positions. Moreover, Habermas has attempted to revise and reconstruct the earlier work of his Frankfurt School colleagues, Theodor Adorno and Max Horkheimer, by revising their pessimistic view of rationality and democratic struggle.

Habermas identifies postmodernity less as a question of style and culture than as one of politics. Postmodernism's rejection of grand narratives, its denial of epistemological foundations, and its charge that reason and truth are always implicated in relations of power are viewed by Habermas as both a retreat and a threat to modernity. For him, postmodernism has a paradoxical relation with modernism. On the one hand, it embodies the worst dimensions of an aesthetic modernism. That is, it extends those aspects of the avant-garde that "live in the experience of rebelling against all that is normative." [26] In this sense, postmodernism echoes surrealism's attempt to undermine the cultural autonomy of art by removing the boundaries that separate it from everyday life. On the other hand, postmodernism represents a negation of the project of social modernity by rejecting its language of universal reason, rights, and autonomy as a foundation for modern social life. According to Habermas, postmodernism's argument that realism, consensus, and totality are synonymous with terror represents a form of political and ethical exhaustion that unjustifiably renounces the task of the rule of reason. [27]

In Habermas's terms, the postmodernist thinkers are conservatives whose philosophical roots are to be found in various irrationalist and counter-Enlightenment theories that resemble a peculiar political kinship with fascism. Hence, postmodernism undermines the still unfolding project of modernity, with its promise of democracy through the rule of reason, communicative competence, and cultural differentiation. Postmodernism is guilty of the dual crime, in this case, of both rejecting the most basic tenets of the modernist ethos and failing to recognize its most emancipatory contributions to contemporary life. In the first instance, postmodernism recklessly overemphasizes the play of difference, contingency, and language against all appeals to universalized and transcendental claims. For the postmodernist, theory without the guarantee of truth redefines the relationship between discourse and power and in doing so destabilizes the modernist faith in consensus and reason. For Habermas, postmodernism represents a revolt against a substantive view of reason and subjectivity and negates the productive features of modernism.

Modernity offers Habermas the promise of integrating the differentiating spheres of science, morality, and art back into society not through an appeal to power, but through the rule of reason, the application of a universal pragmatics of language, and the development of forms of learning based on the dictates of communicative competence. While Habermas accepts the excesses of technological rationality and substantive reason, he believes that it is only through reason that the logic of scientific-technological rationality and domination can be subordinated to the imperatives of modernist justice and morality.[28] Habermas admires Western culture and argues that "bourgeois ideals" contain elements of reason that should be at the center of a democratic society. He writes:

> I mean the internal theoretical dynamic which constantly propels the sciences—and the self-reflection of the sciences as well—beyond the creation of merely technologically exploitable knowledge; furthermore, I mean the universalist foundations of law and morality which have also been embodied (in no matter how distorted and imperfect a form) in the institutions of constitutional states, in the forms of democratic decision-making, and in individualistic patterns of identity formation; finally, I mean the productivity and the liberating force of an aesthetic experience with a subjectivity set free from the imperatives of purposive activity and from the conventions of everyday perception.[29]

Central to Habermas's defense of modernity is his important distinction between instrumental rationality and communicative rationality. Instrumental rationality represents those systems or practices embodied in the state, money, and various forms of power that work through "steering mechanisms" to stabilize society. Communicative rationality refers to the world of common experience and discursive intersubjective interaction, a world characterized by various forms of socialization mediated through language and oriented toward social integration and consensus. Habermas accepts various criticisms of instrumental rationality, but he largely agrees that capitalism, in spite of its problems, represents more acceptable forms of social differentiation, rationalization, and modernization than have characterized past stages of social and instrumental development. On the other hand, he is adamant about the virtues of communicative rationality, with its emphasis on the rules of mutual understanding, clarity, consensus, and the force of argument. Habermas views any serious attack on this form of rationality as irrational itself. In effect, his notion of communicative rationality provides the basis not only for his ideal speech situation but also for his broader view of social reconstruction. With its distinctions between an outer world of systematic steering practices and a privileged inner world of communicative process, rationality in this case represents in part a division between a world saturated with material power expressed in the evolution of ever-growing and complex subsystems of rational modernization and one shaped by universal reason and communicative action. At the core of this distinction is a notion of democracy in which struggle and conflict are not based on a politics of difference and power, but on a conceptual and linguistic search for defining the content of what is rational.[30]

Habermas's defense of modernity is not rooted in a rigorous questioning of the relationship among discourses, institutional structures, and the interests they produce and legitimate within specific social conditions. Instead, he focuses on linguistic competence and the principle of consensus with its guiding problematic defined by the need to uproot the obstacles to "distorted communication." Not only does this point to a particular view of power, politics, and modernity, it also legitimates, as Stanley Aronowitz points out, a specific notion of reason and learning:

> [Habermas] admonishes us to recognize modernity's unfinished task: the rule of reason. Rather than rules of governance based on power or discursive hegemonies, we are exhorted to create a new imaginary, one that would recognize societies able to resolve social conflicts, at least provisionally, so as to permit a kind of collective reflexivity. Characteristically, Habermas finds that the barriers to learning are not found in the exigencies of class interest, but in distorted communication. The mediation of communication by interest constitutes here an obstacle to reflexive knowledge. "Progressive" societies are those capable of learning—that is, acquiring knowledge that overcomes the limits of strategic or instrumental action.[31]

Habermas's work has been both opposed and taken up by a number of critical and radical groups. He has been highly criticized by feminists such as Nancy Fraser[32] and also embraced by radicals who believe that his search for universal values represents a necessary ingredient in the struggle for human emancipation.[33] In many respects, his writing provides a theoretical marker for examining how the debate over foundationalism and democracy, on the one hand, and a politics of difference and contingency, on the other, has manifested itself as a debate on the left between those who line up for or against different versions of modernism or postmodernism.

A more constructive approach to both the specifics of Habermas's work as well as to the larger issue of modernism is that neither should be accepted or rejected as if the only choice was one of complete denial or conversion. Habermas, for example, is both right and wrong in his analyses of modernism and postmodernism. He is right in attempting to salvage the productive and emancipatory aspects of modernism and for attempting to develop a unifying principle that provides a referent for engaging and advancing a democratic society. He is also right in claiming that postmodernism is as much about the issue of politics and culture as it is about aesthetics and style. In this sense, Habermas provides a theoretical service by trying to keep alive as part of a modernist discourse the categories of critique, agency, and democracy. For better or worse, Habermas injects into the modernist versus postmodernist debate the primacy of politics and the role that rationality might play in the service of human freedom and the imperatives of democratic ideology and struggle. As Thomas McCarthy points out, Habermas:

> Believes that the defects of the Enlightenment can only be made good by further enlightenment. The totalized critique of reason undercuts the capacity of reason to be critical. It refuses to acknowledge that modernization bears developments as well as distortions of reason. Among the former, he mentions the "unthawing" and "reflective refraction" of cultural traditions, the universalization of norms and generalization of values, and the growing individuation of personal identities—all prerequisites for that effectively democratic organization of society through which alone reason can, in the end, become practical.[34]

It is around these concerns that postmodern theorists have challenged some of the basic assumptions of modernism. For Habermas, these challenges weaken rather than mobilize the democratic tendencies of modernism. But as I hope to demonstrate in the remainder of this chapter, Habermas is wrong in simply dismissing all forms of postmodernism as antimodernist and neoconservative. Moreover, given his own notion of consensus and social action, coupled with his defense of Western tradition, his view of modernity is too complicitous with a notion of reason that is used to legitimate the superiority of a culture that is primarily white, male, and Eurocentric. Habermas speaks from a position that is not only susceptible to the charge of being patriarchal but is also open to the charge that his work does not adequately engage the relationship between discourse and power and the messy material relations of class, race, and gender. Postmodern and feminist critiques of his work cannot be dismissed simply because they might be labeled as antimodern or antirationalist. In what follows, I want to take up some of the challenges that postmodernism has developed in opposition to some of the central assumptions of modernism.

Postmodern Negations

> If postmodernism means putting the Word in its place . . . if it means the opening up to critical discourse the lines of enquiry which were formerly prohibited, of evidence which was previously inadmissible so that new and different questions can be asked and new and other voices can begin asking them; if it means the opening up of institutional and discursive spaces within which more fluid and plural social and sexual identities may develop; if it means the erosion of triangular formations of power and knowledge with

the expert at the apex and the "masses" at the base; if, in a word, it enhances our collective (and democratic) sense of possibility, then I for one am a postmodernist.[35]

Dick Hebdige's guarded comments regarding his own relationship to postmodernism are suggestive of some of the problems that have to be faced in using the term. As the term is increasingly employed both in and out of the academy to designate a variety of discourses, its political and semantic currency repeatedly becomes an object of conflicting forces and divergent tendencies. Postmodernism has not only become a site for conflicting ideological struggles—denounced by different factions on both the left and the right, supported by an equal number of diverse progressive groups, and appropriated by interests that would renounce any claim to politics—its varied forms have also produced both radical and reactionary elements. Postmodernism's diffuse influence and contradictory character are evident within many cultural fields—painting, architecture, photography, video, dance, literature, education, music, and mass communications—and in the varied contexts of its production and exhibition. Such a term does not lend itself to the usual topology of categories that serve to inscribe it ideologically and politically within traditional binary oppositions. In this case, the politics of postmodernism cannot be neatly labeled under the traditional categories of left and right.

That many groups are making a claim for its use should not suggest that the term has no value except as a buzzword for the latest intellectual fashions. On the contrary, its widespread appeal and conflict-ridden terrain indicate that something important is being fought over, that new forms of social discourse are being constructed at a time when the intellectual, political, and cultural boundaries of the age are being refigured amidst significant historical shifts, changing power structures, and emergent alternative forms of political struggle. Of course, whether these new postmodernist discourses adequately articulate rather than reflect these changes is the important question.

I believe that the discourse of postmodernism is worth struggling over, and not merely as a semantic category that needs to be subjected to evermore precise definitional rigor. As a discourse of plurality, difference, and multinarratives, postmodernism resists being inscribed in any single articulating principle in order to explain either the mechanics of domination or the dynamic of emancipation. At issue here is the need to mine its contradictory and oppositional insights so that they might be appropriated in the service of a radical project of democratic struggle. The value of postmodernism lies in its role as a shifting signifier that both reflects and contributes to the unstable cultural and structural relationships that increasingly characterize the advanced industrial countries of the West. The important point here is not whether postmodernism can be defined within the parameters of particular politics, but how its best insights might be appropriated within a progressive and emancipatory democratic politics.

I want to argue that while postmodernism does not suggest a particular ordering principle for defining a particular political project, it does have a rudimentary coherence with respect to the set of "problems and basic issues that have been created by the various discourses of postmodernism, issues that were not particularly problematic before but certainly are now."[36] Postmodernism raises questions and problems so as to redraw and re-present the boundaries of discourse and cultural criticism. The issues that postmodernism has brought into view can be seen, in part, through its various refusals of all "natural laws" and transcendental claims that by definition attempt to "escape" from any type of historical and normative grounding. In fact, if there is any underlying harmony to various discourses of postmodernism, it is in their rejection of absolute essences. Arguing along similar lines, Laclau claims that postmodernity as a discourse of social and cultural criticism begins with a form of epistemological, ethical, and political awareness based on three fundamental negations:

> The beginning of postmodernity can . . . be conceived as the achievement of multiple awareness: epistemological awareness, insofar as scientific progress appears as a succession of paradigms whose transformation and replacement is not grounded in any algorithmic certainty; ethical awareness, insofar as the defense and assertion of values is grounded on argumentative movements (conversational movements, according to Rorty), which do not lead back to any absolute foundation; political awareness, insofar as historical achievements appear as the product of the hegemonic and contingent—and as such, always reversible—articulations and not as the result of immanent laws of history.[37]

Laclau's list does not exhaust the range of negations that postmodernism has taken up as part of the increasing resistance to all totalizing explanatory systems and the growing call for a language that offers the possibility to address the changing ideological and structural conditions of our time. In what follows, I shall address some of the important thematic considerations that cut across what I define as a series of post-modern negations. I shall address these negations in terms of the challenge they present to what can be problematized as either oppressive or productive features of modernism.

Postmodernism and the Negation of Totality, Reason, and Foundationalism

A central feature of postmodernism has been its critique of totality, reason, and universality. This critique has been most powerfully developed in the work of Jean-François Lyotard. In developing his attack on Enlightenment notions of totality, Lyotard argues that the very notion of the postmodern is inseparable from an incredulity toward metanarratives. In Lyotard's view, "The narrative view is losing its functors, its great hero, its great dangers, its great voyages, it great goal. It is being dispersed in clouds of narrative language elements—narrative, but also denotative, prescriptive, descriptive, and so on."[38] For Lyotard, grand narratives do not problematize their own legitimacy;

rather, they deny the historical and social construction of their own first principles and in doing so wage war on difference, contingency, and particularity. Against Habermas and others, Lyotard argues that appeals to reason and consensus, when inserted within grand narratives that unify history, emancipation, and knowledge, deny their own implications in the production of knowledge and power. More emphatically, Lyotard claims that within such narratives are elements of mastery and control in which "we can hear the mutterings of the desire for a return of terror, for the realization of the fantasy to seize reality."[39] Against metanarratives, which totalize historical experience by reducing its diversity to a one-dimensional, all-encompassing logic, Lyotard posits a discourse of multiple horizons, the play of language games, and the terrain of micropolitics. Against the formal logic of identity and the transhistorical subject, he invokes a dialectics of indeterminacy, varied discourses of legitimation, and a politics based on the "permanence of difference." Lyotard's attack on metanarratives represents both a trenchant form of social criticism and a philosophical challenge to all forms of foundationalism that deny the historical, normative, and the contingent. Nancy Fraser and Linda Nicholson articulate this connection well:

> For Lyotard, postmodernism designates a general condition of contemporary Western civilization. The postmodern condition is one in which "grand narratives of legitimation" are no longer credible. By "grand narratives" he means, in the first instance, overarching philosophies of history like the Enlightenment story of the gradual but steady progress of reason and freedom, Hegel's dialectic of Spirit coming to know itself, and, most important, Marx's drama of the forward march of human productive capacities via class conflict culminating in proletarian revolution. . . . For what most interests [Lyotard] about the Enlightenment, Hegelian, and Marxist stories is what they share with other nonnarrative forms of philosophy. Like ahistorical epistemologies and moral theories, they aim to show that specific first-order discursive practices are well formed and capable of yielding true and just results. True and just here mean something more than results reached by adhering scrupulously to the constitutive rules of some given scientific and political games. They mean, rather, results that correspond to Truth and Justice as they really are in themselves independent of contingent, historical social practices. Thus, in Lyotard's view, a metanarrative . . . purports to be a privileged discourse capable of situating, characterizing, and evaluating all other discourses, but not itself infected by the historicity and contingency that render first-order discourses potentially distorted and in need of legitimation.[40]

What Fraser and Nicholson imply is that postmodernism does more than wage war on totality, it also calls into question the use of reason in the service of power, the role of intellectuals who speak through authority invested in a science of truth and history, and forms of leadership that demand unification and consensus within centrally administered chains of command. Postmodernism rejects a notion of reason that is disinterested, transcendent, and universal. Rather than separating reason from the terrain of history, place, and desire, postmodernism argues that reason and science can only be understood as part of a broader historical, political, and social struggle over the relationship between language and power. Within this context, the distinctions between passion and reason, objectivity and interpretation, no longer exist as separate entities but represent, instead, the effects of particular discourses and forms of social power. This is not merely an epistemological issue, but one that is deeply political and normative. Gary Peller makes this clear by arguing that what is at stake in this form of criticism is nothing less than the dominant and liberal commitment to Enlightenment culture. He writes:

> Indeed the whole way that we conceive of liberal progress (overcoming prejudice in the name of truth, seeing through the distortions of ideology to get at reality, surmounting ignorance and superstition with the acquisition of knowledge) is called into question. Postmodernism suggests that what has been presented in our social-political and our intellectual traditions as knowledge, truth, objectivity, and reason are actually merely the effects of a particular form of social power, the victory of a particular way of representing the world that then presents itself as beyond mere interpretation, as truth itself.[41]

By asserting the primacy of the historical and contingent in the construction of reason, authority, truth, ethics, and identity, postmodernism provides a politics of representation and a basis for social struggle. Laclau argues that the postmodern attack on foundationalism is an eminently political act because it expands the possibility for argumentation and dialogue. Moreover, by acknowledging questions of power and value in the construction of knowledge and subjectivities, postmodernism helps to make visible important ideological and structural forces, such as race, gender, and class. For theorists such as Laclau, the collapse of foundationalism does not suggest a banal relativism or the onset of a dangerous nihilism. On the contrary, Laclau argues that the lack of ultimate meaning radicalizes the possibilities for human agency and a democratic politics. He writes:

> Abandoning the myth of foundations does not lead to nihilism, just as uncertainty as to how an enemy will attack does not lead to passivity. It leads, rather, to a proliferation of discursive interventions and arguments that are necessary, because there is no extra-discursive reality that discourse might simply reflect. Inasmuch as argument and discourse constitute the social, their open-ended character becomes the source of a greater activism and a more radical libertarianism. Humankind, having always bowed to external forces—God, Nature, the necessary laws of History—can now, at the threshold of postmodernity, consider itself for the first time the creator and constructor of its own history.[42]

The postmodern attack on totality and foundationalism is not without its drawbacks. While it rightly focuses on the importance of local narratives and rejects the notion that truth precedes the notion of representation, it also runs the risk of blurring the distinction between master narratives that are monocausal, and formative narratives that provide the basis for historically and relationally placing different groups or local narratives within some common project. To draw out this point further, it is difficult to imagine any politics of difference as a form of radical social theory if it doesn't offer a formative narrative capable of analyzing difference within rather than against unity. I will develop these criticisms in more detail in another section.

Postmodernism as the Negation of Border Cultures

Postmodernism offers a challenge to the cultural politics of modernism at a number of different levels. That is, it not only provides a discourse for retheorizing culture as fundamental to the construction of political subjects and collective struggle, it also theorizes culture as a politics of representation and power. Emily Hicks has presented the postmodern challenge to modernist culture as one framed within the contexts of shifting identities, the remapping of borders, and nonsynchronous memory.[43] In her terms, modernist culture negates the possibility of identities created within the experience of multiple narratives and "border" crossings; instead, modernism frames culture within rigid boundaries that both privilege and exclude around the categories of race, class, gender, and ethnicity. Within the discourse of modernism, culture, in large part, becomes an organizing principle for constructing borders that reproduce relations of domination, subordination, and inequality. In this case, borders do not offer the possibility to experience and position ourselves within a productive exchange of narratives. Instead, modernism constructs borders framed in the language of universals and oppositions. Within the cultural politics of modernism, European culture becomes identified with the center of civilization, high culture is defined in essentialist terms against the popular culture of the everyday, and history as the reclaiming of critical memory is displaced by the proliferation of images. In effect, postmodernism constitutes a general attempt to transgress the borders sealed by modernism, to proclaim the arbitrariness of all boundaries, and to call attention to the sphere of culture as a shifting social and historical construction.

I want to approach the postmodern challenge to a modernist cultural politics by focusing briefly on a number of issues. First, postmodernism has broadened the discussion regarding the relationship between culture and power by illuminating the changing conditions of knowledge embedded in the age of electronically mediated information systems, cybernetic technologies, and computer engineering. In doing so, it has pointed to the development of new forms of knowledge that significantly shape traditional analyses relevant to the intersection of culture, power, and politics. Second, postmodernism raises a new set of questions regarding how culture is inscribed in the production of center/margin hierarchies and the reproduction of postcolonial forms of subjugation. At issue here is not only a reconsideration of the intersection of race, gender, and class, but also a new way of reading history; that is, postmodernism provides forms of historical knowledge as a way of reclaiming power and identity for subordinate groups.[44] Third, postmodernism breaks down the distinction between high and low culture and makes the everyday an object of serious study.[45]

In the first instance, postmodernism points to the increasingly powerful and complex role of the new electronic medium in constituting individual identities, cultural languages, and new social formations. Postmodernism has thus provided a new discourse that enables us to understand the changing nature of domination and resistance in late capitalist societies.[46] This is particularly true in its analyses of how the conditions for the production of knowledge have changed within the last two decades with respect to the electronic information technologies of production, the types of knowledge produced, and the impact they have had at both the level of everyday life and in larger global terms.[47] Postmodern discourses highlight radical changes in the ways in which culture is produced, circulated, read, and consumed; moreover, they seriously challenge those theoretical models that have inadequately analyzed culture as a productive and constituting force within an increasingly global network of scientific, technological, and information-producing apparatuses.

In the second instance, postmodernism has provided an important theoretical service in mapping the relations of the center and periphery with respect to three related interventions into cultural politics. First, it has offered a powerful challenge to the hegemonic notion that Eurocentric culture is superior to other cultures and traditions by virtue of its canonical status as a universal measure of Western civilization. In exposing the particularity of the alleged universals that constitute Eurocentric culture, postmodernism has revealed that the "truth" of Western culture is by design a metanarrative that ruthlessly expunges the stories, traditions, and voices of those who by virtue of race, class, and gender constitute the Other. Postmodernism's war on totality is defined, in this case, as a campaign against Western patriarchal culture and ethnocentricity. To the extent that postmodernism has rejected the ethnocentricism of Western culture, it has also waged a battle against those forms of academic knowledge that serve to reproduce the dominant Western culture as a privileged canon and tradition immune from history, ideology, and social criticism.[48]

Central to such a challenge is a second aspect of postmodernism's refiguring of the politics of the center and the margins. That is, postmodernism not only challenges the form and content of dominant models of knowledge, but it also produces new forms of knowledge through its emphasis on breaking down disciplines and taking up objects of study that were unrepresentable in the dominant discourses of the Western canon.

Postmodern criticism provides an important theoretical and political service in assisting those deemed "Other" to reclaim their own histories and voices. By problematizing the dominant notion of tradition, postmodernism has developed a power-sensitive discourse that helps subordinated and excluded groups to make sense out of their own social worlds and histories, while simultaneously offering new opportunities to produce political and cultural vocabularies by which to define and shape their individual and collective identities. At stake here is the rewriting of history within a politics of difference that substitutes totalizing narratives of oppression with local and multiple narratives that assert their identities and interests as part of a broader reconstruction of democratic public life. Craig Owens captures the project of possibility that is part of reclaiming voices that have been relegated to the marginal and, therefore, seem to be unrepresentable. While women emerge as the privileged force of the marginal in this account, his analysis is equally true for a number of subordinated groups:

> It is precisely at the legislative frontier between what can be represented and what cannot that the postmodernist operation is being staged—not in order to transcend representation, but in order to expose that system of power that authorizes certain representations while blocking, prohibiting, or invalidating others. Among those prohibited from Western representation, whose representations are denied all legitimacy, are women. Excluded from representation by its very structure, they return within it as a figure for—a presentation of—the unrepresentable.[49]

Postmodernism's attempt to explore and articulate new spaces is not without its problems. Marginality as difference is not an unproblematic issue, and differences have to be weighed against the implications they have for constructing multiple relations between the self and the other. Moreover, resistance takes place not only on the margins but also at various points of entry within dominant institutions. Needless to say, any notion of difference and marginality runs the risk of mystifying as well as enabling a radical cultural politics. But what is crucial is that postmodernism does offer the possibility for developing a cultural politics that focuses on the margins, for reclaiming, as Edward Said points out, "the right of formerly un- or misrepresented human groups to speak for and represent themselves in domains defined, politically and intellectually, as normally excluding them, usurping their signifying and representing functions, over-riding their historical reality."[50]

This leads to another dimension of a postmodern cultural politics. As part of a broader politics of difference, postmodernism has also focused on the ways in which modernity functions as an imperialist masternarrative that links Western models of industrial progress with hegemonic forms of culture, identity, and consumption. Within this context, the project of modernity relegates all non-Western cultures to the periphery of civilization, outposts of insignificant histories, cultures, and narratives.

In the discourse of neocolonial modernism, the culture of the Other is no longer inscribed in imperialist relations of domination and subordination through the raw exercise of military or bureaucratic power. Power now inscribes itself in apparatuses of cultural production that easily transgress national and cultural borders. Data banks, radio transmissions, and international communications systems become part of the vanguard of a new global network of cultural and economic imperialism. Modernity now parades its universal message of progress through the experts and intellectuals it sends to Third World universities, through the systems of representations that it produces to saturate billboards all over Latin America, and through advertising images it sends out from satellites to the television sets of inhabitants in Africa, India, and Asia.

Postmodernism makes visible both the changing technological nature of postcolonial imperialism and the new forms of emerging resistance that it encounters. On the one hand, it rejects the notion that the colonial relationship is an "uninterrupted psychodrama of repression and subjugation."[51] There is an attempt to understand how power is not only administered, but also taken up, resisted, and struggled over. The Other in this scenario does not suffer the fate of being generalized out of existence, but bears the weight of historical and cultural specificity. In part, this has resulted in a radical attempt to read the culture of the Other as a construction rather than a description, as a form of text that evokes rather than merely represents.[52] Within this scenario, the relationship between the subject and the object, invention and construction is never innocent and is always implicated in theorizing about the margins and the center. At issue here is an attempt to make problematic the voices of those who try to describe the margins, even when they do so in the interest of emancipation and social justice.[53] This suggests yet another aspect of postcolonial discourse that postmodernism has begun to analyze as part of its own cultural politics.

In the postmodern age, the boundaries that once held back diversity, otherness, and difference, whether in domestic ghettoes or through national borders policed by custom officials, have begun to break down. The Eurocentric center can no longer absorb or contain the culture of the Other as something that is threatening and dangerous. As Renato Rosaldo points out, "the Third World has imploded into the metropolis. Even the conservative national politics of containment, designed to shield 'us' from 'them,' betray the impossibility of maintaining hermetically sealed cultures."[54] Culture in neocolonial discourse becomes something that Others have; it is the mark of ethnicity and difference. What has changed in this hegemonic formulation/strategy is that diversity is not ignored in the dominant cultural apparatus, but promoted in order to be narrowly and reductively defined through dominant stereotypes. Representation does not merely exclude, it also defines cultural difference by *actively constructing* the identity of the Other for dominant and subordinate groups. Postmodernism challenges postcolonial discourse by bringing the margins to the center in terms of their own voices and histories. Representation gives way to opposition and the struggle over questions of identity, place, and values.[55] Difference holds out the possibility of not only bringing the voices and politics of the Other to the centers of power, but also understanding how the center is implicated in the margins. It is an attempt to understand how the radicalizing of difference can produce new forms of displacement and more refined forms of racism and sexism. Understandably, the best work in this field is being done by writers from the "margins."

Finally, it is well-known that postmodernism breaks with dominant forms of representation by rejecting the distinction between elite and popular culture and by arguing for alternative sites of artistic engagement and forms of experimentation.[56] As an antiaesthetic, postmodernism rejects the modernist notion of privileged culture or art; it renounces "official" centers for "housing" and displaying art and culture along with their interests in origins, periodization, and authenticity. Moreover, postmodernism's challenge to the boundaries of modernist art and culture has, in part, resulted in new forms of art, writing, film-making, and various types of aesthetic and social criticism. For example, films like *Whetherby* and television movies like *Twin Peaks* deny the structure of plot and seem to have no recognizable beginning or end, photographer Sherrie Levine uses a "discourse of copy" in her work in order to transgress the notions of origin and originality, and Connie Hatch focuses on the act of looking itself.[57] Writer James Sculley blurs the lines between writing poetry and producing it within a variety of representational forms.[58] The Talking Heads, an American band, adopt an eclectic range of aural and visual signifiers to produce a pastiche of styles in which genres are mixed, identities shift, and the lines between reality and image are purposely blurred.[59]

Most importantly, postmodernism conceives of the everyday and the popular as worthy of serious *and* playful consideration. In the first instance, popular culture is analyzed as an important sphere of contestation, struggle, and resistance. In doing so, postmodernism does not abandon the distinctions that structure varied cultural forms within and between different levels of social practice. Instead, it deepens the possibility for understanding the social, historical, and political foundation for such distinctions as they are played out within the intersection of power, culture, and politics. In the second instance, postmodernism cultivates a tone of irony, parody, and playfulness as part of an aesthetic that desacralizes cultural aura and "greatness" while simultaneously demonstrating that "contingency penetrates all identity" and that "the primary and constitutive character of the discursive is . . . the condition of any practice."[60] Richard Kearney has noted that the postmodern notion of play, with its elements of undecidability and poetical imagining, challenges constricted and egocentric levels of selfhood and allows us to move toward a greater understanding of the Other.

> The ex-centric characteristics of the play paradigm may be construed as tokens of the poetical power of imagination to transcend the limits of egocentric, and indeed anthropocentric, consciousness—thereby exploring different possibilities of existence. Such "possibilities" may well be deemed impossible at the level of the established reality.[61]

Central to the postmodern rejection of elite culture as a privileged domain of cultural production and repository of "truth" and civilization is an attempt to understand modernist cultural practices in their hegemonic and contradictory manifestations.

Postmodernism also rejects the notion of popular culture as structured exclusively through a combination of commodity production and audience passivity, a site for both dumping commercial junk and the creation of consumer robots. Instead, postmodernism views popular culture as a terrain of accommodation and struggle, a terrain whose structuring principles should be analyzed not in the reductionistic language of aesthetic standards, but rather through the discourse of power and politics. Of course, it must be stated that the postmodern elements of a cultural politics that I have provided need to be interrogated more closely for their excesses and absences. I will take up this issue in another section, but in what follows I will analyze the third postmodern negation regarding language and subjectivity.

Postmodernism, Language, and the Negation of the Humanist Subject

Within the discourse of postmodernism, the new social agents become plural; that is, the discourse of the universal agent, such as the working class, is replaced by multiple agents forged in a variety of struggles and social movements. Here we have a politics that stresses differences between groups. But it is worth noting that subjectivities are also constituted within difference. This is an important distinction and offers an important challenge to the humanist notion of the subject as a free, unified, stable, and coherent self. In fact, one of the most important theoretical and political advances of postmodernism is its stress on the centrality of language and subjectivity as new fronts from which to rethink the issues of meaning, identity, and politics. This issue can best be approached by first analyzing the ways in which postmodernism has challenged the conventional view of language.

Postmodern discourse has retheorized the nature of language as a system of signs structured in the infinite play of difference, and in doing so has undermined the dominant, positivist notion of language as either a genetic code structured in permanence or simply a linguistic, transparent medium for transmitting ideas and meaning. Theorists such as Jacques Derrida, Michel Foucault, Jacques Lacan, and Laclau and Mouffe, in particular, have played a major role in retheorizing the relationship among discourse, power, and difference.[62] For example, Derrida has brilliantly analyzed the issue of language through the principle of what he calls "différance." This view suggests that meaning is the product of a language constructed out of and subject to the endless play of differences between signifiers. What constitutes the meaning of a signifier is defined by the shifting, changing relations of difference that characterize the referential play of language. What Derrida, Laclau and Mouffe, and a host of other critics have demonstrated is "the increasing difficulty of defining the limits of language, or, more accurately, of defining the specific identity of the linguistic object."[63] But more is at stake here than theoretically demonstrating that meaning can never be fixed once and for all.

The postmodern emphasis on the importance of discourse has also resulted in a major rethinking of the notion of subjectivity. In particular, various postmodern discourses have offered a major critique of the liberal humanist notion of subjectivity, which is predicated on the notion of a unified, rational, self-determining consciousness. In this view, the individual subject is the source of self-knowledge, and his or her view of the world is constituted through the exercise of a rational and autonomous mode of understanding and knowing. What postmodern discourse challenges is liberal humanism's notion of the subject "as a kind of free, autonomous, universal sensibility, indifferent to any particular or moral contents."[64] Teresa Ebert in her discussion of the construction of gender differences offers a succinct commentary on the humanist notion of identity:

> Postmodern feminist cultural theory breaks with the dominant humanist view . . . in which the subject is still considered to be an autonomous individual with a coherent, stable self constituted by a set of natural and pre-given elements such as biological sex. It theorizes the subject as produced through signifying practices, which precede her, and not as the originator of meaning. One acquires specific subject positions—that is, existence in meaning, in social relations—being constituted in ideologically structured discursive acts. Subjectivity is thus the effect of a set of ideologically organized signifying practices through which the individual is situated in the world and in terms of which the world and one's self are made intelligible.[65]

The importance of postmodernism's retheorizing of subjectivity cannot be overemphasized. In this view, subjectivity is no longer assigned to the apolitical wasteland of essences and essentialism. Subjectivity is now read as multiple, layered, and nonunitary; rather than being constituted in a unified and integrated ego, the self is seen as being "constituted out of and by difference and remains contradictory."[66] No longer viewed as merely the repository of consciousness and creativity, the self is constructed as a terrain of conflict and struggle, and subjectivity is seen as a site of both liberation and subjugation. How subjectivity relates to issues of identity, intentionality, and desire is a deeply political issue that is inextricably related to social and cultural forces that extend far beyond the self-consciousness of the so-called humanist subject. Both the very nature of subjectivity and its capacities for self- and social-determination can no longer be situated within the guarantees of transcendent phenomena or metaphysical essences. Within this postmodern perspective, the basis for a cultural politics and the struggle for power have been opened up to include the issues of language and identity. I now want to take up how various feminist discourses reinscribe some of the central assumptions of modernism and postmodernism as part of a broader cultural practice and political project.

Postmodern Feminism as Political and Ethical Practice

Feminist theory has always engaged in a dialectical relationship with modernism. On the one hand, it has stressed modernist concerns with equality, social justice, and freedom through an ongoing engagement with substantive political issues, specifically the rewriting of the historical and social construction of gender in the interest of an emancipatory cultural politics. In other words, feminism has been quite discriminating in its ability to sift through the wreckage of modernism in order to liberate its victories, particularly the unrealized potentialities that reside in its categories of agency, justice, and politics. On the other hand, postmodern feminism has rejected those aspects of modernism in which universal laws are exalted at the expense of specificity and contingency. More specifically, postmodern feminism opposes a linear view of history that legitimates patriarchal notions of subjectivity and society; moreover, it rejects the notion that science and reason have a direct correspondence with objectivity and truth. In effect, postmodern feminism rejects the binary opposition between modernism and postmodernism in favor of a broader theoretical attempt to situate both discourses critically within a feminist political project.

Feminist theory has both produced and profited from a critical appropriation of a number of assumptions central to both modernism and postmodernism. The feminist engagement with modernism has been taken up primarily as a discourse of self-criticism and has served to radically expand a plurality of positions within feminism itself. Women of color, lesbians, and poor and working-class women have challenged the essentialism, separatism, and ethnocentrism that have been expressed in feminist theorizing and in doing so have seriously undermined the Eurocentricism and totalizing discourse that has become a political straitjacket within the movement. Fraser and Nicholson offer a succinct analysis of some of the issues involved in this debate, particularly in relation to the appropriation by some feminists of "quasi-metanarratives:"

> They tacitly presuppose some commonly held but unwarranted and essentialist assumptions about the nature of human beings and the conditions for social life. In addition, they assume methods and/or concepts that are uninflected by temporality or historicity and that therefore function *de facto* as permanent, neutral matrices for inquiry. Such theories, then, share some of the essentialist and ahistorical features of metanarratives: they are insufficiently attentive to historical and cultural diversity; and they falsely universalize features of the theorist's own era, society, culture, class, sexual orientation, and/ or ethnic or racial group. . . . It has become clear that quasi-metanarratives hamper, rather than promote, sisterhood, since they elide differences among women and among the forms of sexism to which different women are differentially subject. Likewise, it is increasingly apparent that such theories hinder alliances with other progressive movements, since they tend to occlude axes of domination other than gender. In sum, there is a growing interest among feminists in modes of theorizing that are attentive to differences and to cultural and historical specificity.[67]

Fashioning a language that has been highly critical of modernism has not only served to make problematic what can be called totalizing feminisms, but has also called into question the notion that sexist oppression is at the root of all forms of domination.[68] Implicit in this position are two assumptions that have significantly shaped the arguments of mostly Western white women. The first argument simply inverts the orthodox Marxist position regarding class as the primary category of domination with all other modes of oppression being relegated to a second-rate consideration. Here, patriarchy becomes the primary form of domination, while race and class are reduced to its distorted reflection. The second assumption recycles another aspect of orthodox Marxism that assumes that the struggle over power is exclusively waged between opposing social classes. The feminist version of this argument simply substitutes gender for class and in doing so reproduces a form of "us" against "them" politics that is antithetical to developing community building within a broad and diversified public culture.

Both of these arguments represent the ideological baggage of modernism. In both cases, domination is framed in binary oppositions, which suggests that workers or women cannot be complicit in their own oppression and that domination assumes a form that is singular and uncomplicated. The feminist challenge to this ideological straitjacket of modernism is well expressed by bell hooks, who avoids the politics of separatism by invoking an important distinction between the role that feminists might play in asserting their own particular struggle against patriarchy as well as the role they can play as part of a broader struggle for liberation:

> Feminist effort to end patriarchal domination should be of primary concern precisely because it insists on the eradication of exploitation and oppression in the family context and in all other intimate relationships. . . . Feminism, as liberation struggle, must exist apart from and as a part of the larger struggle to eradicate domination in all of its forms. We must understand that patriarchal domination shares an ideological foundation with racism and other forms of group oppression, that there is no hope that it can be eradicated while these systems remain intact. This knowledge should consistently inform the direction of feminist theory and practice. Unfortunately, racism and class elitism among women has frequently led to the suppression and distortion of this connection so that it is now necessary for feminist thinkers to critique and revise much feminist theory and the direction of the feminist movement. This effort at revision is perhaps most evident in the current widespread acknowledgement that sexism, racism, and class exploitation constitute interlocking systems of domination—that sex, race, and class, and not sex alone, determine the nature of any female's identity, status, and circumstance, the degree to which she will or will not be dominated, the extent to which she will have the power to dominate.[69]

I invoke the feminist critique of modernism to make visible some of the ideological territory it shares with certain versions of postmodernism and to suggest the wider implications that a postmodern feminism has for developing and broadening the terrain of political struggle and transformation. It is important to note that this encounter between feminism and postmodernism should not be seen as a gesture to displace a feminist politics with a politics and pedagogy of postmodernism. On the contrary, I think feminism provides postmodernism with a politics, and a great deal more. What is at stake here is using feminism, in the words of Meaghan Morris, as "a context in which debates about postmodernism might further be considered, developed, transformed (or abandoned)."[70] Critical to such a project is the need to analyze the ways in which feminist theorists have used postmodernism to fashion a form of social criticism whose value lies in its critical approach to gender issues and in the theoretical insights it provides for developing broader democratic and pedagogical struggles.

The theoretical status and political viability of various postmodern discourses regarding the issues of totality, foundationalism, culture, subjectivity, and language are a matter of intense debate among diverse feminist groups.[71] I am less concerned with charting this debate or focusing on those positions that dismiss postmodernism as antithetical to feminism. Instead, I want to focus primarily on those feminist discourses that acknowledge being influenced by postmodernism but at the same time deepen and radicalize the assumptions most important in the interest of a theory and practice of transformative feminist democratic struggles.[72]

Feminism's relationship with postmodernism has been both fruitful but problematic.[73] Postmodernism shares a number of assumptions with various feminist theories and practices. For example, both discourses view reason as plural and partial, define subjectivity as multilayered and contradictory, and posit contingency and difference against various forms of essentialism.

At the same time, postmodern feminism has criticized and extended a number of assumptions central to postmodernism. First, it has asserted the primacy of social criticism and in doing so has redefined the significance of the postmodern challenge to founding discourses and universal principles in terms that prioritize political struggles over epistemological engagements. Donna Haraway puts it well in her comment that "the issue is ethics and politics perhaps more than epistemology."[74] Second, postmodern feminism has refused to accept the postmodern view of totality as a wholesale rejection of all forms of totality or metanarratives. Third, it has rejected the postmodern emphasis on erasing human agency by decentering the subject; it has also resisted defining language as the only source of meaning and has therefore linked power not merely to discourse but also to material practices and struggles. Fourth, it has asserted the importance of difference as part of a broader struggle for ideological and institutional change rather than emphasizing the postmodern approach to difference as either an aesthetic (pastiche) or an expression of liberal pluralism (the proliferation of difference without recourse to the language of power). Since it is impossible within this chapter to analyze all of these issues in great detail, I will take up some of the more important tendencies implied in these positions.

Postmodern Feminism and the Primacy of the Political

Working collectively to confront difference, to expand our awareness of sex, race, and class as interlocking systems of domination, of the ways we reinforce and perpetuate these structures, is the context in which we learn the true meaning of solidarity. It is this work that must be the foundation of the feminist movement. Without it, we cannot effectively resist patriarchal domination; without it, we remain estranged and alienated from one another. Fear of painful confrontation often leads women and men active in the feminist movement to avoid rigorous critical encounter, yet if we cannot engage dialectically in a committed, rigorous, humanizing manner, we cannot hope to change the world. . . . While the struggle to eradicate sexism and sexist oppression is and should be the primary thrust of feminist movement, to prepare ourselves politically for this effort we must first learn how to be in solidarity, how to struggle with one another.[75]

bell hooks speaks eloquently to the issue of constructing a feminism that is self-consciously political. In solidarity with a number of feminists, she provides a much-needed corrective to the postmodern tendency to eclipse the political and ethical in favor of issues that center on epistemological and aesthetic concerns. Not only does hooks assert that intellectual and cultural work must be driven by political questions and issues, she also performs the theoretically important task of affirming a feminist politics, which attempts to understand and contest the various ways in which patriarchy is inscribed at every level of daily life. But what is different and postmodern about hooks's commentary is that it argues for a postmodern feminist practice that is oppositional in its appeal "to end sexism and sexist oppression,"[76] and she also calls into question those feminisms that reduce domination to a single cause, focus exclusively on sexual difference, and ignore women's differences as they intersect across other vectors of power, particularly with regards to race and class. In this version of postmodern feminist politics there is an attempt to reaffirm the centrality of gender struggles while simultaneously broadening the issues associated with such struggles. Similarly, there is an attempt to connect gender politics to a broader politics of solidarity. Let me be more specific about some of these issues.

Central to the feminist movement in the United States since the 1970s has been the argument that the personal is political. This argument suggests a complex relationship between material social practices and the construction of subjectivity through the use of language. Within this context, subjectivity was analyzed as a historical and social construction, en-gendered through the historically weighted configurations of power, language, and social formations. The problematization of gender relations in this case has been often described as the most important theoretical advance made by feminists.[77] Postmodern feminism has extended the political significance of this issue in important ways.

First, it has strongly argued that feminist analyses cannot downplay the dialectical significance of gender relations. That is, such relations have to focus not only on the various ways in which women are inscribed in patriarchal representations and relations of power, but also on how gender relations can be used to problematize the sexual identities, differences, and commonalities of both men and women. To suggest that masculinity is an unproblematic category is to adopt an essentialist position that ultimately reinforces the power of patriarchal discourse.[78]

Second, feminist theorists have redefined the relationship between the personal and political in ways that advance some important postmodern assumptions. In part, this redefinition of the relationship has emerged out of an increasing feminist criticism that rejects the notions that sexuality is the only axis of domination and that the study of sexuality should be limited theoretically to an exclusive focus on how women's subjectivities are constructed. For example, theorists such as Teresa de Lauretis have argued that central to feminist social criticism is the need for feminists to maintain a "tension between (the personal and the political) precisely through the understanding of identity as multiple and even self-contradictory."[79] To ignore such a tension often leads to the trap of collapsing the political into the personal and limiting the sphere of politics to the language of pain, anger, and separatism. bell hooks elaborates on this point by arguing that when feminists reduce the relationship between the personal and the political merely to the naming of one's pain in relation to structures of domination they often undercut the possibilities for understanding the multifaceted nature of domination and for creating a politics of possibility. She writes:

> That powerful slogan, "the personal is political," addresses the connection between the self and political reality. Yet it was often interpreted as meaning that to name one's personal pain in relation to structures of domination was not just a beginning stage in the process of coming to political consciousness, to awareness, but all that was necessary. In most cases, naming one's personal pain was not sufficiently linked to overall education for critical consciousness of collective political resistance. Focusing on the personal in a framework that did not compel acknowledgement of the complexity of structures of domination could easily lead to misnaming, to the creation of yet another sophisticated level of non- or distorted awareness. This often happens in a feminist context when race and/or class are not seen as factors determining the social construction of one's gendered reality and most importantly, the extent to which one will suffer exploitation and domination.[80]

The construction of gender must, therefore, be seen in the context of the wider relations in which it is structured. At issue here is the need to deepen the postmodern notion of difference by radicalizing the notion of gender through a refusal to isolate it as a social category while simultaneously engaging in a politics that aims at transforming the self, community, and society. Within this context, postmodern feminism offers the possibility of going beyond the language of domination, anger, and critique.

Third, postmodern feminism attempts to understand the broader workings of power by examining how it functions other than through specific technologies of control and mastery. At issue here is understanding how power is constituted productively. Teresa de Lauretis develops this insight by arguing that while postmodernism provides a theoretical service in recognizing that power is "productive of knowledges, meanings, and values, it seems obvious enough that we have to make distinctions between the positive effects and the oppressive effects of such production."[81] Her point is important because it suggests that power can work in the interests of a politics of possibility, that it can be used to rewrite the narratives of subordinate groups not merely in reaction to the forces of domination but in response to the construction of alternative visions and futures. The exclusive emphasis on power as oppressive always runs the risk of developing as its political equivalent a version of radical cynicism and antiutopianism. Postmodern feminism offers the possibility for redefining both a negative feminist politics[82] and a more general postmodern inclination towards a despair that dresses itself up in irony, parody, and pastiche. Linda Alcoff put it well in arguing that "As the Left should by now have learned, you cannot mobilize a movement that is only and always against: you must have a positive alternative, a vision of a better future that can motivate people to sacrifice their time and energy toward its realization."[83] Central to this call for a language of possibility are the ways in which a postmodern feminism has taken up the issue of power in more expansive and productive terms, one that is attentive to the ways in which power inscribes itself through the force of reason, and constructs itself at the levels of intimate and local associations.

Postmodern Feminism and the Politics of Reason and Totality

Various feminist discourses have provided a theoretical context and politics for enriching postmodernism's analyses of reason and totality. Whereas postmodern theorists have stressed the historical, contingent, and cultural construction of reason, they have failed to show how reason has been constructed as part of a masculine discourse.[84] Postmodern feminists have provided a powerful challenge to this position, particularly in their analyses of the ways in which reason, language, and representation have produced knowledge/power relations, legitimated in the discourse of science and objectivity, to silence, marginalize, and misrepresent women.[85] Feminist theorists have also modified the postmodern discussion of reason in two other important ways. First, while recognizing that all claims to reason are partial, they have argued for the emancipatory possibilities that exist in reflective consciousness and critical reason as a basis for social criticism.[86] In these terms, reason is not merely about a politics of representation structured in domination or a relativist discourse that abstracts itself from the dynamics of power and struggle, it also offers the possibility for self-representation and social reconstruction. For example, Haraway has qualified the postmodern turn towards relativism by theorizing reason within a discourse of partiality that "privileges contestation, deconstruction, passionate construction, webbed connections, and hope for transformation of systems of knowledge and ways of seeing."[87] Similarly, hooks and others have argued that feminists who deny the power of critical reason and abstract discourse often reproduce a cultural practice that operates in the interest of patriarchy.[88] That is, it serves to silence women and others by positioning them in ways that cultivate a fear of theory, which in turn often produces a form of powerlessness buttressed by a powerful anti-intellectualism. Second, feminists such as Jane Flax have modified postmodernism's approach to reason by arguing that reason is not the only locus of meaning:

> I cannot agree . . . that liberation, stable meaning, insight, self-understanding and justice depend above all on the "primacy of reason and intelligence." There are many ways in which such qualities may be attained—for example, political practices; economic, racial and gender equality; good childrearing; empathy; fantasy; feelings; imagination; and embodiment. On what grounds can we claim reason is privileged or primary for the self or justice?[89]

At issue here is not the rejection of reason but a modernist version of reason that is totalizing, essentialist, and politically repressive. Postmodern feminism has also challenged and modified the postmodern approach to totality or master narratives on similar terms. While accepting the postmodern critique of master narratives that employ a single standard and make a claim to embody a universal experience, postmodern feminism does not define all large or formative narratives as oppressive. At the same time, postmodern feminism recognizes the importance of grounding narratives in the contexts and specificities of peoples' lives, communities, and cultures, but supplements this distinctly postmodern emphasis on the contextual with an argument for metanarratives that employ forms of social criticism that are dialectical, relational, and holistic. Metanarratives play an important theoretical role in placing the particular and the specific in broader historical and relational contexts. To reject all notions of totality is to run the risk of being trapped in particularistic theories that cannot explain how the various diverse relations that constitute larger social, political, and global systems interrelate or mutually determine and constrain one another. Postmodern feminism recognizes that we need a notion of large narratives that privileges forms of analyses in which it is possible to make visible those mediations, interrelations, and interdependencies that give shape and power to larger political and social systems. Fraser and Nicholson make very clear the importance of such narratives to social criticism:

> Effective criticism . . . requires an array of different methods and genres. It requires, at minimum, large narratives about changes in social organization and ideology, empirical and social-theoretical analyses of macrostructures and institutions, interactionist analyses

of the micropolitics of everyday life, critical-hermeneutical and institutional analyses of cultural production, historically and culturally specific sociologies of gender. . . . The list could go on.[90]

Postmodern Feminism and the Politics of Difference and Agency

Many feminists exhibit a healthy skepticism toward the postmodern celebration of difference. Many feminist theorists welcome the postmodern emphasis on the proliferation of local narratives, the opening up of the world to cultural and ethnic differences, and the positing of difference as a challenge to hegemonic power relations parading as universals.[91] But at the same time, postmodern feminists have raised serious questions about how differences are to be understood so as to change rather than reproduce prevailing power relations.[92] This is particularly important since difference in the postmodern sense often slips into a theoretically harmless and politically deracinated notion of pastiche. For many postmodern feminists, the issue of difference has to be interrogated around a number of concerns. These include questions regarding how a politics of difference can be constructed that will not simply reproduce forms of liberal individualism, or how a politics of difference can be "rewritten as a refusal of the terms of radical separation?"[93] Also at issue is the question regarding how a theory of difference can be developed that is not at odds with a politics of solidarity. Equally important is the issue of how a theory of the subject constructed in difference might sustain or negate a politics of human agency. And there is the question of how a postmodern feminism can redefine the knowledge/power relationship in order to develop a theory of difference that is not static, one that is able to make distinctions between differences that matter and those that do not. All of these questions have been addressed in a variety of feminist discourses, not all of which support postmodernism. What has increasingly emerged from this engagement is a discourse that radically complicates and amplifies the possibilities for reconstructing difference within a radical political project and set of transformative practices.

In the most general sense, the postmodern emphasis on difference serves to dissolve all pretensions to an undifferentiated concept of truth, man, woman, and subjectivity, while at the same time refusing to reduce difference to "opposition, exclusion, and hierarchic arrangement."[94] Postmodern feminism has gone a long way in framing the issue of difference in terms that give it an emancipatory grounding, that identify the "differences that make a difference" as an important political act. Below, I want to briefly take up the issue of difference and agency that has been developed within a postmodern feminist discourse.

Joan Wallach Scott has provided a major theoretical service by dismantling one of the crippling dichotomies in which the issue of difference has been situated. Rejecting the idea that difference and equality constitutes an opposition, Scott argues that the opposite of equality is not difference but inequality. In this sense, the issue of equality is not at odds with the notion of difference, but depends on an acknowledgment of those differences that promote inequality and those that do not. For Scott, the category of difference is central as a political construct to the notion of equality itself. The implication this has for a feminist politics of difference involves two important theoretical moves:

> In histories of feminism and in feminist political strategies there needs to be at once attention to the operations of difference and an insistence on differences, but not a simple substitution of multiple for binary difference, for it is not a happy pluralism we ought to invoke. The resolution of the "difference dilemma" comes neither from ignoring nor embracing difference as it is normatively constituted. Instead it seems to me that the critical feminist position must always involve two moves: the first, systematic criticism of the operations of categorical difference, exposure of the kinds of exclusions and inclusions—the hierarchies—it constructs, and a refusal of their ultimate "truth." A refusal, however, not in the name of an equality that implies sameness or identity but rather (and this is the second move) of an equality that rests on differences—differences that confound, disrupt, and render ambiguous the meaning of any fixed binary opposition. To do anything else is to buy into the political argument that sameness is a requirement for equality, an untenable position for feminists (and historians) who know that power is constructed on, and so must be challenged from, the ground of difference.[95]

According to Scott, challenging power from the ground of difference by focusing on both exclusions and inclusions allows one to avoid slipping into a facile and simple elaboration or romanticization of difference. In more concrete terms, E. Ann Kaplan takes up this issue in arguing that the postmodern elimination of all distinctions between high and low culture is important, but postmodernism goes too far in overlooking the important differences at work in the production and exhibition of specific cultural works.[96] By not discriminating among differences of context, production, and consumption, postmodern discourses run the risk of suppressing the differences at work in the power relations that characterize these different spheres of cultural production. For example, to treat all cultural products as texts may situate them as historical and social constructions, but it is imperative that the institutional mechanisms and power relations in which different texts are produced be distinguished so that it becomes possible to understand how such texts, in part, make a difference in terms of reproducing particular meanings, social relations, and values.

A similar issue is at work regarding the postmodern notion of subjectivity. The postmodern notion that human subjectivities and bodies are constructed in the endless play of difference threatens to erase not only any possibility for human agency or choice, but also the theoretical means for understanding how the body becomes a site of power and struggle around specific differences that do matter with respect to the issues of race, class, and gender. There is little sensibility in many postmodern accounts toward the ways in which different historical, social, and gendered representations of meaning and desire are actually mediated and taken up subjectively by real, concrete individuals. Individuals are positioned within a variety of "subject positions," but there is no sense of how they actually make choices, promote effective resistance, or mediate between themselves and others. Feminist theorists have extended the most radical principles of modernism in modifying the postmodern view of the subject. Theorists such as de Lauretis, Rita Felski, and others insist that the construction of female experience is not constructed outside of human intentions and choices, however limited. They argue that the agency of subjects is made possible through shifting and multiple forms of consciousness constructed through available discourses and practices, but always open to interrogation through the process of a self-analyzing practice. For de Lauretis and others like Alcoff, such a practice is theoretical and political. Alcoff's own attempt to construct a feminist identity-politics draws on de Lauretis's work and is insightful in its attempt to develop a theory of positionality:

> . . . The identity of a woman is the product of her own interpretation and reconstruction of her history, as mediated through a cultural discursive context to which she has access. Therefore, the concept of positionality includes two points: First . . . the concept of woman is a relational term identifiable only with a (constantly moving) context; but second, that the position that women find themselves in can be actively utilized (rather than transcended) as a location for the construction of meaning, a place where a meaning can be discovered (the meaning of femaleness). The concept . . . of positionality shows how women use their positional perspective as a place from which values are interpreted and constructed rather than as a locus of an already determined set of values.[97]

Feminists have also raised a concern with the postmodern tendency to portray the body as so fragmented, mobile, and boundary-less that it invites a confusion over how the body is actually engendered and positioned within concrete configurations of power and forms of material oppression. The postmodern emphasis on the proliferation of ideas, discourses, and representations underplays both the different ways in which bodies are oppressed and how bodies are constructed differently through specific material relations. Feminists such as Sandra Lee Bartky have provided a postmodern reading of the politics of the body by extending Foucault's notion of how the growth of the modern state has been accompanied by an unprecedented attempt at disciplining the body.[98] Where Bartky differs from Foucault is that she employs a discriminating notion of difference by showing how gender is implicated in the production of the body as a site of domination, struggle, and resistance. For example, Bartky points to the disciplinary measures of dieting, the tyranny of slenderness and fashion, the discourse of exercise, and other technologies of control. She also goes beyond Foucault in arguing that the body must be seen as a site of resistance and linked to a broader theory of agency.

Postmodern feminism provides a grounded politics that employs the most progressive aspects of modernism and postmodernism. In the most general sense, it reaffirms
the importance of difference as part of a broader political struggle for the reconstruction of public life. It rejects all forms of essentialism but recognizes the importance of
certain formative narratives. Similarly, it provides a language of power that engages the
issue of inequality and struggle. In recognizing the importance of institutional structures
and language in the construction of subjectivities and political life, it promotes social
criticism that acknowledges the interrelationship between human agents and social
structures, rather than succumbing to a social theory without agents or one in which
agents are simply the product of broad structural and ideological forces. Finally,
postmodern feminism provides a radical social theory imbued with a language of critique and possibility. Implicit in its various discourses are new relations of parenting,
work, schooling, play, citizenship, and joy. These are relations that link a politics of
intimacy and solidarity, the concrete and the general; they provide a politics that in its
various forms needs to be taken up as central to the development of a critical pedagogy.
That is, critical educators need to provide a sense of how the most critical elements of
modernism, postmodernism, and postmodern feminism might be taken up by teachers,
educators, and cultural workers so as to create a postmodern pedagogical practice. Finally,
I want to briefly outline what some of the principles are that inform such a practice.

Towards a Postmodern Pedagogy

As long as people are people, democracy in the full sense of the word will always be no
more than an ideal. One may approach it as one would a horizon, in ways that may be
better or worse, but it can never be fully attained. In this sense, you too, are merely approaching democracy. You have thousands of problems of all kinds, as other countries
do. But you have one great advantage: You have been approaching democracy uninterrupted for more than 200 years.[99]

How on earth can these prestigious persons in Washington ramble on in their
subintellectual way about the "end of history?" As I look forward into the twenty-first
century I sometimes agonize about the times in which my grandchildren and their children will live. It is not so much the rise in population as the rise in universal material
expectations of the globe's huge population that will be straining its resources to the very
limits. North–South antagonisms will certainly sharpen, and religious and national fundamentalisms will become more intransigent. The struggle to bring consumer greed within
moderate control, to find a level of low growth and satisfaction that is not at the expense
of the disadvantaged and poor, to defend the environment and to prevent ecological
disasters, to share more equitably the world's resources and to insure their renewal—all
this is agenda enough for the continuation of "history."[100]

A striking character of the totalitarian system is its peculiar coupling of human demoral-
ization and mass depoliticizing. Consequently, battling this system requires a conscious
appeal to morality and an inevitable involvement in politics.[101]

All these quotations stress, implicitly or explicitly, the importance of politics and ethics to democracy. In the first, the newly elected president of Czechoslovakia, Vaclav Havel, addressing a joint session of Congress reminds the American people that democracy is an ideal that is filled with possibilities but one that always has to be seen as part of an ongoing struggle for freedom and human dignity. As a playwright and former political prisoner, Havel is the embodiment of such a struggle. In the second, E. P. Thompson, the English peace activist and historian, reminds the American public that history has not ended but needs to be opened up in order to engage the many problems and possibilities that human beings will have to face in the twenty-first century. In the third, Adam Michnik, a founder of Poland's Workers' Defense Committee and an elected member of the Polish parliament, provides an ominous insight into one of the central features of totalitarianism, whether on the Right or the Left. He points to a society that fears democratic politics while simultaneously reproducing a sense of massive collective despair. All of these writers are caught up in the struggle to recapture the Enlightenment model of freedom, agency, and democracy while simultaneously attempting to deal with the conditions of a postmodern world.

These statements serve to highlight the inability of the American public to grasp the full significance of the democraticization of Eastern Europe in terms of what it reveals about the nature of our own democracy. In Eastern Europe and elsewhere there is a strong call for the primacy of the political and the ethical as a foundation for democratic public life, whereas in the United States there is an ongoing refusal of the discourse of politics and ethics. Elected politicians from both sides of the established parties complain that American politics is about "trivialization, atomization, and paralysis." Politicians as different as the late Lee Atwater, the former Republican Party chairman, and Walter Mondale, former vice president, agree that we have entered into a time in which much of the American public believes that "Bull permeates everything . . . (and that) we've got a kind of politics of irrelevance."[102] At the same time, a number of polls indicate that while the youth of Poland, Czechoslovakia, and Germany are extending the frontiers of democracy, American youth are both unconcerned and largely ill-prepared to struggle for and keep democracy alive in the twenty-first century.

Rather than being a model of democracy, the United States has become indifferent to the need to struggle for the conditions that make democracy a substantive rather than lifeless activity. At all levels of national and daily life, the breadth and depth of democratic relations are being rolled back. We have become a society that appears to demand less rather than more of democracy. In some quarters, democracy has actually become subversive. What does this suggest for developing some guiding principles in order to rethink the purpose and meaning of education and critical pedagogy within the present crises? In what follows, I want to situate some of the work I have been developing on critical pedagogy over the last decade by placing it within a broader political context. That is, the principles that I develop below represent educational issues that must be located in a larger framework of politics. Moreover, these principles emerge out of a convergence of various tendencies within modernism, postmodernism, and postmodern feminism. What is important to note here is the refusal to simply play off these various theoretical tendencies against each other. Instead, I try to critically appropriate the most important aspects of these theoretical movements by raising the question of how they contribute to creating the conditions for deepening the possibilities for a radical pedagogy and political project that aim at reconstructing democratic public life so as to extend the principles of freedom, justice, and equality to all spheres of society.

At stake here is the issue of retaining modernism's commitment to critical reason, agency, and the power of human beings to overcome human suffering. Modernism reminds us of the importance of constructing a discourse that is ethical, historical, and political. At the same time, postmodernism provides a powerful challenge to all total-izing discourses, places an important emphasis on the contingent and the specific, and provides a new theoretical language for developing a politics of difference. Finally, postmodern feminism makes visible the importance of grounding our visions in a political project, redefines the relationship between the margins and the center around concrete political struggles, and offers the opportunity for a politics of voice that links rather than severs the relationship between the personal and the political as part of a broader struggle for justice and social transformation. All the principles developed below touch on these issues and recast the relationship between the pedagogical and the political as central to any social movement that attempts to effect emancipatory struggles and social transformations. All of these issues are dealt with in more detail throughout this book.[103]

1. Education needs to be reformulated so as to give as much attention to pedagogy as it does to traditional and alternative notions of scholarship. This is not a question of giving pedagogy equal weight to scholarship as much as it is of assessing the important relationship between them. Education must be understood as the production of iden-tities in relation to the ordering, representation, and legitimation of specific forms of knowledge and power. As Chandra Mohanty reminds us, questions about education cannot be reduced to disciplinary parameters, but must include issues of power, his-tory, self-identity, and the possibility of collective agency and struggle.[104] Rather than rejecting the language of politics, critical pedagogy must link public education to the imperatives of a critical democracy. Critical pedagogy needs to be informed by a public philosophy defined, in part, by the attempt to create the lived experience of empower-ment for the vast majority. In other words, the language of critical pedagogy needs to construct schools as democratic public spheres.

In part, this means that educators need to develop a critical pedagogy in which the knowledge, habits, and skills of critical citizenship, not simply good citizenship, are taught and practiced. This means providing students with the opportunity to develop the critical capacity to challenge and transform existing social and political forms, rather than simply adapt to them. It also means providing students with the skills they will need to locate themselves in history, find their own voices, and provide the convictions and compassion necessary for exercising civic courage, taking risks, and furthering the habits, customs, and social relations that are essential to democratic public forms.

In effect, critical pedagogy needs to be grounded in a keen sense of the importance of constructing a political vision from which to develop an educational project as part of a wider discourse for revitalizing democratic public life. A critical pedagogy for democracy cannot be reduced, as some educators, politicians, and groups have argued, to forcing students either to say the pledge of allegiance at the beginning of every school day or to speak and think only in the language of dominant English. A critical pedagogy for democracy does not begin with test scores but with questions. What kinds of citizens do we hope to produce through public education in a postmodern culture? What kind of society do we want to create in the context of the present shifting cultural and ethnic borders? How can we reconcile the notions of difference and equality with the imperatives of freedom and justice?

2. Ethics must be seen as a central concern of critical pedagogy. This suggests that educators attempt to understand more fully how different discourses offer students diverse ethical referents for structuring their relationship to the wider society. But it also suggests that educators go beyond the postmodern notion of understanding how student experiences are shaped within different ethical discourses. Educators must come to view ethics and politics as a relationship between the self and the other. Ethics, in this case, is not a matter of individual choice or relativism but a social discourse that refuses to accept needless human suffering and exploitation. Ethics becomes a practice that broadly connotes one's personal and social sense of responsibility to the Other. Thus, ethics is taken up as a struggle against inequality and as a discourse for expanding basic human rights. This points to a notion of ethics attentive to both the issue of abstract rights and those contexts that produce particular stories, struggles, and histories. In pedagogical terms, an ethical discourse needs to be taken up with regard to the relations of power, subject positions, and social practices it activates. This is an ethics of neither essentialism nor relativism. It is an ethical discourse grounded in historical struggles and attentive to the construction of social relations free of injustice. The quality of ethical discourse is not simply grounded in difference but in the issue of how justice arises out of concrete historical circumstances and public struggles.

3. Critical pedagogy needs to focus on the issue of difference in an ethically challenging and politically transformative way. There are at least two notions of difference at work here. One, difference can be incorporated into a critical pedagogy as part of an attempt to understand how student identities and subjectivities are constructed in multiple and contradictory ways. In this case, identity is explored through its own historicity

and complex subject positions. The category of student experience should not be limited pedagogically to students exercising self-reflection but opened up as a race, gender, and class specific construct to include the diverse ways in which students' experiences and identities have been constituted in different historical and social formations. Two, critical pedagogy can focus on how differences between groups develop and are sustained around both enabling and disabling sets of relations. In this instance, difference becomes a marker for understanding how social groups are constituted in ways that are integral to the functioning of any democratic society. Examining difference in this context does not only focus on charting spatial, racial, ethnic, or cultural differences structured in dominance, but also analyzes historical differences that manifest themselves in public struggles.

As part of a language of critique, teachers can make problematic how different subjectivities are positioned within a historically specific range of ideologies and social practices that inscribe students in various subject positions. Similarly, such a language can analyze how differences within and between social groups are constructed and sustained within and outside of the schools in webs of domination, subordination, hierarchy, and exploitation. As part of their use of a language of possibility, teachers can explore the opportunity to develop knowledge/power relations in which multiple narratives and social practices are constructed around a politics and pedagogy of difference that offers students the opportunity to read the world differently, resist the abuse of power and privilege, and construct alternative democratic communities. Difference in this case cannot be seen as simply either a register of plurality or a politics of assertion. Instead, it must be developed within practices in which differences can be affirmed *and* transformed in their articulation with historical and relational categories central to emancipatory forms of public life: democracy, citizenship, and public spheres. In both political and pedagogical terms, the category of difference must not be simply acknowledged but defined relationally in terms of antiracist, antipatriarchal, multicentric, and ecological practices central to the notion of democratic community.

4. Critical pedagogy needs a language that allows for competing solidarities and political vocabularies that do not reduce the issues of power, justice, struggle, and inequality to a single script, a master narrative that suppresses the contingent, the historical, and the everyday as serious objects of study. This suggests that curriculum knowledge should not be treated as a sacred text but developed as part of an ongoing engagement with a variety of narratives and traditions that can be reread and reformulated in politically different terms. At issue here is how to construct a discourse of textual authority that is power-sensitive and developed as part of a wider analysis of the struggle over culture fought out at the levels of curricula knowledge, pedagogy, and the exercise of institutional power. This is not merely an argument against a canon, but one that refigures the meaning and use of canons. Knowledge has to be constantly re-examined in terms of its limits and rejected as a body of information that only has

to be passed down to students. As Laclau has pointed out, setting limits to the answers given by what can be judged as a valued tradition (a matter of argument also) is an important political act.[105] What Laclau is suggesting is the possibility for students to creatively appropriate the past as part of a living dialogue, an affirmation of the multiplicity of narratives, and the need to judge those narratives not as timeless or as monolithic discourses, but as social and historical inventions that can be refigured in the interests of creating more democratic forms of public life. Here is opened the possibility of creating pedagogical practices characterized by the open exchange of ideas, the proliferation of dialogue, and the material conditions for the expression of individual and social freedom.

5. Critical pedagogy needs to create new forms of knowledge through its emphasis on breaking down disciplinary boundaries and creating new spheres in which knowledge can be produced. In this sense, critical pedagogy must be reclaimed as a cultural politics and a form of social memory. This is not merely an epistemological issue, but one of power, ethics, and politics. Critical pedagogy as a cultural politics points to the necessity of asserting the struggle over the production and creation of knowledge as part of a broader attempt to create a number of diverse, critical public cultures. As a form of social memory, critical pedagogy starts with the everyday and the particular as a basis for learning. It reclaims the historical and the popular as part of an ongoing effort to critically appropriate the voices of those who have been silenced and to help move the voices of those who have been located within narratives that are monolithic and totalizing beyond indifference or guilt to emancipatory practice. At stake here is a pedagogy that provides the knowledge, skills, and habits for students and others to read history in ways that enable them to reclaim their identities in the interests of constructing more democratic and just forms of life.

This struggle deepens the pedagogical meaning of the political and the political meaning of the pedagogical. In the first instance, it raises important questions about how students and others are constructed as agents within particular histories, cultures, and social relations. Against the monolith of culture, it posits the conflicting terrain of cultures shaped within asymmetrical relations of power, grounded in diverse historical struggles. Similarly, culture has to be understood as part of the discourse of power and inequality. As a pedagogical issue, the relationship between culture and power is evident in questions such as "Whose cultures are appropriated as our own? How is marginality normalized?"[106] To insert the primacy of culture as a pedagogical and political issue is to make central how schools function in the shaping of particular identities, values, and histories by producing and legitimating specific cultural narratives and resources. In the second instance, asserting the pedagogical aspects of the political raises the issue of how difference and culture can be taken up as pedagogical practices and not merely as political categories. For example, how does difference matter as a pedagogical category if educators and cultural workers have to make knowledge meaningful before it can become critical and transformative? Or what does it mean to engage the tension between being theoretically correct and pedagogically wrong? These concerns and tensions offer the possibility for making the relationship between the political and the pedagogical mutually informing and problematic.

6. The Enlightenment notion of reason needs to be reformulated within a critical pedagogy. First, educators need to be skeptical regarding any notion of reason that purports to reveal the truth by denying its own historical construction and ideological principles. Reason is not innocent, and any viable notion of critical pedagogy cannot exercise forms of authority that emulate totalizing form of reason that appear to be beyond criticism and dialogue. This suggests that we reject claims to objectivity in favor of partial epistemologies that recognize the historical and socially constructed nature of their own knowledge claims and methodologies. In this way, curriculum can be viewed as a cultural script that introduces students to particular forms of reason that structure specific stories and ways of life. Reason in this sense implicates and is implicated in the intersection of power, knowledge, and politics. Second, it is not enough to reject an essentialist or universalist defense of reason. Instead, the limits of reason must be extended to recognizing other ways in which people learn or take-up particular subject positions. In this case, educators need to understand more fully how people learn through concrete social relations, through the ways in which the body is positioned through the construction of habit and intuition, and through the production and investment of desire and affect.

7. Critical pedagogy needs to regain a sense of alternatives by combining a language of critique and possibility. Postmodern feminism exemplifies this in both its critique of patriarchy and its search to construct new forms of identity and social relations. It is worth noting that teachers can take-up this issue around a number of considerations. First, educators need to construct a language of critique that combines the issue of limits with the discourse of freedom and social responsibility. In other words, the question of freedom needs to be engaged dialectically not only as one of individual rights but also as part of the discourse of social responsibility. That is, whereas freedom remains an essential category in establishing the conditions for ethical and political rights, it must also be seen as a force to be checked if it is expressed in modes of individual and collective behavior that threaten the ecosystem or produce forms of violence and oppression against individuals and social groups. Second, critical pedagogy needs to explore in programmatic terms a language of possibility that is capable of thinking risky thoughts, that engages a project of hope, and points to the horizon of the "not yet." A language of possibility does not have to dissolve into a reified form of utopianism; instead, it can be developed as a precondition for nourishing convictions that summon up the courage to imagine a different and more just world and to struggle for it. A language of moral and political possibility is more than an outmoded vestige of

humanist discourse. It is central to responding not only with compassion to human beings who suffer and agonize but also with a politics and a set of pedagogical practices that can refigure and change existing narratives of domination into images and concrete instances of a future that is worth fighting for.

There is a certain cynicism that characterizes the language of the Left. Central to this position is the refusal of all utopian images, all appeals to "a language of possibility." Such refusals are often made on the grounds that "utopian discourse" is a strategy employed by the Right and is therefore ideologically tainted. Or the very notion of possibility is dismissed as an impractical and therefore useless category. In my mind, this represents less a serious critique than a refusal to move beyond the language of exhaustion and despair. What is central to develop in response to this position is a discriminating notion of possibility, one that makes a distinction between a language that is "dystopian" and one that is utopian. In the former, the appeal to the future is grounded in a form of nostalgic romanticism that calls for a return to a past, which more often than not serves to legitimate relations of domination and oppression. Similarly, in Constance Penley's terms, a "dystopian" discourse often "limits itself to solutions that are either individualist or bound to a romanticized notion of guerrilla-like small-group resistance. The true atrophy of the utopian imagination is this: we can imagine the future but we *cannot* conceive the kind of collective political strategies necessary to change or ensure that future."[107] In contrast to the language of dystopia, a discourse of possibility rejects apocalyptic emptiness and nostalgic imperialism and sees history as open and society worth struggling for in the image of an alternative future. This is the language of the "not yet," one in which the imagination redeemed and nourished in the effort to construct new relationships fashioned out of strategies of collective resistance based on a critical recognition of both what society is and what it might become. Paraphrasing Walter Benjamin, this is a discourse of imagination and hope that pushes history against the grain. Nancy Fraser illuminates this sentiment by emphasizing the importance of a language of possibility for the project of social change: "It allows for the possibility of a radical democratic politics in which immanent critique and transfigurative desire mingle with one another."[108]

8. Critical pedagogy needs to develop a theory of educators and cultural workers as transformative intellectuals who occupy specific political and social locations. Rather than defining teacher work through the narrow language of professionalism, a critical pedagogy needs to ascertain more carefully what the role of teachers might be as cultural workers engaged in the production of ideologies and social practices. At one level this suggests that cultural workers first renounce the discourse of objectivity and decenteredness and then embrace a practice that is capable of revealing the historical, ideological, and ethical parameters that frame its discourse and implications for the self, society, culture, and the other. Cultural workers need to unravel not only the ideological codes, representations, and practices that structure the dominant order, they

also need to acknowledge "those places and spaces we inherit and occupy, which frame our lives in very specific and concrete ways, which are as much a part of our psyches as they are a physical or geographical placement."[109] The practice of social criticism becomes inseparable from the act of self-criticism; one cannot take place without the other; nor does one have priority over the other, instead they must be seen as both relational and mutually constitutive.

At another level, cultural workers need to develop a nontotalizing politics that makes them attentive to the partial, specific contexts of differentiated communities and forms of power. This is not a call to ignore larger theoretical and relational narratives, but to deepen their power of analyses by making clear the specificity of contexts in which power is operationalized, domination expresses itself, and resistance works in multiple and productive ways. In this case, teachers and cultural workers can undertake social criticism within and not outside of ethical and political discourses; they can address issues that give meaning to the contexts in which they work, but at the same time relate them to broader articulations that recognize the importance of larger formative narratives. Critique, resistance, and transformation in these terms is organized through systems of knowledge and webs of solidarity that embrace the local and the global. Cultural workers need to take seriously Foucault's model of the specific intellectual who acknowledges the politics of personal location. This is important, but not enough; cultural workers must also actively struggle as public intellectuals who can relate to and address wider issues that affect both the immediacy of their location and the wider global context. Transformative intellectuals must create webs of solidarity with those that share localized experiences and identities but must also develop a politics of solidarity that reaches out to those others who live in a global world whose problems cannot be dismissed because they do not occupy a local and immediate space. The issues of human rights, ecology, apartheid, militarism, and other forms of domination against both humans and the planet affect all of us directly and indirectly. This is not merely a political issue; it is also a deeply ethical issue that situates the meaning of the relationships between the self and the other, the margins and the center, and the colonizer and colonized in broader contexts of solidarity and struggle. Educators need to develop pedagogical practices that not only heighten the possibilities for critical consciousness but also for transformative action. In this perspective, teachers and other cultural workers would be involved in the invention of critical discourses, practices, and democratic social relations. Critical pedagogy would represent itself as the active construction rather than transmission of particular ways of life. More specifically, as transformative intellectuals, cultural workers and teachers can engage in the invention of languages so as to provide spaces for themselves, their students, and audiences to rethink their experiences in terms that both name relations of oppression and also offer ways in which to overcome them.

9. Central to the notion of critical pedagogy is a politics of voice that combines a postmodern notion of difference with a feminist emphasis on the primacy of the political. This engagement suggests taking-up the relationship between the personal and the political in a way that does not collapse the political into the personal but strengthens the relationship between the two so as to engage rather than withdraw from addressing those institutional forms and structures that contribute to forms of racism, sexism, and class exploitation. This suggests some important pedagogical interventions. First, the self must be seen as a primary site of politicization. That is, the issue of how the self is constructed in multiple and complex ways must be analyzed as part of both a language of affirmation and a broader understanding of how identities are inscribed in and between various social, cultural, and historical formations. To engage issues regarding the construction of the self is to address questions of history, culture, community, language, gender, race, and class. It is to raise questions regarding what pedagogical practices need to be employed that allow students to speak in dialogical contexts that affirm, interrogate, and extend their understandings of themselves and the global contexts in which they live. Such a position recognizes that students have several or multiple identities, but also affirms the importance of offering students a language that allows them to reconstruct their moral and political energies in the service of creating a more just and equitable social order, one that undermines relations of hierarchy and domination.

Second, a politics of voice must offer pedagogical and political strategies that affirm the primacy of the social, intersubjective, and collective. To focus on voice is not meant to simply affirm the stories that students tell, nor to simply glorify the possibility for narration. Such a position often degenerates into a form of narcissism, a cathartic experience that is reduced to naming anger without the benefit of theorizing in order both to understand its underlying causes and what it means to work collectively to transform the structures of domination responsible for oppressive social relations. Raising one's consciousness has increasingly become a pretext for legitimating hegemonic forms of separatism buttressed by self-serving appeals to the primacy of individual experience. What is often expressed in such appeals is an anti-intellectualism that retreats from any viable form of political engagement, especially one willing to address and transform diverse forms of oppression. The call to simply affirm one's voice has increasingly been reduced to a pedagogical process that is as reactionary as it is inward looking. A more radical notion of voice should begin with what bell hooks calls a critical attention to theorizing experience as part of a broader politics of engagement. In referring specifically to feminist pedagogy, she argues that the discourse of confession and memory can be used to "shift the focus away from mere naming of one's experience . . . to talk about identity in relation to culture, history, and politics."[110] For hooks, the telling of tales of victimization, or the expression of one's voice is not enough; it is equally imperative that such experiences be the object of theoretical and critical analyses so that they can be connected rather than severed from broader notions of solidarity, struggle, and politics.

Conclusion

This chapter attempts to analyze some of the central assumptions that govern the discourses of modernism, postmodernism, and postmodern feminism. But in doing so, it rejects pitting these movements against each other and tries instead to see how they converge as part of a broader political project linked to the reconstruction of democratic public life. Similarly, I have attempted here to situate the issue of pedagogical practice within a wider discourse of political engagement. Pedagogy is not defined as simply something that goes on in schools. On the contrary, it is posited as central to any political practice that takes up questions of how individuals learn, how knowledge is produced, and how subject positions are constructed. In this context, pedagogical practice refers to forms of cultural production that are inextricably historical and political.

Pedagogy is, in part, a technology of power, language, and practice that produces and legitimates forms of moral and political regulation that construct and offer human beings particular views of themselves and the world. Such views are never innocent and are always implicated in the discourse and relations of ethics and power. To invoke the importance of pedagogy is to raise questions not simply about how students learn but also how educators (in the broad sense of the term) construct the ideological and political positions from which they speak. At issue here is a discourse that both situates human beings within history and makes visible the limits of their ideologies and values. Such a position acknowledges the partiality of all discourses so that the relationship between knowledge and power will always be open to dialogue and critical self-engagement. Pedagogy is about the intellectual, emotional, and ethical investments we make as part of our attempt to negotiate, accommodate, and transform the world in which we find ourselves. The purpose and vision that drives such a pedagogy must be based on a politics and view of authority that link teaching and learning to forms of self- and social empowerment that argue for forms of community life that extend the principles of liberty, equality, justice, and freedom to the widest possible set of institutional and lived relations.

As defined within the traditions of modernism, postmodernism, and postmodern feminism, pedagogy offers educators an opportunity to develop a political project that embraces human interests that move beyond the particularistic politics of class, ethnicity, race, and gender. This is not a call to dismiss the postmodern emphasis on difference as much as it is an attempt to develop a radical democratic politics that stresses difference within unity. This effort means developing a public language that can transform a politics of assertion into one of democratic struggle. Central to such a politics and pedagogy is a notion of community developed around a shared conception of social justice, rights, and entitlement. Such a notion is especially necessary at a time in our history in which the value of such concerns has been subordinated to the priorities of the market and used to legitimate the interests of the rich at the expense of the poor, the unemployed, and the homeless. A radical pedagogy and transformative democratic politics must go hand in hand in constructing a vision in which liberalism's emphasis on individual freedom, postmodernism's concern with the particularistic, and feminism's concern with the politics of the everyday are coupled with democratic socialism's historic concern with solidarity and public life.

As I mentioned previously, we live at a time in which the responsibilities of citizens extend beyond national borders. The old modernist notions of center and margin, home and exile, and familiar and strange are breaking apart. Geographic, cultural, and ethnic borders are giving way to shifting configurations of power, community, space, and time. Citizenship can no longer ground itself in forms of Eurocentrism and the language of colonialism. New spaces, relationships, and identities have to be created that allow us to move across borders, to engage difference and otherness as part of a discourse of justice, social engagement, and democratic struggle. Academics can no longer retreat into their classrooms or symposiums as if they were the only public spheres available for engaging the power of ideas and the relations of power. Foucault's notion of the specific intellectual taking-up struggles connected to particular issues and contexts must be related to broader social concerns that deeply affect how people live, work, and survive.

But there is more at stake here than defining the role of the intellectual or the relationship of teaching to democratic struggle. The struggle against racism, class structures, sexism, and other forms of oppression needs to move away from simply a language of critique, and redefine itself as part of a language of transformation and hope. This shift suggests that educators combine with other cultural workers engaged in public struggles in order to invent languages and provide critical and transformative spaces both in and out of schools that offer new opportunities for social movements to come together. By doing this, we can rethink and re-experience democracy as a struggle over values, practices, social relations, and subject positions that enlarge the terrain of human capacities and possibilities as a basis for a compassionate social order. At issue here is the need for cultural workers to create a politics that contributes to the multiplication of sites of democratic struggles. Within such sites cultural workers can engage in specific struggles while also recognizing the necessity to embrace broader issues that enhance the life of the planet while extending the spirit of democracy to all societies.

In rejecting certain conservative features of modernism, the apoliticism of some postmodern discourses, and separatist versions of feminism, I attempt to critically appropriate the most emancipatory features of these discourses in the interest of developing a postmodern feminist pedagogy. Of course, the list of principles I provide is far from complete; I develop them in greater depth theoretically throughout this book.

But the critical appropriation of emancipatory features does offer the opportunity for educators to analyze how it might be possible to reconceive as pedagogical practice some of the insights that have emerged from the discourses I analyze in this chapter. Far from being exhaustive, the principles offered are only meant to provide some fleeting images of a pedagogy that can address the importance of democracy as an ongoing struggle, the meaning of educating students to govern, and the imperative of creating pedagogical conditions in which political citizens can be educated within a politics of difference that supports rather than opposes the reconstruction of radical democracy.

Notes

1. Representative analyses of the range of disciplines, genres, and writers who inhabit the slippery landscape known as postmodernism can be found in H. Foster, ed., *The Anti-Aesthetic: Essays on Postmodern Culture* (Port Townsend, Wash.: Bay Press, 1983); Ihab Hassan, *The Postmodern Turn: Essays in Postmodern Theory and Culture* (Columbus: Ohio State University Press, 1987); Dick Hebdige, "Postmodernism and the Other Side," *Journal of Communication Inquiry* 10:2 (1986), 78–99; Andreas Huyssen, *After the Great Divide* (Bloomington: Indiana University Press, 1986); Dick Hebdige, *Hiding in the Light* (New York: Routledge,1989); Linda Hutcheon, "Postmodern Problematics," in R. Merrill, *Ethics/Aesthetics: Post-Modern Positions* (Washington, D.C.: Maisonneuve Press, 1988), 1–10; Linda Hutcheon, *The Politics of Postmodernism* (London: Routledge, 1989); Linda Hutcheon, *The Poetics of Postmodernism* (London: Routledge, 1988); L. Appignanesi and G. Bennington, eds., *Postmodernism: ICA Documents 4* (London: Institute of Contemporary Arts, 1986); Stanley Aronowitz, "Postmodernism and Politics," *Social Text* No. 18 (1987/1988), 94–114; Steven Connor, *Postmodernist Culture: An Introduction to Theories of the Contemporary* (New York: Basil Blackwell, 1989); Fredric Jameson, *Postmodernism, or, the Cultural Logic of Late Capitalism* (Durham: Duke University, 1990); Scott Lash, *Sociology of Postmodernism* (New York: Routledge, 1990); Jane Flax, *Thinking Fragments: Psychoanalysis, Feminism, and Postmodernism in the Contemporary West* (Berkeley: University of California Press, 1990).
2. Mark Poster, *Critical Theory and Poststructuralism* (Ithaca: Cornell University Press, 1989).
3. Jean-François Lyotard, *The Postmodern Condition* (Minneapolis: University of Minnesota Press, 1984).
4. Ernesto Laclau and Chantal Mouffe, *Hegemony and Socialist Strategy* (London: Verso Press, 1985).
5. Mark Hannam, "The Dream of Democracy," *Arena* No. 90 (1990), 113.
6. Ibid.
7. Eugene Lunn, *Marxism and Modernism* (Berkeley: University of California Press, 1982); David Kolb, *The Critique of Pure Modernity* (Chicago: University of Chicago Press, 1986); Neil Larsen, *Modernism and Hegemony* (Minneapolis: University of Minnesota Press, 1990); Anthony Giddens, *The Consequences of Modernity* (Stanford: Stanford University Press, 1990).
8. Lyotard, *The Postmodern Condition.*
9. Charles Newman, *The Post-Modern Aura* (Evanston: Northwestern University Press, 1985); Charles Newman, "Revising Modernism, Representing Postmodernism," in L. Appignanesi and G. Bennington, eds., *Postmodernism: ICA Documents 4* (London: Institute of Contemporary Arts, 1986), 32–51.

10. Jürgen Habermas, "Modernity Versus Postmodernity," *New German Critique* 8:1 (1981), 3–18; Jürgen Habermas, "The Entwinement of Myth and Enlightenment," *New German Critique* 9:3 (1982), 13–30; Jürgen Habermas, "Modernity—An Incomplete Project," in H. Foster, ed., *The Anti-Aesthetic: Essays on Postmodern Culture* (Port Townsend, Wash.: Bay Press, 1983), 3–16; Jürgen Habermas, *The Philosophical Discourse of Modernity*, trans. by F. Lawrence (Cambridge: MIT Press, 1987).
11. The now-classic defense of modernity in the postmodern debate can be found in Habermas, "An Incomplete Project" and *Philosophical Discourse*. An interesting comparison of two different views on modernity can be found in Marshall Berman, "Why Modernism Still Matters," *Tikkun* 4:11 (1988), 81–86, and Nelly Richard, "Postmodernism and Periphery," *Third Text, No.* 2 (1987/88), 5–12.
12. Matei Calinescu, *Five Faces of Modernity: Modernism, Avant-Garde, Decadence, Kitsch, Postmodernism* (Durham, N.C.: Duke University Press, 1987), 41.
13. Jean Baudrillard, "Modernity," *Canadian Journal of Political and Social Theory* 11:3 (1987), 65.
14. Aronowitz, "Postmodernism and Politics," No. 18 (1987/1988), 94–114.
15. Cited in Calinescu, *Five Faces of Modernity*, 117.
16. Roland Barthes, *Critical Essays* (New York: Hill and Wang, 1972).
17. Marshall Berman, *All That is Solid Melts into Air: The Experience of Modernity* (New York: Simon & Schuster, 1982); Marshall Berman, "Why Modernism Still Matters," *Tikkun* 4:1 (1988), 81–86.
18. Berman, *All That is Solid*, 11.
19. Robert Merrill, "Forward-Ethics/Aesthetics: A Post-Modern Position," in R. Merrill, ed., *Ethics/Aesthetics: Post-Modern Positions*, 9.
20. See, for example, Chantal Mouffe, "Radical Democracy: Modern or Postmodern?" in A. Ross, ed., *Universal Abandon? The Politics of Postmodernism* (Minneapolis: University of Minnesota Press, 1988), 31–45.
21. Mark Warren, *Nietzsche and Political Thought* (Cambridge: MIT Press, 1988), 9–10.
22. Habermas, "Modernity versus Postmodernity," "An Incomplete Project," *Philosophical Discourse*.
23. Richard Rorty, "Habermas and Lyotard on Postmodernity," in Richard Bernstein, ed., *Habermas and Modernity* (Cambridge: MIT Press, 1985), 161–76.
24. Perry Anderson, "Modernity and Revolution," *New Left Review* No. 144 (1984), 96–113.
25. Nancy Hartsock, "Rethinking Modernism: Minority vs. Majority Theories," *Cultural Critique* No. 7 (1987), 187–206.
26. Habermas, "An Incomplete Project," 5.
27. Jürgen Habermas, *Communication and the Evolution of Society* (Boston: Beacon Press, 1979).
28. Douglas Kellner, "Postmodernism as Social Theory: Some Challenges and Problems," *Theory, Culture, and Society* 5:2 & 3 (1988), 239–69.
29. Habermas, "Myth and Enlightenment," 18.
30. Michael Ryan, *Politics and Culture: Working Hypotheses for a Post-Revolutionary Society* (Baltimore: The Johns Hopkins University Press, 1989).
31. Aronowitz, "Postmodernism and Politics," 103.
32. Nancy Fraser "What is Critical about Critical Theory? The Case of Habermas and Gender," *New German Critique* 12:2 (1985), 97–131.
33. Barbara Epstein, "Rethinking Social Movement Theory," *Socialist Review* 20:1 (1990), 35–65.
34. Thomas McCarthy, "Introduction," in Habermas, *Philosophical Discourse*, xvii.

35. Hebdige, *Hiding in the Light* (1989), 226.
36. Hutcheon, "Postmodern Problematics," in R. Merrill, ed., *Ethics/Aesthetics: Post-Modern Positions*, 5. For a more extensive treatment of Hutcheon's work on postmodernism, see *The Politics of Postmodernism* and *The Poetics of Postmodernism*.
37. "Building a New Left: An Interview with Ernesto Laclau," *Strategies* 1:1 (1988), 10–28.
38. Lyotard, *The Postmodern Condition*, xxiv.
39. Ibid., 82.
40. Nancy Fraser and Linda Nicholson, "Social Criticism Without Philosophy: An Encounter Between *Feminism and Postmodernism*," in A. Ross, ed., *Universal Abandon? The Politics of Postmodernism*, 86–87.
41. Gary Peller, "Reason and the Mob: the Politics of Representation," *Tikkun* 2:3 (1987), 30.
42. Ernesto Laclau, "Politics and the Limits of Modernity," in A. Ross, ed., *Universal Abandon? The Politics of Postmodernism*, 79–80.
43. Emily Hicks, "Deterritorialization and Border Writing," in R. Merrill, ed., *Ethics/Aesthetics: Post-Modern Positions*, 47–58.
44. This issue is taken up in a number of brilliant essays in Russell Ferguson, Martha Gever, Trinh T. Minh-ha, and Cornel West, eds., *Out There: Marginalization and Contemporary Cultures* (Cambridge: MIT Press, 1990). See also bell hooks, *Yearning: Race, Gender, and Cultural Politics* (Boston: South End Press, 1990); Stanley Aronowitz and Henry A. Giroux, *Postmodern Education: Politics, Culture, and Social Criticism* (Minneapolis: University of Minnesota Press, 1991).
45. Jim Collins, *Uncommon Cultures: Popular Culture and Post-Modernism* (New York: Routledge, 1989).
46. Scott Lash and John Urry, *The End of Organized Capitalism* (Madison: University of Wisconsin Press, 1987).
47. Poster, *Critical Theory and Poststructuralism*.
48. Aronowitz and Giroux, *Postmodern Education*.
49. Craig Owens, "The Discourse of Others: Feminists and Postmodernism," in H. Foster, ed., *The Anti-Aesthetic: Essays on Postmodern Culture*, 59.
50. Edward W. Said, quoted in Connor, *Postmodernist Culture*, 233.
51. Richard Roth, "The Colonial Experience and its Postmodern Fate," *Salmagundi* 84 (Fall 1989), 250.
52. James Clifford and George Marcus, eds., *Writing Culture: The Poetics and Politics of Ethnography* (Berkeley: University of California Press, 1986); James Clifford, *The Predicament of Culture: Twentieth Century Ethnography, Literature, and Art* (Cambridge: Harvard University Press, 1988).
53. Trinh Minh-ha. *Woman, Native, Other: Writing Postcoloniality and Feminism* (Bloomington: Indiana University Press, 1989).
54. Renato Rosaldo, *Culture and Truth: The Remaking of Social Analysis* (Boston: Beacon Press, 1989), 44.
55. Gayatri Spivak, *In Other Worlds: Essays in Cultural Politics* (New York: Methuen, 1987); Gayatri Spivak, *The Post-Colonial Critic*, Sarah Harasym, ed. (London: Routledge, 1990); Minh-ha, *Woman, Native, Other*.
56. Hal Foster, *Recordings, Art, Spectacle, Cultural Politics* (Seattle: Bay Press, 1985); Brian Wallis, ed., *Art After Modernism: Rethinking Representation* (New York: Godine, 1989).
57. See the discussion of various postmodern photographers in Abigail Solomon-Godeau, *Photography at the Dock* (Minneapolis: University of Minnesota Press, 1990).
58. James Sculley, *Line Break: Poetry as Social Practice* (Seattle: Bay Press, 1988).
59. Hebdige, *Hiding in the Light*, 1988.

60. Laclau, "Building a New Left," 17.
61. Kearney, *The Wake of Imagination* (Minneapolis: University of Minnesota Press, 1988), 366–367.
62. Jacques Derrida, *Of Grammatology*, G. Spivak, trans. (Baltimore: The Johns Hopkins University Press, 1976); Michel Foucault, *Language, Counter-Memory, Practice: Selected Essays and Interviews*, D. Bouchard, ed., (Ithaca: Cornell University Press, 1977); *Power/ Knowledge: Selected Interviews and Other Writings*, G. Gordon, ed., (New York: Pantheon, 1977). *Discipline and Punish: The Birth of the Prison* (New York: Vintage Books, 1979); *The History of Sexuality, Volume 1: An Introduction* (New York: Vintage Books, 1980); Jacques Lacan, *Speech and Language in Psychoanalysis*, A. Wilden, trans. (Baltimore: The Johns Hopkins University Press, 1988); Laclau & Mouffe, *Hegemony and Socialist Strategy*.
63. Laclau, "Politics and the Limits of Modernity," 67.
64. Terry Eagleton, "The Subject of Literature," *Cultural Critique* No. 2 (1985/86), 101.
65. Teresa Ebert, "The Romance of Patriarchy: Ideology, Subjectivity, and Postmodern Feminist Cultural Theory," *Cultural Critique* 10 (Fall 1988), 22–23.
66. Lawrence Grossberg, "On Postmodernism and Articulation: An Interview with Stuart Hall," *Journal of Communication Inquiry* 10:2 (1986), 56.
67. Fraser and Nicholson, "Social Criticism Without Philosophy," in A. Ross, ed., *Universal Abandon? The Politics of Postmodernism*, 92, 99.
68. M. Malson, J. O'Barr, S. Westphal-Wihl, and M. Wyer, "Introduction," in M. Malson, J. O'Barr, S. Westphal-Wihl, and M. Wyer, eds., *Feminist Theory in Practice and Process* (Chicago: University of Chicago Press, 1989), 1–13.
69. hooks, *Talking Back*, 22.
70. Meaghan Morris, *The Pirate's Fiancee: Feminism, Reading, Postmodernism* (London: Verso Press, 1988), 16.
71. A number of feminist theorists take-up these issues while either rejecting or problematizing any relationship with postmodernism. For instance, see Nancy Hartsock, "Postmodernism and Political Change: Issues for Feminist Theory," *Cultural Critique* No. 14 (Winter 1989–1990), 15–33; Rita Felski, "Feminism, Postmodernism, and the Critique of Modernity," *Cultural Critique* No. 13 (Fall 1989), 33–56. For a range of feminist theoretical analyses concerning the construction of gender and modes of social division, see the two special issues of *Cultural Critique*, Nos. 13 and 14 (1989, 1989–90).
72. Of course, as a number of feminists have pointed out, many of the issues taken-up in postmodernist discourses have also been analyzed, albeit in different ways, in much of the literature written by feminists since the 1970s. See Morris, *The Pirate's Fiancee*, and hooks, *Yearnings*, for comments and references on this issue.
73. E. Ann Kaplan, "Introduction," in E. Ann Kaplan, ed., *Postmodernism and Its Discontents* (London: Verso Press, 1988), 1–6.
74. Donna Haraway, "Situated Knowledges: The Science Question in Feminism and the Privilege of Partial Perspective," *Feminist Studies* 14:3 (1989), 579.
75. hooks, *Talking Back*, 25.
76. Ibid., 23.
77. Elaine Showalter, "Introduction: The Rise of Gender," in E. Showalter, ed., *Speaking of Gender* (New York: Routledge, 1989), 1–13.
78. This issue is taken-up in a number of feminist works. Some important and varied analyses include: hooks, *Yearning*; Rita Felski, *Beyond Feminist Aesthetics* (Cambridge: Harvard University Press, 1989); Judith Butler, *Gender Trouble* (New York: Routledge, 1990); Carol Pateman, *The Sexual Contract* (Stanford: Stanford University Press, 1988); and Michele Wallace, *Invisibility Blues* (London: Verso Press, 1990).

79. Teresa de Lauretis, "Feminist Studies/Critical Studies: Issues, Terms, Contexts," in T. de Lauretis, ed., *Feminist Studies/Critical Studies* (Bloomington: Indiana University Press, 1986), 9.
80. hooks, *Talking Back*, 32. See also Felski, *Beyond Feminist Aesthetics*.
81. de Lauretis, *Feminist Studies/Critical Studies*, 18.
82. Julia Kristeva, "Oscillation between Power and Denial," in E. Marks and I. de Courtivron, eds., *New French Feminisms* (New York: Schocken Books, 1988), 165–67.
83. Linda Alcoff, "Cultural Feminism vs. Poststructuralism: The Identity Crisis in Feminist Theory," *Signs* 13:3 (1988), 418–19.
84. Irene Diamond and Lee Quinby, "American Feminism and the Language of Control," in I. Diamond and L. Quinby, eds., *Feminism & Foucault: Reflections on Resistance* (Boston: Northeastern University Press, 1988), 193–206.
85. For example, see the work of Alison Jaggar, *Feminist Politics and Human Nature* (Totawa, N.J.: Rowman & Allanheld, 1983); Sandra Harding, *The Science Question in Feminism* (Ithaca: Cornell University Press, 1986); Patricia Jagentowicz Mills, *Women, Nature, and Psyche* (New Haven: Yale University Press, 1987); Donna Haraway, *Primate Visions: Gender, Race, and Nature in the World of Modern Science* (New York: Routledge, 1989); Sandra Harding, *Whose Science? Whose Knowledge? Thinking from Women's Lives* (Ithaca, N.Y.: Cornell University Press, 1991).
86. For example, see Sharon Welch, *Communities of Resistance and Solidarity: A Feminist Theology of Liberation* (Maryknoll: Orbis Books, 1985); Sharon Welch, *A Feminist Ethic of Risk* (Minneapolis: Fortress Press, 1990); de Lauretis, *Feminist Studies/Critical Studies*.
87. Haraway, "Situated Knowledges," 585.
88. For example, see hooks, *Talking Back; Yearning*; Felski, *Beyond Feminist Aesthetics*; Nancy Fraser, *Unruly Practices: Power, Discourse and Gender in Contemporary Social Theory* (Minneapolis: University of Minnesota Press, 1989).
89. Jane Flax, "Reply to Tress," *Signs* 14:1 (1988), 202.
90. Fraser and Nicholson, "Social Criticism Without Philosophy," 91.
91. See, for example, Jane Flax, "Postmodernism and Gender Relations in Feminist Theory," in M. Malson et al., eds., *Feminist Theory in Practice and Process*, 51–73; hooks, *Yearning*; Harding, *The Science Question*.
92. For example, see Audre Lorde, *Sister Outsider* (Freedom, CA: The Crossing Press, 1984); hooks, *Talking Back*; Trinh T. Minh-ha, *Woman, Native, Other* (Bloomington: Indiana University Press, 1989).
93. Caren Kaplan, "Deterritorializations: The Rewriting of Home and Exile in Western Feminist Discourse," *Cultural Critique* No. 6 (1987), 194.
94. Malson et al., "Introduction," in M. Malson, et al., eds., *Feminist Theory in Practice and Process*, 4.
95. Joan Scott, *Gender and the Politics of History* (New York: Columbia University Press, 1988), 176–77.
96. Kaplan, "Introduction," in E. Ann Kaplan, ed., *Postmodernism and Its Discontents*.
97. Alcoff, "Cultural Feminism vs. Poststructuralism," 434.
98. Sandra Lee Bartky, "Foucault, Femininity, and the Modernization of Patriarchal Power," in Diamond and Quinby, eds., *Feminism and Foucault*, 61–86.
99. Vaclav Havel quoted in M. Oreskes, "America's Politics Loses Way as Its Vision Changes World," *New York Times* (1990), 16.
100. E. P. Thompson, "History Turns on a New Hinge," *The Nation* (January 29, 1990), 120.
101. Adam Michnik, "Notes on the Revolution," *New York Times Magazine*, March 11, 1990, 44.

102. Oreskes, "America's Politics Loses Way," 16.
103. Some representative collections of current literature on diverse discourses in critical peda-
gogy can be found in: Cary Nelson, ed., *Theory in the Classroom* (Urbana: University of
Illinois Press, 1986); David Livingstone, ed., *Critical Pedagogy and Cultural Power* (New
York: Bergin and Garvey Press, 1986); Henry A. Giroux and Roger Simon, eds., *Popular
Culture, Schooling and Everyday Life* (New York: Bergin and Garvey, 1988); Henry A. Giroux
and Peter McLaren, eds., *Critical Pedagogy, the State, and Cultural Struggle* (Albany: SUNY
Press, 1989); Patricia Donahue and Ellen Quandahl, eds., *Reclaiming Pedagogy: The Rhetoric
of the Classroom* (Carbondale: Southern Illinois University Press, 1989); Susan L. Gabriel
and Isaiah Smithson, eds., *Gender in the Classroom* (Urbana: University of Illinois Press,
1990); Donald Morton and Mas'ud Zavarzadeh, eds., *Theory/Pedagogy/Politics: Texts for
Change* (Urbana: University of Illinois Press, 1991). See also Roger I. Simon, *Teaching
Against the Grain* (New York: Bergin and Garvey, 1992).
104. Chandra T. Mohanty, "On Race and Voice: Challenges for Liberal Education in the 1990s,"
Cultural Critique No. 14 (Winter 1989–1990), 179–208.
105. Laclau, "Politics and the Limits of Modernity," in A. Ross, ed., *Universal Abandon? The
Politics of Postmodernism*, 63–82.
106. Thomas Popkewitz, "Culture, Pedagogy, and Power: Issues in the Production of Values
and Colonialization," *Journal of Education* 170:2 (1988), 77.
107. Constance Penley, *The Future of an Illusion: Film, Feminism, and Psychoanalysis* (Minneapolis: University of Minnesota, 1989), 122.
108. Fraser, *Unruly Practices*, 107.
109. Joan Borsa, "Towards a Politics of Location," *Canadian Women Studies* (Spring 1990), 36.
110. hooks, *Talking Back*, 110.

3

Redefining the Boundaries of Race and Ethnicity

Beyond the Politics of Pluralism

Introduction

Within the current historical conjuncture, the political and cultural boundaries that have long constituted the meaning of race and cultural politics are beginning to shift. The question of race figures much differently in the United States at the beginning of the 1990s than it did a decade ago for a number of reasons. First, the legacies of anticolonial and postcolonial struggles have ruptured the ability of Eurocentric discourses to marginalize and erase the many-faceted voices of those Others who have struggled under the yoke of colonial oppression. Second, the population of America's subordinated groups are changing the cultural landscapes of our urban centers. According to recent demographic projections, Blacks and Hispanics will "constitute a decided majority in nearly one-third of the nation's 50 largest cities . . . and Blacks alone will be the major racial group in at least nine major cities, notably Detroit, Baltimore, Memphis, Washington, D.C., New Orleans, and Atlanta."[1] In this case, populations traditionally defined as the Other are moving from the margin to the center and challenging the ethnocentric view that people of color can be relegated to the periphery of everyday life.

Third, while people of color are redrawing the cultural demographic boundaries of the urban centers, the boundaries of power appear to be solidifying in favor of rich, white, middle and upper classes. The consequences of this solidification will have a dramatic effect on race relations in the next decade. For example, escalating unemployment among Afro-American teenage youth poses a serious threat to an entire generation of future adults; in many urban cities the dropout rate for nonwhite children exceeds 60 percent (with New York City at 70%);[2] the civil rights gains of the 1960s are slowly being eroded by the policy-makers and judicial heirs of the Reagan Era, and the tide of racism is aggressively rising in the streets, schools, workplaces, and campuses of the United States.[3] In the Reagan and Bush Eras, equity and social justice are given low priority next to the "virtues" of collective greed, individual success, and expanding the defense budget. As class divisions grow deeper, intraclass and racial tensions mask the need for collective struggles for social and political justice. As the white working class sees its dream of moving up the social and economic ladder imperiled, it is increasingly coming to view affirmative action, social policy programs, and the changing nature of national and cultural identity as a threat to its own sense of security and possibility. Instead of embracing Afro-Americans and other ethnic groups as allies in the struggle to dismantle the master narratives of Eurocentric domination with the discourse of democratic struggle and solidarity, the legacy of institutional and ideological racism appears to have once again reached a dangerous threshold that impedes rather than extends such a goal. As we move into a postmodern world that is progressively redrawing the boundaries established by nationalism, ethnocentrism, and Eurocentric culture, the United States appears to be refiguring its political, social, and cultural geography in a manner that denies rather than maintains a democratic community. Instead of engaging a politics of difference, community, and democracy with respect to the principles of justice, equality, and freedom, the current neoconservative government appears eager to sever "the links between democracy and political equality."[4]

The shadow of totalitarianism is darkening the future of American democracy. Its primary expression is found in the resurgence of racism in this country. Racial slurs are now regularly incorporated into the acts of some rock stars and stand-up comedians;[5] the dominant culture seems indifferent or even hostile to the deepening poverty and despair affecting a growing population of Afro-Americans in the underclass in our nation's cities; the growing dropout rate among Afro-American students is met with insulting diatribes and the refusal to engage the racism prevalent in our nation's schools;[6] the Afro-American family is not highlighted for its resiliency amidst the most degrading economic and social conditions but is condemned as a cause of its own misery.[7] Increasingly, racial hatred is erupting into racist terror. Growing racial tensions have resulted in outbreaks of violence in Chicago's Marquette Park, Baltimore's Hampden section, Philadelphia's Fishtown and Feltonville, and a number of other cities in the last decade. In two highly publicized murders, black youths Michael Griffith and Yusuf Hawkins were killed by racists in Howard Beach and Bensonhurst, New York. Civil rights demonstrations have been met by overt white hostility and racist attacks. What needs to be stressed is not only that minorities are increasingly open to ideological and physical assaults, but that the very fate of our society as a democratic nation is at risk. Central to the effort to reconstruct this nation as a democratic society is the need to rethink the project of race, and cultural and economic justice. Moreover, this is not merely a political issue; it is eminently a pedagogical one as well. Racism is an ideological poison that is learned; it is a historical and social construction that seeps into social practices, needs, the unconscious, and rationality itself. If it is to be challenged at the institutional level, at the very centers of authority, racism must first be addressed as an ideological concern for the ways in which it is produced, sustained, and taken-up within a cultural politics secured within wider dominant relations of power.

These are not new insights and generations of Afro-American leaders have raised them in elegant and courageous ways. The fight against racism has always been seen as an important political objective by those committed to democratic struggle. But in most cases, this concern has been framed within a discourse of modernism that has failed to place race and ethnicity at the center of a radical politics of democracy, difference, and cultural struggle. In what follows, I want to argue for a postmodern discourse of resistance as a basis for developing a cultural politics and antiracist pedagogy as part of a larger theory of difference and democratic struggle. In developing this perspective, I will first address in general terms the failings of various versions of modernist discourse; next I will argue that the foundations for an antiracist pedagogy can be taken-up by drawing selectively upon the discourses of a critical postmodernism, the discourse of narrative and difference that has largely emerged in the work of Afro-American feminist writers, and a neo-Gramscian discourse that links difference with the notion of a democratic public philosophy. I will conclude by suggesting how these discourses provide some important elements for developing specific pedagogical practices.

Refiguring the Boundaries of Race as Modernism

The dominant discourses of modernity have rarely been able to address race and ethnicity as ethical, political, and cultural markers in order to understand or self-consciously examine the notions of justice inscribed in the modernist belief in change and the progressive unfolding of history.[8] In fact, race and ethnicity have been generally reduced to a discourse of the Other, a discourse that, regardless of its emancipatory or reactionary intent, often essentialized and reproduced the distance between the centers and margins of power. Within the discourse of modernity, the Other not only sometimes ceases to be a historical agent, but is often defined within totalizing and universalistic theories that create a transcendental rational, white, male, Eurocentric subject that occupies the centers of power while simultaneously appearing to exist outside of time and space. Read against this Eurocentric transcendental subject, the other is shown to lack any redeeming community traditions, collective voice, or historical weight—and is reduced to the imagery of the colonizer. By separating the discourse of the Other from the epistemic and material violence that most postmodernist critics have identified as central to the character and definition of Western notions of progress, modernist discourses were never able to develop an adequate understanding of racism that could serve as a form of cultural criticism capable of redefining the boundaries and articulations between modernism and the subordinate groups it continually oppressed. In this sense, modernism in its various forms served to repress the possibility of linking the construction of its own master narratives and relations of power with the simultaneous creation of alternative narratives woven out of the pain, misery, and struggle of subordinate groups.[9] Modernist discourses, in part, have served to solidify the boundaries of race and ethnicity either by creating biological and scientific theories that "proved" the inferiority of Afro-American and other subordinated groups, or in their more liberal forms by creating the self-delusion that the boundaries of racial inequality and ethnicity were always exclusively about the language, experiences, and histories of the Other and had little to do with power relations at the core of modernism's own cultural and political identity as the discourse of white authority. In the first instance, the ideology of racism and degraded Otherness can be found, as Cornel West points out, in the logics of three central European traditions: the Judeo-Christian, scientific, and psychosexual. He is worth quoting at length on this issue:

> The Judeo-Christian racist logic emanates from the biblical account of Ham looking upon and failing to cover his father Noah's nakedness and thereby receiving divine punishment in the form of blackening his progeny. Within this logic, black skin is a divine curse owing to disrespect for and rejection of paternal authority. The scientific racist logic rests upon a modern philosophical discourse guided by Greek ocular metaphors, undergirded by Cartesian notations of the primacy of the subject and the preeminence of representation and buttressed by Baconian ideas of observation, evidence, and confirmation that promote and encourage the activities of observing, comparing, measuring, and ordering physical characteristics of human bodies. Given the renewed appreciation and appropriation of classical aesthetic and cultural norms within this logic, the notions of black ugliness, cultural deficiency, and intellectual inferiority are legitimated by the value laden, yet prestigious, authority of science. The psychosexual racist logic arises from the phallic obsessions, Oedipal projections, and anal-sadistic orientations in European culture that endow African men and women with sexual prowess; view Africans as either cruel, revengeful fathers; frivolous, carefree children; or passive, long-suffering mothers; and identify Africans with dirt, odious smell, and feces. In short, Africans are associated with acts of bodily defecation, violation, and subordination. Within this logic, Africans are walking abstractions, inanimate things or invisible creatures. For all three white supremacist logics, which operate simultaneously in the modern West, Africans personify degraded Otherness, exemplify radical alterity, and embody alien difference.[10]

It is important to emphasize that the Eurocentric drive to systematize the world by mastering the conditions of nature and human life represents a form of social modernism that must not be confused with the more emancipatory elements of political modernism. On the one hand, the project of social modernity has been carried out under the increasing domination of relations of capitalist production characterized by a growing commodification, bureaucraticization, homogenization, and standardization of everyday life. Such a project has been legitimized, in part, through an appeal to the Enlightenment project of rationality, progress, and humanism. On the other hand, the legacy of political modernism provides a discourse that inaugurates the possibility of developing social relations in which the principles of liberty, justice, and equality provide the basis for democratic struggles. If the ravages of modernism have led to overt forms of racism and colonialization, its victories have provided a discourse of rights, universal education, and social justice.

As I mentioned in Chapter 2, modernity is not a unified discourse, and its networks of meanings and social practices have included a Western-style counterdiscourse that also offered liberals and radicals spaces for challenging racist practices and ideologies.[11] This challenge can be seen, of course, in the traditions of rupture and dissent in this country that extend from the abolitionist movement to the civil rights legislation of the 1960s and to the more recent efforts by contemporary activists and artists to counter the increasing racism of the 1980s and perhaps the 1990s as well. As noble as these responses have been, at least in intent, few of them have adequately theorized racism as part of a wider discourse of ethics, politics, and difference.[12] Unable to step beyond the modernist celebration of the unified self, totalizing notions of history, and universalistic models of reason, liberal and radical discourses have generally failed to explore the limits of the absolutist character of their own narratives regarding race and difference. Within these discourses, ethics and politics have been removed from any serious attempt to engage contingency, particularity, partiality, and community within a notion of difference free from binary oppositions, hierarchical relations, and narratives of mastery and control. But modernity has also failed to challenge with any great force the white supremacist logics embedded in the ideological traditions cited by Cornel West. Similarly, it has failed to account for the power of its own authority as a central component in structuring the very notion of Otherness as site for objectification and marginalization.

The emancipatory promise of plurality and heterogeneity as the basis for new forms of conversation, solidarity, and public culture never fully materialized within the more liberal and radical discourses of Western modernity. Caught within the limiting narratives of European culture as the model of civilization and progress, liberal and radical theorists have never been able to break away from Western models of authority that placed either the individual white male at the center of history and rationality or viewed history as the unproblematic progressive unfolding of science, reason, and technology.

For example, dominant strains of liberal ideology have fashioned their antiracist discourses on a Eurocentric notion of society that subordinates the discourse of ethics and politics to the rule of the market, an unproblematic acceptance of European culture as the basis of civilization, and a notion of the individual subject as a unified, rational self that is the source of all cultural and social meaning. The central modernist political ideology at work here, as Stanley Aronowitz has pointed out, is "that a free market and a democratic state go hand in hand."[13] Unfortunately for liberals, it is precisely this assumption that prevents them from questioning how they, as a dominant group, actually benefit from racist ideologies and social relations, even as they allegedly contest such practices. By assuming that the middle class, which bears the values of individualism and free-market rationality, is the only agent of history, liberals are blind to the corruptions implicated in the exercise of their own authority and historical actions.[14]

Within this multilayered liberal discourse, the attack on racism is often reduced to policy measures aimed at eliminating racist institutional barriers in the marketplace, providing compensatory programs to enhance the cultural capital and skills of Afro-Americans as in various remedial programs in education or the workplace such as Headstart or the now defunct Job Corps project, or is relegated to patronizing calls for Afro-Americans to muster the courage and fortitude to compete in a manner consistent with the drive and struggle of other ethnic groups who have succeeded in American society.

Though the theoretical sweep is broad and oversimplified here, the basic issue is that modernist discourse in its various forms rarely engages how white authority is inscribed and implicated in the creation and reproduction of a society in which the voices of the center appear either invisible or unimplicated in the historical and social construction of racism as an integral part of their own collective identity. Rather than recognizing how differences are historically and socially constructed within ideologies and material practices that connect race, class, and gender within webbed connections of domination, liberals consign the struggle of subordinate groups to master narratives that suggest that the oppressed need to be remade in the image of a dominant white culture in order to be integrated into the heavenly city of Enlightenment rationality.

Eurocentric radical discourses of modernity have also failed to develop a complex and adequate theory of racism as part of a wider theory of difference and democratic struggle. The classic instance in this case is represented by those versions of Marxism that have reduced struggle and difference to a reductionist logocentricism that universalizes the working class as the collective agent of history. Marxism buys the productivist discourse of modernity but rejects the liberal notion of the middle class as the agent of history. Marxist economics rejects the rule of the market as the end of ideology and inserts in its place the rule of the working class as the projected end of history. In this view, racism is historically tied to the rise of capitalism and is afforded no independent status as an irreducible source of either exploitation or struggle. In this instance, the notion of historical agency loses its pluralist character. As a consequence, racism is subsumed within the modernist logic of essentialism in which reason and history seem to move according to some inner logic outside of the play of difference and plurality.

In effect, class struggle becomes the all-embracing category that relegates all other struggles, voices, and conflicts to simply a distraction in the march of history.[15]

Radical social theorists have long offered a challenge to the classical Marxist theory of race, but it is only within the last few decades that such work has advanced the category of difference beyond the essentialism of Afro-American nationalism, cultural separatism, staged pluralism, and the discourse of avant-garde exoticism.[16] The failure of modernism around race can be seen in the ways in which it has structured the discourse of educational reform on this issue.

Educational Theory and the Discourse of Race and Ethnicity

Within the discourse of modernism, dominant educational approaches to race and ethnicity imitate many of the worst dimensions of liberal ideology and radical essentialism.[17] Questions of Otherness are generally fashioned in the discourse of multicultural education, which in its varied forms and approaches generally fails to conceptualize issues of race and ethnicity as part of the wider discourse of power and powerlessness. Questions of representation and inclusion suppress any attempts to call into question the norm of whiteness as an ethnic category that secures its dominance by appearing to be invisible. Modernism's emancipatory potential within multicultural education finds expression in the call to reverse negative images of Afro-American and other ethnic groups as they appear in various forms of texts and images. Missing here is any attempt to either critique forms of European and American culture that situate difference in structures of domination or reconstruct a discourse of race and ethnicity in a theory of difference that highlights questions of equality, justice, and liberty as part of an ongoing democratic struggle. Multiculturalism is generally about Otherness, but is written in ways in which the dominating aspects of white culture are not called into question and the oppositional potential of difference as a site of struggle is muted.[18] Modernism and dominant forms of multicultural education merge in their refusal to locate cultural differences in a broader examination of how the boundaries of ethnicity, race, and power make visible how whiteness functions as a historical and social construction, "an unrecognized and unspoken racial category that secures its power by refusing to identify culture as a problem of politics, power, and pedagogy."[19] As a critical discourse of race and pedagogy, multiculturalism needs to break its silence regarding its role in masking how white domination colonizes definitions of the normal.[20] In effect, critical educators need to move their analyses and pedagogical practices away from an exotic or allegedly objective encounter with marginal groups and raise more questions with respect to how the dominant self is always present in the construction of the margins. As Toni Morrison points out, the very issue of race requires that the bases of Western civilization will require rethinking.[21] It means that the central question may not be why Afro-Americans are absent from dominant narratives, but "What intellectual feats had to be performed by the author or his critic to erase (Afro-Americans) from a society seething with (their) presence, and what effect has that performance had on the work? What are the strategies of escape from knowledge?"[22] This means refiguring the map of ethnicity and difference outside of the binary oppositions of modernism. What is at stake here is more than the politics of representation. Issac Julien and Kobena Mercer state the issue clearly:

> One issue at stake, we suggest, is the potential break-up or deconstruction of structures that determine what is regarded as culturally central and what is regarded as culturally marginal. . . . Rather than attempt to compensate for the "structured absences" of previous paradigms, it would be useful to identify the relations of power/knowledge that determine which cultural issues are intellectually prioritized in the first place. The initial stage in any deconstructive project must be to examine and undermine the force of the binary relation that produces the marginal as a consequence of the authority invested in the centre.[23]

Implicit in this perspective are a number of political and pedagogical challenges that can be taken up by radical educators as part of a broader theoretical attempt to deconstruct and displace some of the more powerful ideological expressions of a hegemonic theory of multicultural education. First, critical educators need to reveal the political interests at work in those forms of multicultural education that translate cultural differences into learning styles; the ideological task here is to challenge those mystifying ideologies that separate culture from power and struggle while simultaneously treating difference as a technical rather than a political category. Second, critical educators need to challenge those educational discourses that view schooling as a decontextualized site free from social, political, and racial tensions. What has to be stressed here is the primacy of the political and the contextual in analyzing issues of culture, language, and voice. Third, critical educators must ideologically engage theories of multicultural education that attempt to smother the relationship between difference and power/empowerment under the call for harmony and joyful learning. At the same time, they must further the development of a theory of difference that takes as its starting point issues of power, domination, and struggle.[24] But an antiracist pedagogy must do more than reconceptualize the political and pedagogical struggle over race, ethnicity, and difference as merely part of the language of critique. It must also retrieve and reconstruct possibilities for establishing the basis for a progressive vision that makes schooling for democracy and critical citizenship an unrealized yet possible reality. In doing so, it is necessary to provide some central theoretical principles for developing the foundation for an antiracist pedagogy. In what follows, I will argue that there are elements of a postmodern discourse that offer valuable insights for engaging in such a task.

Postmodernism and the Shifting Boundaries of Otherness

Postmodernism is a culture and politics of transgression. It is a challenge to the bound-aries in which modernism has developed its discourses of mastery, totalization, repre-sentation, subjectivity, and history.[25] Whereas modernism builds its dream of social engineering on the foundations of universal reason and the unified subject, post-modernism questions the very notion of meaning and representation. Postmodernism not only opens up a new political front within discourse and representation. It also criticizes the notion of the unified subject as a Eurocentric construct designed to provide white, male, Christian bosses and workers with a legitimating ideology for colonizing and marginalizing those Others who do not measure up to the standards of an "I" or "We" wielding power from the center of the world.[26]

Postmodernism also rejects the modernist distinction between art and life. In doing so, it also rejects the modernist distinctions between elite culture and the culture of everyday life. As a discourse of disruption and subversion, postmodernism does not argue that all referents for meaning and representation have disappeared; rather, it seeks to make them problematic and reinscribes and rewrites the boundaries for estab-lishing the conditions for the production of meaning and subjectivity.[27] For example, in treating cultural forms as texts, postmodernism multiplies both the possibilities of constructing meaning as well as the status of meaning itself. In this sense, postmodernism redraws and retheorizes the objects and experiences of politics by ex-tending the reach of power and meaning to spheres of the everyday that are often excluded from the realm of political analysis and pedagogical legitimation. In this case, the field of political contestation is not restricted to the state or the workplace, but also includes the family, mass and popular culture, the sphere of sexuality, and the terrain of the refused and forgotten. In the discourse of modernism, there is a world held together by the metanarrative of universal reason and social engineering.[28] Therefore, the central questions for modernists have been, "How can I interpret and master this world? How do I constitute myself within it?" Postmodernism does not begin from such a comfortable sense of place and history. It subordinates reason to uncertainty and pushes its sense of distrust into transgressions that open up entirely different lines of inquiry.

Zygmunt Bauman captures the political and epistemological shifts between mod-ernism and postmodernism in the different questions and lines of inquiry they each pursue. He writes:

> [Postmodernists] have hardly any axioms they may use as a confident start, nor do they
> have a clear address. Before they turn to exploring the world, they must find out what
> world(s) there is (are) to be explored. Hence: "What world is it? What is to be done in it?
> Which of my selves is to do it?"—in this order . . . the typically modern questions are,

among others: "What is there to be known? Who knows it? How do they know it, and with what degree of certainty?" The typically postmodern questions do not reach that far. Instead of locating the task for the knower, they attempt to locate the knower himself [sic]. "What is a world? What kinds of worlds are there? How are they constituted, and how do they differ?" Even when sharing concern about knowledge, the two types of inquiry articulate their problems differently: "How is knowledge transmitted from one knower to another, and with what degree of reliability?" as against "What happens when different worlds are placed in confrontation, or when boundaries between worlds are violated?" Note that postmodern questions have no use for "certainty"; not even reliability. The one-upmanship of modernist epistemology looks hopelessly out of place in that pluralist reality to which the postmodern ontological inquiry is first reconciled and then addressed. Here that overwhelming desire of power which animated the search for the ultimate (and which alone could animate it) raises little passion. Only eyebrows are raised by the self-confidence, which once made the pursuit of the absolute look as a plausible project.[29]

Bauman articulates an antagonism that has become a central feature of postmodernist discourse. That is, postmodernism rejects those aspects of the Enlightenment and Western philosophical tradition that rely on master narratives "which set out to address a transcendental subject, to define an essential human nature, to prescribe a global human destiny or to proscribe collective human goals."[30] Within this perspective, all claims to universal reason and impartial competence are rejected in favor of the partiality and specificity of discourse. Abstractions that deny the specificity and particularity of everyday life, that generalize out of existence the particular and the local, and that smother difference under the banner of universalizing categories are rejected as totalitarian and terroristic.

But there is more at stake here than simply an argument against master narratives or the claims of universal reason. There is also an attack on those intellectuals who would designate themselves as the emancipatory vanguard, members of an intellectual elite who have deemed themselves to be above history only to attempt to shape it through their pretensions to what Dick Hebdige calls an "illusory Faustian omnipotence."[31] In some versions of the postmodern, not only do totality and foundationalism not lead to the truth or emancipation; they actually lead to periods of great suffering and violence. The postmodernist attack on master narratives is simultaneously a criticism of an inflated teleological self-confidence, a dangerous transcendentalism, and a rejection of the omniscient narrator.[32] Read in more positive terms, critical postmodernists are arguing for a plurality of voices and narratives, that is, for narratives of difference that recognize their own partiality and present the unrepresentable, those submerged and dangerous memories that provide a challenge to white supremacist logic and recover the legacies of historically specific struggles against racism. Similarly, postmodern discourse is attempting with its emphasis on the specific and the normative to situate reason and knowledge within rather than outside particular configurations of space, place, time, and power. Partiality in this case becomes a political necessity as part of the discourse of locating oneself within rather than outside of history and ideology.

Related to the critique of master narratives and theories of totality is another major concern of critical postmodernism: the development of a politics that addresses popular culture as a serious object of aesthetic and cultural criticism on the one hand and one that signals and affirms the importance of minority cultures as historically specific forms of cultural production on the other.[33] Postmodernism's attack on universalism, in part, has translated into a refusal of modernism's relentless hostility to mass culture and its reproduction of the elitist division between high and low culture.[34] Not only has postmodernism's reaffirmation of popular culture challenged the aesthetic and epistemological divisions supportive of academic disciplines and the contours of what has been considered "serious" taste, it has also resulted in new forms of art, writing, film-making, and types of aesthetic and social criticism.[35] Similarly, postmodernism has provided the conditions necessary for exploring and recuperating traditions of various forms of Otherness as a fundamental dimension of both the cultural and the sociopolitical sphere. In other words, postmodernism's stress on the problematic of Otherness has included a focus on the importance of history as a form of counter-memory;[36] an emphasis on the value of the everyday as a source of agency and empowerment;[37] a renewed understanding of gender as an irreducible historical and social practice constituted in a plurality of self and social representation;[38] and an insertion of the contingent, the discontinuous, and the unrepresentable as coordinates for remapping and rethinking the borders that define one's existence and place in the world.

Another important aspect of postmodernism is that it provides a series of referents both for interrogating the notion of history as tradition and for redrawing and rewriting how individual and collective experience might be struggled over, understood, felt, and shaped. For example, postmodernism points to a world in which the production of meaning has become as important as the production of labor in shaping the boundaries of human existence. Three issues are at stake here. First, the notion that ideological and political structures are determined and governed by a single economic logic is rejected. Cultural and social forms contain a range of discursive and ideological possibilities that can only be grasped within the contextual and contradictory positions in which they are taken-up; moreover, while such forms are reproduced under the conditions of capitalist production, they influence and are influenced by such relations. This is not a rejection of materialist analyses of culture as much as a rejection of the vulgar reductionism that often accompanies its classical interpretation. Second, labor does not provide the exclusive basis either for meaning or for understanding the multiple and complex ensemble of social relations that constitute the wider society. In this case, social antagonisms grounded in religious, gender, racial, and ethnic conflicts, among others, possess their own dynamism and cannot be reduced to the logic of capitalist relations. More specifically, the various discourses of historical materialism no longer describe the social order. Third, how subjects are constituted in language is no less important than how they are constructed as subjects within relations of production. The world of the discursive, with its ensemble of signifying terms and practices, is essential to how people relate to themselves, Others, and the world around them. It is a textual world through which people develop a sense of self and collective identity and relate to each other, not a world that can be explained merely in terms of causal events that follow the rule-bound determinations of physical and economic laws.[39] The political economy of the sign does not displace political economy; it simply assumes its rightful place as a primary category for understanding how identities are forged within particular relations of privilege, oppression, and struggle. In pursuing this line of inquiry, postmodernism serves to deterritorialize the map of dominant cultural understanding. That is, it rejects European tradition as the exclusive referent for judging what constitutes historical, cultural, and political truth. There is no tradition or story that can speak with authority and certainty for all of humanity. In effect, critical postmodernism argues that traditions should be valued for their attempts to name the partial, the particular, and the specific; in this view, traditions demonstrate the importance of constituting history as a dialogue among a variety of voices as they struggle within asymmetrical relations of power. Traditions are not valued for their claims to truth or authority, but for the ways in which they serve to liberate and enlarge human possibilities. In other words, tradition does not represent the voice of an all-embracing view of life; instead, it serves to place people self-consciously in their histories by making them aware of the memories constituted in difference, struggle, and hope. Tradition in postmodern terms is a form of counter-memory that recovers those complex yet submerged identities that constitute the social and political construction of public life.[40]

Postmodernism rejects the modernist discourse on history that views it as uniform, chronological, and teleological. In contrast, postmodernism argues for a view of history that is decentered, discontinuous, fragmented, and plural. Jim Collins rightly argues that postmodernism challenges this view of historiography by problematizing "histories that seek to minimize heterogeneity in pursuit of a dominant style, collective spirit, or any other such unitary conception."[41] He elaborates on this by arguing:

> The common denominator of all such histories, from Oswald Spengler's *The Decline of the West* to Will Wright's *Six Guns and Society,* has been the privileging of homogeneous structures that allow historians to draw rather neat generalizations that support far more grandiose claims about culture "as a whole." Emphasis has been placed repeatedly on the diachronic changes between periods, movements, moods, etc., instead of on synchronic tensions within those subdivisions—which would naturally undermine any unitary formulations concerning a particular period's representation of itself in a specific time. . . . The chief way to break this spell is to begin with a different set of priorities—specifically that most periods are a "mixture of inconsistent elements," and that different

art forms, discourses, etc., all have their own history as well as a societal history . . . To account for these differences, histories that have been predicated on theories of evolution, mass consciousness, or Zeitgeist, must be replaced by histories that emphasize synchronic tensions, the fragmentation of mass consciousness, and the possibility of more than one Zeitgeist per culture.[42]

It is worth emphasizing that postmodernism not only raises central questions about not simply how to rethink the meaning of history and traditions. It also forces us in the absence of a discourse of essences and foundationalism to raise new and different questions. As Chantal Mouffe has pointed out, postmodernism provides the possibility of understanding the limits of traditions so we can enter into dialogue with them, particularly with respect to how we may think about the construction of political subjects and the possibility of democratic life.[43]

Finally, as I have stated in Chapter 3, and at the risk of great simplification, a postmodernism of resistance challenges the liberal, humanist notion of the unified, rational subject as the bearer of history.[44] In this instance, the subject is neither unified nor can such a subject's action be guaranteed in metaphysical or transhistorical terms. Postmodernism not only views the subject as contradictory and multilayered, it also rejects the notion that individual consciousness and reason are the most important determinants in shaping human history. It posits instead a faith in forms of social transformation that are attentive to the historical, structural, and ideological limits that shape the possibility for self-reflection and action. It points to solidarity, community, and compassion as essential aspects of how we develop and understand the capacities we have for how we experience the world and ourselves in a meaningful way.[45] But it does so by stressing that in the absence of a unified subject, we can rethink the meaning of solidarity through a recognition of the multiple antagonisms and struggles that characterize both the notion of the self and the wider social reality. By recognizing the multiplicity of subject positions that mediate and are produced by and through contradictory meanings and social practices, it becomes possible to create a discourse of democratic values that requires a "multiplication of democratic practices, institutionalizing them into ever more diverse social relations . . . [so that] we will be able not only to defend democracy but also to deepen it."[46] In different terms, postmodernism offers a series of referents for rethinking how we are constituted as subjects within a rapidly changing set of political, social, and cultural conditions.

What does this suggest for the way we look at the issue of race and ethnicity? Postmodern discourse provides a theoretical foundation for deconstructing the master narratives of white supremacist logics and for redrawing the boundaries between the construction of experience and power. In the first instance, by challenging the concept of master narratives, critical postmodernism has opened up the possibility for launching a renewed attack on the underlying assumptions that have allowed the dominant culture to enforce its own authority and racist practices through an unproblematic appeal to the virtues of Western civilization. In challenging the notions of universal reason, the construction of a white, humanist subject, and the selective legitimation of high culture as the standard for cultural practice, postmodern criticism has illuminated how Eurocentric-American discourses of identity suppress difference, heterogeneity, and multiplicity in the effort to maintain hegemonic relations of power. Not only does postmodernism provide new ways to understand how power works in constructing racist identities and subjectivities, but it also redefines culture and experience within multiple relations of difference that offer a range of subject positions from which people can struggle against racist ideologies and practices. By calling into question the themes of "degraded Otherness and subaltern marginality" postmodernism offers new theoretical tools for attacking "notions of exclusionary identity, dominating heterogeneity, and universality—or in more blunt language, white supremacy."[47] Postmodern engagements with foundationalism, culture, difference, and subjectivity provide the basis for questioning the modernist ideal of what constitutes a decent, humane, and good life. Rather than celebrate the narratives of the "masters," postmodernism raises important questions about how narratives get constructed, what they mean, how they regulate particular forms of moral and social experience, and how they presuppose and embody particular epistemological and political views of the world. Similarly, postmodernism attempts to delineate how borders are named; in fact, it attempts to redraw the very maps of meaning, desire, and difference, inscribing the social and individual body with new intellectual and emotional investments and calling into question traditional forms of power and their accompanying modes of legitimation. All of these developments redefine theory by moving it far beyond—and in opposition to—the concerns embodied in the ideologies and questions that have defined the underlying racist principles that have remained unchallenged as a central aspect of modernist discourse.

For educators interested in developing an antiracist pedagogy, postmodernism offers new epistemologies for rethinking both the broader and specific contexts in which democratic authority is defined; it offers what Richard Bernstein calls a healthy "suspiciousness of all boundary-fixing and the hidden ways in which we subordinate, exclude, and marginalize."[48] Postmodernism also offers educators a variety of discourses for interrogating modernism's reliance on totalizing theories based on a desire for certainty and absolutes.

In order for postmodernism to make a valuable contribution to the development of critical pedagogy of race, educators must combine its most important theoretical insights with those stories and narratives that illuminate how difference and resistance are concretely expressed within communities of struggle organized around specific antiracist practices. In this way, the project of an antiracist pedagogy can be deepened by expanding its discourse to increasingly wider spheres of social relations and practices. But postmodern discourse must do more than redefine difference as an integral aspect of the construction of educational life. It must also do more than reconstruct the theoretical discourse of resistance by recovering knowledge, histories, and experiences that have traditionally been left out of dominant accounts of schooling, everyday life, and history. Most important, it is vital that postmodernism open up and establish public spheres among nonacademic audiences and work with them as part of the struggle to fight racism and other forms of domination while simultaneously struggling to revitalize democratic public life. What is important to recognize is that a critical postmodernism needs to provide educators with a more complex and insightful view of the relationship between culture, power, and knowledge. When linked with the language of democratic public life, the notions of difference, power, and specificity can be understood as part of a public discourse that broadens and deepens individual liberties and rights through rather than against a radical notion of democracy.

In what follows, I want to develop how a postmodern discourse of resistance might be elaborated and advanced through the discourse of Afro-American feminists and writers whose work serves to rewrite and reinscribe the relations between power and issues of difference, struggle, identity-politics, and narrative. In choosing to focus on the writings of Afro-American feminists, I make no claim to speak as, for, or within a similar politics of location. My own politics of location as a white, academic male positions me to speak to issues of racism and gender by self-consciously recognizing my own interests in taking-up these practices as part of a broader political project to expand the scope and meaning of democratic struggle and a politics of solidarity. Border crossing in this instance is part of an attempt to further rupture a politics of historical silence and theoretical erasure that serves to repress and marginalize the voices of the Other. At stake here is the need to understand the specificity of cultural production in its own terms as it is produced through the diverse voices of Afro-American feminists constituted in different relations of power. In addition, border crossings of this sort need to challenge the authority and practices of dominant representation in order to refigure the possibility for building new forms of identification and solidarity across a politics of difference. What is at issue here is not an attempt to merely develop forms of self-criticism and understanding, although these are not to be easily discounted, but to rewrite the conditions for forms of solidarity by making visible the varied contributions that women of color are developing in their attempts both to come to voice and to voice critical and transformative narratives that deeply refigure the meaning of justice, liberty, and freedom as a condition for making difference essential to democratic life. Such a position rewrites the relationship between the margins and the centers by resisting the tendency to construct the world through the conceptual baggage of Eurocentric colonial discourse while simultaneously creating new critical public spheres as sites of resistance and transformation that challenge existing neocolonial, ideological and institutional centers of power.

Afro-American Feminist Writers and the Discourse of Possibility

Afro-American women feminists have been writing against the grain for a long time in this country.[49] Most importantly, they have given the politics of resistance and solidarity a new meaning in the diverse ways in which they have struggled, as Barbara Christian puts it, "to define and express our totality rather than being defined by Others."[50] Within the diverse body of material that makes up their work, there is a language both of critique and possibility. It is woven out of forms of testifying, narrativizing, and theorizing that reconstruct the meaning of difference while simultaneously rewriting the meaning of history as a basis for sustaining community memories and enveloping viable forms of collective struggle. The tensions that permeate this work range from suffering and resistance to a sense of healing and transcendence. For example, in the work of the novelist Paule Marshall we encounter the attempts to reconstruct "the past and the need to reverse the present social order."[51] In the work of political writers such as June Jordan, Audre Lorde, bell hooks, Michele Wallace, and Hazel Carby there is an ongoing attempt to retheorize the notion of voice as part of the shifting construction of identities forged in differences, especially those constituted out of class, race, and gender.[52] There is also an attempt to theorize voice as a historically specific cultural site from which one learns to create an oppositional consciousness and identity, a standpoint that exists not only as one that opposes domination, but one that also enables and extends individual and social capacities and possibilities for making human connections and compassionate communities of resistance and liberation.[53]

Within this work, a discourse of difference and solidarity emerges which is multilayered and dialectical. First, all of these Afro-American women offer, in different ways, a critique of difference as it is constructed through the codes and relations of the dominant culture. Second, Afro-American feminist writers have criticized the emancipatory notion of difference put forward by white feminists in the last decade while simultaneously developing a more radical notion of the politics of difference and identity politics. Third, there is a brilliant reconstruction of difference in these works through the development of narratives as forms of dangerous memory that provide the foundation for communities of resistance and a radical ethics of accountability. In what follows, I will analyze each of these elements of difference before addressing their pedagogical implications for developing what I call a border pedagogy of resistance.

Unlike many radical and postmodern theories, the work of Afro-American feminists is deeply concerned with developing a politics of difference that locates the dynamics of domination in the center of rather than on the margins of power. In effect, Afro-American feminists have attempted to uncover how complex modes of inequality are structured through racial, class, and gender divisions that lie at the heart of the dominant culture and that by definition serve to shape its most basic institutional and ideological forms. A number of issues are at work here. First, there is the need to establish that racial identities are also white and must be seen as specific historical and social constructions. It is imperative to see questions of ethnicity as part of a broader discussion of racism in order to understand how whiteness serves as a norm to privilege its own definitions of power while simultaneously concealing the political and social distinctions embedded in its essentialist constructions of difference through the categories of race, gender, and class.

Within this perspective, difference cannot be understood outside of the dynamics of silencing, subjugation, and infantilization. By focusing on the ways in which white ethnicity exercises power, designates Otherness in terms that degrade and cheapen human life, and hides its own partiality in narratives of universality and common sense, Afro-American feminists have been able to redefine what it means for people of color to come to voice and to speak in their own terms. To struggle within a politics of voice, within these practices, means that Afro-Americans have to reject a politics of the center in which the Other is reduced to an object whose experiences and traditions are either deemed alien by whites or whose identity has to bear exclusively the historical weight of Otherness and racialization. Hazel Carby suggests that:

> one way to rethink the relationship between the social, political, and cultural construction of blackness and marginality, on the one hand, and assumptions of a normative whiteness within the dominant culture, on the other, is to examine the ways in which that dominant culture has been shaped and transformed by the presence of the marginalized. This means a public recognition that the process of marginalization itself is central to the formation of the dominant culture. The first and very important stage is . . . to recognize the cultural and political category of whiteness. It seems obvious to say it but in practice the racialization of our social order is only recognized in relation to racialized "others."[54]

What Carby points to is part of a broader theoretical attempt by Afro-American feminists to reject narrow notions of Afro-American identity while also calling into question the cultural absences that historically and socially locate white ethnicity within subject positions that blind many whites to the mechanisms of cultural apartheid and relations of power that are constitutive of what it means to be part of a dominant Eurocentric culture in America. As Coco Fusco puts it, "Endemic to this history are structured absences that function to maintain relations of power. To put it bluntly, no one has yet spoken of the 'self' implicit in the 'other,' or of the ones who are designating the 'others.' Power, veiled and silent, remains in place."[55] Afro-American feminists have provided an enormous service by shifting the discussion of difference away from an exclusive concern with the margins and in doing so have made it clear that any analysis of racial identity must include an analysis of how the dominant Other functions to actively and systematically conceal its own historical and cultural identity while devaluing the identity of other racial groups. By challenging how boundaries of difference have been constructed through dominant Eurocentric codes and binarisms, it becomes possible to deepen our understanding of not only how white ethnicity is constructed

in its attempts to position others. It also becomes possible to rethink the issue of subjectivity and resistance outside of the crippling essentialisms that have characterized
dominant humanist theory. Identity is no longer something that is fixed but fluid,
shifting, and multiple. At the same time, oppression can now be seen in its multiple
antagonisms and social relations. Once dominant culture is racialized within the discourse of ethnicity and existing power relations, it becomes possible to write history
from the perspective of those engaged in the struggle against cultural genocide. Voices
now begin to emerge from different locations and are no longer authorized to speak
only through a Eurocentric perspective that defines them in its own interests. bell hooks
links this emergence of multiple voices as part of a wider struggle for a politics and
identity that is crucial to the reconstruction of Afro-American subjectivity. She writes:

> We return to "identity" and "culture" for relocation, linked to political practice—identity
> that is not informed by a narrow cultural nationalism masking continued fascination
> with the power of the white hegemonic other. Instead identity is evoked as a stage in a
> process wherein one constructs radical black subjectivity. Recent critical reflections on a
> static notion of black identity urge transformation of our sense of who can we be and
> still be black. Assimilation, imitation, or assuming the role of rebellious exotic other are
> not the only available options and never have been. This is why it is crucial to radically
> revise notions of identity politics, to explore marginal locations as spaces where we can
> best become whatever we want to be while remaining committed to liberatory black
> liberation struggle.[56]

Central to the notion of difference put forth by many black theorists is a notion
of antiracism that refigures the meaning of ethnicity as a social and historical construct.
Such a view signals the end of the essentialist black subject as well as the structured
absence of whiteness as a racial category. For example, Stuart Hall suggests that the
notion of the black subject as a social and historical construction points to a new conception of identity and a redefinition of a cultural politics of difference. He writes:

> Constituting oneself as "black" is another recognition of self through difference: certain
> clear polarities and extremities against which one tries to define oneself. . . . It has long
> been thought that this is really a simple process: a recognition—a resolution of
> irresolutions, a coming to rest in some place which was always there waiting for one. The
> "real me.". . . The fact is "black" has never been just there either. It has always been an
> unstable identity, psychically, culturally, and politically. It, too, is a narrative, a story, a
> history. Something constructed, told, spoken, not simply found.[57]

The strategic importance of making Afro-American identity both complex and
visible has been theoretically developed in the writing of a number of Afro-American
feminists. More specifically, these writers have criticized the ways in which the notion
of difference and race have been taken-up in essentialist terms by many white middle-

class feminists in the struggle over sexuality and gender. Audre Lorde is a powerful voice in this struggle:

> Those of us who have been forged in the crucibles of difference—those of us who are poor, who are lesbians, who are Black, who are older—know that survival is not an academic skill. It is learning how to stand alone, unpopular and sometimes reviled, and how to make common cause with those others identified as outside the structures in order to define and seek a world in which we can all flourish. It is learning how to take our differences and make them strengths. For the master's tools will never dismantle the master's house. They may allow us temporarily to beat him at his own game, but they will never enable us to bring about change.[58]

In this quote, she uses the notion of difference as a referent for critique and as a basis for advancing the emancipatory possibilities in a radicalized notion of difference. In the first instance, she argues against various versions of contemporary feminism that limit domination to the sphere of sexual relations and, in doing so, develop a discourse of difference that excludes questions of racism, class domination, and homophobia. Under the banner of feminist struggle and liberation, many contemporary feminists have unconsciously reconstructed the Eurocentric logocentrism they claimed they were attacking. In effect, while the center was being reconstructed as an affirmation of feminism in the service of an attack on patriarchy, it functioned to recreate existing margins of power while denying the voices of working-class women, lesbians, and women of color. As Lorde points out:

> The absence of these considerations weakens any feminist discussion of the personal and the political. It is a particular academic arrogance to assume any discussion of feminist theory without examining our many differences, and without a significant input from poor women, Black and Third World Women, and lesbians.[59]

Lorde is not merely criticizing a feminist perspective that refuses to examine differences as they are constructed outside of the world of white, middle-class women. She is also arguing that in this refusal of difference lie the seeds of racism and homophobia. She recognizes that whites have a heavy cultural, political, and affective investment in ignoring differences. To recognize such differences is to immediately call into play the asymmetrical relations of power that structure the lives of white and Afro-American women differently. For white middle-class women, this often invokes guilt and forces them to "allow women of Color to step out of stereotype . . . [and] it threatens the complacency of these women who view oppression only in terms of sex."[60] Lorde is eloquent on this issue:

> Poor women and women of Color know there is a difference between the daily manifestations of marital slavery and prostitution because it is our daughters who line 42nd

Street. If white American feminist theory need not deal with the differences between us, and the resulting difference in our oppressions, then how do you deal with the fact that the women who clean your houses and tend your children while you attend conferences on feminist theory, are for the most part, poor women and women of Color? What is the theory behind racist feminism? In a world of possibility for us all, our personal visions help lay the groundwork for political action. The failure of academic feminists to recognize difference as a crucial strength is a failure to reach beyond the first patriarchal lesson. In our world, divide and conquer must become define and empower.[61]

But Lorde, like a number of Afro-American writers, is not content either to limit her analysis to the racism inherent in narrowly defined feminist theories of difference or to deconstruct forms of cultural separatism that argue that Afro-Americans only need to bear witness to the positive moments in their own stories. These are important political and strategic issues, but Lorde is also concerned about developing a politics of solidarity and identity that views difference as a dynamic human force that is "enriching rather than threatening to the defined self when there are shared goals."[62] In this case, Afro-American women writers have attempted to develop a politics of difference that celebrates its creative function while simultaneously arguing for new forms of community rooted in definitions of power and patterns of relating that allow diverse groups of people to reach out beyond their own interests to forge living connections with a multitude of differences for the purpose of developing a democratic culture and society.

At issue here is a politics of resistance in which difference is explored through the category of voice and solidarity. It is important to stress, even at the expense of overstating the issue, that Afro-American feminists have attempted to develop a notion of Afro-American subjectivity and voice that portrays Afro-American women outside of the narrow confines of an essentialist and stereotypical reading. In this case, there is an attempt to develop a notion of self and identity that links difference to the insistence of speaking in many voices, to fasten a notion of identity that is shifting and multiple rather than static and singular. Central here is the need to engage voice as an act of resistance and self-transformation, to recognize that as one comes to voice one establishes the precondition for becoming a subject in history rather than an object.[63] In analyzing a portion of her own experience in attending all-black segregated schools, hooks comments on how she learned to recognize the value of an education that allowed her to speak in many voices. She writes:

> In part, attending all-black segregated schools with black teachers meant that I had come to understand black poets as being capable of speaking in many voices . . . The black poet, as exemplified by Gwendolyn Brooks and later Amiri Baraka, had many voices—with no single voice being identified as more or less authentic. The insistence on finding one voice, one definitive style of writing and reading one's poetry, fits all too neatly with a static notion of self and identity that was pervasive in university settings. It seemed

that many black students found our situations problematic precisely because our sense of self, and by definition our voice, was not unilateral, monologist, or static but rather multidimensional. We were as at home in dialect as we were in standard English. Individuals who speak languages other than English, who speak patois as well as standard English, find it a necessary aspect of self-affirmation not to feel compelled to choose one voice over another, not to claim one as more authentic, but rather to construct social realities that celebrate, acknowledge, and affirm differences, variety . . . to claim all the tongues in which we speak, to make speech of the many languages that give expression to the unique cultural reality of a people.[64]

As part of a politics of difference, an antiracist pedagogy would have to investigate the relationship between language and voice as part of a wider concern with democratic struggle and antagonisms. Instead of talking about literacy, radical educational theory would have to educate teachers and administrators to speak and listen to many languages and ways of understanding the world. Not only would this open up the possibility for many people to speak from the decided advantage of their own experiences, it would also multiply and decidedly transform the discursive and nondiscursive sites from which administrators, teachers, students, parents, and neighborhood people could engage in dialogue and communities of solidarity. A radical educational discourse would also educate people to the tyranny that lies beneath logocentric narratives, truths that appear to exist beyond criticism, and language that undermines the force of democratic encounters. In this context, June Jordan is illuminating in sharply contrasting the implications of a language difference with the reality that most people find themselves in at the current historical juncture in the United States:

I am talking about majority problems of language in a democratic state, problems of a currency that someone has stolen and hidden away and then homogenized into an official "English" language that can only express non-events involving nobody responsible, or lies. If we lived in a democratic state our language would have to hurtle, fly, curse, and sing, in all the common American names, all the undeniable and representative participating voices of everybody here. We would not tolerate the language of the powerful and, thereby, lose all respect for words, per se. We would make our language conform to the truth of our many selves and we would make our language lead us into the equality of power that a democratic state must represent . . . This is not a democratic state. And we put up with that. We have the language of the powerful that perpetuates that power through the censorship of dissenting views.[65]

Another important element in the theory and politics of difference that has emerged in the writings of Afro-American feminists is the importance of stories, of narrative forms that keep alive communities of resistance while also indicting the collective destruction that mobilizes racism, sexism, and other forms of domination. Barbara Christian argues that Afro-American people have always theorized in narrative forms, "in the stories we create, in riddles and proverbs, in the play with language,

since dynamic rather than fixed ideas seem more to our liking."[66] The narratives that
are at work here are grounded in the discourse of everyday life—they are polyphonic,
partial, and vibrant. And yet they are produced amid relations of struggle. Toni Cade
Bambara claims that such stories are grounded in relations of survival, struggle, and
wide-awake resistance. She writes:

> Stories are important. They keep us alive. In the ships, in the camps, in the quarters,
> field, prisons, on the road, on the run, underground, under siege, in the throes, on the
> verge—the story teller snatches us back from the edge to hear the next chapter. In which
> we are the subjects. We, the hero of the tales. Our lives preserved. How it was, how it be.
> Passing it along in the relay. That is what I work to do: to produce stories that save our
> lives.[67]

The development of narrative forms and stories in the work of writers like Zora
Neale Hurston, Paule Marshall, Toni Morrison, Alice Walker, and Toni Cade Bambara
challenge the ways in which knowledge is constructed, illuminate the relationship between knowledge and power, and redefine the personal and the political so as to rewrite
the dialectical connection between what we learn and how we come to learn given our
specific location in history, experience, and language.[68] The literature of Afro-American
feminist writers extends and challenges postmodernism's view of narratives. Their
writings link the form and substance of narrative storytelling with issues of survival
and resistance and add a more progressive political character to narrative structure
and substance than is developed in postmodern analyses. The development of these
stories becomes a medium for developing forms of historical consciousness that provide
the basis for new relations of solidarity, community, and self-love. For example, Michelle
Gibbs Russell links the political and the pedagogical in the use of storytelling and, in
doing so, demonstrates the radical potential it assumes as a form of self and social
empowerment:

> The oldest form of building historical consciousness in community is storytelling. The
> transfer of knowledge, skill, and value from one collective memory, has particular sig-
> nificance in diaspora culture. . . . Political education for Black women in America be-
> gins with the memory of four hundred years of enslavement, diaspora, forced labor,
> beatings, bombings, lynchings, and rape. It takes on inspirational dimensions when we
> begin cataloguing the heroic individuals and organizations in our history who have battled
> against those atrocities, and triumphed over them. It becomes practical when we are
> confronted with the problem of how to organize food cooperatives for women on food-
> stamp budgets or how to prove one's fitness as a mother in court. It becomes radical
> when, as teachers, we develop a methodology that places daily life at the center of history
> and enables Black women to struggle for survival with the knowledge that they are making
> history. One setting where such connections can be made is the classroom. In the ab-
> sence of any land, or turf, which we actually control, the classroom serves as a temporary

space where we can evoke and evaluate our collective memory of what is done to us, and what we do in turn.[69]

As a pedagogical practice, the recovery and affirmation of stories that emanate from the experience of marginal groups can also serve in an emancipatory way to recenter the presence of white authority. Such stories cannot be used exclusively as a basis for whites to examine their own complicity in the construction of racism; they can also help privileged groups listen seriously to the multiple narratives that constitute the complexity of Others historically defined through reifications and stereotypes that smother difference within and between diverse subordinate groups. Of course, such stories also need to provide the opportunity to raise questions about what kinds of common claims regarding a discourse of ethics, accountability, and identity politics can be developed between whites and people of color around such narrative forms. I believe that by making visible and interrogating the variety of textual forms and voices that inform such narratives, students can deconstruct the master narratives of racism, sexism, and class domination while simultaneously questioning how these narratives contribute to forms of self-hatred and contempt that surround the identities of blacks, women, and other subordinated groups.[70] Similarly, the stories of marginal groups provide counter-narratives that call into question the role that whites and other dominant groups have and continue to play in perpetuating oppression and human suffering. Sharon Welch is instructive on this issue. She argues that listening to and engaging the stories of the other can educate members of white, Eurocentric culture to a redefinition of responsibility through what she calls an ethic of risk and resistance. She writes:

> Particular stories call us to accountability. As dangerous memories of conflict, oppression, and exclusion, they call those of us who are, often unknowingly, complicit in structures of control to join in resistance and transformation. For those of us who are members of the Western elite, by reason of race, gender, education, or economic status, we are challenged by the stories of the marginalized and oppressed to grasp the limits of our ethical and political wisdom–the limited appeal of our capitalist economic system, our limited appreciation of the vitality and determination of the other people to shape their own identities. . . . We in the First World are not responsible for others; we are responsible for ourselves—for seeing the limits of our own vision and for rectifying the damages caused by the arrogant violation of those limits.[71]

Welch is arguing for a dialectical notion of narrative. She rightly argues that the narratives of subordinate groups needs to be recovered as "dangerous memories" that rewrite and reinscribe the historical threads of community forged in resistance and struggle. She also argues that such stories are needed to construct an ethical discourse that indicts Eurocentric-American master narratives so they can be critically interrogated and discarded when necessary in the interests of constructing social relations and communities of struggle that provide healing, salvation, and justice. At the same time, Michele Wallace offers a critical qualification on the praise and use of narrative structure in the writings of Afro-American women.[72.] She argues that the success of contemporary Afro-American women's novel writing is privileged by dominant groups to the exclusion of other forms of discursive representation. This is not to undermine what I have said about the importance of narrative structure in Afro-American feminist works. I mean only to locate how such work can be appropriated by the dominant culture in ways that reproduce and reinforce forms of inequality and racism. In this case, theoretical cultural criticism becomes the exclusive discourse of mostly white academics, while theoretical cultural criticism by Afro-American feminists is either ignored or marginalized.

Border Pedagogy as the Practice of Struggle and Transformation

If the construction of antiracist pedagogy is to escape from a notion of difference that is silent about other social antagonisms and forms of struggle, it must be developed as part of a wider public discourse that is simultaneously about the discourse of an engaged plurality and the formation of critical citizenship. This must be a discourse that breathes life into the notion of democracy by stressing a notion of lived community that is not at odds with the principles of justice, liberty, and equality.[73] Such a discourse must be informed by a postmodern concern with establishing the material and ideological conditions that allow multiple, specific, and heterogeneous ways of life to come into play as part of a border pedagogy of postmodern resistance. In other words, educators must prepare students for a type of citizenship that does not separate abstract rights from the realm of the everyday and does not define community as the legitimating and unifying practice of a one-dimensional historical and cultural narrative. Postmodernism radicalizes the emancipatory possibilities of teaching and learning as part of a wider struggle for democratic public life and critical citizenship. It does this by refusing forms of knowledge and pedagogy wrapped in the legitimizing discourse of the sacred and the priestly; rejecting universal reason as a foundation for human affairs; claiming that all narratives are partial; and performing a critical reading on all scientific, cultural, and social texts as historical and political constructions.

In this view, the broader parameters of an antiracist pedagogy are informed by a political project that links the creation of critical citizens to the development of radical democracy; that is, a political project that ties education to the broader struggle for a public life in which dialogue, vision, and compassion remain critically attentive to the rights and conditions that organize public space as a democratic social form rather than as a regime of terror and oppression. It is important to emphasize that difference and pluralism in this view do not mean reducing democracy to the equivalency of diverse interests; on the contrary, what is being argued for is a language in which different voices and traditions exist and flourish to the degree that they listen to the voices of Others; a language that engages in an ongoing attempt to eliminate forms of subjective and objective suffering and maintains those conditions in which the act of communicating and living extends rather than restricts the creation of democratic public spheres. This is as much a political project as it is a pedagogical project, one that demands that antiracist pedagogical practices be developed within a discourse that combines a democratic public philosophy with a postmodern theory of resistance. Within this perspective, the issue of border pedagogy is located within those broader cultural and political considerations that are beginning to redefine our traditional view of community, language, space, and possibility. It is a pedagogy that is attentive to developing a democratic public philosophy that respects the notion of difference as part of a common struggle to extend and transform the quality of public life. In short, the notion of border pedagogy presupposes not merely an acknowledgment of the shifting borders that both undermine and reterritorialize dominant configurations of power and knowledge. It also links the notion of pedagogy with the creation of a society in which there is available a multiplicity of democratic practices, values, and social relations for students to take-up within different learning situations. At stake here is a view of democracy and learning in which multiplicity, plurality, and struggle become the raison d'etre of democratic public life. Chantal Mouffe has elaborated this position in neo-Gramscian terms:

> If the task of radical democracy is indeed to deepen the democratic revolution and to link together diverse democratic struggles, such a task requires the creation of new subject-positions that would allow the common articulation, for example, of antiracism, antisexism, and anticapitalism. These struggles do not spontaneously converge, and in order to establish democratic equivalences, a new "common sense" is necessary, which would transform the identity of different groups so that the demands of each group could be articulated with those of others according to the principle of democratic equivalence. For it is not a matter of establishing a mere alliance between given interests but of actually modifying the very identity of those forces. In order that the defense of workers' interests is not pursued at the cost of the rights of women, immigrants, or consumers, it is necessary to establish an equivalence between these different struggles. It is only under these circumstances that struggles against power become truly democratic.[74]

Mouffe's position should not suggest that this is merely a political task to be established and carried out by an elite, a party, or a specific group of intellectuals. It is more importantly a pedagogical task that has to be taken-up and argued for by all cultural workers who take a particular political stand on the meaning and importance of radical democracy as a way of life. Such a position not only rejects the one-sided and undemocratic interests that inform the conservative argument that collapses democracy into the logic of the market or buttresses the ideology of cultural uniformity, but also rejects leftist versions of an identity politics that excludes the Other as part of a reductive discourse of assertion and separatism. Stanley Aronowitz extends Mouffe's emphasis on difference as a central feature of democracy by linking democracy with citizenship understood as a form of self-management constituted in all major economic, social, and cultural spheres.[75] Democracy in this context takes-up the issue of transferring power from elites and executive authorities, who control the economic and cultural apparatuses of society, to those producers who wield power at the local levels. Aronowitz's argument is important because he not only critiques the discourse of liberal pluralism and "chic" difference in his analysis of democratic struggle and calls for the construction of popular public spheres, but he also places the issue of power, politics, and struggle at the heart of the debate over radical democracy. What is being called for here is a notion of border pedagogy that provides educators with the opportunity to rethink the relations between the centers and the margins of power. That is, such a pedagogy must address the issue of racism as one that calls into question not only forms of subordination that create inequities among different groups as they live out their lives, but as I have mentioned previously, also challenges those institutional and ideological boundaries that have historically masked their own relations of power behind complex forms of distinction and privilege.

What does this suggest for the way we develop the basic elements of an antiracist pedagogy? First, the notion of border pedagogy offers students the opportunity to engage the multiple references that constitute different cultural codes, experiences, and languages. This means providing the learning opportunities for students to become media-literate in a world of changing representations. It means offering students the knowledge and social relations that enable them to critically read not only how cultural texts are regulated by various discursive codes, but also how such texts express and represent different ideological interests. In this case, border pedagogy establishes conditions of learning that define literacy inside of the categories of power and authority. This suggests developing pedagogical practices that address texts as social and historical constructions; it also suggests developing pedagogical practices that allow students to analyze texts in terms of their presences and absences. Most important, such practices should provide students with the opportunity to read texts dialogically through a configuration of many voices, some of which offer resistance, some of which provide support. Border pedagogy also stresses that students must be provided with the opportunity to critically engage the strengths and limitations of the cultural and social codes that define their own histories and narratives. In this case, partiality becomes the basis for recognizing the limits built into all discourses. At issue here is the need for students to not merely develop a healthy skepticism toward all discourses of authority, but also to recognize how authority and power can be transformed in the interest of creating a democratic society.

Within this discourse, students engage knowledge as border-crossers, as people moving in and out of borders constructed around coordinates of difference and power.[76] These are not only physical borders, but cultural borders historically constructed and socially organized within maps of rules and regulations that serve to either limit, exclude, or pathologize particular identities, individual capacities, and social forms. Students cross borders of meaning, maps of knowledge, social relations, and values that are increasingly being negotiated and rewritten as the codes and regulations that organize them become destabilized and reshaped. Border pedagogy decenters as it remaps. The terrain of learning becomes inextricably linked to the shifting parameters of place, identity, history, and power. By reconstructing the traditional radical emphasis of the knowledge–power relationship away from the limited emphasis of mapping domination to the politically strategic issue of engaging the ways in which knowledge can be remapped, reterritorialized, and decentered, in the wider interests of rewriting the borders and coordinates of an oppositional cultural politics, educators can redefine the teacher–student relationship in ways that allow students to draw upon their own personal experience as real knowledge.

At one level this means giving students the opportunity to speak, locate themselves in history, and become subjects in the construction of their identities and the wider society. It also means defining voice not merely as an opportunity to speak, but to engage critically with the ideology and substance of speech, writing, and other forms of cultural production. In this case, "coming to voice" for students from both dominant and subordinated cultures means engaging in rigorous discussions of various cultural texts, drawing upon one's personal experience, and confronting the process through which ethnicity and power can be rethought as a political narrative that challenges racism as part of a broader struggle to democratize social, political, and economic life. In part, this means looking at the various ways in which race implicates relations of domination, resistance, suffering, and power within various social practices and how these are taken-up in multiple ways by students who occupy different ethnic, social, and gender locations. In this way, race is never discussed outside of broader articulations nor is it merely about people of color.

Second, a border pedagogy of postmodern resistance needs to do more than educate students to perform ideological surgery on master narratives based on white, patriarchal, and class-specific interests. If the master narratives of domination are to be effectively deterritorialized, it is important for educators to understand how such narratives are taken-up as part of an investment of feeling, pleasure, and desire. The syntax of learning and behavior must be rethought outside of the geography of rationality and reason. For example, this means that racism cannot be dealt with in a purely limited analytical way. An antiracist pedagogy must engage how and why students both make particular ideological and affective investments and occupy particular subject positions that give them a sense of meaning, purpose, and delight. As Hall argues, this means uncovering both for ourselves as teachers as well as for the students we are teaching "the deep structural factors which have a tendency persistently not only to generate racial practices and structures but to reproduce them through time which therefore account for their extraordinarily immovable character."[77] In addition to engaging racism within a politics of representation, ideology, and pleasure, any serious analysis of racism must also be historical and structural. It has to chart-out how racist practices develop, where they come from, how they are sustained, how they affect dominant and subordinate groups, and how they can be challenged. This is not a discourse about personal preferences or dominant tastes but a discourse about economics, culture, politics, and power.

Third, a border pedagogy offers the opportunity for students to air their feelings about race from the perspective of the subject positions they experience as constitutive of their own identities. Ideology in this sense is treated not merely as an abstraction but as part of the student's lived experience. This does not mean that teachers either reduce their role to that of intellectual voyeur or collapse their authority into a shabby form of relativism. Nor does border pedagogy suggest that students merely express or assess their own experiences. Rather, it points to a particular form of teacher authority grounded in a respect for a radically decentered notion of democratic public life, a view of authority that rejects the notion that all forms of authority are expressions of unwarranted power and oppression. Instead, border pedagogy argues for forms of authority that are rooted in democratic interests and emancipatory social relations. Authority, in this case, rejects politics as aesthetics, and retains instead the significance of the knowledge/power relationship as a discourse of criticism and politics necessary for the achievement of equality, freedom, and struggle. This is not a form of authority based on an appeal to universal truths; rather, it is a form of authority that recognizes its own partiality while simultaneously asserting a standpoint from which to engage the discourses and practices of democracy, freedom, and domination. Put another way, this is a notion of authority rooted in a political project that ties education to the broader struggle for public life in which dialogue, vision, and compassion remain critically attentive to the liberating and dominating relations that organize various aspects of everyday life.[78]

This suggests that teachers use their authority to establish classroom conditions in which different views about race can be aired but not treated as simply an expression of individual views or feelings.[79] Andrew Hannan rightly points out that educators must refuse to treat racism as a matter of individual prejudice and counter such a position by addressing the "structural foundations of [the] culture of racism."[80] An antiracist pedagogy must demonstrate that the views we hold about race have different historical and ideological weight, forged in asymmetrical relations of power, and that they always embody interests that shape social practices in particular ways. In other words, an antiracist pedagogy cannot treat ideologies as simply individual expressions of feeling, but as historical, cultural, and social practices that serve to either undermine or reconstruct democratic public life. These views must be engaged without silencing students, but they must also be interrogated next to a public philosophy that names racism for what it is and calls racist ideologies and practices into account on political and ethical terms.

Fourth, educators need to understand how the everyday experience of marginality lends itself to forms of oppositional and transformative consciousness. For those designated as Others need to both reclaim and remake their histories, voices, and visions as part of a wider struggle to change those material and social relations that deny radical pluralism as the basis of democratic political community. It is only through such an understanding that teachers can develop a border pedagogy that opens up the possibility for students to reclaim their voices as part of a process of empowerment and not merely as what some have called an initiation into the culture of power.[81] It is not enough for students to learn how to resist power that is oppressive, that names them in a way that undermines their ability to govern rather than serve, and that prevents them from struggling against forms of power that subjugate and exploit. For example, Lisa Delpit's call for educators to integrate Afro-American students into what she unproblematically addresses as "the culture of power" appears to be linked to how such power is constructed in opposition to democratic values and used as a force for domination.[82]

I do not mean to suggest the authority of white dominant culture is all of one piece, nor do I mean to imply that it should not be an object of study. What is at stake here is forging a notion of power that does not collapse into a form of domination, but is critical and emancipatory, which allows students to both locate themselves in history and to critically, not slavishly, appropriate the cultural and political codes of their own and other traditions. Moreover, students who have to disavow their racial heritage in order to succeed are not becoming "raceless" as Signithia Fordham has argued; they are being positioned to accept subject positions that are the source of power for a white, dominant culture.[83] The ability of white, male, Eurocentric culture to normalize and universalize its own interests works so well that Fordham underemphasizes how whiteness as a cultural and historical construction, as a site of dominant narratives, exercises the form of authority that prevents black students from speaking through their own memories, histories, and experiences. Delpit and Fordham are right in attempting to focus on issues of powerlessness as they relate to pedagogy and race, but they both obscure this relation by not illuminating more clearly how power works in this society within the schools to secure and conceal various forms of racism and subjugation. Power is multifaceted, and we need a better understanding of how it works not simply as a force for oppression but also as a basis for resistance and self and social empowerment. Educators need to fashion a critical postmodern notion of authority, one that decenters essentialist claims to power while simultaneously fighting for relations of authority and power that allow many voices to speak so as to initiate students into a culture that multiplies rather than restricts democratic practices and social relations as part of a wider struggle for democratic public life.

Fifth, educators need to analyze racism not only as a structural and ideological force, but also in the diverse and historically specific ways in which it emerges. This is particularly true of the most recent and newest expressions of racism developing in the United States and abroad among youth, in popular culture, and in racism's resurgence in the highest reaches of the American government.[84] Any notion of antiracist pedagogy must arise out of specific settings and contexts and must allow its own character to be defined, in part, by historically specific and contextual boundaries from which it emerges. At the same time, such a pedagogy must disavow all claims to scientific method or for that matter to any objective or transhistorical claims. As a political practice, an antiracist pedagogy has to be constructed not on the basis of essentialist or universal claims but on the concreteness of its specific encounters, struggles, and engagements. Roger Simon outlines some of the issues involved here in his discussion of critical pedagogy:

> Such a form of educational work is at root contextual and conditional. A critical pedagogy can only be concretely discussed from within a particular "point of practice"; from within a specific time and place and within a particular theme. This means doing critical pedagogy is a strategic, practical task not a scientific one. It arises not against a background of psychological, sociological, or anthropological universals—as does much educational theory to pedagogy—but from such questions as: "how is human possibility being diminished here?"[85]

Sixth, an antiracist border pedagogy must redefine how the circuits of power move in a dialectical fashion among various sites of cultural production.[86] That is, we need a clearer understanding of how ideologies and other social practices that bear down on classroom relations emerge from and articulate with other spheres of social life. As educators, we need a clearer understanding of how the grounds for the production and organization of knowledge are related to forms of authority situated in political economy, the state, and other material practices. We also need to understand how circuits of power produce forms of textual authority that offer readers particular subject positions, that is, ideological references that provide but do not rigidly determine particular views of the world.[87] In addition, educators need to explore how the reading of texts is linked with the forms of knowledge and social relations that students bring into the classroom. In other words, we need to understand in terms of function and substance those social and cultural forms outside of the classroom that produce the multiple and often contradictory subject positions that students learn and express in their interaction with the dominant cultural capital of American schools.

Finally, central to the notion of border pedagogy is a number of important pedagogical issues regarding the role that teachers might take-up in making a commitment to fight racism in their classrooms, schools, communities, and the wider society. The concept of border pedagogy can help to locate teachers within social, political, and cultural boundaries that define and mediate in complex ways how they function as intellectuals who exercise particular forms of moral and social regulation. Border pedagogy calls attention to both the ideological and the partial as central elements in the construction of teacher discourse and practice. To the degree that teachers make the construction of their own voices, histories, and ideologies problematic, they become more attentive of Otherness as a deeply political and pedagogical issue. In other words, by deconstructing the underlying principles that inform their own lives and pedagogy, educators can begin to recognize the limits underlying the partiality of their own views. Such a recognition offers the promise of allowing teachers to restructure their peda- gogical relations in order to engage in an open and critical fashion fundamental ques- tions about how knowledge is taught, how knowledge relates to students' lives, how students can engage with knowledge, and how pedagogy actually relates to empowering both teachers and students. Within dominant models of pedagogy, teachers are often silenced through a refusal or inability to make problematic with students the values that inform how they teach and engage the multifaceted relationship between knowl- edge and power. Without the benefit of dialogue and understanding of the partiality of their own beliefs, teachers are cut-off from any understanding of the effects their pedagogies have on students. In effect, their infatuation with certainty and control serves to limit the possibilities inherent in their own voices and visions. In this case, dominant pedagogy serves not only to disable students, but teachers as well. In short, teachers need to take-up a pedagogy that provides a more dialectical understanding of their own politics and values; they need to break down pedagogical boundaries that silence them in the name of methodological rigor or pedagogical absolutes; more im- portant, they need to develop a power-sensitive discourse that allows them to open up their interactions with the discourses of various Others so that their classrooms can engage, rather than negate, the multiple positions and experiences that allow teachers and students to speak in and with many complex and different voices.[88]

What border pedagogy makes undeniable is the relational nature of one's own politics and personal investments. But at the same time, border pedagogy emphasizes the primacy of a politics in which teachers assert rather than retreat from the pedagogies they use in dealing with the differences represented by the students who come into their classes. For example, it is not enough for teachers to merely affirm uncritically their students' histories, experience, and stories. To take student voices at face value is to run the risk of idealizing and romanticizing them. It is equally important for teachers to help students find a language for critically examining the historically and socially constructed forms by which they live. Such a process involves more than allowing stu- dents to speak from their own histories and social formations. It also raises questions about how teachers use power to cross borders that are culturally strange to them.

At issue here is not a patronizing notion of understanding the Other, but a sense of how the self is implicated in the construction of Otherness, how exercising critical attention to such a relationship might allow educators to move out of the center of the dominant culture toward its margins in order to analyze critically the political, social, and cultural lineaments of their own values and voices as viewed from different ideo- logical and cultural spaces. It is important for teachers to understand both how they wield power and authority and how particular forms of authority are sedimented in the construction of teachers' own needs along with the limited subject positions offered them in schools. Border pedagogy is not about engaging just the positionality of our students but about the nature of our own identities as they have emerged and are emerging within and between various circuits of power. If students are going to learn how to take risks, to develop a healthy skepticism towards all master narratives, to recognize the power relations that offer them the opportunity to speak in particular ways, and to be willing to critically confront their role as critical citizens who can animate a democratic culture, they need to see such behavior demonstrated in the social practices and subject positions that teachers live out and not merely propose.

If an antiracist pedagogy is to have any meaning as a force for creating a democratic society, teachers and students must be given the opportunity to put into effect what they learn outside of the school. In other words, they must be given the opportunity to engage in antiracist struggles in their effort to link schooling with real life, ethical discourse to political action, and classroom relations to a broader notion of cultural politics. School curriculum should make antiracist pedagogies central to the task of educating students to enliven a wider and more critically engaged public culture. It should allow students not merely to take risks but also to push against the boundaries of an oppressive social order. Such projects can be used to address the relevance of the school curriculum and its role as a significant public force for linking learning and social justice with the daily institutional and cultural traditions of society and reshaping them in the process. All schools should have teachers and students participate in antiracist curriculum that in some way links with projects in the wider society. This approach redefines not only teacher authority and student responsibility, but places the school as a major force in the struggle for social, economic, and cultural justice. A critical postmodern pedagogy of resistance can challenge not only the oppressive boundaries of racism, but all of those barriers that undermine and subvert the construction of a democratic society.

Notes

1. Editorial, "The Biggest Secret of Race Relations: The New White Minority," *Ebony Magazine* (April 1989), 84; John B. Kellog, "Forces of Change," *Phi Delta Kappan* (November 1988), 199–204.
2. Michelle Fine, *Framing Dropouts* (Albany: SUNY Press, 1991).
3. Kirk Johnson, "A New Generation of Racism Is Seen," *The New York Times* (August 27, 1989), 20; Kathy Dobie, "The Boys of Bensonhurst," *The Village Voice* 54:36 (September 5, 1989), 34–39.
4. Chantal Mouffe, "Hegemony and New Political Subjects: Toward a New Concept of Democracy," in Cary Nelson and Lawrence Grossberg, eds., *Marxism and the Interpretation of Culture* (Urbana: University of Illinois Press, 1988), 102. For a lengthy discussion of a notion of democracy similar to my own, see Stanley Aronowitz, *The Crisis in Historical Materialism* (Minneapolis: University of Minnesota Press, 1990), especially Chapter 8.
5. John Pareles, "There's a New Sound in Pop Music: Bigotry," *The New York Times* Sect. 2 (Sunday, September 10, 1989), 10, 32. See also Lawrence Grossberg, *We Gotta Get Out of This Place: Popular Conservatism and Postmodern Culture* (Routledge, 1995).

6. This theme is taken up in Stanley Aronowitz and Henry A. Giroux, *Postmodern Education: Politics, Culture, and Social Criticism* (Minneapolis: University of Minnesota Press, 1991).

7. This position was first made famous in Daniel Moynihan, *The Negro Family: The Case for National Action* (Washington, D.C.: U.S. Department of Labor, 1985). For two critical responses to this report, see Marian Wright Edelman, *Families in Peril: An Agenda for Social Change* (Cambridge: Harvard University Press, 1987), and Hortense J. Spillers, "Mamma's Baby, Papa's Maybe: An American Grammar Book," *Diacritics* 17:2 (Summer 1987), 65–81. See also a special issue of *The Nation* (July 24/31, 1989), entitled "Scapegoating the Black Family: Black Women Speak."

8. Ernesto Laclau, "Politics and the Limits of Modernity," in Andrew Ross, ed., *Universal Abandon? The Politics of Postmodernism* (Minneapolis: University of Minnesota Press), 63–82; Nelly Richard, "Postmodernism and Periphery," *Third Text* 2 (1987/1988), 5–12.

9. Gayatri C. Spivak, *In Other Worlds: Essays in Cultural Politics* (London: Metheun, 1987). See also Abdul R. JanMohamed and David Lloyd, eds., *The Nature and Context of Minority Discourse* (New York: Oxford University Press, 1990).

10. Cornel West, "Marxist Theory and the Specificity of Afro-American Oppression," in Nelson and Grossberg , eds., *Marxism and the Interpretation of Culture*, 17–26.

11. David Kolb, *The Critique of Pure Modernity: Hegel, Heidegger, and After* (Chicago: University of Chicago Press, 1986), especially the first and last chapters. See also Anthony Giddens, *The Consequences of Modernity* (Stanford: Stanford University Press, 1990).

12. Stuart Hall, "Gramsci's Relevance for the Study of Race and Ethnicity," *Journal of Communication Inquiry* 10:2 (Summer 1986), 5–27. Of course, a number of writers, especially those of color, have begun to place the issue of race within a broader context. In addition to the feminist works cited in this chapter, see bell hooks, *Yearning: Race, Gender, and Cultural Politics* (Boston: South End Press, 1990); Michele Wallace, *Invisibility Blues* (London: Verso Press, 1991); Trinh T. Minh-ha, *Woman, Native, Other* (Bloomington: Indiana University Press, 1989). See also the various articles in Russell Ferguson, Martha Gever, Trinh T. Minh-ha, Cornel West, eds., *Out There: Marginalization and Contemporary Cultures* (Cambridge: MIT Press, 1990); David Theo Goldberg, ed., *Anatomy of Racism* (Minneapolis: University of Minnesota Press, 1990); Henry Louis Gates, Jr., ed., *Reading Black, Reading Feminist* (New York: Meridian, 1991); Gloria Anzaldua, ed., *Making Face, Making Soul: Creative and Critical Perspectives by Women of Color* (San Francisco: An Aunt Lute Foundation Book, 1990); Chandra Talpade Mohanty, Ann Russo, & Lourpes Torres, eds., *Third World Women and the Politics of Feminism* (Bloomington: Indiana University Press, 1991).

13. Stanley Aronowitz, "Postmodernism and Politics," *Social Text* 18 (1987/88), 113.

14. Scott Lash and John Urry, *The End of Organized Capitalism* (Madison: University of Wisconsin Press, 1987); Scott Lash, *Sociology of Postmodernism* (New York: Routledge, 1990).

15. Of course, this type of economistic crudeness is a bit exaggerated but its spirit lives on in more updated orthodoxies; for example, see Jim Sleeper, "The Economics Beyond Race," *Democratic Left* 19:2 (March–April 1991), 9, 19. See also Jim Sleeper, *The Closest of Strangers: Liberalism and the Politics of Race in New York* (New York: W. W. Norton, 1989). For a critique of this position, see Stanley Aronowitz, *The Crisis of Historical Materialism* (Minneapolis: University of Minnesota Press, 1990); Ernesto Laclau and Chantal Mouffe, *Hegemony and Socialist Strategy* (London: Verso Books, 1985).

16. See sources listed in note #12. In addition, two important references on these issues are Cornel West, *Prophesy Deliverance: An Afro-American Revolutionary Christianity* (New York: Westminister Press, 1982); Cornel West, *The American Evasion of Philosophy* (Madison: University of Wisconsin Press, 1989); Coco Fusco, "Fantasies of Oppositionality: Reflections on Recent Conferences in Boston and New York," *Screen* 29:4 (Autumn 1988), 80–93.

17. This theme is taken up in Henry A. Giroux, *Schooling and the Struggle for Public Life* (Min-

116 Border Crossings

neapolis: University of Minnesota Press, 1989). See also Aronowitz and Giroux, *Postmodern Education*.

18. Some exceptions include John Young, ed., *Breaking the Mosiac: Ethnic Identities in Canadian Society* (Toronto: Garamond Press, 1987); Lisa Albrecht and Rose Brewer, eds., *Bridges of Power: Women's Multicultural Alliances* (Santa Cruz, CA: New Society Publishers, 1990); Cameron McCarthy, *Race and Curriculum: Social Inequality and the Theories and Politics of Difference in Contemporary Research on Schooling* (New York: Falmer Press, 1990); Christine E. Sleeter, ed., *Empowerment Through Multicultural Education* (Albany: SUNY Press, 1991); Lucy R. Lippard, *Mixed Blessings: New Art in Multicultural America* (New York: Pantheon Books, 1990).

19. Hazel V. Carby, "The Canon: Civil War and Reconstruction," *Michigan Quarterly Review* 28:1 (Winter 1989), 39.

20. On the issue of engaging whiteness as a central racial category in the construction of moral power and political/cultural domination, see Richard Dyer, "White," *Screen*: 29:4 (Autumn 1988), 44–64; Cornel West , "The New Cultural Politics of Difference," *October* 53 (Summer 1990), 93–109, especially 105; Russell Ferguson, "Introduction: Invisible Center," in Russell Ferguson, et al., *Out There* (Cambridge: MIT Press, 1991), 9–14; Robert Young, *White Mythologies: Writing History and the West* (New York: Routledge, 1990).

21. Toni Morrison, "Unspeakable Things Unspoken: The Afro-American Presence in American Literature," *Michigan Quarterly Review* 28:1 (Winter 1989), 34.

22. Ibid., 11.

23. Isaac Julien and Kobena Mercer, "Introduction: De Margin and de Centre," *Screen* 8:2 (1987), 3.

24. Hazel V. Carby, "Multi-Culture," *Screen Education* 34 (Spring 1980), 3; hooks, *Yearning*.

25. For an elaboration of the distinction between critical and conservative forms of postmodernism, see Stanley Aronowitz and Henry A. Giroux, *Postmodern Education*.

26. Robert Merrill, "Ethics/Aesthetics: A Post-Modern Position," in Robert Merrill, ed., *Ethics/Aesthetics: Postmodern Positions* (Washington, D.C.: Maisonneuve Press, 1988), 7–13.

27. Hal Foster, ed., *The Anti-Aesthetic: Essays on Postmodern Culture* (Townsend, Washington: Bay Press, 1983); Hal Foster, ed., *Discussions in Contemporary Culture* No. 1 (Seattle: Bay Press, 1987); Linda Hutcheon, *A Poetics of Postmodernism* (New York: Routledge, 1988).

28. Jean-François Lyotard, *The Postmodern Condition: A Report on Knowledge* (Minneapolis: University of Minnesota Press, 1984).

29. Zygmunt Bauman, "Strangers: The Social Construction of Universality and Particularity," *Telos* 78 (Winter 1988–1989), 12.

30. Dick Hebdige, "Postmodernism and 'the Other Side,'" *Journal of Communication Inquiry* 10:2 (1986), 81.

31. Ibid., 91.

32. Frenc Feher, "The Status of Postmodernity," *Philosophy and Social Criticism* 13:2 (1988), 195–206.

33. Jim Collins, *Uncommon Cultures: Popular Culture and Post-Modernism* (New York: Routledge, 1989).

34. For a variety of essays on this issue, see Brian Wallis, ed., *Art After Modernism: Rethinking Representation* (Boston: Godine Publishing, 1989); Foster, *The Anti-Aesthetic*.

35. For instance, Dennis Farber employs painting and photography in a way that makes the distinction between them seem moot. In photography, this tradition is most manifest in the work of Sherri Levine, Barbara Kruger, and Cindy Sherman. For both examples and analyses of the new forms of representation and social criticism that has emerged out of postmodernism, see Hutcheon, *A Poetics of Postmodernism;* Brian Wallis, ed., *Blasted Allegories* (Cambridge: MIT Press, 1988); Brian Wallis, ed., *Art After Modernism;* Hal Foster, *Recordings: Art, Spectacle, Cultural Politics* (Seattle: Bay Press, 1985); Robert Hewison, *Future*

Tense: A New Art for the Nineties (London: Methuen, 1990); Abigail Solomon-Godeau, *Photography at the Dock* (Minneapolis: University of Minnesota Press, 1994); Hugh J. Silverman, *Postmodernism: Philosophy and the Arts* (New York: Routledge, 1990).

36. Caren Kaplan, "Deterritorializations: The Rewriting of Home and Exile in Western Feminist Discourse," *Cultural Critique* 6 (1987), 187–98; Iain Chambers, *Border Dialogues: Journeys in Postmodernity* (New York: Routledge, 1990).

37. See especially the excellent treatment of this issue in Grossberg, *We Gotta Get Out of This Place.*

38. Teresa de Lauretis, *Technologies of Gender* (Bloomington: Indiana University Press, 1987); Meaghan Morris, *The Pirate's Fiancee: Feminism, Reading, Postmodernism* (London: Verso Press, 1988).

39. These themes are taken-up in Ernesto Laclau and Chantal Mouffe, *Hegemony and Socialist Strategy* (London: Verso Press, 1985); Ernesto Laclau, *New Reflections on the Revolution of Our Time* (London: Verso Books, 1990); Stanley Aronowitz, *The Crisis in Historical Materialism.* On different interpretations of the changing economic, political, and cultural conditions that characterize the postmodern condition, see Lash Urry, *The End of Organized Capitalism;* David Harvey, *The Condition of Postmodernity* (New York: Basil Blackwell, 1989); Steven Connor, *Postmodernist Culture* (New York: Blackwell, 1989).

40. Richard Terdiman, *Discourse/Counter-Discourse* (New York: Cornell University Press, 1985); George Lipsitz, *Time Passages: Collective Memory and American Popular Culture* (Minneapolis: Unversity of Minnesota Press, 1990); Renato Rosaldo, *Culture and Truth* (Boston: Beacon Press, 1989).

41. Jim Collins, *Uncommon Cultures,* 115.

42. Ibid.

43. Chantal Mouffe, "Radical Democracy: Modern or Postmodern," in Ross ed., *Universal Abandon?,* 41.

44. Of course, this theme is taken up in an endless number of discussions of postmodernism. One important analysis can be found in Laclau and Mouffe, *Hegemony and Socialist Strategy.* See also Slavoj •i•ek, *The Sublime Object of Ideology* (London: Verso Books, 1989).

45. Sharon Welch, *A Feminist Ethic of Risk* (Minneapolis: Fortress Press, 1990).

46. Mouffe, Op. cit., in Ross, ed., 1988, 41.

47. Cornel West, "Black Culture and Postmodernism," in Barbara Kruger and Phil Mariani, eds., *Remaking History* (Seattle: Bay Press, 1989), 90.

48. Richard Bernstein, "Metaphysics, Critique, and Utopia," *The Review of Metaphysics* 42 (1988), 267.

49. The literature on this issue is vast. Three representative works on black women writers include: Paula Giddings, *When and Where I Enter: The Impact of Black Women on Race and Sex in America* (New York: Bantam Books, 1984); Mari Evans, ed., *Black Women Writers (1950–1980): A Critical Evaluation* (New York: Anchor Press, 1984); Henry Louis Gates, Jr., ed., *Reading Black, Reading Feminist.* Important theoretical works discussing the writings of black women include: Barbara Christian, *Black Feminist Criticism* (New York: Pergamon, 1985); Susan Willis, *Specifying: Black Women Writing—The American Experience* (Madison: University of Wisconsin, Press, 1987); Hazel V. Carby, *Reconstructing Womanhood: The Emergence of the Afro-American Woman Novelist* (New York: Oxford University Press, 1987); Michele Wallace, *Black Macho and the Myth of the Superwoman* (London: Verso Books, 1990); Michele Wallace, *Invisibility Blues,* especially 129–225; Sharon Welch, *A Feminist Ethic of Risk.*

50. Christian, *Black Feminist Criticism,* 159.

51. Cited in John McCluskey, Jr., "And Call Every Generation Blessed: Theme, Setting and Ritual in the Works of Paule Marshall," in Evans, ed., *Black Women Writers,* 316.

52. See, for example, Audre Lorde, *Sister Outsider* (Freedom, CA: The Crossing Press, 1984);

hooks, *Talking Back* (Boston: South End Press, 1989), *Yearning* (Boston: South End Press, 1990); Wallace, *Black Macho*; June Jordan, *On Call* (Boston: South End Press, 1989); and Carby, *Reconstructing Womanhood.*

53. Lorde, *Sister Outsider.*
54. Carby, "The Canon: Civil War and Reconstruction," 39.
55. Fusco, "Fantasies of Oppositionality," 90.
56. bell hooks, "The Politics of Radical Black Subjectivity," *Talking Back* (Boston: South End Press, 1989), 54.
57. Stuart Hall, "Minimal Selves," in *ICA Documents* 6, *Postmodernism and the Question of Identity* (London: ICA, 1987), 45.
58. Lorde, *Sister Outsider*, 112.
59. Ibid.
60. Ibid., p. 118.
61. Ibid.
62. Ibid., p. 45.
63. Christian, *Black Feminist Criticism.*
64. bell hooks, *Talking Back*, 11–12.
65. June Jordan, *On Call*, 30–31.
66. Barbara Christian, "The Race for Theory," *Cultural Critique* 6 (Spring 1987), 52.
67. Toni Cade Bambara, "Evaluation Is the Issue," in Evans, *Black Women Writers*, 46.
68. See Willis, *Specifying.*
69. Michelle Gibbs Russell, "Black Eyed Blues Connections; From the Inside Out," in Charlotte Bunch and Sandra Pollack, eds., *Learning Our Way: Essays in Feminist Education* (Trumansburg, N.Y.: The Crossing Press, 1983), 274, 275.
70. June Jordan, "Where Is the Love?" in Barbara H. Andolsen, Christine Gurdorf, and Mary Pellauer, eds., *Women's Consciousness Women's Conscience* (New York: Harper and Row, 1985), 203.
71. Welch, *A Feminist Ethic of Risk, 139.*
72. Michele Wallace, *Invisibility Blues*, 1–10.
73. Henry A. Giroux, *Schooling and the Struggle for Public Life*; Mouffe, "Hegemony and New Political Subjects: Toward a New Concept of Democracy," in Nelson and Grossberg, eds., *Marxism and the Interpretation of Culture*, 89–104.
74. Mouffe, "Radical Democracy," *Marxism and the Interpretation of Culture*, in Ross, ed., *Universal Abandon?*, 42.
75. Aronowitz, *The Crisis in Historical Materialism.*
76. D. Emily Hicks, "Deterritorrialization and Border Writing," in Robert Merrill, ed., *Ethics/ Aesthetics: Postmodern Positions* (Washington, D.C.: Maisonneuve Press, 1988), 47–58.
77. Stuart Hall, "Teaching Race," in Alan Jones and Robert Jeffcoate eds., *The School in Multicultural Society* (London: Harper and Row, 1981), 61.
78. I have taken-up this issue in Giroux, *Schooling and the Struggle for Public Life*, especially chapters 2 & 3. See also two excellent pieces on authority and pedagogy in Patricia Bizzell, "Classroom Authority and Critical Pedagogy," *American Literary History* 3 (1991), 847–63; Patricia Bizzell, "Power, Authority, and Critical Pedagogy," *Journal of Basic Writing* 10:2 (1991), 54–70.
79. Chandra Mohanty is excellent on this issue. See "On Race and Voice: Challenges for Liberal Education in the 1990s," *Cultural Critique* 14 (Winter 1989–1990), 179–208.
80. Andrew Hannan, "Racism, Politics, and the Curriculum," *British Journal of Sociology of Education* 8:2 (1987), 127.
81. Lisa Delpit, "The Silenced Dialogue: Power and Pedagogy in Educating Other People's Children," *Harvard Educational Review* 58:3 (1988), 280–98.

82. Ibid.

83. Signithia Fordham, "Racelessness as a Factor in Black Student's School Success: Pragmatic Strategy or Pyrrhic Victory?" *Harvard Educational Review* 58:3 (1988), 54–82.

84. Hall, "Teaching Race," in Jones and Jeffcoate, eds., *The School in Multicultural Society,* 58–69.

85. Roger, I. Simon, "For a Pedagogy of Possibility," *Critical Pedagogy Networker* 1:1 (1981), 54–82.

86. Richard Johnson, "What is Cultural Studies Anyway?" *Social Text* 16 (Winter 1986/87), 38–80.

87. These issues are taken up in Catherine Belsey, *Critical Practice* (New York: Methuen, 1980); Tony Bennett, "Texts in History: The Determinations of Readings and Their Texts," in Derek Atridge, Geoff Bennington, and Robert Young, eds., *Post-Structuralism and the Question of History* (New York: Cambridge University Press, 1987); Aronowitz and Giroux, *Postmodern Education.*

88. For specific ways in which voice and difference are treated in critical pedagogical terms, see various chapters in this book. Also see hooks, *Talking Back*; hooks, *Yearning*; Giroux, *Schooling and the Struggle for Public Life.*

Cultural Workers
and Cultural Pedagogy

4

Critical Pedagogy
and Cultural Power

An Interview
*with Henry A. Giroux**

For nearly two decades education theorist Henry A. Giroux has worked to broaden our understanding of the relationship between schooling and political life. In challenging traditional roles of students, teachers, and the institutional structures that bring them together, Giroux has formulated a range of radical educational subject positions and new discursive spaces for learning. Giroux's work is of particular interest to artists for the way he draws cultural workers into the circle of pedagogy, whether they practice in the classroom, the gallery, or the street. As discussed in the conversation below, such efforts to form alliances among progressive artists and educators have assumed even greater urgency in recent years, as conservatives have recognized the strategic role of arts and humanities education in producing identities.

At the center of Giroux's writing and teaching lies a moral commitment to a set of democratic practices that engages all citizens in common governance. He argues that these practices can never be inherited but must be learned and re-learned by each successive generation. In espousing these views, Giroux has emerged as one of the most outspoken proponents of the "critical pedagogy" movement, an amalgam of educational philosophies that first gained wide public recognition in the 1960s through the writings of Brazilian expatriate Paulo Freire. At the heart of this philosophy lies a belief in the centrality of education in

---

*David Trend is a professor and director of University of California Institute of Research for the Art.

determining political and social relations. As practiced by Freire in countries through-out the third world, the doctrines of critical pedagogy were used by colonized citizens to analyze their roles in relations of oppression and to devise programs for revolutionary change.

During the 1970s and 1980s the philosophies of critical pedagogy were adapted throughout the industrialized world as a means of addressing power imbalances there. As a result much of the vocabulary of "empowerment," "dialogue," and "voice" has entered the lexicon of Western social reform movements. At the same time the principles of critical pedagogy have undergone significant modifications that adapt them to the needs of contemporary technocratic societies. In a world that is rapidly redefining relations between its centers and margins and questioning the legitimacy of master narratives, critical pedagogy has borrowed significantly from postmodernism, feminism, literary theory, cultural studies, and psychoanalysis.

Since 1983 Giroux has taught in the School of Education and Allied Professions at Miami University in Oxford, OH, where he is a professor of education and director of the Center for Education and Cultural Studies. A secondary school teacher from 1969 to 1975, he earned his Ph.D. in curriculum theory, sociology of education, and history at Carnegie-Mellon University in 1977. He later taught at Boston and Tufts universities.

Giroux is the author of numerous books, five of which were named by the American Educational Studies Association as among the most significant books in education in the years of their publication: *Ideology, Culture and the Process of Schooling, Education Under Siege: The Conservative, Liberal, and Radical Debate over Schooling* (with Stanley Aronowitz), *Theory and Resistance in Education, Education Under Siege* (co-authored with Stanly Aronowitz), *The Abandoned Generation,* and *Schooling and the Struggle for Public Life: Critical Pedagogy in the Modern Age.* His other works include *Curriculum Discourse as Postmodernist Critical Practice, Postmodern Education: Politics, Culture, and Social Criticism* (with Stanley Aronowitz),[1] and over 150 articles and essays.

Giroux has edited books including *Critical Pedagogy, the State, and the Struggle for Culture* (with Peter McLaren), *Popular Culture, Schooling and Everyday Life* (with Roger Simon), and *Postmodernism, Feminism, and Cultural Politics: Rethinking Educational Boundaries.*[2] He is a member of the consulting editorial board of the Boston University *Journal of Education* and a contributing editor of *Curriculum Inquiry.* He is coeditor with Freire of the series *Critical Studies in Education,* published by Bergin and Garvey Press, and coeditor with Peter McLaren of *Teacher Empowerment and School Reform,* a series published by SUNY Press.

David Trend: By way of introduction, I think we should discuss the language of critical pedagogy and perhaps address the issue of discursive terminology itself.

Henry Giroux: The struggle over language in these fields often stems from arguments about clarity, complexity, and the redefinition of terms. Many people reading pedagogical language mistakenly say that you simply have to explain it or write in a style that is clear and uncomplicated. This position is too reductionist. Actually, we're talking about how educational paradigms begin to generate a new language and raise new questions. These points shouldn't be confused. We're pointing to a theory that examines how you view the very realities you engage. When people say that we write in a language that isn't as clear as it could be, while that might be true they're also responding to the unfamiliarity of a paradigm that generates questions suppressed in the dominant culture.

     When you discuss language, you must consider what public you are addressing. Is there one public? What's the relationship between intellectuals and the public sphere? Is there a universalized standard of language that becomes a referent for all others? How do you begin to ask that question in a way that remains aware of the possibility of ghettoization on one hand but that also recognizes different publics in different contexts? You should consider those multiple publics and their multiple political strategies. I think the question is a very important one.

Producing Knowledge and Power

DT: What are the new paradigms that pedagogical language conveys? Isn't the discourse of critical pedagogy based on critiques of conventional models of schooling, the interests they embody, the values they promote, the groups they favor and disfavor?

HG: Critical pedagogy has arisen from a need to name the contradiction between what schools claim they do and what they actually do. This position has both strengths and weaknesses.

DT: You mean that it's a reactive discussion?

HG: Historically schools were rarely self-critical about their purposes and means, and the few movements challenging them were very marginal. But something happened in the 1970s. Samuel Bowles and Herbert Gintis published a book called *Schooling in Capitalist America: Educational Reform and the Contradictions of Economic Life*[3] that launched a form of analysis tied to theories of social reproduction. This wasn't critical pedagogy but an attempt to unravel certain political and economic injustices within education. As important as it was in politicizing the issue of school, it was still built upon an Orwellian notion of domination that was overpowering and without a discourse of resistance.

Also it focused almost exclusively on labor functions. Schools were said to reproduce the social relations necessary for maintaining a market economy. Rather than creating managers they produced passive workers who adjust to the imperatives of the capitalist order. That language exercised a powerful influence in mobilizing the critical pedagogy movement, but it exhausted itself in its inability to take-up power dialectically or to consider what schools could do to apply power productively. So it doesn't have much of an impact except in academic circles. In 1978 I could count 10 people in education who had established public reputations writing about those ideas.

DT: In this country?

HG: Yes. And those whose works were imported from abroad you could count on one hand: people like Paul Willis, Geoff Witty, and Basil Bernstein. The new feminist work wasn't emerging then in education because the emphasis was on materialist theories of class reproduction. Also no one addressed the question of pedagogy outside the realm of schooling.

DT: This is in the late 1970s? Why was educational thinking evolving in such a vacuum?

HG: Marxism seemed to offer the only discourse available to people interested in analyzing the relationship of schools and politics. Even the most radical educational theory was overwhelmed by an economic orthodoxy. The importance of other discourses wasn't recognized. However, you have to remember that, while orthodox Marxism reigned from around 1977 to 1980, a new version of reproductive theory emerged in the work of Pierre Bourdieu and others. It wasn't simply about laborers being socialized by the hidden curriculum into dead-end futures. It also addressed cultural reproduction. Bourdieu brought forward an old Gramscian line in which schools were said to create cultural capital for those who occupy positions of power as intellectuals within the cultural apparatus of the larger society. Dominant forms of cultural capital had a certain exchange rate on the market but were accessible to very few people—those who are white and upper middle class. Regrettably, Bourdieu's work was similarly overdetermined by theories of domination and had no programmatic notion of power in the Foucauldian sense.

DT: Coincidentally, this was also a period of great government largesse. It's difficult to discuss the era without considering its very generous social programs: educational initiatives, CETA (Comprehensive Employment and Training Act) programs, and the growth of the National Endowment for the Arts, for example. What about the impact of the Reagan revolution in catalyzing some of this thinking, perhaps some of your thinking?

HG: Reagan comes along and introduces the idea of education as a popular struggle. The Reagan administration said that social reproduction is a terrific idea: We absolutely need workers, and that's what schools should do. We'll define education precisely in those terms; we believe that progressives really missed the point of living in a capitalist society. Schools aren't neutral. They're political sites, and we're going to fight for them on those grounds. We're going to engage the notion of power by saying that schools create character and identities, and we're going to show you how to inscribe students in specific roles. And they will take them up very cheerfully. After all, students are not just dupes. What are you people on the Left talking about? It's demeaning to say that people are stupid and that they don't make choices.

Then comes Allan Bloom. This is one of the most important moments in the history of education in the United States, as the Right begins to wage an over-active struggle on the cultural front. It says that schools exist to preserve Western civilization. We need not only a structure to train workers but also a means of taking up the issues of ideology and cultural formations, particularly as they are linked to traditions that we think are vital to American hegemony. But the con-servative argument goes even further and says that probably the place in which traditions are most dangerously undermined is within the discourse of democracy.

DT: Turning democracy on its head?

HG: Yes, invoking the infamous Trilateral Commission Study of 1965, the one that said that we should limit the excesses of democracy, control social criticism, and police the universities. Bloom offers no apology at all. He argues that the nation is engaged in a cultural politics in which democracy becomes subversive, criticism becomes dangerous, and intellectuals who do not take-up the mantle of tradition should not teach in the university. So it seems to me that what Bloom and E.D. Hirsch Jr. did—along with Dianne Ravitch, John Silber, Chester Finn Jr., and William Bennett—was really to help us rethink schooling as a form of cultural politics—as opposed to simply thinking of it as a form of cultural domination.

They certainly forced me, among others, to rethink how we were going to redefine schools as sites of struggle, where power is productive and where the axis isn't simply between reproduction and resistance. It's more about the com-plexity with which power works and the multilayered and contradictory identities that are taken-up. It's about the production of particular ways of life. Because of the attack from the Right, we began to make this incredible shift. We no longer simply said, in classic Left pedagogical terms, "Okay, here's a school, let's identify the dominant ideological interests at work that serve to oppress teachers and students."

DT: Nevertheless, that is an important point to reach.

HG: Of course; it's an essential moment. But there are at least two other central ques-tions in the configuration of cultural politics. Beyond identifying interests, we need to ask how these interests function. How do they produce particular ways of life? Even more importantly, we need to consider how they're taken-up. Without considering the question of how they're taken-up, we assume that ideologies are absorbed by virtue of their existence rather than fought over continually.

DT: By "taken up" do you mean how they are integrated into everyday life?

HG: Yes, how people respond to them. Where does a theory of agency come in here? Simply because a curriculum is racist, does this mean everyone in the class will become a racist? Simply because a curriculum is based on an *Afterimage* notion of culture, does this mean that everyone will come out thinking that way? We should be concerned with how students actually construct meaning, what the categories of meaning are, and what ideologies students bring to their encounters with us. In the interaction between text, teacher, and student something is always created around the specificity of the situation in which you find yourself.

DT: Meaning is a negotiated part of the transaction.

HG: Given the different variables in each context, people are writing meaning rather than simply receiving it. That seems dangerous to the Right because it makes knowledge problematic. It means taking the identities of subordinate cultures seriously. It means you can't have standardized curricula. When we enlarge our notion of how ideology works, a circle of power begins to develop that has more to do with what a cultural politics of schooling should be about. For me there are four major points. First, obviously there's a material apparatus at work in the state, in textbook companies, in banks, etc. Second, there is the question of text. Who authorizes them, who produces them, what is the historical weight of the range of meanings they make available or legitimize? And texts include everything from visual images to curricula. Third, there is the question of ideology. What ideologies and lived experiences enter the context of a particular classroom? Finally, there are communities. One should examine communities to understand how ideologies accumulate historical weight for kids, how they provide the conditions for specific intellectual and emotional investments. Beyond addressing the ideologies that kids bring to the classroom, I'm concerned with the historical, social and political conditions that create lived experiences for those kids in the first place. Although those four issues circle round and round, unfortunately most people on the Left are focused on the first moment.

Struggle and Democracy

DT: What about the ways theories of schooling and cultural politics work in practical application? How do these premises actually function in schools, for instance?

HG: Schools and teachers need to gain a vision of why they're doing what they're doing. For this reason you need to define intellectual work within some notion of authority that you can fight for. That means that it has to have an ethical and political referent. For me this means defining schools as democratic public spheres. We need to make a link between schooling and the reconstruction of public life, because in this country the language of democracy has been removed from the language of schooling except as a pejorative term.

DT: The Right has appropriated the language of democracy. They say its values bind us all together, that its heritage is what makes us whole. Of course, we both know that isn't so, but they've adopted that terminology.

HG: Actually there are two versions of that position. The Blooms say that democracy is dangerous to higher education.

DT: Ultimately anarchistic.

HG: Yes; then there are the Ravitches and the Hirsches who, while they use the language of democracy, always manipulate it in a way that does the same thing. They remove its central and basic tenets and substitute expressions like "tradition" or "common culture." By never discussing democracy as a radical social practice, they recode the term and displace its meaning.

Left cultural workers need to address democracy as a site of struggle and to reclaim it in terms that take seriously issues of quality, justice, freedom, and difference. That's a very practical matter for me. We need to reclaim progressive notions of the *public* in public schooling so that education can become a real public service, just as one might say maybe the arts need to be taken-up pedagogically in the same ways.

In this regard the debate over Robert Mapplethorpe's photographs isn't simply a matter of censorship. The real issue concerns a fight for democracy beyond the arts. It's also about difference as it's constituted in public life and in schools. This business that cultural works or intellectual knowledge can only be ordered in very particular ways according to government mandates and surveillances—I see the struggle against this idea as central to the notion of democracy itself.

What I find in my field, and I know this may sound terribly bizarre, is that teachers have no vocabulary to link schools to a critical notion of democracy. The language is absent. Even when democracy is evoked, it is evoked in a way that doesn't expand human capacities to engage issues of justice and struggle.

DT: What do you mean they don't have a language?

HG: The language of teacher education, the language in the places where they're educated or trained.

DT: But it's like that in every field.

HG: Some have more room than others. Where you get a field that defines itself as applied, you often find a confused relationship between principles and applications.

Larger questions of vision can be relegated quickly to the dustbin of academic involvement. So teachers come along and demand 25 different ways to teach social studies or deconstruction. They become focused on a fetishized methodology that precludes examination of their roles as public intellectuals, of the institutions in which they work, and of society at large. The language they learn or take-up is depoliticized; it is largely a language or procedure and technique.

DT: What would you say makes that happen? The commodification of knowledge? Is it job standardization and professionalization?

HG: The ideology of positivism is very powerful in American education. It represents strong interests, and it complements capitalist social relations very well. It breaks knowledge down. It makes people into consumers. It exalts the language of commodification. At the same time there's a legacy of McCarthyism in American education that is making a comeback.

DT: Not to mention books like Charles Sykes's *Profscam* (1988) that cast the university as a hideout for lazy, tenured academics.

HG: The attack on tenure is really an attack on the civil rights of educators who dare to raise their voices. It's another form of censorship that is forcing educators and cultural workers to rethink the function of struggle in an ongoing reconstruction of democratic public life. As a pedagogue I am constantly working to remind people both inside and outside my field that just as democracy is given, it can also be taken away.

You can define democracy within the narrow limits of electoral politics, or you can define it as an ongoing contest within every aspect of daily life. By understanding that, we can make articulations between the specific cultural work we do and other fields. You and I know that knowledges and identities always concern the relationships among power, language, imagery, social relations, and ethics. Although we may do different things, there's something connecting us when we have the sense of being in the fight for democracy. We operate in different terrains, but that difference doesn't become antagonistic, it becomes a basis for articulation.

DT: You've made the point before that this is always a dynamic process. Conservatives often argue that we're now in a democracy that's perfect and shouldn't be questioned.

HG: The Mapplethorpe case brings the point home so powerfully. In Cincinnati, curator Dennis Barrie was actually put on trial. His life is on the line not for a particular photography exhibition but for the kind of social criticism that's endemic to the very nature of democracy. His struggle is much broader than the arts. [Barrie and the Cincinnati Contemporary Arts Center have since been acquitted.] The fight is over our ability to name realities in ways that aren't simply functions of government surveillance. When you say that democracy has reached its ultimate from you're stepping into the world of terrorism. The U. S. is getting closer to describing democracy as a totality of one, a democracy in which social criticism is no longer pragmatic because it's dangerous. Ironically, we've reached a point where democracy actually can be taken up in terms that suggest that any struggle for it is a struggle against it—which immediately proves that it's always a struggle.

But there's also the other side. No tradition should ever be seen as received, because when it is received it becomes sacred, its terms suggest reverence, silence, and passivity. Democratic societies are noisy. They're about traditions that need to be critically reevaluated by each generation. The battle to extend democratic possibilities has to be fought in education at a very primal level. The very notions of knowledge, values, testing, evaluation, ethics are all ultimately related to social criticism and its role in democratic struggle.

Authority and Agency

DT: To play the devil's advocate for a minute, what about the argument that teaching operates within relations of unequal power, despite theories of agency and resistance, and that even the principles of critical pedagogy are transmitted through a dominant teacher to a student? If we're talking about what constructs us all and motivates us in what we do, how does a teacher practicing critical pedagogy not deliver an ideology to someone else in his or her own interests?

HG: Two issues. I would reiterate that knowledge is produced rather than received. That raises a very interesting question about the notion of authority. You can exercise authority in ways that do not establish the conditions for knowledge to be produced and engaged. I would call that authoritarianism. Or you can exercise authority to establish conditions in which a central tension lies at the heart of how we teach. The latter method encourages self-reflection, learning from others, and refiguring forms of cultural practice.

Therefore it's conceivable to be theoretically correct and pedagogically wrong. It's conceivable that I can go into a class and say that this knowledge is absolutely worthwhile because it's an antiracist pedagogy that takes up questions of difference in a profoundly utopian way. We can certainly justify doing that but what we can't justify is assuming that that's all we should do. We also have to consider how knowledge can be taken-up in ways that make it the object of analyses rather than of reverence. We also need to consider how knowledge is understood within the contexts of the experiences students bring to our classes. We are there not merely to produce knowledge so that it can be debated but also to be self-critical ourselves and learn from the forms of knowledge produced as they come from the class, from our students, from the community, and from their texts.

Nevertheless, we should always be mindful of our obligation not to run away from authority but to exercise it in the name of self- and social formation. That means always reminding ourselves that power must be exercised within a framework that allows students to inform us and to be more critical about their own voices, as well as aware of the codes and cultural representations of others outside the immediacy of their experience. As cultural workers we must be aware of the partial nature of our own views.

I don't want to argue simply that as a white, middle-class intellectual I have no right to do anything but listen to the voices of the oppressed. That suggests that social location and identity politics absolutely determine and guarantee the way one takes up political questions. I have no trouble at all in exercising authority as long as I'm constantly self-critical about the limits of my own knowledge. One needs to recognize what it means to place students in relations of difference and articulation that consistently push them toward forms of struggle with themselves, teachers, and the society at large.

DT: That's a very difficult question. I know teachers who have become frustrated with student-centered techniques because they don't work. Students resist because they don't really believe the teacher is yielding authority to them. They instinctively recognize that the institution is exerting an overdetermining influence over what happens in the classroom.

HG: It's naive to deny the existence of authority. Instead one should investigate how it is exercised.

DT: You can't avoid authority, because it's a psychological condition. It creates a relationship of transference.

HG: The problem of authority raises several other issues. We're not merely free-floating intellectuals. We're inscribed within institutions that have the historical weight of particular kinds of power. Whether we like it or not, particularly as university professor or people involved in other cultural institutions, we don't just represent ourselves. We are representations of authority, and to say to students that institutions and practices of power don't exist is actually to be deceptive about the ways those institutions shape our own roles. This is why we must become self-conscious through the exercise of oppositional forms of authority: not only to question those roles but to undo them where necessary.

I find too many students who come from places where they're afraid to speak. They've been silenced all their lives. It is now becoming very popular to say that intellectuals have no right to speak, that we have no right to appropriate the voice of the other. I certainly have no right to totalize the other and to say that I can speak for the other. I can speak to and about racism, sexism, and other issues as considerations that must be challenged in democratic society, but what happens when we find ourselves in classes with students who have been mutilated and are afraid to speak? How do we raise issues that encourage them to speak? If I try to do so, does that mean that as a white man I've violated some category that says that only blacks can speak about oppression?

Experience has to be read critically; it never speaks for itself. This points to the need to exercise authority as a politics of engagement rather than as politics of assertion or as a politics of the personal/confessional. Authority must be used to provide the pedagogical conditions that empower students not only to speak but also to develop the critical capacities and courage to transform the conditions that oppress them and others in the first place.

DT: Obviously one has to be very careful about doing this.

HG: Given the power that public intellectuals sometimes have, I'm suggesting that we have obligations at least to inaugurate a discourse around the unrepresentable, that which cannot be spoken within social relations, particularly within groups that know that generally to speak is to be punished. I want to help create those oppositional spaces without dominating them. I don't want to say this is the only truth that will prevail. But as a public intellectual I have the obligation to rewrite the narratives of possibility for those who have occupied subject positions where that hasn't been possible before.

Teachers and Communities

DT: At his point we should move our theoretical discussion to other issues of practice.

HG: A specific point that we've just begun to discuss is the notion of teachers as intellectuals. How do teachers assume positions in which they can engage in real struggles over what forms of knowledge count? How do we approach questions of social relations? How do racism, sexism, and classism work? How do we begin to deconstruct textbooks in order to identify the ways of life and the stories that they tell?

DT: This applies perfectly to artists and other cultural workers.

HG: Yes; how can we begin to produce our own materials? How do we begin to take seriously the production of content-specific curricula? We see this happening all over the San Francisco Bay Area, as Mexican, Chicano, and Latino kids are suddenly becoming historians of their own cultures, going out and doing oral histories, taking photographs. They're reappropriating their own identifies within forms of historical memory that represent a complete reconfiguration of how they look at knowledge. Another example is Tim Rollins's KOS (Kids of Survival) project in the Bronx. In their classrooms knowledge is not simply about something that's been produced in New York City or about Dick and Jane and their little dog in Greenwich, CT. It's about reappropriating history as part of the struggle over power, knowledge, culture, and identity.

The fight for curricular democracy and our roles as public intellectuals requires more than rethinking the relationship between knowledge and power. It also means that educators must form alliances with people like you who are doing this work in other ways. We need to enlarge the possibility for other groups to see schools as political sites where they can make a contribution.

There are a number of things we can do in this regard. First, the historical isolation of people who work in schools from other cultural workers needs to be overcome. This means we must make an attempt to develop a shared language around the issue of pedagogy and struggle, develop a set of relevancies that can be recognized in each other's work, and articulate a common political project that addresses the relationship between pedagogical work and the reconstruction of oppositional public spheres. Second, we need to form alliances around the issue of censorship both in and out of the schools. The question of representation is central to the issue of pedagogy as a form of cultural politics and cultural politics as a practice related to the struggles of everyday life. Third, we need to articulate these issues in a public manner, in which *Artforum* and *Afterimage* can say we're really addressing a variety of cultural workers and not simply a narrowly defined audience. This points to the need to broaden the definition of culture and political struggle and in doing so invite others to participate in both the purpose and practice central to such tasks.

DT: How do we do that? It's a question many people have been grappling with.

HG: There are at least three ways in which it has to be done. First we begin to talk about an organization that frames itself around the struggle for democracy and cultural politics.

DT: What kind of organization?

HG: I'm not sure if it is a formal organization or not. As a loose entity the cultural studies movement might yield some answers, but it has no frame or political project. Cultural studies for what? It should involve issues like the reconstruction of public life, questions of pedagogy, politics, identity, and power, breaking down the disciplines and bringing groups together, and ways to explore the perimeters or borderlands where they can meet.

Maybe we should discuss a public sphere created in the form of conferences or in new kinds of journals, or new kinds of relationships in neighborhoods.

Maybe we should focus on breaking down the lines between academics and cultural workers around different kinds of local projects.

DT: Unfortunately, it sounds like this revolution is going to take place inside a university. There are many factors preventing it from taking place elsewhere. It's difficult to get people to think otherwise, because there are so few support structures to encourage people to bridge these gaps.

HG: The gaps need to be bridged by people who have the resources and time to do so. That's why people both inside and outside academia should begin to reformulate the ghettoization of academic public life. Politics is not simply about theoretical work that takes place around symposia. The academy is important, but there is also a network of people who work in communities. Since I work primarily in public education, I find myself addressing communities of people, and they don't just talk about school. They talk about drugs and crime, and they want to know where resources can be found in their communities. We need academics to come into our communities with their resources and possibilities so that we can begin to create borderlands for dialogue and struggles.

DT: We try to name these new discursive spaces, but it's difficult because they don't exist.

HG: There are many things that stand in the way. How do the notions of professionalism and expertise get perpetuated even in the most radical of languages? How are we implicated in these forms of exclusions? A battle has to be fought in the academic sector, because it has resources that other communities don't really have.

DT: One of the saddest things is the strength of material pressure. You and I both know people who began their careers as grassroots radicals only to find themselves at a point in their lives with very few choices. Very few support structures, and very few places to go except the university. And that's where they go, because it's the only place where they can practice what they want. But the tacit understanding is that you keep your practice sequestered within the academy.

HG: That's why pedagogy is both exhilarating and dangerous. It's one of the few forms of cultural politics that cannot simply be consigned to academia. Its central questions of ideology and politics ask how people take-up what they take-up; that is, how they participate in, produce, and challenge particular ways of life. The issue is not simply how people are inserted into particular subject positions but also how they create them. To raise that question is automatically to engage the language of specificity, community, diversity, difference, and the struggle for public life.

Notes

1. Published by, respectively, Temple University Press (1981), Bergin and Garvey (1983), Bergin and Garvey (1985), Bergin and Garvey (1988), University of Minnesota Press (1988), Deakin University Press (1990), and University of Minnesota (1991).
2. Published by, respectively, SUNY Press (1989), Bergin and Garvey (1989), and SUNY Press (1991).
3. Published simultaneously by Basic Books (New York) and Routledge and Kegan Paul (London) in 1976.

5

Cultural Studies,
Resisting Difference, and
the Return of Critical Pedagogy

All those men and women in South Africa, Namibia, Zaire, Ivory Coast, El Salvador, Chile, Philippines, South Korea, Indonesia, Grenada, Fanon's 'Wretched of the Earth', who have declared loud and clear that they do not sleep to dream, 'but dream to change the world'.[1]

Introduction

American public education is in crisis. It is not an isolated crisis affecting a specific aspect of American society; it is a crisis that is implicated in and produced by a transformation in the very nature of democracy itself. This is not without a certain irony. As a number of countries in Eastern Europe move toward greater forms of democratization, the United States presents itself as the prototype for such reforms and leads the American people to believe that democracy in the United States has reached its penultimate form. The emptiness of this type of analysis is best revealed by the failure of the American public to actively participate in the election of its own government officials, to address the growing illiteracy rates among the general population, and to challenge the increasing view that social criticism and social change are irrelevant to the meaning of American democracy. In part, this is an illiteracy built on the refusal of a large segment of the American public to "dream to change the world." But the failure of formal democracy is most evident in the refusal of the American government and general population to view public schooling as fundamental to the life of a critical democracy. At stake here is the refusal to grant public schooling a significant role in the ongoing process of educating people to be active and critical citizens capable of fighting for and reconstructing democratic public life.

The struggle over public schools cannot be separated from the social problems currently facing this society. These problems are not only political in nature but are pedagogical as well. That is, whenever power and knowledge come together, politics not only functions to position people differently with respect to the access of wealth and power, but it also provides the conditions for the production and acquisition of learning. Put another way, it offers people opportunities to address and reflect on the conditions that shape themselves and their relationship with others. The pedagogical in this sense is about the production of meaning and the primacy of the ethical and the political as a fundamental part of this process. This means that any discussion of public schooling has to address the political, economic, and social realities that construct the contexts that shape the institution of schooling and the conditions that produce the diverse populations of students who constitute its constituencies. This perspective suggests making visible the social problems and conditions that affect those students who are at risk in our society while recognizing that such problems need to be addressed in both pedagogical and political terms, inside and outside of the schools.

The problems that are emerging do not augur well for either the fate of public schooling or the credibility of the discourse of democracy itself as it is currently practiced in the United States. For example, it has been estimated that nearly 20% of all children under the age of 18 live below the poverty line. In fact, the United States ranks first among the industrialized nations in child poverty; similarly, besides South Africa, the United States is the only industrialized country that does not provide universal health care for children and pregnant women. Moreover, economic inequality is worsening with the poor getting poorer while the rich are getting richer. In fact, the division of wealth was wider in 1988 than at any other time since 1947. As Sally Reed and Craig Sautter have pointed out, "the poorest 20% of families received less than 5% of the national income, while the wealthiest 20% received 44% . . . 1% of families own 42% of the net wealth of all U.S. families."[2] At the same time, it is important to note that neoconservative attempts to dismantle public schooling in this country during the last decade have manifested themselves not only in the call for vouchers and the development of school policy based on the market logic of choice, but also in the ruthless cutbacks that have affected those most dependent on the public schools, i.e., the poor, people of color, minorities, the working class, and other subordinated groups. The Reagan "commitment" to education and the underprivileged manifested itself shamefully in policies noted for slashing federal funds to important programs such as Aid to Families with Dependent Children, drastically reducing federal funding for low income housing and, in general, cutting over 10 million dollars from programs designed to aid the poor, homeless, and the hungry. At the same time the Reagan government invested $1.9 trillion dollars in military spending.

Within this perspective, the discourse of democracy was reduced to conflating patriotism with the cold war ideology of military preparedness, and the notion of the public good was abstracted from the principles of justice and equality in favor of an infatuation with individual achievement. Greed became respectable in the 1980s while notions of community and democratic struggle were either ignored or seen as subversive. Absent from the neoconservative public philosophy of the 1980s was any notion of democracy that took seriously the importance of developing a citizenry that could think critically, struggle against social injustices, and develop relations of community based on the principles of equality, freedom, and justice. This should not suggest that as educational and cultural workers we have nothing to do but to offer a language of critique. On the contrary, we need a new language of educational and cultural criticism that provides the basis for understanding how different social formations are structured in dominance within specific pedagogical and cultural practices. Cultural workers also need to rupture the relationship between difference and exploitation through a vision and social movement that transform the material and ideological conditions in which difference, structured in the principles of justice, equality, and freedom, becomes central to a postmodern conception of citizenship and radical democracy.[3]

In what follows, I want to argue that cultural studies needs to be reconstructed as part of a broader discourse of difference and pedagogical transformation, one that is forged in the dialectic of critique and possibility. In effect, I want to argue that cultural studies offers a theoretical discourse for a new cultural politics of difference, pedagogy, and public life. Central to the reconstruction of cultural studies is the need to develop a discourse that accentuates the organic connections between cultural workers and everyday life on the one hand and schooling and the reconstruction of democratic public culture on the other. In effect, I develop the proposition that cultural studies provides the opportunity for educators and other cultural workers to rethink and transform how schools, teachers, and students define themselves as political subjects capable of exhibiting critical sensibilities, civic courage, and forms of solidarity rooted in a strong commitment to freedom and democracy.

Cultural Studies as Pedagogical Practice

When I moved into internal University Teaching . . . we started teaching in ways that . . . [related] history to art and literature, including contemporary culture, and suddenly so strange was this to the Universities that they said 'My God, here is a new subject called Cultural Studies.'. . . The true position . . . was not only a matter of remedying deficit, making up for inadequate educational resources in the wider society, nor only a case of meeting new needs of the society, though those things contributed. The deepest impulse was the desire to make learning part of the process of social change itself.[4]

Raymond Williams reminds us that the relationship between cultural studies and education has a long history, one that appears to have been forgotten in the United States. More specifically, the theoretical and historical legacy of cultural studies has largely been ignored by progressive American educators. In part, this is because radical educational theory has never adequately escaped from an overly orthodox concern with the relationship between schooling and political economy and has refused to engage the complex and changing traditions that have informed the diverse formations and projects in which cultural studies has developed.[5]

While it is not my intention to reconstruct either the history of cultural studies or to present an analysis of its everchanging theoretical strengths and weaknesses, I do want to focus on some of the implications it has for providing a set of categories that deepens the radical democratic project of schooling while theoretically advancing the discourse and practice of critical pedagogy as a form of cultural politics. In what follows, I want to cast cultural studies as a political and pedagogical project that provides a convergence between a species of modernism that takes up questions of agency, voice, and possibility with those aspects of a postmodern discourse that have critically deconstructed issues of subjectivity, language, and difference. In effect, I will argue that cultural studies offers a theoretical terrain for rethinking schooling as a form of cultural politics and provides a discourse of intervention and possibility.

Cultural studies is important to critical educators because it provides the grounds for making a number of issues central to a radical theory of schooling. First, it offers the basis for creating new forms of knowledge by making language constitutive of the conditions for producing meaning as part of the knowledge/power relationship. Knowledge and power are reconceptualized in this context by reasserting not merely the indeterminacy of language but also the historical and social construction of knowledge itself. In this case, the cultural studies strategy of interrogation points to an evaluation of the disciplines within which intellectual knowledge is configured. Holding these disciplines to be constructed under historically specific circumstances leads to the discovery that as these conditions have been surpassed, the legitimacy of dominant forms of knowledge are in doubt. Therefore, efforts to preserve the distinctions among natural, social, and human sciences and the arts can be viewed as exemplars of the politics and historicity of the academic disciplines. Rather than holding knowledge in some kind of correspondence with a self-enclosed objective reality, a critical cultural study views the production of knowledge in the context of power. The consequences of these views are: to reshape knowledge according to the strategy of transgression; to define the traditional disciplines as much by their exclusions as by their inclusions; and to reject the distinctions between high and low culture.

Of central concern is not merely how aesthetic standards emerge, but how "our interpretations of society, culture, history and our individual lives, hopes, dreams, passions and sensations, involve attempts to *confer* sense rather than to *discover* it."[6] There is more at stake here than the crisis of representation. What cultural studies makes visible is the need to underscore questions of culture, change, and language with the equally important concerns of agency and ethics. Questions of culture are deeply political and ethical and necessitate theoretical and pedagogical practices in which educators and cultural workers engage in a continual dialogue and struggle that address the obligations of critical citizenship and the construction of public spheres that provide "the justification for a cultural pluralism, which seeks to address the needs and interests of a range of audiences . . . and be effective on a range of levels."[7] This suggests more than a politics of discourse and difference. It also points to a politics of social and cultural forms in which new possibilities open up for naming in concrete terms what struggles are worth taking-up, what alliances are to be formed as a result of these struggles, and how a discourse of difference can deepen the political and peda-gogical struggle for justice, equality, and freedom.

Second, by defining culture as a contested terrain, a site of struggle and transfor-mation, cultural studies offers critical educators the opportunity for going beyond cultural analyses that romanticize everyday life or engage culture as merely the reflex of the logic of domination.[8] A more critical version of cultural studies raises questions about the relations between the margins and the center of power, especially as they are configured through and around the categories of race, class, and gender. In doing so, a critically and politically informed version of cultural studies offers educators the oppor-tunity to challenge hegemonic ideologies, to read culture oppositionally, and to deconstruct historical knowledge as a way of reclaiming social identities that give collec-tive voice to the struggles of subordinate groups. In this case, culture is taken up not merely as a marker for the specificity of different cultural identities. Culture also refig-ures itself as a political and pedagogical discourse for calling into question not only forms of subordination that create inequities among different groups as they live out their lives, but also as a basis for challenging those institutional and ideological bound-aries that have historically masked their own relations of power behind complex forms of distinction and privilege. Hence, cultural studies points to the need to analyze the relationship between culture and power as historical differences that manifest themselves in historical, textual, and public struggles.

Third, cultural studies offers the opportunity to rethink the relationship between the issue of difference as it is constituted within subjectivities and between social groups. This suggests understanding more clearly how questions of subjectivity can be ad-dressed so as not to erase the possibility for individual and social agency. As such, subjectivities are seen as contradictory and multiple, produced rather than given, and are both taken-up and received within particular social and historical circumstances. What is important to note is developing a pedagogical practice based on what Larry Grossberg calls a theory of articulation. He writes:

A theory of articulation denies an essential human subject without giving up the active individual who is never entirely and simply 'stitched' into its place in social organizations of power. . . . There are always a multiplicity of positions, not only available but occupied, and a multiplicity of ways in which different meanings, experiences, powers, interests, and identities can be articulated together.[9]

Finally, cultural studies provides the basis for understanding pedagogy as a form of cultural production rather than as the transmission of a particular skill, body of knowledge, or set of values. In this context, critical pedagogy is understood as a cultural practice engaged in the production of knowledge, identities, and desires. As a form of cultural politics, critical pedagogy suggests inventing a new language for resituating teacher/student relations within pedagogical practices that open up rather than close down the borders of knowledge and learning. Disciplines can no longer define the boundaries of knowledge or designate the range of questions that can be asked. Similarly, critical pedagogy within the tradition of an older cultural study ruptures the dominant notion that culture as pedagogy is about transmission and consumption. As risky as this approach is, it serves to reinvent the project and possibility of teaching and learning within a context that engages its own ideological assumptions rather than suppresses them. In doing so, critical pedagogy can assert itself on the terrain of convictions through forms of ethical address and cultural work that freely engage real problems confronting everyday life. In effect, as a form of cultural production, critical pedagogy becomes a critical referent for understanding how various practices in the circuit of power inscribe institutions, texts, and lived cultures in particular forms of social and moral regulation which presuppose particular visions of the past, present and future. In what follows, I want to further develop the relationship between cultural studies and some of the issues mentioned above as part of a broader debate on language, difference, voice, and pedagogy.

Schooling and the Politics of Language

Education may well be, as of right now, the instrument whereby every individual, in a society like our own, can gain access to any kind of discourse. But we all know that in its distribution, in what it permits and prevents, it follows the well-trodden battle lines of social conflict. Every educational system is a political means of maintaining or modifying the appropriation of discourse with the knowledge and powers it carries with it.[10]

There is a long tradition in the United States of viewing schools as relatively neutral institutions whose language and social relations mirror the principles of equal opportunity. For example, liberal theories of education are grounded upon the belief that students have open access to the language and knowledge that schools provide as part of their public responsibility to educate. More recently, radical educators have drawn on a number of theoretical traditions that link language and power to disprove this assumption.[11] Not only do they expose the naivete of such views by revealing the social and political constraints that operate upon language, they also provide an intricate reading of how school language functions through a web of hierarchies, prohibitions, and denials to reward some students and deny other students access to what can be both learned and spoken within the confines of dominant schooling.[12] For radical educators, schools are sites where knowledge and power enter into relations that articulate with conflicts being fought out in the wider society. Central to this thesis is the assumption that the language of schooling is implicated in forms of racism that attempt to silence the voices of subordinated groups whose primary language is not English and whose cultural capital is either marginalized or denigrated by the dominant culture of schooling.

There are three important elements in this view of language that need to be reiterated. First, language has a social foundation and must be viewed as a site of struggle implicating the production of knowledge, values, and identities. Second, as a social phenomenon, language cannot be abstracted from the forces and conflicts of social history. In other words, the historicity of the relationship between dominant and subordinate forms of language offers insights into countering the assumption that the dominant language at any given time is simply the result of a naturally given process rather than the result of specific historical struggles and conflicts. In effect, the literature on social linguistics, deconstruction, and post-structuralism provides an important lesson in refusing to analyze the language/power relationship in simply synchronic and structural terms. While radical educators are acutely concerned with analyzing the ideologies that structure dominant language paradigms and the ways of life they legitimate, they do not abstract this type of inquiry from particular forms of historical and social analyses. That is, rather than developing an analysis that is simply concerned with the codes, classifications, orderings, and distribution of discourse, they also attend to the historical contexts and conflicts that are central to the purpose and meaning of discourse.[13] In effect, this work builds upon Bakhtin's insight that specific languages cannot be uprooted from the historical struggles and conflicts that make them heteroglossic rather than unitary. Bakhtin is clear on this issue and argues that:

> at any given moment of its historical existence, language is heteroglot from top to bottom:
> it represents the coexistence of socio-ideological contradictions between the present and
> the past, between differing epochs of the past, between different socio-ideological groups
> in the present, between tendencies, schools, circles, and so forth, all given a bodily form.
> These 'languages' of heteroglossia intersect each other in a variety of ways, forming new
> socially typifying 'languages.'[14]

More recent analyses have argued that any claim to a totalizing and unitary language is the result of forms of social, moral, and political regulation that attempt to erase their own histories.[15] At stake here is the need to make clear that language is always implicated in power relationships expressed, in part, through particular historical struggles over how established institutions such as education, law, medicine, social welfare, and the mass media produce, support, and legitimate particular ways of life that characterize a society at a given time in history. Language makes possible both the subject positions that people use to negotiate their sense of self and the ideologies and social practices that give meaning and legitimacy to institutions that form the basis of a given society.

Third, radical educators more recently have not been content to simply situate the analysis of language in the discourse of domination and subjugation. They are also concerned with developing a "language of possibility."[16] In this case, the emphasis is on perceiving language as both an oppositional force and an affirmative force. That is, discursive practices are viewed as deconstructing and reclaiming not only new forms of knowledge but also providing new ways of reading history through the reconstruction of suppressed memories that offer identities that challenge and contest the very conditions through which history, desire, voice, and place are experienced and lived. It is within this context that radical education offers educators a critical approach to pedagogy forged in the discourse of difference and voice.

The Politics of Voice and Difference

So, if you want to really hurt me, talk badly about my language. Ethnic identity is twin skin to linguistic identity—I am my language. Until I can accept as legitimate Chicano Texas Spanish, Tex-Mex and all the other languages I speak, I cannot accept the legitimacy of myself . . . and as long as I have to accommodateEnglish speakers rather than having them accommodate me, my tongue will be illegitimate. I will no longer be made to feel ashamed of existing. I will have my voice: Indian, Spanish, White. I will have my serpent's tongue—my woman's voice, my sexual voice, my poet's voice. I will overcome the tradition of silence.[17]

Difference must be not merely tolerated, but seen as a fund of necessary polarities between which our creativity can spark like a dialectic. Only then does the necessity for interdependency become unthreatening. . . . Within the interdependence of mutual (nondominant) differences lies that security, which enables us to descend into the chaos of knowledge and return with true visions of our future, along with the concomitant power to effect those changes, which can bring that future into being. . . . As women, we have been taught either to ignore our differences, or to view them as causes for separation and suspicion rather than as forces for change. Without community there is no liberation, only the most vulnerable and temporary armistice between an individual and her oppression. But community must not mean a shedding of our differences, nor the pathetic pretense that these differences do not exist.[18]

The discourse of difference as used by both Gloria Anzaldua and Audre Lorde provides a glimpse of the multiple and shifting ground that the term suggests. Defined in opposition to hegemonic codes of culture, subjectivity, and history, a number of social theorists have begun recently to use a discourse of difference to challenge some of the most fundamental dominant assertions that characterize mainstream social science. As I have pointed out in other chapters, theorists writing in anthropology, feminism, liberation theology, critical education, literary theory, and a host of other areas firmly reject mainstream assumptions regarding culture as a field of shared experiences defined in Western ethnocentric terms; in addition, critical theorists have rejected the mainstream humanist assumption that the individual is both the source of all human action and the most important unit of social analysis; moreover, many critical theorists reject the view that objectivity and consensus are the privileged and innocent concerns of dominant social science research. Reading in opposition to these assumptions, the notion of difference has played an important role in making visible how power is inscribed differently in and between zones of culture, how cultural borderlands raise important questions regarding relations of inequality, struggle, and history, and how differences are expressed in multiple and contradictory ways within individuals and between different groups.

While theories of difference have made important contributions to a discourse of progressive politics and pedagogy, they have also exhibited tendencies that have been theoretically flawed and politically regressive. In the first instance, the most important insights have emerged primarily from feminist women of color. These include: "the recognition of a self that is multiplicitous, not unitary; the recognition that differences are always relational rather than inherent; and the recognition that wholeness and commonality are acts of will and creativity, rather than passive discovery."[19] In the second instance, the discourse of difference has contributed to paralyzing forms of essentialism, ahistoricism, and a politics of separatism. In what follows, I first want to explore the dialectical nature of the relationship between difference and voice that informs a discourse of critical pedagogy. I conclude by pointing to some of the broader implications that a discourse of difference and voice might have for what I call a liberatory border pedagogy.

It is important for critical educators to take-up culture as a vital source for developing a politics of identity, community, and pedagogy. In this perspective, culture is not seen as monolithic or unchanging, but as a site of multiple and heterogeneous borders where different histories, languages, experiences, and voices intermingle amidst diverse relations of power and privilege. Within this pedagogical cultural borderland known as school, subordinated cultures push against and permeate the alleged unproblematic and homogeneous borders of dominant cultural forms and practices. It is important to note that critical educators cannot be content just to merely map how ideologies are inscribed in the various relations of schooling, whether they be the curriculum, forms of school organization, or in teacher-student relations. While these should be important concerns for critical educators, a more viable critical pedagogy needs to go beyond them by analyzing how ideologies are actually taken-up in the voices and lived experiences of students as they give meaning to the dreams, desires, and subject positions that they inhabit. In this sense, radical educators need to provide the conditions for students to speak so that their narratives can be affirmed and engaged along with the consistencies and contradictions that characterize such experiences. More specifically, the issue of student experiences has to be analyzed as part of a broader politics of voice and difference.

As bell hooks points out, coming to voice means "moving from silence into speech as a revolutionary gesture . . . the idea of finding one's voice or having a voice assumes a primacy in talk discourse, writing, and action. . . . Only as subjects can we speak. As objects, we remain voiceless—our beings defined and interpreted by others. . . . Awareness of the need to speak, to give voice to the varied dimensions of our lives, is one way [to begin] the process of education for critical consciousness."[20] This suggests that educators need to approach learning not merely as the acquisition of knowledge but as the production of cultural practices that offer students a sense of identity, place, and hope. To speak of voice is to address the wider issue of how people either become agents in the process of making history or function as subjects under the weight of oppression and exploitation within the various linguistic and institutional boundaries that produce dominant and subordinate cultures in any given society. In this case, voice provides a critical referent for analyzing how students are made voiceless in particular settings by not being allowed to speak, or how students silence themselves out of either fear or ignorance regarding the strength and possibilities that exist in the multiple languages and experience that connect them to a sense of agency and self-formation. At the same time, voices forged in opposition and struggle provide the crucial conditions by which subordinated individuals and groups can reclaim their own memories, stories, and histories as part of an ongoing collective struggle to challenge those power structures that attempt to silence them.

By being able to listen critically to the voices of their students, teachers become border-crossers through their ability to not only make different narratives available to themselves and other students but also by legitimating difference as a basic condition for understanding the limits of one's own voice. By viewing schooling as a form of cultural politics, radical educators can bring the concepts of culture, voice, and difference together to create a borderland where multiple subjectivities and identities exist as part of a pedagogical practice that provides the potential to expand the politics of democratic community and solidarity. Critical pedagogy serves to make visible those marginal cultures that have been traditionally suppressed in American schooling. Moreover, it provides students with a range of identities and human possibilities that emerge among, within, and between different zones of culture. Of course, educators cannot approach this task by merely giving equal weight to all zones of cultural difference; on the contrary, they must link the creation, sustenance, and formation of cultural difference as a fundamental part of the discourse of inequality, power, struggle, and possibility. Difference is not about merely registering or asserting spatial, racial, ethnic, or cultural differences but about historical differences that manifest themselves in public and pedagogical struggles. The possibilities for making difference and voice central aspects of critical pedagogy can be further elaborated around a number of concerns that are integral to a politics of border pedagogy.

Resisting Difference: Toward a Liberatory Theory of Border Pedagogy

Difference is not difference to some ears, but awkwardness or incompleteness. Aphasia. Unable or unwilling? Many have come to tolerate this dissimilarity and have decided to suspend their judgments (only) whenever the other is concerned. Such an attitude is a step forward. But it is a very small step indeed, since it serves as an excuse for their complacent ignorance and their reluctance to involve themselves in the issue. You who understand the dehumanization of forced removal, relocation, reeducation, redefinition, and the humiliation of having to falsify your own reality, your voice—you know. And often cannot *say* it. You try and keep on trying to unsay it, for if you don't, they will not fail to fill in the blanks on your behalf, and you will be said.[21]

To take up the issue of difference is to recognize that it cannot be analyzed unproblematically. In effect, the concept has to be used to resist those aspects of its ideological legacy used in the service of exploitation and subordination as well as to develop a critical reference for engaging the limits and strengths of difference as a central aspect of a critical theory of education. In what follows, I want to look briefly at how the concept of difference has been used by conservatives, liberals, and radicals in ways that either produce relations of subordination or undermine its possibility for developing a radical politics of democracy.

Conservatives have often used the term difference in a variety of ways to justify relations of racism, patriarchy, and class exploitation by associating difference with the notion of deviance while simultaneously justifying such assumptions through an appeal to science, biology, nature, or culture. In many instances, difference functions as a marker of power to name, label, and exclude particular groups while simultaneously being legitimated within a reactionary discourse and politics of public life, i.e., nationalism, patriotism, and "democracy."[22] What needs to be noted here is that there is more at stake than the production of particular ideologies based on negative definitions of identity. When defined and used in the interests of inequality and repression, difference is "enacted in violence against its own citizens as much as it is against foreigners."[23]

Liberals generally take up a dual approach to the issue of difference. This can be illuminated around the issue of race. On the one hand, liberals embrace the issue of difference through a notion of cultural diversity in which it is argued that race is simply one more form of cultural difference among many that make up the population of a country like the United States. The problem with this approach is that "by denying both the centrality and uniqueness of race as a principle of socio-economic organization, it redefines difference in a way that denies the history of racism in the United States and, thus, denies white responsibility for the present and past oppression and exploitation of people of color."[24] In this view, the systems of inequalities, subordination, and terror that inform the dominant culture's structuring of difference around issues of race, gender, and class are simply mapped out of existence. On the other hand, liberals often attempt to both appropriate and dissolve cultural differences into the melting pot theory of culture. The history, language, experiences, and narratives of the Other are relegated to invisible zones of culture, borderlands where the dominant culture refuses to hear the voice of the Other while celebrating a "white, male, middle-class, European heterosexuality [as] the standard of and the criteria for rationality and morality."[25] Under the rubric of equality and freedom, the liberal version of assimilation wages "war" against particularity, lived differences, and imagined futures that challenge culture as unitary, sacred, and unchanging, and identity as unified, static, and natural.

On the other hand, radical educational theorists have addressed the issue of difference around two basic considerations. First, difference has been elaborated as part of an attempt to understand subjectivity as fractured and multiple rather than as unified and static.[26] Central to this approach is the notion that subjectivities and identities are constructed in multilayered and contradictory ways. Identity is seen not only as a historical and social construction, but also as part of a continual process of transformation and change. This position is of enormous significance for undermining the humanist notion of the subject as both unified and the determinate source of human will and action. As significant as this position is, it is fraught with some theoretical problems.

By arguing that human subjectivities are constructed in language through the production and availability of diverse subject positions, many radical theorists have developed a theory of subjectivity that erases any viable notion of human agency. In effect, subjectivity becomes an effect of language, and human agency disappears into the discredited terrain of humanist will. Lost here is any understanding of how agency works within the interface of subject positions made available by a society and the weight of choices constructed out of specific desires, forms of self-reflection, and concrete social practices. There is little sense of how people actually invest in particular subject positions, what individuals and groups are privileged in having access to particular positions, and what the conditions are that make it impossible for some groups to take up, live, and speak particular discourses.[27]

The second approach to difference that radical educational theorists have taken-up centers on the differences between groups. A number of theorists, particularly feminists, have developed what can be called a discourse of identity politics.[28] In the most general sense, identity politics refers to "the tendency to base one's politics on a sense of personal identity—as gay, as Jewish, as Black, as female."[29] This politics of identity celebrates differences as they are constructed around the categories of race, class, gender, and sexual preference. Again, I will first point to the limitations that have emerged around this position and then later highlight the importance of identity politics within a broader notion of difference, politics, and culture.

Initially, identity politics offered a powerful challenge to the hegemonic notion that Eurocentric culture is superior to other cultures and traditions by offering political and cultural vocabularies to subordinated groups by which they could reconstruct their own histories and give voice to their individual and collective identities. This was especially true for the early stages of the feminist movement when the slogan, "the personal is the political," gave rise to the assumption that lived experience offered women the opportunity to insert themselves back into history and everyday life by naming the injustices they had suffered within a society constructed in patriarchal social relations. A number of problems emerged from the conception of difference that informed this view of identity politics. A number of theorists argued that there was a direct correlation between one's social location and one's political position. At stake here was the assumption that one's identity was rooted in a particular set of experiences that led rather unproblematically to a particular form of politics. This position is questionable on a number of grounds. To accept the authority of experience uncritically is to forget that identity itself is complex, contradictory, and shifting and does not unproblematically reveal itself in a specific politics. Second, the emphasis on the personal as a fundamental aspect of the political often results in highlighting the personal through a form of confessional politics that all but forgets how the political is constituted in social and cultural forms outside of one's own experiences. bell hooks puts the issue well:

> While stating "the personal is the political" did highlight feminist concern with the self, it did not insist on a connection between politicization and the transformation of consciousness. It spoke most immediately to the concerns women had about self and identity. . . . Feminist focus on self was then easily linked not to a process of radical politicization, but to a process of depoliticization. Popularly, the important quest was not to radically change our relationship to self and identity, to educate for critical consciousness, to become politically engaged and committed, but to explore one's identity, to affirm and assert the primacy of the self as it already existed.[30]

Another problem with the radical notion of difference is that it sometimes produces a politics of assertion that is both essentialist and separatist. By ignoring the notion that "the politics of any social position is not guaranteed in advance,"[31] identity politics often reproduced the very problems it thought it was attacking. As I have pointed out in another chapter, the essentialism at work in particular constructions of feminism has been made clear by Audre Lorde, Angela Harris, bell hooks, and others who have criticized white women not only for privileging patriarchy over issues of race, class, sexual preference, and other forms of oppression, but also for defining patriarchy and the construction of women's experiences in terms that excluded the particular narratives and stories of women of color.[32] In this case, racial and class differences among women are ignored in favor of an essentializing notion of voice that romanticizes and valorizes the unitary experience of white, middle-class women who assumed the position of being able to speak for all women. Moreover, forms of identity politics that forgo the potential for creating alliances among different subordinated groups run the risk of reproducing a series of hierarchies of identities and experiences, which serves to privilege their own form of oppression and struggle. All too often this position results in totalizing narratives that fail to recognize the limits of their own discourse in explaining the complexity of social life and the power such a discourse wields in silencing those who are not considered part of the insider group. June Jordan captures this sentiment well in her comment that "Traditional calls to 'unity' on the basis of only one of these factors—race or class or gender—will fail, finally, and again and again, I believe, because no simple one of these components provides for a valid fathoming of the complete individual."[33]

Far from suggesting that critical educators should dispense with either the notion of difference or an identity politics, I believe that we need to learn from the theoretical shortcomings analyzed above and begin to rethink the relationship among difference, voice, and politics. What does this suggest for a liberatory theory of border pedagogy? I want to end by pointing briefly to a number of suggestions.

First, the notion of difference must be seen in relational terms that link it to a broader politics that deepens the possibility for reconstructing democracy and schools as democratic public spheres. This means organizing schools and pedagogy around a sense of purpose and meaning that makes difference central to a critical notion of citizenship and democratic public life. Rather than merely celebrating specific forms of difference, a politics of difference must provide the basis for extending the struggle for equality and justice to broader spheres of everyday life. This suggests that the discourse of difference and voice be elaborated within, rather than against, a politics of solidarity. By refusing to create a hierarchy of struggles, it becomes possible for critical educators to take-up notions of political community in which particularity, voice, and difference provide the foundation for democracy. Chantal Mouffe persuasively argues that this view of difference is central to developing a postmodern notion of citizenship:

> An adequate conception of citizenship today should be "postmodern" if we understand by that the need to acknowledge the particular, the heterogeneous, and the multiple. . . . Only a pluralistic conception of citizenship can accommodate the specificity and multiplicity of democratic demands and provide a pole of identification for a wide range of democratic forces. The political community has to be viewed, then, as a diverse collection of communities, as a forum for creating unity without denying specificity.[34]

Second, critical educators must provide the conditions for students to engage in cultural remapping as a form of resistance. That is, students should be given the opportunity to engage in systematic analyses of the ways in which the dominant culture creates borders saturated in terror, inequality, and forced exclusions. Similarly, students should be allowed to rewrite difference through the process of crossing over into cultural borders that offer narratives, languages, and experiences that provide a resource for rethinking the relationship between the center and margins of power as well as between themselves and others. In part, this means giving voice to those who have been normally excluded and silenced. It means creating a politics of remembrance in which different stories and narratives are heard and taken-up as lived experiences. Most importantly, it means constructing new pedagogical borders where difference becomes the intersection of new forms of culture and identity.

Third, the concept of border pedagogy suggests not simply opening diverse cultural histories and spaces to students, but also understanding how fragile identity is as it moves into borderlands crisscrossed with a variety of languages, experiences, and voices. There are no unified subjects here, only students whose voices and experiences intermingle with the weight of particular histories that will not fit into the master narrative of a monolithic culture. Such borderlands should be seen as sites for both critical analysis and as a potential source of experimentation, creativity, and possibility. This is not a call to romanticize such voices. It is instead a suggestion that educators construct pedagogical practices in which the ideologies that inform student experiences be both heard and interrogated.[35] There is more at risk here than giving dominant and subordinated subjects the right to speak or allowing the narratives of excluded differences to be heard. There is also the issue of making visible those historical, ideological, and institutional mechanisms that have both forced and benefited from such exclusions. It is here that the borderland between school and the larger society meet, where the relevancies between teachers and cultural workers come into play, and where schooling is understood within the larger domain of cultural politics. More specifically, the pedagogical borderlands where blacks, whites, latinos, and others meet demonstrate the importance of a multicentric perspective that allows teachers, cultural workers, and students to not only recognize the multilayered and contradictory ideologies that construct their own identities but to also analyze how the differences within and between various groups can expand the potential of human life and democratic possibilities.

Fourth, the notion of border pedagogy needs to highlight the issue of power in a dual sense. First power has to be made central to understanding the effects of difference from the perspective of historically and socially constructed forms of domination. Second, teachers need to understand more clearly how to link power and authority in order to develop a pedagogical basis for reading differences critically. Difference cannot be merely experienced or asserted by students. It must also be read critically by teachers who, while not being able to speak as or for those who occupy a different set of lived experiences, can make progressive use of their authority by addressing difference as a historical and social construction in which all knowledges are not equally implicated in relations of power. Teacher authority can be used to provide the conditions for students to engage difference not as the proliferation of equal discourses grounded in distinct experiences, but as contingent and relational constructions that produce social forms and identities that must be made problematic and subject to historical and textual analyses. Teachers and cultural workers must take responsibility, as Stuart Hall points out, for the knowledge they organize, produce, mediate, and translate into the practice of culture.[36]

At the same time, it is important for teachers and cultural workers to construct pedagogical practices that neither position students defensively nor allow students to speak simply by asserting their voices and experiences. A pedagogy of affirmation is no excuse for refusing students the obligation to interrogate the claims or consequences their assertions have for the social relationships they legitimate. Larry Grossberg is correct in arguing that teachers who refuse to assert their authority or take up the issue of political responsibility as social critics and committed intellectuals often end up "erasing themselves in favor of the uncritical reproduction of the audience [students]."[37]

Fifth, border pedagogy also points to the importance of offering students the opportunity to engage the multiple references and codes that position them within various structures of meaning and practice. In part, this means educating students to become media literate in a world of changing representations. It also means teaching students to critically read not only how cultural texts and images are regulated by various discursive codes but also how such texts express and represent different ideological interests and how they might be taken up differently by students. More generally, border pedagogy points to the need to establish conditions of learning that define literacy inside rather than outside of the categories of power and authority. This suggests providing students with the opportunities to read texts as social and historical constructions, to engage texts in terms of their presences and absences, and to read texts oppositionally. This means teaching students to resist particular readings while simultaneously learning how to write their own narratives. At issue here is not merely the need for students to develop a healthy skepticism towards all discourses of authority, but also to recognize how authority and power can be transformed in the interest of creating a democratic society.

Finally, border pedagogy points to the need for educators to rethink the syntax of learning and behavior outside of the geography of rationality and reason. For example, racist, sexist, and class discriminatory narratives cannot be dealt with in a purely limited, analytical way. As a form of cultural politics, border pedagogy must engage how and why students make particular ideological and affective investments in these narratives. But this should not suggest that educators merely expand their theoretical and pedagogical understanding of how meaning and pleasure interact to produce particular forms of investment and student experience; rather, it points to a pedagogical practice that takes seriously how ideologies are lived, experienced, and felt at the level of everyday life as a basis for student experience and knowledge.[38] It means restructuring the curriculum so as to redefine the everyday as an important resource for linking schools to the traditions, communities, and histories that provide students with a sense of voice and relationship to others.

All of these concerns are relevant to the discourses of cultural studies. While it is true that cultural studies cannot be characterized by a particular ideology or position, it does offer a terrain through which cultural borders can be refigured, new social relations constructed, and the role of teachers and cultural workers as engaged critics rethought within the parameters of a politics of resistance and possibility. It is within this shifting and radical terrain that schooling as a form of cultural politics can be reconstructed as part of a discourse of opposition and hope.

Notes

1. Ngugi Wa Thiong'o, *Decolonizing the Mind: The Politics of Language in African Literature* (Portsmouth, NH: Heinemann, 1986), 3.
2. Sally Reed and R. Craig Sautter, "Children of Poverty: The Status of 12 Million Young Americans," *Phi Delta Kappan* (June 1990), K5.
3. The issue here is to develop a politics of difference that would allow various cultural workers to rethink and deepen the purpose and meaning of a radical democracy. Chantal Mouffe is useful on this issue:

   If the task of radical democracy is indeed to deepen the democratic revolution and to link together diverse democratic struggles, such a task requires the creation of new subject-positions that would allow the common articulation, for example, of antiracism, antisexism, and anticapitalism. These struggles do not spontaneously converge, and in order to establish democratic equivalences, a new "common sense" is necessary, which would transform the identity of different groups so that the demands of each group could be articulated with those of others according to the principle of democratic equivalence. For it is not a matter of establishing a mere alliance between given interests but of actually modifying the very identity of these forces. In order that the defense of workers' interests is not pursued at the cost of the rights of women, immigrants, or consumers, it is necessary to establish an equivalence between these different struggles. It is only under these circumstances that struggles against power become truly democratic.

   In Chantal Mouffe, "Radical Democracy: Modern or Postmodern," in Andrew Ross, ed., *Universal Abandon? The Politics of Postmodernism* (Minneapolis: University of Minnesota Press, 1988), 42.
4. Raymond Williams, "Adult Education and Social Change," *What I Came to Say* (London: Hutchinson-Radus, 1989), 162, 158.
5. Some of the better commentaries on both the history and central assumptions that informed cultural studies, at least in its British versions, since the 1950s can be found in Lawrence Grossberg, "The Formations of Cultural Studies: An American in Birmingham," *Strategies* 2 (1989), 114–49; Lawrence Grossberg, *It's a Sin* (Sydney, Australia: Power Publications, 1988); Richard Johnson, "The Story So Far: and Further Transformations?" in David Punter, ed., *Introduction to Cultural Studies* (New York: Longman, 1986), 277–313; Stuart Hall, "Cultural Studies: Two Paradigms," *Media, Culture and Society* 2 (1980), 57–82; Meaghan Morris, "Banality in Cultural Studies," *Discourse* 10:2 (1988), 3–29.
6. Iain Chambers, *Border Dialogues: Journeys in Postmodernity* (New York: Routledge, 1990), 11.
7. Rita Felski, "Feminism, Realism, and the Avant-Garde," in Andrew Milner, Philip Thomson, and Chris Worth, eds., *Postmodern Conditions* (New York: Berg Publishers, 1990), 76, 75.
8. For an excellent analysis of some of the theoretical pitfalls various forms of cultural studies have fallen into, see Meaghan Morris, "Banality in Cultural Studies," *Discourse* 10:2 (1988),

3–29; Cary Nelson, "Always Already Cultural Studies: Two Conferences and a Manifesto," *The Journal of the Midwest Modern Language Association* 24:1 (1991), 24–38.

9. Lawrence Grossberg, "The Formations of Cultural Studies," 137.

10. Michel Foucault, "The Discourse on Language," *The Archaeology of Knowledge* (London: Tavistock, 1972), 227.

11. For a summary of the various discourses now being taken-up by radical educators, see Diane Macdonell, *Theories of Discourse* (London: Blackwell, 1986).

12. I take this issue up in Henry A. Giroux, *Schooling and the Struggle for Public Life*, (Minneapolis: University of Minnesota Press, 1988).

13. See, for example, Noelle Bisseret, *Education, Class Language, and Ideology* (London: Routledge & Kegan Paul, 1979); Cleo Cherryholmes, *Power and Criticism: Poststructural Investigations in Education* (New York: Teachers College Press, 1988); Tony Crowley, *Standard English and the Politics of Language* (Urbana: University of Illinois Press, 1989).

14. M.M. Bakhtin, *The Dialogic Imagination* (Austin: University of Texas Press, 1981), 291.

15. Stanley Aronowitz and Henry A. Giroux, *Postmodern Education: Politics, Culture, and Social Criticism*, (Minneapolis: University of Minnesota Press, 1991).

16. Henry A. Giroux *Teachers as Intellectuals* (New York: Bergin and Garvey Press, 1988).

17. Gloria Anzaldua, *Borderlands/La Frontera: The New Mestizo* (San Francisco: Spinsters/Aunt Lute Press, 1987), 59.

18. Audre Lorde, *Sister Outsider* (Freedom, CA.: The Crossing Press, 1984), 111–12.

19. Angela P. Harris, "Race and Essentialism in Feminist Legal Theory," *Stanford Law Review* 42 (February 1990), 581. For an analysis of women of color who have contributed significantly to a theory of difference, see Kimberle Crenshaw, "Demarginalizing the Intersection of Race and Sex: A Black Feminist Critique of Antidiscrimination Doctrine, Feminist Theory and Antiracist Politics," *The University of Chicago Legal Forum* (1989), 139–67; Regina Austin, "Sapphire Bound!" *Wisconsin Law Review* (Fall 1989), 539–78. I am deeply indebted to Linda Brodkey for bringing this literature to my attention. Also see Linda Brodkey's excellent piece, "Toward a Feminist Rhetoric of Difference" (University of Texas at Austin, 1990).

20. bell hooks, *Talking Back* (Boston: South End Press, 1989), 12.

21. Trinh T. Minh-ha, *Woman, Native, Other* (Bloomington: Indiana University Press, 1989), 80.

22. Of course, we have a vast literature of anticolonialism that points this out very clearly. For example, see Chapter 2 in this book and Frantz Fanon, *Black Skin, White Masks* (New York: Grove Weidenfeld, 1967); Albert Memmi, *The Colonizer and the Colonized* (Boston: Beacon Press, 1965). For a particularly powerful example of the use of language in the production of difference as a marker of colonialism, see Wa Thiong'o, *Decolonizing the Mind*. See also Edward W. Said, *Orientalism* (New York: Vantage Books, 1979). Of course, most of the anti-colonial literature constructs difference through the modernist dichotomies of colonized versus colonizer, enemy versus foe. More recently, especially in the racist discourse being developed by the French Right, the concept of difference is being affirmed through themes that appear to eschew racism (the right to be different), while in actuality are used to reproduce its effects. On this issue, see Alain Policar, "Racism and Its Mirror Images," *Telos* No. 83 (Spring 1990), 99–108; Pierre-Andre Taguieff, "The New Cultural Racism in France," *Telos* No. 83 (Spring 1990), 109–22.

23. Sean Cubitt, "Introduction: Over the Borderlines," *Screen* 30:4 (Autumn 1989), 5.

24. Paula Rothenberg, "The Construction, Deconstruction, and Reconstruction of Difference," *Hypatia* 5:1 (Spring 1990), 47.

25. Ibid., 43.

26. Julian Henriques, Wendy Hollway, Cathy Urwin, Couze Venn, and Valerie Walkerdine, *Changing the Subject: Psychology, Social Regulation, and Subjectivity* (New York: Methuen, 1984).

27. Lawrence Grossberg, "The Context of Audiences and the Politics of Difference," *Australian Journal of Communication* No. 16 (December 1989), 29.

28. For some insightful comments on this issue, see hooks, *Talking Back*; Brodkey, "Toward a Feminist Rhetoric of Difference"; Regina Austin, "Sapphire Bound!" *Wisconsin Law Review* (Fall 1989), 539–78; Henry A. Giroux, "Rethinking the Boundaries of Educational Discourse: Modernism, Postmodernism, and Feminism," *College Literature* 17:2/3 (1990), 1–50.

29. Diana Fuss, "Lesbian and Gay Theory: The Question of Identity Politics," in D. Fuss, *Essentially Speaking: Feminism, Nature, and Difference* (New York: Routledge, 1989), 97.

30. hooks, *Talking Back*, 106.

31. Lawrence Grossberg, "The Context of Audience and the Politics of Difference," 28.

32. In this book, see Chapter 5, "Redefining the Boundaries of Race and Ethnicity."

33. June Jordan, "Waiting for a Taxi," *The Progressive* (June 1989), 16. Of course, the call to move beyond a politics of difference and identity that reproduces totalizing narratives should not be mistaken as a criticism of all theorists and social movements that take-up particular issues in order to promote specific struggles against racism, sexism, or class exploitation. Such a criticism is warranted only when these issues are developed as part of a politics of assertion and separatism that functions to silence other progressive voices and oppressed groups. In this case, identity politics and the discourse of difference collapse into a hegemonic narrative. The complexity of the issues surrounding the relationship between a politics of location, difference, and essentialism are taken-up in Teresa de Lauretis, "The Essence of the Triangle or, Taking the Risk of Essentialism Seriously: Feminist Theory in Italy, the U.S., and Britain," *Difference* 1:1 (Summer 1989), 3–37; Cornel West, "The New Cultural Politics of Difference," *October* No. 53 (Summer 1990), 93–109; Rita Felski, "Feminism, Postmodernism, and the Critique of Modernity," *Cultural Critique* No. 13 (Fall 1989), 33–56.

34. Chantal Mouffe, "The Civics Lesson," *The New Statesman and Society* (October 7, 1988), 30.

35. Renato Rosaldo, *Culture and Truth* (Boston: Beacon Press, 1989).

36. Stuart Hall, "The Emergence of Cultural Studies and the Crisis of the Humanities," *October* 53 (Summer 1990), 11–23.

37. Lawrence Grossberg, "The Context of Audiences and the Politics of Difference," 30.

38. Lawrence Grossberg, "Teaching the Popular," Cary Nelson, ed., *Theory in the Classroom* (Urbana: University of Illinois Press, 1986), 177–200; Henry A. Giroux and Roger Simon, eds., *Popular Culture, Schooling and Everyday Life* (New York: Bergin and Garvey Press, 1989).

6

Popular Culture as a Pedagogy of Pleasure and Meaning

*Decolonizing the Body**

In the past decade, radical educators have begun to take seriously the issue of student experience as a central component in developing a theory of schooling and cultural politics.[1] The ways in which student experience is produced, organized, and legitimated in schools has become an increasingly important theoretical consideration for understanding how schools function to produce and authorize particular forms of meaning and to implement teaching practices consistent with the ideological principles of the dominant society. Rather than focusing exclusively on how schools reproduce the dominant social order through forms of social and cultural reproduction or how students contest the dominant logic through various forms of resistance, radical educators have attempted more recently to analyze the terrain of schooling as a struggle over particular ways of life. In this view the process of being schooled cannot be fully conceptualized within the limiting parameters of the reproduction/resistance model. Instead, being schooled is analyzed as part of a complex and often contradictory set of ideological and material processes through which the transformation of experience takes place. In short, schooling is understood as part of the production and legitimation of social forms and subjectivities as they are organized within relations of power and meaning that either enable or limit human capacities for self and social empowerment.[2]

---

*Roger I. Simon co-author.

While the theoretical service that this position has provided cannot be overstated, radical educational theorists have nonetheless almost ignored the importance of popular culture both for developing a more critical understanding of student experience and for posing the problem of pedagogy in a critical and theoretically expanded fashion. The irony of this position is that while radical educators have argued for the importance of student experience as a central component for developing a critical pedagogy, they have generally failed to consider how such experience is shaped by the terrain of popular culture. Similarly, they have been reluctant to raise the question of why popular culture has not been a serious object of study either in the school curriculum or in the curriculum reforms put forth by critically minded liberal educators. This lacunae can be partly explained by the fact that radical educators often legitimate in their work a theory of pedagogy in which the ideological correctness of one's political position appears to be the primary determining factor in assessing the production of knowledge and exchange that occurs between teachers and students. Guided by a concern with producing knowledge that is ideologically correct, radical theorists have revealed little or no understanding of how a teacher can be both politically correct and pedagogically wrong. Nor can there be found any concerted attempts by radical theorists to analyze how relations of pedagogy and relations of power are inextricably tied not only to what people know but also to how they come to know in a particular way within the constraints of specific social forms.[3]

We want to argue in this chapter that the lack of an adequate conception of critical pedagogical practice is in part responsible for the absence of an adequate politics of popular culture. Within critical educational theories, the issue of pedagogy is often treated in one of two ways: (1) as a method whose status is defined by its functional relation to particular forms of knowledge or (2) as a process of ideological deconstruction of a text. In the first approach, close attention is given to the knowledge chosen for use in a particular class. Often the ways in which students actually engage such knowledge is taken for granted. It is assumed that if one has access to an ideologically correct comprehension of that which is to be understood, the only serious question that needs to be raised about pedagogy is one of procedural technique; that is, should one use a seminar, lecture, or some other teaching style?[4] In the second approach, pedagogy is reduced to a concern with and analysis of the political interests that structure particular forms of knowledge, ways of knowing, and methods of teaching. For example, specific styles of teaching might be analyzed according to whether or not they embody sexist, racist, and class-specific interests, serve to silence students, or promote practices that deskill and disempower teachers.[5] In both approaches, what is often ignored is the notion of pedagogy as a form of cultural production and exchange that addresses how knowledge is produced, mediated, refused, and represented within relations of power both in and outside of schooling.

In our view, the issue of critical pedagogy demands an attentiveness to how students actively construct the categories of meaning that prefigure how they produce and respond to classroom knowledge. By ignoring the cultural and social forms that are both authorized by youth and simultaneously serve to empower or disempower them, educators run the risk of complicity in silencing and negating their students. This is unwittingly accomplished by educators' refusing to recognize the importance of those sites and social practices outside of schools that actively shape student experiences and through which students often define and construct their sense of identity, politics, and culture. The issue at stake is not one of relevance but of empowerment. We are not concerned with simply motivating students to learn, but rather with establishing the conditions of learning that enable students to locate themselves in history and to interrogate the adequacy of that location as both a pedagogical and political question.[6]

Educators who refuse to acknowledge popular culture as a significant basis of knowledge often devalue students by refusing to work with the knowledge that students actually have. In doing so, these educators eliminate the possibility of developing a pedagogy that links school knowledge with the differing subject relations that help to constitute students' everyday lives. A more critical pedagogy demands that pedagogical relations be seen as relations of power structured primarily through dominant but always negotiated and contested forms of consent.

We wish to stress that the basis for a critical pedagogy cannot be developed merely around the inclusion of particular forms of knowledge that have been suppressed or ignored by the dominant culture, nor can it only center on providing students with more empowering interpretations of the social and material world. Such a pedagogy must be attentive to ways in which students make both affective and semantic investments as part of their attempts to regulate and give meaning to their lives.[7] This is an important insight that both problematizes and provides a corrective to the traditional ways in which radical educators have explained how dominant meanings and values work as part of a wider ideology to position, address, and limit the ways in which students view both themselves and their relationships to the larger society. The value of including popular culture in the development of a critical pedagogy is that it provides the opportunity to further our understanding of how students make investments in particular social forms and practices. In other words, the study of popular culture offers the possibility of understanding how a politics of pleasure serves to address students in a way that shapes and sometimes secures the often contradictory relations students have to both schooling and the politics of everyday life. If one of the central concerns of a critical pedagogy is understanding how student identities, cultures, and experiences provide the basis for learning, we need to grasp the totality of elements that organize such subjectivities.

In this chapter we shall particularly emphasize that while the production of meaning provides one important element in the production of subjectivity, it is not enough. The production of meaning is also tied to emotional investments and the production of pleasure. In our view, the production of meaning and the production of pleasure are mutually constitutive of who students are, the view they have of themselves, and how they construct a particular version of their future. In what follows, we first want to argue that critical educators need to retheorize the importance of popular culture as a central category for both understanding and developing a theory and practice of critical pedagogy. In developing this position, we first want to examine some conservative and radical views of popular culture and then analyze the pedagogical practices implicit in these positions. Second, we will attempt to develop the basic elements that constitute a theory of popular culture, one that would support a critical pedagogical practice. Third, we will analyze a particular Hollywood film as a popular form, treating the film as an exemplary text in order to demonstrate how the formation of identities takes place through attachments and investments that are as much a question of affect and pleasure as they are of ideology and rationality. Finally, we will discuss the implications of this analysis for the practice of a critical pedagogy.

Radical and Conservative Approaches to Popular Culture

Historically, the concept of popular culture has not fared well either as part of the discourse of the Left or of the Right.[8] For the Left, two positions have held center stage in different terrains of Marxist theory. In the first, popular culture lacks the possibility for creative, productive, or authentic forms of expression. In this view, popular culture is simply that terrain of ideology and cultural forms imposed by the culture industry on the masses in order to integrate them into the existing social order. Within this discourse, popular culture becomes commodified and produces people in the image of its own logic, a logic characterized by standardization, uniformity, and passivity. The structuring principle at work in this view of popular culture is one of total dominance and utter resignation. People become synonymous with cultural dupes incapable of either mediating, resisting, or rejecting the imperatives of the dominant culture.

The paradigmatic example of this position comes from Theodor Adorno and Max Horkheimer.[9] Within their discourse, popular culture was equated with mass culture. This was seen as a form of psychoanalysis in reverse; that is, instead of curing socially induced neuroses, mass culture produced them. Similarly, popular forms such as television, radio, jazz, or syndicated astrology columns were seen as nothing more than a form of ideological shorthand for those social relations that reproduced the social system as a whole. For Adorno, in particular, popular culture was simply a form of mass culture whose effects had no redeeming political possibilities. The people or "masses" in this view lacked any culture through which they could offer either resistance or an alternative vision of the world. Adorno is clear on this issue:

> The total effect of the culture industry is one of antienlightenment, in which, as Horkheimer and I have noted, enlightenment, that is the progressive technical domination of nature, becomes mass deception and is turned into a means for fettering consciousness.

It impedes the development of autonomous, independent individuals who judge and decide consciously for themselves. . . . If the masses have been unjustly reviled from above as masses, the culture industry is not among the least responsible for making them into masses and then despising them, while obstructing the emancipation for which human beings [might be] ripe.[10]

Adorno's views represent one of the central paradoxical theses of the Frankfurt School theorists. According to them, reason is not only in eclipse in the modern age, it is also the source of crisis and decline. Progress has come to mean the reification, rationalization, and standardization of thought itself, and the culture industry plays a key role in transforming culture and reason into their opposite, culture as ignorance and commodification. Within this perspective, the distinction between high culture and mass/popular culture is preserved. In this case, high culture becomes a transcendent sphere, one of the few terrains left in which autonomy, creativity, and opposition can be thought and practiced. While arguing that mass culture is an expression of the slide into ignorance, Frankfurt theorists such as Adorno and Horkheimer fall back upon an unfortunate legitimation of high culture in which particular versions of art, music, literature, and the philosophic tradition become a utopian refuge for resisting the new barbarism.[11]

The second view of popular culture that is predominant in Marxist theory is developed mostly in the work of historians and sociologists who focus on various aspects of "peoples' history" or the practices of subcultural groups. In this view, popular culture becomes a version of folk culture and its contemporary variant. That is, as an object of historical analysis, working-class culture is excavated as an unsullied expression of popular resistance. Within this form of analysis the political and the pedagogical emerge as an attempt to reconstruct a "radical and 1/4 popular tradition in order that 'the people' might learn from and take heart from the struggles of their forebears," or it appears as an attempt to construct "'the people' as the supporters of [a] 'great culture' so that they might eventually be led to appropriate that culture as their own."[12]

A similar and more contemporary version of this discourse opposes the high or dominant culture to the alternative culture of the working class or various subcultural groups. This is the culture of authenticity, one which is allegedly uninfluenced by the logic and practices of the culture industry or the impositions of a dominant way of life. At work here is a romanticized view of popular experience that somehow manages to escape from the relations and contradictions at work in the larger society. This view falls prey to an essentialist reading of popular culture. It deeply underestimates the most central feature of cultural power in the twentieth century. In failing to acknowledge popular culture as one sphere in a complex field of domination and subordination, this view ignores the necessity of providing an understanding of how power produces different levels of cultural relations, experience, and values that articulate the multilayered ideologies and social practices of any society.[13]

Both of these leftist traditions have played a powerful role in defining popular culture within a theoretical framework that helps to explain why the people have not risen up against the inequities and injustices of capitalism. Ironically, the Right has not ignored the underlying logic of this position, and, in fact, has appropriated it for its own ideological interests. For example, as Patrick Brantlinger points out, the category of popular culture has been "just as useful for helping to explain and condemn the failures of egalitarian schools and mass cultural institutions such as television and the press to educate 'the masses' to political responsibility."[14] Conservative critics such as Arnold Toynbee, José Ortega Y Gasset, Ezra Pound, and T. S. Eliot have viewed popular culture as a threat to the very existence of civilization as well as an expression of the vulgarization and decadence of the masses.

In the conservative attack on mass culture, the category of true culture is treated as a warehouse filled with the goods of antiquity, waiting patiently to be distributed anew to each generation. Knowledge in this perspective becomes sacred, revered, and removed from the demands of social critique and ideological interests.[15] The pedagogical principles at work here are similar to those at work in the Left's celebration of high culture. In both cases, the rhetoric of cultural restoration and crisis legitimates a transmission pedagogy consistent with a view of culture as an artifact and students as merely bearers of received knowledge. Though starting from different political positions, advocates of high culture on the Left and Right often argue that the culture of the people has to be replaced with forms of knowledge and values that are at the heart of ruling culture. In these perspectives, the modalities of revolutionary struggle and conservative preservation seem to converge around a view of popular culture as a form of barbarism, a notion of "the people" as passive dupes, and an appeal to a view of enlightenment that reduces cultural production and meaning to the confines of high culture. Questions regarding the multidimensional nature of the struggles, contradictions, and reformations that inscribe in different ways the historically specific surface of popular cultural forms are completely overlooked in both the dominant radical and conservative positions developed above.

Dominant Left views of popular culture have not provided an adequate discourse for developing a theory of cultural analysis that begins with the issue of how power enters into the struggles over the domains of common sense and everyday life.[16] Nor do such accounts provide sufficient theoretical insight into how the issues of consent, resistance, and the production of subjectivity are formed by pedagogical processes whose structuring principles are deeply political. Of course, in the exaggerations that characterize popular culture as one that is either imposed from above or generated spontaneously from below there are hints of the political reality of cultural power both as a force for domination and as a condition for collective affirmation and struggle. The point is not to separate these different elements of cultural power from each other as binary oppositions but to capture the complexity of cultural relations as they are manifested in practices that both enable and disable people within sites and social forms that give meaning to the relations of popular culture.[17]

Hegemony as a Pedagogical Process

The work of Antonio Gramsci represents an important starting point for both redefining the meaning of popular culture and for advancing its pedagogical and political importance as a site of both struggle and domination.[18] Gramsci did not directly address himself to modern manifestations of popular culture such as cinema and radio, nor did he write anything noteworthy on the symbolic forms of popular culture that existed in the urban centers of Europe in the early part of the twentieth century; but he did formulate an original and profound theory of culture, power, and hegemony that provides a theoretical basis for moving beyond the impasse of viewing popular culture within the bipolar alternatives of a celebratory populism or a debilitating cultural stupor.[19] Gramsci's theory of hegemony redefines the structuring principles that maintain relations between dominant and subordinate classes in the advanced capitalist societies. For Gramsci, the exercise of control by the ruling classes is characterized less by the excessive use of officially sanctioned force than it is through what he calls the struggle for hegemonic leadership. Hegemonic leadership refers to the struggle to win the consent of subordinated groups to the existing social order. In substituting hegemonic struggle for the concept of domination, Gramsci points to the complex ways in which consent is organized as part of an active pedagogical process on the terrain of everyday life. In Gramsci's view such a process must work and rework the cultural and ideological terrain of subordinate groups in order to legitimate the interests and authority of the ruling bloc.

Gramsci's concept of hegemony broadens the question of which social groups will hold and exert power. More importantly, it raises a number of theoretical considerations regarding how power as a cultural, economic, and political set of practices works to define, organize, and legitimate particular conceptions of common sense.[20] Gramsci's hegemony needs to be articulated as both a political and pedagogical process. Moral leadership and state power are tied to a process of consent, as a form of learning, which is secured through the elaboration of particular discourses, needs, appeals, values, and interests that must address and transform the concerns of subordinated groups. In this perspective hegemony is a continuing, shifting, and problematic historical process. Consent is structured through a series of relations marked by an ongoing political struggle over competing conceptions and views of the world between dominant and subordinated groups. What is worth noting here is that this is not a political struggle framed within the polarities of an imposing dominant culture and weak or "authentic" subordinate cultures. On the contrary, by claiming that every relation of hegemony is necessarily an educational relationship, Gramsci makes clear that a ruling bloc can only engage in a political and pedagogical struggle for the consent of subordinate groups if it is willing to take seriously and articulate some of the values and interests of these groups.[21]

Inherent in the attempt by dominant groups to transform rather than displace the ideological and cultural terrain of subordinated groups, dominant ideology itself is compromised and exists in a far from pure, uncontaminated state. Needless to say, the culture of subordinated groups never confronts the dominant culture in either a completely supine or totally resistant fashion. In the struggle to open up its own spaces for resistance and affirmation, subordinated cultures have to negotiate and compromise around *both* those elements they give over to the dominant culture and those they maintain as representative of their own interests and desires.[22]

From this view of struggle within the hegemonic process, it is clear that the relationship between popular culture and the processes of consent require rejecting any concept of popular culture articulated in essentialist terms. That is, the concept of popular culture cannot be defined around a set of ideological meanings permanently inscribed in particular cultural forms. On the contrary, because of the location of cultural forms within and as part of the dynamics of consent, their meaning can only be ascertained through their articulation into a practice and set of historically specific contextual relations that determine their political meaning and ideological interests. Break dancing, punk dress codes, or heavy metal music may be sufficiently oppositional and congruent within one social and historical context to be considered a legitimate radical expression of popular culture and yet in another social field may be mediated through the consumer ideology and investments of mass culture. What is important to recognize here is that *the key structuring principle of popular culture does not consist in the contents of particular cultural forms*. Stuart Hall illuminates this issue well:

> The meaning of a cultural form and its place or position in the cultural field is not inscribed inside its form. Nor is its position fixed once and forever. This year's radical symbol or slogan will be neutralized into next year's fashion; the year after, it will be the object of a profound cultural nostalgia. Today's rebel folksinger ends up, tomorrow, on the cover of *The Observer* color magazine. The meaning of the cultural symbol is given in part by the social field into which it is incorporated, the practices with which it articulates and is made to resonate. What matters is not the intrinsic or historically fixed objects of culture, but the state of play in cultural relations.[23]

We want to extend further this insight and argue that not only are popular cultural forms read in complex ways, but they also mobilize multiple forms of investment. In other words, the popular has a dual form of address: it serves as a semantic and ideological referent for marking one's place in history and also brings about an experience of pleasure, affect, and corporeality. This is not to suggest that these forms of address posit a distinction in which pleasure takes place outside of history or forms of representation. What is being posited is that the popular as both a set of practices and a discursive field has a variety of effects that may be mediated through a combination of corporeal and ideological meanings or through the primacy of one of these determinants. For instance, while popular cultural forms are productive around historically constructed sets of meanings and practices, their effects may be primarily affective. That is, how these forms are mediated and addressed, how they work to construct a particular form of investment, may depend less on the production of meanings than on the affective relations that they construct with their audiences. For example, pleasure as a terrain of commodification and struggle never exists completely free from the technology of gendered representations, but its power as a form of investment cannot be reduced to its signifying effects. This means that the practices associated with a particular cultural form such as punk can never be dismissed as being merely ideologically incorrect or as simply a reflex of commodity logic. The importance of both the semantic and the affective in the structuring of the investments in popular cultural forms provides new theoretical categories for linking the terrain of the everyday with the pedagogical processes at work in the notion of consent.

In summary, we are arguing that there is no popular culture outside of the interlocking processes of meaning, power, and desire that characterize the force of cultural relations at work at a given time and place in history. What this suggests more specifically is that the content of popular culture cannot be understood as prespecified content; instead, its content is produced as the ideological and institutional structuring relations of a given society's function to sustain the differences between what constitutes the dominant culture and what does not. Underlying this struggle in North America today to maintain both a difference and an accommodation of dominant and subordinate cultures is a configuration of institutions, ideologies, and social practices that constitute those features that mark a generic distinction between the realms of popular and dominant culture.

In the context of this distinction, popular culture is, in a sense, an empty cultural form. That is, its form or representation does not guarantee an unproblematic, transcendent meaning. At the same time, popular culture can be understood as a social practice constituted by a particular site and features that point to a distinctive field of political action. The general distinctiveness of popular culture as a sphere of social relations can be made more clear by further elaborating its basic theoretical features.

To begin with the concept of hegemony clarifies how cultural power is able to penetrate into the terrain of daily life, transforming it into both a struggle over and accommodation to the culture of subordinate groups. Second, it is important to acknowledge that the cultural terrain of everyday life is not only a site of struggle and accommodation, but one in which the production of subjectivity can be viewed as a pedagogical process whose structuring principles are deeply political. Third, the notion of consent that lies at the heart of the process of hegemony underscores the importance of specifying the limits and possibilities of the pedagogical principles at work within cultural forms that serve in contradictory ways to empower and disempower various groups. In what follows, we want to extend these insights by pointing to those specific features and activities that illuminate more specifically what constitutes popular culture as both a site and field of pedagogical work.

Culture as a Site of Struggle and Power Relations

We enter the process of theorizing the relation between popular culture and critical pedagogy by arguing for educational practice as both a site and form of cultural politics. In this regard, our project is the construction of an educational practice that expands human capacities in order to enable people to intervene in the formation of their own subjectivities and to be able to exercise power in the interest of transforming the ideological and material conditions of domination into social practices that promote social empowerment and demonstrate possibilities. Within this position we are emphasizing popular culture as a site of differentiated politics; a site with multiple ideological and affective weightings. It represents a particular historical place where different groups collide in transactions of dominance, complicity, and resistance over the power to name, legitimate, and experience different versions of history, community, desire, and pleasure through the availability of social forms structured by the politics of difference. Some of the theoretical and political implications at work in this view of popular culture are captured in Larry Grossberg's discussion of a theory of articulation:

> . . . people are never merely passively subordinated, never entirely incorporated. People are engaged in struggles with, within, and sometimes against, real tendential forces and determinations, in their efforts to appropriate what they are given. Consequently, their relations to particular practices and texts are complex and contradictory: they may win something in the struggle against sexism and lose something in the struggle against economic exploitation; they may both gain and lose something economically; and while they lose ideological ground, they may win some emotional strength. If peoples' lives are never merely determined by the dominant position, and their subordination is always complex and active, then understanding [popular] culture requires us to look at how they are actively inserted at particular sites of everyday life and at how particular articulations empower and disempower its audience.[24]

The key theoretical concepts for further specifying popular culture as a particular site of struggle and accommodation can be initially organized around the category of what we label "the productive." In the more general sense, we use the term "productive" to refer to the construction and organization of practices engaged in by dominant *and* subordinated groups to secure a space for producing and legitimating experiences and social forms constitutive of different ways of life forged in asymmetrical relations of power. The term "productive" points to two distinctly different sets of relations within the sphere of the popular.

The first set of relations refers to the ways in which the dominant culture functions as a structuring force within and through popular forms. In this case, the dominant culture attempts to secure both semantically and affectively, through the production of meaning and the regulation of pleasure, the complicity of subordinated groups. Rather than merely dismiss and ignore the traditions, ideologies, and needs that emerge from the cultures of subordinated groups, the dominant culture attempts to appropriate and transform the ideological and cultural processes that characterize the terrain of the popular. At issue here are processes of selective production, controlled distribution, and regulated notions of narrative and consumer address.

In the second set of relations, the notion of the productive refers to the ways in which subordinated groups articulate a distinct set of contents and/or a level of involvement in popular forms that is less distancing and more social in nature than that found in the cultural forms of dominant bourgeois groups. This articulation and set of relations are characterized by a refusal to engage in social practices defined by an abstract rationality, a theoretical mapping, so to speak, that structures cultural forms through a denial of the familiar affective investments and pleasures. For the dominant class, such refusal is often understood as a surrender to the moment, the fun of the event, or the "horror of the vulgar." A more critical reading might suggest that the affective investment and level of active involvement in popular forms such as neighborhood sports and punk dancing, or at working-class weddings represent an important theoretical signpost. In this case, it is a particular form of sociality that signals something more than vulgarity, cooption, or what Bloch calls the swindle of fulfillment. Instead, the sociality that structures popular forms may contain the unrealized potentialities and possibilities necessary for more democratic and humane forms of community and collective formation.[25] This can be made clearer by analyzing the structuring principles that often characterize dominant cultural forms.

Pierre Bourdieu argues that the cultural forms of dominant bourgeois groups can be characterized by the celebration of a formalism, an elective distance from the real world, with all of its passions, emotions, and feelings. The social relations and attendant sensibility at work in bourgeois cultural forms are those that often maintain an investment of form—a celebration of stylized detachment. On the other hand, there is often a space in cultural forms embraced by subordinated groups that is organized around a sensibility in which the needs, emotions, and passions of the participants largely resonate with the material and ideological structures of everyday life. Underlying these social relations one often finds a richly textured collective investment of play and affective engagement in which there is no great disjunction/interruption between the act and its meaning. In other words, there is an active, communal set of experiences and social practices at work in subordinated cultural forms, including a form of public participation in which the dominant practice of distancing the body from reflection is refused. This is the productive moment of corporeality. Mercer illuminates this point in his discussion of Bourdieu's concept of "popular forms:"

> 'Nothing,' argues Pierre Bourdieu, 'more radically distinguishes popular spectacles—the football match, Punch and Judy, the circus, wrestling, or even in some cases the cinema—from bourgeois spectacles, than the form of participation of the public.' For the former, whistles, shouts, pitch invasions are characteristic, for the latter the gestures are distant, heavily ritualized—applause, obligatory but discontinuous and punctual cries of enthusiasm—'author, author' or 'encore.' Even the clicking of fingers and tapping of feet in a jazz audience are only a 'bourgeois spectacle, which mimes a popular one' since the participation is reduced to 'the silent allure of the gesture.' A certain distance, Bourdieu argues, has been central in the bourgeois economy of the body: a distance between 'reflexion' and corporeal participation.[26]

Since corporeality may be inscribed in either repressive or emancipatory actions, any uncritical celebration of the body is theoretically and politically misplaced. At the same time, it is important to recognize that a discourse of the body is needed that recognizes a sensibility and set of social practices that both define and exhibit a possibility for extending unrealized and progressive moments in the production of corporeality. For example, punk culture's lived appropriation of the everyday as a refusal to let the dominant culture encode and restrict the meaning of daily life suggests the first instance of a form of resistance that links play with the reconstruction of meaning. This particular popular form, filled as it is with abortive hopes, signifies within bourgeois culture a "tradition of the scorned." That is, punk culture (or for that matter any lived relation of difference that doesn't result in dominance or infantilization) ruptures the dominant order symbolically and refuses to narrate *with* permission. It is scorned by the bourgeoisie because it not only challenges the dominant order's attempt to suppress all differences through a discourse that asserts the homogeneity of the social domain but presents the possibility of a social imaginary in which a politics of democratic difference offers up forms of resistance in which it becomes possible to rewrite, rework, recreate, and reestablish new discourses and cultural spaces that revitalize rather than degrade public life. Whether conscious or not, punk culture partly expresses social practices that contain the basis for interrogating and struggling to overthrow all those forms of human behavior in which difference becomes the basis for subjecting human beings to forms of degradation, enslavement, and exploitation. Of course, there is more at work in punk culture than the affirmation of difference; there is also the difference of affirmation, that is, affirmation becomes the precondition for claiming one's experience as a legitimate basis for developing one's own voice, place, and sense of history. It is this dialectic of affirmation, pleasure, and difference that constitutes some of the basic elements of the notion of the productive. Bourdieu is helpful here, for he defines the productive as that dialectical mixture of pleasure, consent, and unselfconscious involvement that maps out a significant aspect of the popular within everyday life. As Bourdieu points out,

> The desire to enter into the game, identifying with the characters' joys and sufferings, worrying about their fate, espousing their hopes and ideals, living their life, is based on a form of investment, a sort of deliberate "naivety", ingenuousness, good-natured credulity ("we're here to enjoy ourselves"), which tends to accept formal experiments and specifically artistic effects only to the extent that they can be forgotten and do not get in the way of [the affirmation and dignity of everyday life].[27]

As we have stressed, it would be a political mistake to place too much faith in the level of participation and nature of spontaneity that characterizes many cultural forms of subordinated groups. Many of these forms are not innocent. As an area and site of exchange between the dominant and subordinated classes, popular culture embodies a violence inherent in both sides of the processes of hegemony as well as the unrealized potentiality of those needs and desires that reflect a respect for human dignity and a commitment to extend their most ethical and empowering capabilities. We stress here that innocence is not an intrinsic feature of the popular. There is a violence inextricably inscribed in popular forms that must also be addressed as part of the multilayered and contradictory investments and meanings that constitute its changing character.

Popular Culture and Consent: The Dialectic of Ideology and Pleasure

If the popular is to be understood in terms of the unrealized potentialities that inform it, critical educators need to analyze how the production of subjectivity and cultural alliances can emerge within the grammar and codes that make the terrain of the popular significant in peoples' everyday lives. As a site of struggle and possibility, popular culture needs to be understood not only in terms of its productive elements, but also in terms of how its cultural forms articulate processes through which the production, organization, and regulation of consent take place around various social practices and struggles at the level of everyday life. These processes can be elaborated through the category we call "the persuasive." In the most general sense, the term refers to the ways in which hegemony functions on the terrain of popular culture through a variety of pedagogical processes that work not only to secure dominant interests but to offer as well the possibility of a politics of resistance and social transformation.

The notion of the persuasive illuminates the insight that political power never works without an ideological mediation. For example, instances of domination and hegemony raise questions as to how domination is produced and organized within processes of motivation and legitimation. By introducing the element of persuasion—

that is, how ideological mediation actually functions as a pedagogical process—domination along with resistance can be connected to a broader notion of cultural politics in which the very act of learning can be analyzed as a fundamental aspect of hegemony. More specifically, the category of the persuasive in popular culture is important because it provides a starting point for understanding how the complex relations of dominance and resistance are organized and structured through particular pedagogical forms and practices. Theorizing about popular culture in this way helps to lay bare the practical grounds on which transformations are worked and represented through the important and related categories of consent, investment, ideology, and pleasure.

Consent is an important feature of the practice of persuasion. As the term is generally defined in radical theories of hegemony, consent refers to two somewhat different perspectives on how people come to be engaged within the ideologies and social relations of the dominant culture. In the more orthodox version, consent often refers to the ways in which the dominant logic is imposed on subordinated groups through the mechanizations of the culture industry. In the revisionist radical version, consent is defined through more active forms of complicity in that subordinated groups are now viewed as partly negotiating their adaptation and place within the dominant culture. As either imposition or negotiated complicity, consent defines the relationship between power and culture as nothing more than the equivalence of domination. We want to modify these notions of consent so as to illuminate its dialectical importance as a political and pedagogical process.

In our view, the notion of consent rightly points to the ways in which people are located within and negotiate elements of place and agency as a result of their investments in particular relations of meaning constructed through popular forms. At work in this notion of consent is the central question of what it is that people know, how they come to know, and how they come to feel in a particular way that secures for the hegemonic or counter-hegemonic order their loyalties and desires. This perspective is important as a political and social practice and as a framework of inquiry because it raises important questions about how the modern apparatuses of moral and social regulation, as well as resistance and counter-discourse, define what kind of knowledge counts, how it is to be taught, how subjectivities are defined, and how the very dynamic of moral and political regulation is constantly worked and reworked. The political implications of these insights for a politics of popular culture are significant and need further theoretical elaboration.

That consent is learned begs the question of what kinds of pedagogical processes are at work through which people actively rather than passively identify their own needs and desires with particular forms and relations of meaning. Unfortunately, the pedagogical issue of how people come to learn such identities and pleasures through particular forms of identification and cathexis has not been the central focus of study in most radical analyses of culture. Instead, radical analyses have often focused either on deconstructing the ideologies at work in particular cultural forms or on how readers organize texts according to their own meanings and experiences. In both cases, the issue of pedagogy has been subordinated to and subsumed within a rather limited notion of ideology production. The concern over ideology is limited to a particular view of consent in which the study of popular culture is reduced to analyses of texts or to popular culture as merely forms of consumption.[28] Ideology as a pedagogical process in this case is restricted to how meanings are produced by texts and mediated by audiences or to analyses that attempt to uncover how the market organizes needs in order to commodify popular culture.

What is particularly missing from these perspectives are questions regarding how cultural forms can be understood as mobilizing desire in a way that elaborates how such forms are engaged. For example, through what processes do cultural forms induce an anger or pleasure that has its own center of gravity as a form of meaning? How can we come to understand learning outside of the limits of rationality, as a form of engagement that mobilizes and sometimes reconstructs desire? These questions suggest that pedagogy is not so neatly ensconced in the production of discourse. Rather, pedagogy also constitutes a moment in which the body learns, moves, desires, and longs for affirmation. These questions also suggest a rejection of the pedagogy of modernism, one that serves up "ideal" forms of communication theory in which the tyranny of discourse becomes the ultimate pedagogical medium,[29] that is, talk embodied as a logic abstracted from the body itself. We need to reemphasize that the issue of consent opens up pedagogy to the uncertain, that space that refuses the measurable, that legitimates the concrete in a way that is felt and experienced rather than merely spoken. In this argument, we are not trying to privilege the body or a politics of affective investments over discourse as much as we are trying to emphasize their absence in previous theorizing as well as their importance for a critical pedagogy.

It is worth stressing that the relationship we are posing between affective and discursive investment is neither ahistorical nor ideologically innocent. Nor are we suggesting that ideology and affect as particular forms of investment can best be understood by positing a rigid conceptual opposition between meaning and desire. The cultural forms that mobilize desire and affect along with the struggles that take place over reproducing and investing desire, pleasure, and corporeality are constructed within power relations, which are always ideological *in nature* but which produce an experience or form of investment that cannot be understood merely as an ideological construction— an experience re-presented and enjoyed through the lens of meaning rather than through the primacy of pleasure and affect. Put another way, interpellations in the Althusserian sense are not merely ideological, they are also a summons to particular forms of pleasure, which are always historically situated but not discursively privileged. In what follows, we will argue that by retheorizing the notion of ideology through a reconstructed theory of pleasure, educators can begin to develop a pedagogy that offers a more critical possibility for addressing the purpose and meaning of popular culture as a terrain of struggle and hope.

We are arguing that the relationship between power and complicity is not framed simply around the organization of knowledge and meaning. The power of complicity and the complicity of power are not exhausted simply by registering how people are positioned and located through the production of particular ideologies structured through particular discourses. The relationships that subordinated groups enter into with respect to cultural forms cannot be understood and exhausted simply through what often amounts to a search and destroy mission based on uncovering the particular meanings and messages that mediate between a particular film, popular song, or text and its audience. The limits of ideology and rationality as the interests that structure behavior and move us within particular social forms are neither understood nor made problematic in this position. This position represents a basic misrecognition of the central and important role that pleasure (or its absence) plays in structuring the relationships and investments that one has to a particular cultural form. Colin Mercer emphasizes the point we are trying to make here:

> Barthes has it that 'ideology passes over the text and it's reading like the blush over a face (in love, some take erotic pleasure in this colouring)' and this signals something of the contemporary concern for the contradictory play of ideology. There is a general unease that, within the plethora of ideology analysis, which has emerged in recent years, something has quite crucially been missed out: that it may now be important to look over our shoulders and try to explain a certain 'guilt' of enjoyment of such and such in spite of its known ideological and political provenance. . . . Any analysis of the pleasure, the modes of persuasion, the consent operative with a given cultural form would have to displace the search for an ideological, political, economic or, indeed subjective, meaning and establish the coordinates of that 'formidable underside' (i.e., pleasure, joy) . . . because what we are really concerned with here is a restructuring of the theoretical horizon within which a cultural form is perceived.[30]

Drawing upon the work of Walter Benjamin, Roland Barthes, and others, Mercer has called attention to an issue that is central to a politics of popular culture. That is, he has focused on the ways in which consent is articulated not only through the structuring of semantically organized meanings and messages, but also through the pleasures invoked in the mechanisms and structuring principles of popular forms. The theoretical insight at work in this position is in part revealed through the question of why "we not only consent to forms of domination which we know, rationally and politically, are 'wrong', but even enjoy them."[31] The importance of this issue is made somewhat clear in the limits of an ideological analysis that might reveal the sexist nature of the lyrics in a popular song or video. Such a critique is important but it does not tell us or even seem capable of raising the question as to why people enjoy the song or video even though they might recognize the sexist ideologies that such texts embody. It is important to stress that an overreliance on ideology critique has limited our ability to understand how people actively participate in the dominant culture through processes of accommodation, negotiation, and even resistance.

In short, the investments that tie students to popular cultural forms cannot be ascertained simply through an analysis of the meanings and representations that we decode in them. On the contrary, affective investments have a real cultural hold and such investments may be indifferent to the very notion of meaning itself as constructed through the lens of the ideological. This suggests a number of important political and pedagogical principles. First, in hegemonic and counter-hegemonic struggles, the production and regulation of desire is as important as the construction of meaning. This means that the constitution and the expression of such desire is an important starting point for understanding the relations that students construct to popular and dominant forms. Second, the idea and experience of pleasure must be constituted politically so that we can analyze how the body becomes not only the object of (his-patriarchal) pleasure,[32] but also the subject of pleasure. In this case "pleasure becomes the consent of life in the body," and provides an important corporeal condition of life affirming possibility.[33] This argues for a discriminatory notion of pleasure that is not only desirable in and of itself, but that also suggests "at one and the same time . . . a figure for utopia in general, and for the systemic revolutionary transformation of society as a whole."[34] Third, we must recognize how popular culture can constitute a field of possibilities within which students can be empowered so as to appropriate cultural forms on terms that dignify and extend their human possibilities.

We realize that this raises enormously difficult questions about how, as teachers, we come to analyze a politics of feeling within sites that are at odds with the very notion of the popular. To make the popular the object of study within schools is to run the risk of not only reconstituting the meaning and pleasures of cultural forms but also of forcing students into a discourse and form of analysis that is at odds with their notion of what is considered pedagogically acceptable and properly distant from their everyday lives outside of school. At the same time, the popular cannot be ignored because it points to a category of meanings and affective investments that shape the very identities, politics, and cultures of the students we deal with. Subjectivity and identity are in part constituted on the ground of the popular and their force and effects do not disappear once students enter school. The political issue at stake here and its pedagogical relevance are suggested by Larry Grossberg:

> . . . It is only if we begin to recognize the complex relations between affect and ideology that we can make sense of people's emotional life, their desiring life, their struggles to find the energy to survive, let alone struggle. It is only in the terms of these relations that we can understand people's need and ability to maintain a "faith" in something beyond their immediate existence.[35]

In the section that follows, we will consider a particular Hollywood film as a demonstrative text in order to illuminate how the formation of multiple identities takes place through attachments and investments that are structured as much by affect and pleasure as they are by ideology and rationality. The importance of this cultural text is in part due to the opportunity it offers for further elaborating the elements of a critical pedagogical practice and our affirmation of the centrality of the body in the processes of knowing and learning.

Investment and Pleasure in *Dirty Dancing*

We have argued throughout this chapter that popular forms both shape and are mediated through the investments of rationality and affect. In attempting to make this observation more concrete as both a way of analyzing popular forms as well as using them as part of a critical pedagogical process, we want to take-up a specific consideration of the film, *Dirty Dancing*, written by Eleanor Bergstein and released into the North American market during the summer of 1987.

As we have stressed earlier in this chapter, the concept of popular culture cannot be defined around a set of ideological meanings permanently inscribed in particular cultural forms. Rather, the meaning of cultural forms can only be ascertained through their articulation into a practice and set of historically specific contextual relations that determine their pleasures, politics, and meanings. This position straightforwardly implies Roland Barthes' encouragement that "whenever it's the body which writes, and not ideology, there's a chance the text will join us in our modernity."[36] Thus our comments on the text of *Dirty Dancing* are not offered as abstract observations without an observer, but rather as a fully embodied account. The pedagogical significance of this statement should not be minimized. It means that when we engage students through a critical consideration of particular cultural forms (whether they be commodity texts such as films or lived social relations such as local peace or environmental movements), we must begin with an acknowledgement and exploration of how we—our contradictory and multiple selves [fully historical and social]—are implicated in the meanings and pleasures we ascribe to those forms. The interest here is not so much self-knowledge as it is the understanding and consideration of the possibilities and limitations inherent in lived social differences.

The following interpretation of *Dirty Dancing* has been produced through a recognition of our own investments in this film. This combination of reason and pleasure is organized not only by our shared work as educators interested in elaborating the complexities of a critical pedagogical practice but as well by biographies within which our earliest sense of social contradiction was formed within the juxtaposition of body movements, textures, timbre, and clothing. We have lived our lives within and against the grain of very different conjunctions of class, gender, and ethnic relations. But what we have shared is the shock, awe, and production of desire in confronting bodies that knew something we did not. For Simon, this experience of difference and desire was organized, in part, through being born to a marriage constituted across class divisions. Thus, the infrequent visits and family celebrations with working-class relatives and the more frequent moments when adult bodies—father and friends—[in the syntax, semantics, and very volume of speech; in the expansive gestures and use of space]—articulated forms of passion and pleasure suppressed by the detachment offered with middle-class rituals of politeness and formalism. For Giroux, the experience of having a different culture inscribe the body in terms that were at odds with one's own social positioning occurred when affiliations organized through high school sport led to hanging out with working-class blacks. Attending weekend parties, dancing to the music of black blues singers such as Etta James, and learning how to dance without moving one's feet made manifest the fact that the body could speak with a rhythm vastly different from that which structured the Catholic Youth Organization dances organized for white working-class youth. In both of our situations, our bodies were positioned within different sets of experiences and practices that embodied contradictions that we neither understood nor were able to articulate.

Unlike many of the teenage films that have swept the North American and European markets, *Dirty Dancing* locates the formation of youth within a material and social set of contradictory and conflicting practices. That is, this film does not treat youth as an isolated social stratum lacking any wider referent than itself. Questions of class and sexism, culture and privilege come together in a tapestry of social relations that emerge within the unlikely location of an affluent summer resort for the families of the rising class of Jewish businessmen and professionals.[37]

The year is 1963 and Frances "Baby" Houseman, her sister, mother, and father arrive at Kellerman's Resort for their summer vacation. We sense after a few moments into the film that Baby [who is soon to start a university program in the economics of international development and later plans to join the U.S. Peace Corps] is bored and alienated from the pleasures and pastimes of the nouveau Jewish-bourgeoisie who make up the majority of the patrons at Kellerman's. But we also quickly learn that Baby's idealistic political commitments to equality and fairness are just as surely rooted in the rhetorical discourse of liberal democracy historically embraced by her class (embodied particularly by her physician father). Baby is proudly introduced as someone who "is going to change the world" and do it with reason and intelligence.

Except for the college students hired by Kellerman to work the dining room, the hotel staff consists of young people whose experience and corporeality define a location across a solid class and ethnicity barrier that marks the landscape of the resort. Such barriers are familiar to us; we have been on both sides.

One evening after escaping the inanities of "entertainment night" at Kellerman's, Baby wanders the grounds and inadvertently discovers what to her is an unknown, astonishing, and mesmerizing corner of the site of the popular. What she discovers is the terrain of "dirty dancing," a form of music and movement whose coded desires and productive pleasures crumble what to her seem like an empty bourgeois body, only to reconstitute it with new meanings and pleasures. What Baby discovers at this working-class party is the overt sensuality of rock and soul. She learns what we have learned in that shock of displacement when one's ignorant body is called to new forms of participation that promise unfamiliar pleasures. She discovers in Barthes' words that "the human body is not an eternal object, written forever in nature . . . for it is really a body that was constructed by history, by societies, by regimes, by ideologies."[38]

The articulations between Baby's class position and the class location of the working-class help are first felt as differences of affective investment in the body. By placing her body within the terrain of working-class pleasures, Baby begins to feel and identify her body as a terrain of struggle, one that suggests a need to reject her family's view of bodily pleasure and desire for the more pronounced terrain of sexuality and bodily abandonment offered by the culture of the working-class help. It is through the sociality of "dirty dancing" that Baby first engages her own class-specific cultural capital and attempts to reclaim her body as a terrain of struggle through a redefined sense of pleasure and identity. For Baby, the body becomes the referent not only for redefining and remaking a sense of her own class and gender identity, but also for investing in a notion of desire and pleasure that reconstitutes her sense of self and social empowerment.

It is from this position of being amazed and attracted to a particular body of knowledge that the film's narrative begins to unfold. Baby is attracted to both the male and female personifications of the new cultural terrain: the dance instructor Johnny Castle and his partner Penny. As the story proceeds, Baby is transformed both by a new body knowledge and a new knowledge of her body and its pleasures. Baby seems to embrace the "abandon" of working-class cultural terrain, finding in it perhaps an arena of feeling and emotion that cannot be totally colonized by the expectations of rationality within which her identity has been formed.[39]

Baby learns that Penny is pregnant and that money is needed to illegally terminate the pregnancy. A "doctor" is only available on the night Penny and Johnny are to perform at a nearby hotel. If they miss the performance, Penny would most likely be fired. Deceiving her family (who places perfect faith in her reason and honesty), Baby obtains the abortion money from her father and agrees to take Penny's place as Johnny's partner. As Johnny begins to teach her the dance routine, their relationship develops.

Baby's substitution for Penny as Johnny's partner is a form of lived fantasy that works a reconstitution of explicitly who and what she is. As McRobbie has written:

> Dance evokes fantasy because it sets in motion a dual relationship projecting both internally towards the self and externally towards the 'other'; which is to say that dance as a leisure activity connects desires for the self with those for somebody else. It articulates adolescence and girlhood with femininity and female sexuality and it does this by and through the body. This is especially important because it is the one pleasurable arena

where women have some control and know what is going on in relation to physical sensuality and to their own bodies. Continually bombarded with images and with information about how they should be and how they should feel, dance offers an escape, a positive and vibrant sexual expressiveness.[40]

That Baby's investment in the dance of the Other is being anchored through affect seems clear enough from the often cliched dialogue. As Johnny emphasizes, "it is not enough to know the steps; you have to feel the music." And as Baby acknowledges as their relationship deepens: "I'm afraid of never feeling the rest of my whole life as I do when I'm with you."

Even in a setting so well defined to privilege the wealthy, the constraints of class and power move across the terrains of pleasure and work so as to lay bare the relationship between wider social constraints and the formation of differentiated class-specific dreams. In *Dirty Dancing* the desire mobilized by relations of domination runs both ways. Johnny confides to Baby, "I dreamed you and I were walking along and we met your father and he put his arm around me just like Robby [one of the Kellerman dining room staff who attends medical school]."

Baby's new investments, however, are not independent from the identity position regulated and organized by liberal discourse. Within the complications of the plot [when Johnny is falsely accused of theft], she acts on the belief that she can and should help those in trouble and less fortunate than herself, fully expecting Johnny and his friends to be treated with the same credibility and fairness as anyone else. When they are not, her naivete is shattered and the film seems about to conclude with an honest appraisal of the relations of class power. Even though he is cleared of the theft charge, Johnny is fired when Baby admits to their relationship. They say good-bye to each other and he drives off.

But screenwriter Bergstein was evidently unsatisfied by such a limited sense of possibility. Consequently, she closes the film with what can be either dismissed as Hollywood schmaltz or celebrated as a glimpse of Utopian hope keyed by the recognition of the importance of investments in the pleasures of sensuality. Johnny returns to find the closing talent night in progress. Confronting Baby's parents, he leads her on to the stage for a final dance performance that evolves into total audience participation. The film thus ends, magically erasing all social divisions [including the patriarchal one between Mr. and Mrs. Houseman] as all the assembled staff and guests rock and roll to the final dissolve into the film's credits.

This concluding scene constitutes dance as a collectivizing process within which individual differences disappear. Rock and roll, like religious singing, seems to deftly bind people together, uniting young and old, performers and audiences, white and black, the rulers and the ruled in an expression of celebration of the American dream in which the relationship between social power and inequality simply fades away.

What then does our understanding of *Dirty Dancing* display regarding the processes of persuasion? Our argument is that Baby's lived relation to the working-class people she engages is mediated by a dual investment mobilized by both the subject position she takes up within the discourse of liberalism *and* the popular cultural forms of working-class life within which she experiences the pleasures of the body. The emphasis here is how popular cultural forms are important in constituting the identities that influence how we engage new challenges and construct new experiences. In this context we are referring to popular culture as a field within which is mobilized a form of investment that is an elaboration of how any given cultural form (text, song, film, and event) is engaged. It is worth noting how important it is to be able to hold analytically separate both semantic and affective aspects of investment, since they can be mutually contradictory. Thus it is not uncommon to experience contrary investments in relation to a specific cultural text: for example, rock music can provide pleasure while being comprehended as very sexist and racist. Such internal contradictions are integral to experiences of guilt.[41]

Implications for Critical Pedagogical Practice

Everyday moments of teaching . . . incorporate the minds and bodies of subjects, as knowers and as learners. When we are at our best as teachers we are capable of speaking to each of these ways of knowing in ourselves and our students. We may override precedents in the educational project that value the knowing of the mind and deny the knowing of the heart and of the body. Students, the partners in these enterprises of knowing, are whole people with ideas, with emotions and with sensations . . . the project must not be confined to a knowing only of the mind; it must address and interrogate what we think we know from the heart and the body.[42]

While we are in agreement with McDade, it is important to clarify that when we consider the relationship between popular cultures and pedagogy, we have a particular form of teaching and learning in mind. This is a critical pedagogical form that affirms the lived reality of difference as the ground on which to pose questions of theory and practice. It is a form that claims the experience of lived difference as an agenda for discussion and a central resource for a pedagogy of possibility.[43] The discussion of lived difference, if pedagogical, will take on a particular tension. It implies a struggle over assigned meaning, a struggle over in what direction to desire, a struggle over particular modes of expression, and ultimately a struggle over multiple and even contradictory versions of "self." It is this struggle that makes possible and hence can redefine the possibilities we see both in the conditions of our daily lives and in those conditions that are "not yet." This is a struggle that can never be won, or pedagogy stops.[44]

What we are stressing is the absolutely crucial dimension of a critical pedagogy in which knowledge is conceived as an integral aspect of teaching-learning. As David Lusted writes:

> Knowledge is not produced in the intentions of those who believe they hold it, whether in the pen or in the voice. It is produced in the process of interaction, between writer and reader at the moment of reading, and between teacher and learner at the moment of classroom engagement. Knowledge is not the matter that is offered so much as the matter that is understood. To think of fields or bodies of knowledge as if they are the property of academics and teachers is wrong. It denies an equality in the relations at moments of interaction and falsely privileges one side of the exchange, and what that side 'knows' over the other.[45]

This position *does not require teachers to suppress or abandon what and how they know*. Indeed, the pedagogical struggle is lessened without such resources. However, within this position teachers and students are challenged to find forms within which a single discourse does not become the locus of certainty and certification. Rather, teachers need to find ways of creating a space for mutual engagement of lived difference that does not require the silencing of a multiplicity of voices by a single dominant discourse. Indeed, this is precisely the pedagogical motive in stressing that our account of *Dirty Dancing* must be seen as an embodied interpretation that provides an invaluable resource from which to engage lived difference as a possibility for critical dialogue and self and social formation.

What might a teacher need to understand in order to engage in such a struggle? What might she or he wish to find out? If we take popular culture as that terrain of images, knowledge forms, and affective investments within which meaning and subjectivity function, there are several questions a teacher might pursue. What are the historical conditions and material circumstances within which the practices of popular culture are pursued, organized, asserted, and regulated? Do such practices open up new notions of identities and possibilities? What identities and possibilities are disorganized and excluded? How are such practices articulated with forms of knowledge and pleasure legitimated by dominant groups? What interests and investments are served by a particular set of popular cultural practices and critiqued and challenged by the existence of such? What are the moral and political commitments of such practices, and how are these related to one's own commitments as a teacher [and if there is a divergence, what does this imply]?

What all this means is that we think the analysis of popular culture is not simply a question of "reading" off ideology from either commodity forms or forms of lived everyday relations. Rather, we are moving toward a position within which one would inquire into the popular as a field of practices that constitute Foucault's indissoluble triad of knowledge, power, and pleasure.[46] At the same time we want to raise a note of caution. The teacher engaged in a pedagogy that requires some articulation of knowledge and pleasures integral to student everyday life is walking a dangerous road. Too easily perhaps, encouraging student voice can either become a form of voyeurism or satisfy a form of ego-expansionism constituted on the pleasures of understanding those who appear as "Other" to us. This is why we must be clear on the nature of the pedagogy we pursue. Popular culture and social difference can be taken up by educators either as a pleasurable form of knowledge/power, which allows for more effective individualizing and administration of forms of physical and moral regulation, or as the terrain on which we must meet our students in a critical and empowering pedagogical encounter.

As teachers committed to the project of a critical pedagogy, we have to read the ground of the popular for investments that both distort and constrict human potentialities and those that give "voice" to unrealized possibilities. This is what the pedagogical struggle is all about—opening up the material and discursive basis of particular ways of producing meaning and representing ourselves, our relations to others, and our relation to our environment so as to consider possibilities not yet realized. This is a utopian practice both to be embraced for its urgent necessity and scrutinized for its inherent limitations, a sentiment captured by John Berger in his short story, "The Accordion Player." He writes:

> Music demands obedience. It even demands obedience of the imagination when a melody comes to mind. You can think of nothing else. It's a kind of tyrant. In exchange it offers its own freedom. All bodies can boast about themselves with music. The old can dance as well as the young. Time is forgotten. And that night, from behind the silence of the last stars, we thought we heard the affirmation of a Yes.
>
> "La belle Jacqueline" once more! the dressmaker shouted at Felix. I love music! With music you can say everything!
>
> You can't talk to a lawyer with music, Felix replied.[47]

Notes

1. For example, see Ira Shor, *Critical Teaching and Everyday Life* (Boston: South End Press, 1980); Paul Willis, *Learning to Labor: How Working Class Kids Get Working Class Jobs* (New York: Columbia University Press, 1981); R.W. Connell, D.J. Ashenden, S. Kessler, and G.W. Dowsett, *Making the Difference: Schools, Families, and Social Division* (Sydney, Australia: George Allen & Unwin, 1982); Michael Apple, *Education and Power* (New York: Routledge and Kegan Paul, 1982); Henry A. Giroux, *Theory and Resistance in Education* (South Hadley, Mass.: Bergin and Garvey Publishers, 1983); Peter McLaren, *Schooling as a Ritual Performance* (New York: Routledge and Kegan Paul, 1986).
2. Examples of this work include: Michael W. Apple and Lois Weis, eds., *Ideology and Practice in Schooling* (Philadelphia: Temple University Press, 1983); Margo Culley and Catherine Portuges, eds., *Gendered Subjects: The Dynamics of Feminist Teaching* (New York: Routledge and Kegan Paul, 1985); David Livingstone et al., *Critical Pedagogy and Cultural Power* (South Hadley, Mass.: Bergin and Garvey Publishers, 1988); Kathleen Weiler, *Women Teaching for*

Change (South Hadley, Mass.: Bergin and Garvey Publishers, 1988); Jay MacLeod, *Ain't No Makin It* (Boulder: Westview Press, 1988).

3. Exceptions include the work done in *Screen Education* in England during the late 1970s and early 1980s, and the U203 Popular Culture course and writings first offered by the Open University in 1982 (and only recently terminated). For example, see the entire issue of *Screen Education* No. 34 (Spring 1980), especially Tony Bennett, "Popular Culture: A Teaching Object," *Screen Education* No. 34 (Spring 1980), 17–29; Iain Chambers, "Rethinking 'Popular Culture,'" *Screen Education* No. 36 (Autumn 1980), 113–17; Iain Chambers, "Pop Music: A Teaching Perspective," *Screen Education* No. 39 (Summer 1981), 35–44; Len Masterman, *Teaching About Television* (London: Macmillan, 1980); Len Masterman, "TV Pedagogy," *Screen Education* No. 40 (Autumn/Winter 1981/2), 88–92; David Davies, *Popular Culture, Class, and Schooling* (London: Open University Press, 1981).

4. Both of these positions can be found in Theodore Mills Norton and Bertell Ollman eds., *Studies in Socialist Pedagogy* (New York: Monthly Review Press, 1987). A classic example of the privileging of knowledge in the educational encounter can be found in Pierre Bourdieu and Jean-Claude Passeron, *Reproduction in Education, Society, and Culture* (London: Sage Publishers, 1977); Rachel Sharp, *Knowledge, Ideology, and the Politics of Schooling* (New York: Routledge and Kegan Paul, 1980).

5. Much of the radical work dealing with the hidden curriculum fell into the theoretical trap of privileging social relations and pedagogical processes over the relations between knowledge and power; the most well-known example is Samuel Bowles and Herbert Gintis, *Schooling in Capitalist America* (New York: Basic Books, 1976); another example can be found in Robert V. Bullough, Jr., Stanley L. Goldstein, and Ladd Holt, *Human Interests in the Curriculum* (New York: Teachers College Press, 1984).

6. This issue is taken-up in detail in Henry A. Giroux, *Schooling and the Struggle for Public Life* (Minneapolis: University of Minnesota Press, 1988); Valerie Walkerdine, "On the Regulation of Speaking and Silence: Subjectivity, Class, and Gender in Contemporary Schooling," in *Language, Gender and Childhood*, Carolyn Steedman, Cathy Urwin, and Valerie Walkerdine, eds. (London: Routledge and Kegan Paul, 1985), 203–41; Roger I. Simon, "Empowerment as a Pedagogy of Possibility," *Language Arts* 64:4 (April 1987), 370–82; Michelle Fine, *Framing Dropouts* (Albany: SUNY Press, 1991).

7. The issue of the politics and pedagogy of emotional investment is developed in Larry Grossberg, "Teaching the Popular," in *Theory in the Classroom*, Cary Nelson, ed. (Urbana: University of Illinois Press, 1986), 177–200. For an exceptional analysis of the relationship between pleasure and the popular, see Colin Mercer "Complicit Pleasure," in *Popular Culture and Social Relations*, Tony Bennett, Colin Mercer, and Janet Woollacoot, eds. (London: Open University Press, 1986), 50–68; See also various articles in Fredric Jameson, et al., *Formations of Pleasure* (London: Routledge and Kegan Paul, 1983); Roger I. Simon, *Teaching Against the Grain* (New York: Bergin and Garvey Press, 1992).

8. For a historical treatment of this theme, see Patrick Brantlinger, *Bread and Circuses: Theories of Mass Culture as Social Decay* (Ithaca: Cornell University Press, 1983). This subject has been treated extensively and we cannot repeat all of the sources here, but excellent analyses of the theoretical and political shortcomings of left and right positions on popular culture can be found in Stuart Hall, "Deconstructing 'the Popular,'" in *People's History and Socialist Theory*, Raphael Samuel, ed. (London: Routledge and Kegan Paul, 1981), 227–40; Tony Bennett and Graham Martin, eds., *Popular Culture: Past Present* (London: Croom Helm/ Open University, 1982); Bennett, Mercer, and Woollacoot eds., *Popular Culture and Social Relations*. It is worth noting that a more recent version of left cultural elitism that disdains the masses can be found in Jean Baudrillard, *In the Shadow of the Silent Majorities*, Paul Foss, trans. (New York: Semiotext(e), Inc., 1983); Jean Baudrillard, *Simulations*, Paul Foss,

et al., trans. (New York: Semiotext(e), Inc., 1983). The epitome of cultural conservatism and hatred for popular culture, along with the class content it signifies, can be found in Allan Bloom, *The Closing of the American Mind* (New York: Simon and Schuster, 1987) and in various issues of the American journal, *The New Criterion*.

9. Max Horkheimer and Theodor W. Adorno, *Dialectic of Enlightenment* (New York: Herder and Herder, [1944], 1972) (see especially "The Culture Industry: Enlightenment as Mass Deception," 120–67); Theodor W. Adorno, "Television and the Patterns of Mass Culture," in *Mass Culture: The Popular Arts in America*, Bernard Rosenberg and David Manning White, eds. (Glencoe, New York: The Free Press, 1957), especially 483–84; Theodor W. Adorno, *Minima Moralia* (London: New Left Books, [1951], 1974).

10. Theodor W. Adorno, "Culture Industry Reconsidered," *New German Critique* No. 6 (Fall 1975), 18–19.

11. Horkheimer and Adorno, *Dialectic of the Enlightenment*.

12. Tony Bennett, "The Politics of the 'Popular' and Popular Culture," in *Popular Culture and Social Relations*, Bennett, Mercer, and Woollacott, eds., 15.

13. Examples of this tradition in the United States can be found in the *Journal of Popular Culture*. See also John G. Cawelti, *The Six-Gun Mystique* (Bowling Green: Bowling Green State University Press, 1984). For a discussion of this issue, see Stuart Hall, "Deconstructing 'the Popular.'" Examples of work that integrates history and theoretical analyses include John F. Kasson, *Amusing the Million: Coney Island at the Turn of the Century* (New York: Hill and Wang, 1978); Duncan Webster, *Looka Yonder: The Imaginary America of Populist Culture* (New York: Routledge, 1988).

14. Brantlinger, *Bread and Circuses*, 23.

15. For an excellent commentary on this issue, see Robert Scholes, "Aiming a Canon at the Curriculum," *Salmagundi* No. 72 (Fall 1986), 101–17.

16. Lawrence Grossberg, *We Gotta Get Out of This Place: Popular Conservatism and Postmodern Culture* (New York: Routledge, 1995).

17. This issue is taken-up in a variety of essays in Henry A. Giroux and Roger I. Simon, eds., *Popular Culture, Schooling, and Everyday Life* (New York: Bergin and Garvey Press, 1989).

18. See Antonio Gramsci, *Selections from Prison Notebooks*, Quintin Hoare and Geoffrey Nowell-Smith, eds. and trans. (New York: International Publishers, 1971); Antonio Gramsci, *Selections From Cultural Writings*, David Forgacs and Geoffrey Nowell-Smith, eds., William Boelhower, trans. (Cambridge: Harvard University Press, 1985).

19. Larry Grossberg provides a useful theoretical elaboration of hegemony as a struggle for the popular:

> Hegemony is not a universally present struggle; it is a conjunctural politics opened up by the conditions of advanced capitalism, mass communication and culture. . . . Hegemony defines the limits within which we can struggle, the field of "common sense" or "popular consciousness." It is the struggle to articulate the position of "leadership" within the social formation, the attempt by the ruling bloc to win for itself the position of leadership across the entire terrain of cultural and political life. Hegemony involves the mobilization of popular support, by a particular social bloc, for the broad range of its social projects. In this way, the people assent to a particular social order, to a particular system of power, to a particular articulation of chains of equivalence by which the interest of the ruling bloc come to define the leading positions of the people. It is a struggle over "the popular."

Larry Grossberg, "History, Politics, and Postmodernism: Stuart Hall and Cultural Studies," *Journal of Communication Inquiry* 10:2 (Summer 1986), 69.

20. By focusing on the relationship between power and domination on the one hand and consent and struggle on the other, Gramsci highlights not only the contradiction between the interests of the ruling bloc and the powerlessness of subordinated groups, but also the

contradictions between the choices that subordinated groups make and the reality of the conduct they live out at the level of everyday life. Thought and action, common sense and lived experience, become for Gramsci elements of a contradictory consciousness that should be at the heart of political and pedagogical struggle. Gramsci clarifies what he means by contradictory consciousness in the following passage:

> The active man-in-the-mass has a practical activity, but has no clear theoretical consciousness of his practical activity, which nonetheless involves understanding the world insofar as it transforms it. His theoretical consciousness can indeed be historically in opposition to his activity. One might almost say that he has two theoretical consciousnesses (or one contradictory consciousness); one which is implicit in his activity and which in reality unites him with all his fellow workers in the practical transformation of the real world; and one, superficially explicit or verbal, which he has inherited from the past and uncritically absorbed. But this verbal conception is not without consequences. It holds together a specific social group, it influences moral conduct and the direction of will, with varying efficacy but often powerfully enough to produce a situation in which the contradictory state of consciousness does not permit of any action, any decision or any choice, and produces a condition of moral and political passivity.

Antonio Gramsci, *Selections from Prison Notebooks*, Hoare and Smith, eds., 333.
21. Ibid., 350.
22. Bennett, "Introduction: Popular Culture and 'the Turn to Gramsci,'" 15.
23. Hall, "Notes on Deconstructing 'the Popular,'" 235.
24. Lawrence Grossberg, "Putting the Pop Back into Postmodernism," in Andrew Ross, ed., *Universal Abandon? The Politics of Postmodernism* (Minneapolis: University of Minnesota Press, 1988), 169–70.
25. Ernst Bloch, *The Principle of Hope* (Cambridge, Mass.: MIT Press [1959] 1986).
26. Mercer, "Complicit Pleasure," 59.
27. Pierre Bourdieu, "The Aristocracy of Culture," in *Media, Culture, and Society* 2:2 (1980), 237–38.
28. The emphasis on the study of texts can be seen most clearly in Roland Barthes, *S/Z* (New York: Hill and Wang, 1974); the emphasis on the relationship between popular culture and consumption is exemplified in Judith Williamson, *Decoding Advertisements: Ideology and Meaning in Advertising* (New York: Marion Boyars, 1978); Judith Williamson, *Consuming Passions: The Dynamics of Popular Culture* (New York: Marion Boyars, 1986).
29. Jürgen Habermas, *The Theory of Communicative Action*, Vol. 1, Thomas McCarthy, trans. (Boston: Beacon Press, 1973).
30. Colin Mercer, "Complicit Pleasure," 54–55.
31. Colin Mercer, "A Poverty of Desire: Pleasure and Popular Politics," in *Formations of Pleasure*, 84.
32. Laura Mulvey, "Visual Pleasure and Narrative Cinema," *Screen* 16:3 (Autumn 1986), 6–18.
33. Jameson, "Pleasure: A Political Issue," in *Formations of Pleasure*, 10.
34. Ibid., 13.
35. Grossberg, "Putting the Pop Back into Postmodernim," 179.
36. Roland Barthes, *The Grain of the Voice: Interviews 1962–80*, Linda Coverdale, trans. (New York: Hill & Wang, 1985), 191.
37. Two qualifications must be made here. First, we reject the notion that class portrayed in *Dirty Dancing* embodies a class nostalgia. That is, class formations in this case are not developed along representative ethnic and racial lines and as such portray class conflict in relatively white, waspy terms. Second, there is a complex articulation of gender differences in this film that we have not addressed. These represent an important subtext regarding the articulation of class and gender relations, particularly in Baby's relationship with Penny.
38. Roland Barthes, "Encore le Corps," *Critique* 35:425 (August–September 1982), 10.

39. The worst aspect of *Dirty Dancing* is its construction of the polarities of reason and passion as congruent with the class dichotomy portrayed in the film.
40. Angela McRobbie, "Dance and Social Fantasy," in Angela McRobbie and Mica Nava, eds., *Gender and Generation* (London: MacMillan, 1984), 144–45.
41. Larry Grossberg, "Teaching the Popular," in Cary Nelson, ed., *Theory in the Classroom* (Urbana: University of Illinois Press, 1986).
42. Laurie McDade, "Sex, Pregnancy and Schooling: Obstacles to a Critical Teaching of the Body," *Journal of Education* 69 (1987), 58–79.
43. Simon, "Empowerment as a Pedagogy of Possibility."
44. Magda Lewis and Roger Simon, "A Discourse Not Intended for Her: Learning and Teaching With Patriarchy," *Harvard Educational Review* 56:4 (1986), 457–72.
45. David Lusted, "Why Pedagogy," *Screen* 27 (September–October 1986), 4–5.
46. Michel Foucault, *Power/Knowledge: Selected Interviews and Other Writings, 1972–1980,* Colin Gordon, ed. (New York: Pantheon Books, 1980).
47. John Berger, *Once in Europa* (New York: Pantheon Books, 1987), 35.

III

Neoliberalism and the Militarization of Public Space

7

Interview

Politics of Radical Pedagogy*

Carlos Alberto Torres: What have you done in your life in terms of your formal training and the different positions that you've held as a teacher and a researcher?

Henry Giroux: I never intended to be a teacher. After high school, I received a basketball scholarship to a junior college but dropped out and then worked for two years in various jobs. Fortunately, I received another basketball scholarship and it happened to be at a teachers' college. I then went on scholarship to Appalachian State University for a Master's in history, and my education began in earnest because I was assigned as a teaching assistant to a professor who was extremely progressive and radical politically. I learned more from him than I did in all of my formal education up to that point. When I started graduate school in 1967, the country was in turmoil. It was a great period to learn about politics, power, and knowledge outside of the university. After getting my Master's, I taught secondary school for one year in a small town outside of Baltimore. The town was marked by deep racial divisions, economically and culturally, and the school was heavily segregated in the sense that very few blacks were placed in the college-bound track. I found myself confronted with an institutional and cultural register of racism that I didn't have a language to understand or confront. Tracking seemed so natural to me at that point that I did not equate it at

---

*Carlos Alberto Torres is Professor of Education at UCLA and Director of the UCLA Latin American Center.

first with a form of racial, gender, and class injustice. The experience radicalized me. In 1967, I became a community organizer trying to change the school. I worked in the black community for one year. And I got fired because of that— because I tried to democratize the school organization and the curriculum. So I came back to New England and got a job in a suburban school. Coming from a working-class background, I found it very difficult to work with students who were upper middle class, white, and extremely privileged. This proved to be a very difficult terrain for me to negotiate.

The school was in Barrington, Rhode Island. I taught there for about six years. These kids were on the fast track for academic and economic mobility. I certainly provided them with alternative ways of seeing the world, but the work just was not entirely rewarding for me. I was also getting tired as a high school teacher. The work was overbearing. It was exhausting. Moreover, I was starting to seriously study radical social theory. I felt it was time to move on and do something that would have a more profound impact.

CT: What were you teaching?

HG: I was teaching in the social studies department. The schools were experimenting with their curricula. I was given the freedom to teach courses out of the usual run-of-the-mill orthodoxy. I taught a course on society and alienation, as well as courses on race and feminism. My course on feminism garnered the attention of some right-wing fundamentalists in the community, and the school board held a public hearing because of all the furor over the course. The story made the local news and a number of right-wing fundamentalist preachers announced on their radio programs that a left-wing feminist was teaching in a local high school. The Right mobilized and managed to convince the school to take my class texts off the library reserve shelves. I didn't use the prescribed books. I would buy five copies of each book and put them on reserve. We were reading books you couldn't get through normal channels. Plus, I was renting films from the American French Service Committee at five bucks a whack. Even though I had to finance my own courses, it was a great teaching experience, but it caused quite an uproar in the community. My days were numbered after that.

Soon afterwards, I attended a conference on the new social studies and met a wonderful guy named Ted Fenton. I raised a number of questions at his conference and after it ended, he invited me to join the doctoral program at Carnegie Mellon University. He was a very gracious and kind guy, and in many ways helped change my life. He arranged a scholarship for me and off I went. It was truly by happenstance.

I got my doctorate in 1977. Soon afterwards, I landed a job at Boston University. My theoretical life took a very specific turn while there. It was a very exciting time to be teaching and studying critical educational theory and practice. The new politics and sociology of education were taking very critical turns. While attempting to take up a critical position on schooling and curriculum, I was enormously influenced by the work done by Herb Gintis and Sam Bowles, Maxine Greene, David Purpel, Jonathan Kozol, Stanley Aronowitz, and Michael Apple. Equally important was the critical work developed in the New Sociology of Education movement in England by Michael Young, Basil Bernstein, Geoff Whitty, Paul Willis, and others at the Cultural Studies Center in Birmingham. Such work was crucial in rearticulating a new critical discourse on educational theory and practice. Within a few years, I wrote my first book, *Ideology, Culture and the Process of Schooling*, which was a real initiation into the necessity of doing rigorous theoretical work. Even now, the book seems relevant to me.

I had an enormous number of students coming to my classes—50 to 100— while only 20 people would be registered. Students came from Harvard, Boston College, Northeastern, and they were all interested in the new work on social reproduction and schooling. The philosophy department was extraordinary, with many of the faculty doing Frankfurt School theory and other critical work. The excitement of reading critical work, having culturally diverse and highly motivated students, and being in the middle of a vibrant city was like a dream come true for me. I got married while at Boston University and life seemed a struggle, but it was good to us. Then in 1983 my life changed dramatically. Quite unexpectedly, I was denied tenure by John Silber, the president of Boston University. My tenure process was relatively straightforward. I was given an unanimous vote at all levels of academic review. At the university level, the vote was 13 to 0 in my favor. There were twenty-seven cases up for tenure that year and only three were unanimous. I was one of them. My dean told me he would resign if I did not get tenure and he publicly announced his intentions. I guess he was quite surprised when the provost informed him that I would not be given tenure, in spite of the reviews. In order to avoid any academic embarrassment, Silber decided to go beyond the normal channels of the review process and established his own ad hoc review committee, which included Nathan Glazer, Chester Finn, David Cohen, and others, all of whom were quite slimy. I chose one member of the committee—Michael Apple. The other two choices were out of my hands. Once the reviews came back, I had a meeting with Silber. He made the following offer to me: if I didn't publish or write anything for two years and studied the history of logic and science with him personally as my tutor he would maintain my current salary and I could be reconsidered for tenure. Of course, I declined and started applying for jobs, eventually landing one at Miami University.

CT: If my recollection is correct, Silber attempted to bolster his charge against your scholarship by referring to a serious mistake in one of your books.

HG: He had a copy of *Ideology, Culture and the Process of Schooling*, and he said, "I hear you're such a great teacher. Why do you write such shit? One of the reasons you're not getting tenure is because of this. Turn to page 34." Or whatever page it was. I'm thinking, "God, what is on this page that is so serious?" Then it dawned on me. I had ended a sentence or quote with a reference something like "Horkheimer (1965)." He argued that I should have put in the original publication date instead of the later publication date. I was flabbergasted. I said, "Is this a joke?" And he said, "No, this is what scholarship is about." Of course, it was a cheap shot, an attempt to make his case when in fact he didn't have one.

I later got back the copy of my book that Silber had used. The book looked brand new. He had only read and marked up the first half of the introduction. The rest of the book was unmarked and appeared to have been unread. Nathan Glazer actually admitted that he didn't have time to read *Theory and Resistance*. He just glanced through it. His recommendation to Silber was that I was fit to be a good high school teacher but not a college educator. This was more than simply two examples of meanspiritedness—it pointed to the kind of censorship the right wing was willing to exercise to restrict freedom of speech, especially as it applied to integrating intellectually rigorous work with social criticism.

My scholarship was so out of the ordinary that at the time my dean, Paul Warren, told me it was the strongest case in the School of Education that he had ever seen. Both of my books were widely reviewed and *Theory and Resistance in Education* became something of a standard referent in the field. Moreover, the fifty articles I had published were placed in journals of the highest academic quality: *Harvard Education Review, Educational Theory, and Curriculum Inquiry*, which was then a very powerful journal. It was a simple matter of being punished because I was a critical working-class intellectual on the Left.

I went to Miami University (in Ohio) in September of '83. It was a very traumatic experience for me because I lost most of my friends. I had to sell my house, and my wife had to give up a wonderful job, and, of course, the trauma caused considerable stress in our personal relationship. We had to leave a vibrant city and ended up in a rather rural, homogenous, semi-suburban, middle-class college. It was an alienating experience. It also marked the beginning of the second phase of my career, characterized by my being located away from the inner city. I don't particularly like living in rural areas or homogeneous communities. The urban context is really exciting and important to my psychological health and mental growth. I love public schools, urban students, and the excitement of cities.

So I found myself in this really remote town inhabited almost exclusively by a very conservative white student body. Ironically, Miami had a number of top notch faculty that were quite left and progressive—Paul Smith, Michael Ryan, Jim Sosnoski, and others. I was working with a faculty whose ideological beliefs were largely at odds with the climate of the town and certainly at odds with the student body. So we formed a very tight-knit community that had an enormous number of study groups. In that sense, Miami was very good for me.

Unfortunately, the place was too far-off the beaten path to attract good students. Moreover, I didn't have any resources to bring students in and give them financial support. It wasn't until the last four years of my career there that I started getting some very powerful students. By then my reputation had become more public, and there were people who really wanted to study with me. Stephen Haymes, Joe Kretovics, and David Trend came along with some students from Ireland, Poland, South Africa. At the same time, Peter McLaren joined the faculty and we started a cultural studies center at Miami. It was one of the first in the country. I brought in people like Stuart Hall, Lawrence Grossberg, Stanley Aronowitz, Ellen Willis, and others. Things finally started to come together during the last few years of my stay at Miami. I must also point out that I had a great department chair, Nelda Cameron McCabe, and a wonderful Dean named Jan Kettlewell. Both were enormously progressive and provided me with great intellectual and emotional support.

I would have stayed at Miami if I had received a prestigious university professorship. But I was denied it on the grounds that I was still too young. That decision convinced me it was time to leave Miami. I arrived at Penn State in 1992 and found myself in a very different intellectual and political context than when I first arrived at Miami.

CT: Tell me about the intellectual influences in your life.

HG: I had been heavily influenced by the work of Beat poets and writers, and by the work of James Baldwin. But it was Paulo Freire's work that gripped me theoretically, because I read him at that period in my life when I was a high school teacher struggling with the politics of education as part of my own life. When I found Freire's work, I discovered a language that I could use to give forceful expression to my own emotions, to the gut-wrenching feelings about the contradictions in which I found myself as an educator. Through Stanley Aronowitz's work I embraced the full range of neo-Marxist scholarship that was emerging in the United States in the 1970s. When I moved into the university environment, I think that the British sociologists certainly had an enormous influence on my work. And Richard Johnson, Stuart Hall, and the cultural studies group at Birmingham certainly alerted me to the changing historical and political conditions that demanded the need for a new discourse in educational theory and practice.

So, Paulo's and Stanley's works completely changed my perception of problems in education, particularly regarding positivism, ideology, the role of the state, and the politics and culture of capitalism. Martin Carnoy's work was also very important for me in the early stages of my work. Bowles and Gintis were enormously influential in my life in bringing to the surface the question of hidden curriculum. And the later theorists, such as Phil Corrigan and Roger Simon, were very important in my own self-formation. Antonio Gramsci increasingly played a prominent role in my writing, along with the work of the Frankfurt School. I remember publishing a piece on Gramsci in *Telos* as a young assistant professor and feeling it was one of the high points of my political journey. It was then, also, that I started reading, and became friends with, Stanley Aronowitz. He, in many ways, became my mentor before he became my friend. My own career and ideological interests have shifted in ways that parallel some of the shifts in Stanley's work. Once we became friends, many of the shifts in my thinking often came out of extensive conversations with Stanley.

Once I started teaching at B.U., my work radically changed. Existing theories of cultural and socio-cultural reproduction seemed too one-dimensional to me. Though I read Basil Bernstein, I was never highly influenced by his work. I thought his work was too mechanistic. He had an enormous influence on people like Michael Apple, Jean Anyon, and others. And though I thought their work was very important, it lacked a critical cultural politics. As a result, I found myself writing in opposition to some of that work and during that time produced *Theory and Resistance in Education*. After splitting with the social and cultural reproduction theorists, I was highly influenced by the cultural studies discourse that was coming on the scene in the United States around 1983. While at Miami, I joined in study groups with other faculty and students on Foucault and Derrida. This helped me develop a more dialectical theory of power, one that I could use to understand the limits of the functionalist model that was dominating critical educational theory at that time. Walter Benjamin was also enormously significant in helping me refigure my position in education, particularly his view of popular culture and the media.

At that point, I began to shift out of the reproduction versus resistance paradigm. I became more interested in schooling and democracy, reading Dewey and the social reconstructionists. There was little work linking democracy and schooling at that time, and there were very few theorists developing a language of critique and possibility. It was then that I began to develop a language of resistance and possibility. I wanted to explore the ways in which power functioned productively, how it could be theorized as part of a complex theory of agency, and what these issues meant for developing a theory of schooling, authority, and critical pedagogy. It was about talking about agency in ways that expanded the possibility for talking about hope as the precondition for agency. Feminism had a significant influence on my thinking, especially the work of feminist thinkers such as Chandra Mohanty, bell hooks, Michele Wallace, Nancy Fraser, Teresa de Lauretis, and Gayatri Spivak.

This was also a period when the postmodern debate exploded and I was enormously attracted to its more critical strains. Language, identity, race, media, postcolonialism, literary studies, and art were being refigured. And I found myself trying to appropriate critically from postmodernism its most critical theoretical contributions. Postmodern discourses allowed many of us to recognize and understand how the mechanisms of schools functioned around the legacy of certainty and control—concepts that were so much a part of the modernist paradigm. Postmodern discourses made it clear how racism is central to modernism and its hatred of difference. It put into perspective questions regarding how, as educators, we explain the school's fear of difference, indeterminacy, and its obsession with the notion of time that completely rejects the notion of space as a constructive force in shaping human relations.

As time went on, I became dissatisfied with the postmodern work because it increasingly was being depoliticized by people appropriating it as anaesthetic discourse. In order to recover the primacy of the political, I turned to cultural studies and found it much more interesting and suspicious, so to speak, of its own politics, while rarely compromising on its concern for specificity and theory. My recent emphasis on working with concrete texts was part of an attempt to refigure the relationship between theory and practice, and between the abstract and the concrete. It was also part of a theoretical effort to move more dialectically between the particular and a series of expanding historical and social relations when talking about power, ideology, and agency. It seemed to me that unless, in some fundamental way, you make something meaningful in order to make it critical and transformative, it would be very difficult to move students through the pedagogies we were attempting to use critically in our classrooms.

CT: What do you see as your key contributions to the debate on cultural studies?

HG: It is important to stress that I draw upon and work in a critical tradition to which many people have contributed. If my work has been selected by some as expressing, in a forceful way, that position, that's different than saying that I'm responsible for that position. I'm not. I was lucky enough to be writing about issues at a historical time when a number of important theoretical considerations were being debated and many brilliant people were on the scene. I would not have had those ideas if other people weren't doing it as well.

First, I tried to reinvigorate the debates in the 1970s around theory and resistance by challenging the notion that domination was so oppressive that schools could only be talked about as either prisons or total institutions in the service of oppression. It was an unproductive discourse, and, because it ignored any space for resistance or the complex ways in which power worked, I also wanted to broaden the relationship between schooling and society beyond class by reasserting the issue of general emancipation, and specifically the issue of democracy. Democracy as an articulation was capable of engaging class, race, and gender, but in a way that related them to the broader concerns of public life. I wanted to tie the concept of resistance not merely to the language of critique but also to the language of possibility, one that engaged what it meant to deepen and expand the possibilities of democratic public life. I also wanted to connect rather than separate issues of political economy and cultural politics. Cultural criticism and economic analyses worked on and through each other and any easy divide between them had to be refused.

Second, my long-time concern with the role of teachers as intellectuals has certainly been an organizing principle for much of my work. It underwent a number of revisions, moving from a concern with teachers as transformative intellectuals to the more political role of teachers and other activists as public intellectuals. This provided me with the theoretical tools to talk about public intellectuals as cultural workers who inhabited a diverse number of pedagogical sites, including, but not reduced to, schools.

Third, my work on popular culture made it possible for me to cross disciplines and write and publish in other fields outside of education. Popular culture became a central category for me in order to stress the powerful educational force of the larger culture and the rise and pedagogical importance of the new information technologies.

Fourth, I think my work contributed to a growing recognition of the importance of pedagogy in other fields, including composition, literary studies, speech communication, media studies, and so on. This is not to suggest that people were not doing important work in these fields around education, but my work helped bring a number of these fields together in recognizing the scholarly work going on in education. The first edition of *Border Crossings* was a very influential text in this regard because it was used and referenced by a great number of theorists across a wide range of disciplines. Hopefully, my most recent work on children's culture, cultural studies, film, and neoliberalism will have some impact on other fields as well.

I think my attempts to address the interrelated issues of the politics of representation and the representation of politics has made a small contribution to how the issue of difference matters as part of a broader cultural politics. This is especially true in books such as *Public Spaces/Private Lives*. In this work, there is a serious attempt to link the politics of difference to the larger issue of how to reinvigorate public life. And this is the fifth contribution, in that my work has always taken an amazingly strong stand for developing the discourse of ethics. Not an ethical discourse that makes a claim to some universal essence, but one that is provisional and constantly re-examining itself in the light of the historical conditions and contexts that we inherit and move within. That has always been a major concern of my work. I'm not interested in forms of relativism that simply collapse into an aesthetic discourse. I find that abhorrent. If educators can't address the question of agency and ethics, then we're in big trouble, to say the least.

I always took criticism of my work very seriously while at the same time trying to discern serious from irrelevant criticisms. And much of this criticism has helped me to reformulate a range of issues. Certainly, the move away from a strictly economistic position, the incorporation of a critical feminism, and the attempt to make my discourse more public can all be seen in the paths my books took. *Border Crossings* is a very different book from *Living Dangerously*, and both bear little resemblance to concerns I took up in *Take Back Higher Education* and *The Abandoned Generation*.

The Abandoned Generation focuses on the politics and representation of youth in the United States, particularly the demonization of youth and the more specific attacks on black youth in urban areas. I look at the false separation of entertainment and politics, principally as it is defended by the Disney Corporation, Hollywood filmmakers, and important domains of popular culture. I try to show how matters of race are utterly privatized in films such as *Baby Boy*. In *Breaking Into the Movies*, I examine critically the emergence of racism in the media, talk radio, and other public spheres and demonstrate how the larger media are anything but innocent and often work to demonize young people, especially minorities of color.

We need more work on how these new pedagogical machines are rewriting the texts of power and identity and how such texts resonate with broader public discourses about race, gender, class, and national identity. We need more work on the meaning and politics of democracy. The question of democracy strikes me as so central to what's going on in this country and what's going on globally. I also think that youth in this country are really under attack. Just look at the social policies being enacted in the 94th Congress and the effects they are having on the young and poor. Nobody wants to acknowledge this. Giving up on youth is tantamount to giving up on democracy.

These are two interrelated issues that demand a certain amount of pedagogical and political urgency. What are the implications of this—politically, pedagogically, intellectually, socially, culturally? And how do we begin to raise that question in a way that mobilizes people who do not just have kids in school but also are concerned about democracy and the quality of civic life? I'm very concerned about children's culture and how so few adults speak for and with children. I have three teenage boys and I'm very concerned about what they are learning, what they're reading, and how their own sense of identity and agency are being constructed within a culture that basically says they don't count because the future doesn't count. It is the relationship among youth, democracy, and social justice that will drive much of my new work.

CT: How do you relate to the notion of critical pedagogy?

HG: I've always felt that whatever contribution I made to critical pedagogy was very modest compared to others in the field. I associate critical pedagogy with the work of Paulo Freire. And I think that anyone who took up that field, in some way, had to begin with him whether they liked him or not. Regardless of Paulo's initial theoretical flaws, especially around gender, the fact of the matter is that he gave the term a political importance and international significance that it had lacked until his work appeared.

Paulo was crucial in forecasting a number of theoretical interventions, including work in postcolonial theory, cultural studies, critical adult education, literacy and language studies, and the primacy of politics in education. Moreover, his was a social and theoretical project, it was not simply about methodology or practice. Paulo's work suggests at least three important interventions: One, he exemplified what it meant to be a broader intellectual. Paulo was never at home in one place. Paulo's gaze around the questions of power and possibility cut across continents and borders. Second, he revitalized the relationship between theory and practice as an act of politics and struggle for social justice. Third, Paulo gave us a sense of what commitment was. Paulo was a provocateur who gave his life over to struggling for, and with, others and made pedagogy the central defining principle of how you take-up questions of agency, power, and politics. Paulo was, for me, a great teacher, a model of humility and inspiration. Many people have labeled me a Freirian, but that label is antithetical to everything Paulo represents. One didn't imitate Paulo, one tried to use his work as a theoretical resource rather than as a method, and this meant one had to be a producer of theory rather than one who simply implements other's theories. I used his work along with the work of others within a political project that was specific to my own context, problems, and concerns. At the same time, my work on critical pedagogy was inspired by the work of social reconstructionists such as John Dewey, George Counts, and others in the critical American education tradition.

CT: Paulo has said over and over, "You don't have to follow me. You have to reinvent me."

HG: We always, if our work is in any way worthwhile, are involved in translations when we use the work of others. We create something new out of the old. My relationship with Paulo has never been one of simply being imitative in any way. But certainly my work translates some of Paulo's work in a way that offers it up for another kind of cultural politics and another kind of emphasis that suggests the multifaceted way in which people learn from his work.

CT: You come from a working-class family. Some people have said, "Why have you drifted away from the key issue of class?"

HG: I certainly admit that my work gives less emphasis to class as a universal category of domination, but I never 'drifted' from class as a crucial social category. I think it is difficult after twenty-five years of critical work in feminism, race theory, postcolonialism, popular culture, and other areas to view class as the only or most important category for explaining the dynamics of social struggle. I never thought that class was an unimportant social determinant, I simply refused to believe that class as a category, or any other category of social analysis taken alone, could provide an explanation for everything. Moreover, those who did cling to such a position were often guilty of a kind of sexism and racism that betrayed the limits of their thinking. Is class important? Yes. Is it any more important than race? No, I don't think so. I think we live in an enormously complicated world. And I find myself being concerned about the inter-relationships among categories more than I do on the legitimate focus on single narratives such as class. But, I must say I have been disturbed about how class has disappeared from much of educational theory, especially under the ruthless emergence of neoliberalism in the last twenty-five years, and more importantly under the regime of George W. Bush.

CT: In the same vein, some years ago you and I talked about the claim that your work does not take feminism in education very seriously.

HG: I have written a number of articles dealing with the issue of feminism and have edited books on the subject, particularly *Postmodernism, Feminism, and Cultural Politics*. Of course, there are also some very important feminist essays in *Between Borders*, which I coedited with Peter McLaren. I am always a bit baffled by critics who claim I don't include feminism in my work. I can only assume that they are familiar with my early work but none of the books or articles I wrote after 1985. Looking back on that period, feminist theory and discourse was not as widely available as it is today. And I didn't think about gender as much as class because I was moving within the then dominant language of the Left. It wasn't that I didn't care about gender—I simply didn't have access to the language in order to rework my own identity as a cultural worker. Madeline Grumet, Maxine Greene, and a few of the British feminists in education were taking it up in the later 1970s, but at that time it was not a prominent discourse. I realized very quickly that there was an enormous gap in my work regarding gender issues, particularly in *Ideology, Culture, and the Process of Schooling and Theory and Resistance in Education*. After the latter book, I began to address the absence, and such work has played an influential role in shaping my own thinking and writing. I also learned a great deal from those feminists who refused to define feminism through a paralyzing binarism that simply appropriated the worse aspects of identity politics. Rather than engage in dialogue and foster a general notion of emancipation, a number of feminists in the late 1980s and early 1990s engaged in dubious forms of scapegoating and in some ways closed down the possibilities for a constructive dialogue about the relevance of feminist theory for a broader and more critical theory of education. Fortunately, a number of feminists and others have responded to this type of discourse and now recognize how unproductive it was theoretically and politically. It was a terrible moment in critical education theory and practice in which a very unproductive form of identity politics exercised a prominent, if not, almost fundamentalist, influence on many educational theorists in and out of the United States. From the perspective of 2005, these people appear as caricatures of a radical educational discourse and most of them have faded into oblivion theoretically.

CT: One of the criticisms you have heard is that your written expression is too obscure, wordy, and doesn't follow the rules of logic—like too many notes in a symphony. What is your response to the criticism that your written expression is not clear?

HG: There are a number of issues at stake in this question of language and clarity. First, there is the historical context. In the early years of my work, I was working through some difficult theoretical discourses, especially around the Frankfurt School, and the work of people like Georg Lukács, Gramsci, Marcuse, and others. Very early on, I learned that language is a terrain of struggle, and that the appeal to clarity often undertheorized important political insights regarding language's critical and rupturing qualities. When language is used to raise questions that have not been raised, or is struggling to name problems outside of traditional critical discourses, people will always feel uncomfortable with such a discourse. This is a price one pays for pushing the edge of language. It is not a popular place to be in and may cost one some readers. But when I first started writing, I thought it was important to push the rhetorical and theoretical boundaries of common sense for both the Left and the Right. Most people who read that kind of language are going to be uncomfortable with it because it's a new language. I made an attempt to bring a new set of theoretical concerns to the language of critical education, and the language that I brought to the field at that time was relatively new to educators. I have no apologies for that work because it emerged at a very specific historical moment, and at that moment it seemed perfectly appropriate for me.

Moreover, I never made a claim to be writing for the same audience that reads *Reader's Digest*. I knew that the people who would be reading that work would probably be relatively select, highly theoretical, intellectually engaged people who read those kinds of discourses. My audience, in the early phase of my career, was relatively limited. But that's the direction in which I wanted to work because that language was the most opportune vehicle for me to address the project in which I had located myself. As time went on, especially after the publication of *Education Under Siege* in 1993, my language became more public. I found myself then writing for a variety of audiences. I wrote for the *Village Voice, Educational Leadership, Cultural Studies,* and the *Educational Forum.* These journals represent a range of audiences and readers. When I write for *Cultural*

Critique, it is quite different than when I write for *Educational Leadership* or *Phi Delta Kappan*. It's an incredibly different audience, which induces different demands on language. So we have to recognize there are multiple languages and multiple audiences. Do I want to write like Frank Rich, a writer for the *New York Times*? No. That's not for me. Rich's public discourse speaks to a different audience than my work does, so there is no need for me to apologize because my writing style is less accessible. That's the practical, experiential, conditional, historical argument.

The theoretical argument is more complicated, but very important. In this country, the question of clarity is not one that needs to be a burden on the Left. The question of clarity is the burden of the Right because the Right uses clarity all the time to produce a set of images, a language, a discourse, a set of representations that promote literacy. They simplify to the point of ignorance. If you are really going to take the question of clarity seriously, as a political issue, maybe the question here is: What does the Left have to do to employ a language that demands that people struggle over that language without merely being passive voyeurs to a language that utterly erases history, complexity, and possibility? So, I'm very curious about why the Left has ignored that issue, in many cases, and focused on the issue of clarity as a way to attack leftists or radical thinkers or critical thinkers who are somewhat more complex. Also, it seems to me, the notion of clarity suggests that there is a universal reference for clarity. That's a very peculiar argument coming from people who write in English because English is a colonial language. I mean, it is *the* colonial language. Think about this. Toni Morrison writes in an idiom of black language, black vernacular. That's not a clear language. I mean, when you read *Beloved*, you're not reading standard English. So this appeal for clarity in some way imitates a colonialist logic because it argues that standard English, in its unadorned blessing, is somehow the privileged motif of intellectuals. I think it is sad and misguided, theoretically and politically, when leftist intellectuals argue for a notion of clarity that seems to suggest that there is some universal referent for understanding language, or that clarity is an unproblematic comfort zone where all discourses meet with an equally shared response. This position does violence to the multiple reading audiences that make up any society, underplays the importance of language as a site of struggle, and minimizes the political dangers inherent in an appeal to clarity that shuts down rather than opens up multiple spheres for different forms of writing and literacy.

CT: English was not your first language and you had to learn it to cross a particular border, to enter into the dialogues going on in another society.

HG: I had to cross a class-specific border; that is, I had to learn how to speak elaborated English because I grew up speaking and writing in a restricted coded language that was unacceptable in the schools I attended. You came from another language, but I came from restricted English. Language for me was about the body, identity, speaking to different audiences. I had to learn the skills of middle-class language usage to survive. My identity was on trial with this language. Hence, to talk about clarity without talking about one's identity is to subordinate the political issue of language, narrative, and identity to the procedural issue of clarity. Clarity doesn't tell me anything. Clarity is a false, bogus argument that often privileges the traces of colonialism, anti-intellectualism, and a refusal to deal with multiple sites of literacy. The appeal to clarity doesn't understand the political importance for a Carlos Torres, for example, to write for a variety of audiences and magazines. And the more people he can address in those different sites, switching, and translating and hybridizing his language, the more he fulfills his role as a public intellectual. I enjoy reading people like Homi Bhabha, Stuart Hall, Nancy Fraser, Judith Butler, and others who are theoretically complex. I have no intention of joining the clarity brigade and arguing that language should function to make people stupid, especially in an age when the "dumb and dumber" syndrome seems to be everywhere in the mass culture. But, at the same time, I have in recent years tried to make my language more accessible without simplifying my ideas. My books on Disney, youth, film, and neoliberalism are all published as trade books and are aimed at a more general audience. Oddly enough, I am now often accused of being *too* public in my work.

CT: Some liberal intellectuals have argued that the Left tend to be ideological and therefore tend to be less prone to negotiation when developing a position. What would you say are your politics and alliances?

HG: There are basically three sites in which my politics emerge. They emerge within the university itself and the struggles that go on in a university; they emerge in public life through my talks and through the vast number of meetings I have with people all over the country; and finally in the work that I do with others through some kind of collective project. My politics are grounded in my role as a teacher, writer, and public intellectual. So, the question for me is how does the political emerge in one's life in order to generate, legitimate, mobilize, create, and extend multiple critical public spheres that may contribute to a range of critical capacities, social movements, and political action that people might engage in to deepen and expand democratic relations within nonhierarchical forms of life. That's how I define my politics. For me, it is impossible to be a critical intellectual and not be self-critical, open to debate, and be willing *always* to take a position, but never to stand still.

CT: What can you tell me about your personal biography and the issue of power and higher education?

HG: One of the things that became very dear to me within a very short time was what I needed to do in order not to be appropriated by the university. How could I be part of the university and still be able to maintain a space of resistance? In some fundamental way you've got to learn how to work in an institution with one foot in and one foot out. If you have two feet in, they've appropriated you. You're one of them. If you have two feet out you've given up taking risk and offering resistance both within and against what the university often represents in its alignment with the most commercial and reactionary interests of the broader society. Of course, there are some people on the Left who consider working in the university or public education in general as unworthy of being significant political work. This is an entirely bogus and self-serving argument. The fact of the matter is that the university does reach an enormous number of people who have an impact on society, and I have no interests in turning it over to either corporate interests or religious and right-wing fanatics (all of whom are on the rise under George W. Bush).

Rather than abandon the university, the Left should take it seriously as a site of struggle and engage the difficult task of trying to negotiate that terrain, as much as possible to expand those rights and possibilities within that terrain while always grappling over what that university or institution actually does compared to what it might do. In other words, you really have to be, in some ways, an unsettling voice in the institution but never a voice that is so unsettling that you completely disempower yourself. So, you have to build alliances, you have to work with people. You have to know what the limits are for political work and constantly try to push the limits further. You have to know what to expect and what not to expect if you are critical and risk-taking. You have to draw a fine line between maintaining your own integrity and in some way recognizing that there are limits to what one can do in these institutions. These are not just strategic issues, but also political and ethical considerations.

The second issue is one of integrity. You always have to be conscious of the politics of your own location and the politics you have to employ to work with people out there. At some point, you have to focus on yourself, not just on fear, and ask yourself, can I live with this? And how can I, in solidarity with others, do more to link my political work in the university with the broader society? Have I compromised my integrity out of existence?

Third, it seems to me that you avoid working alone at all costs. I think that when you find yourself operating like some kind of romantic intellectual you are in trouble. The late Edward Said, to whom I am theoretically indebted, sometimes falls into this trap. He paints a picture of political work that is too isolated, individualized, and removed from collective struggle at the site of theoretical and ideological production. The intellectual is a figure who works in a community of people who give him or her support and nourishment. Cultural workers in any field have to find communities and social movements that nourish them, that enliven them, that work with them, that unsettle them, that question them, and help them grow intellectually, spiritually, and ethically.

Fourth, intellectuals have got to make some kind of connection outside of the university. Intellectuals need to cross borders in order to live and learn with others, to get a sense of what the struggles are that we teach about, represent, and engage. Finally, political work is about having a passion, feeling connected to the dynamics of social justice, and being happy with what one does. If we can't live with ourselves and be happy, if we can't find a sense of joy in what we do in the places in which we find ourselves, I don't think any notion of politics justifies the pain it often causes. I don't care how noble the cause is. I think that once you become dead spiritually, one is not very useful politically or pedagogically to anybody, regardless of what you believe in. If you're politically brilliant and enormously mean-spirited as a person, I think that the personal often cancels out the commitment to any notion of transformative politics. We often see such contradictions in people who are opportunists, in people whose politics seem to be theoretically correct but who are constantly badmouthing others on the Left or are caught up in the most egregious forms of careerism. Or we see it in people who have lost themselves in notions of celebrity and are no longer connected organically to anything but their own publicity machines. These people are constantly citing or interviewing themselves. Anybody who takes the role of the public intellectual seriously has to take risks, be suspicious of one's own politics, and be willing to take a lot of crap from leftists who assume the role of petty careerists. I think that you also have to be enormously sensitive to what it means to form communities and alliances of people who are also taking risks. You can't do this type of work alone. I think that in my own academic life I have spent far too many years in isolation by virtue of my getting fired, living in places that were isolated, and having few colleagues in the colleges of education in which I worked. Whatever public recognition I received came at an enormous toll emotionally and physically.

CT: In the formulation of educational policy in the United States, I see a reliance on instrumental rationality from a fairly technocratic perspective. How would you criticize this amalgam of perspectives? What kind of alternatives can we offer in education?

HG: It seems to me that there's a legacy of rational choice that is wedded to a kind of liberal philosophy that is central to modernist thought. We need to have the freedom to make choices about our future. Inherent in that argument is an emphasis on equality, justice, and freedom. These are not irrelevant principles. But what often happens in this argument is that it loses any attempt to formulate those considerations within a broader public discourse and is trapped in an utterly individualized discourse and set of market values. So we lose those ethical referents that celebrate not simply the notion of freedom as it pertains to the individual making his or her way through the world, but as it pertains to communities in which people have to understand their obligations to each other around ethical and public considerations. We need to reinvigorate the relationships among public life, social justice, and communities steeped in differences as a way of expressing freedom through a notion of the social.

The principles of social justice should articulate a notion of community that is far more democratic than the modernist, ethnocentric notion of community, which always saw difference as a threat to democracy and order. Differences need to become the basis for negotiation, for communication, and for the ongoing construction of democratic public life. Put another way, the central issue around rational choice is how we take the notion of difference, in its individualist paradigm, and reconcile that with the notion of democratic community. How can we remove choice from the narrow liberal emphasis on market values and link it to forms of empowerment in which choices without power and justice become meaningless or simply oppressive to large parts of a society?

The current fascination in the U.S. with the logic of the market and its absolute refusal of the notion of the public and social justice, along with all those principles that cannot be measured in merely instrumental terms, pave the way for the worst kinds of barbarisms. Where you have no ethical referents outside of instrumental rationality, you have no basis for distinguishing between consuming subjects—bearers of the market—and social subjects—those who actively work to expand the principles of democratic community and social equality. You have no way of translating, as Hannah Arendt and Zygmunt Bauman point out, private issues into public considerations. When you have no language of public life, the citizen has no way of inserting him/herself within traditions in which compassion, empathy, and justice become the overriding principles that define our individual and collective existence. And it seems to me that this problem has become more pronounced at the present time than at any other time in our history, especially under the Bush/Cheney regime. And so the question here is not what I think of rational choice, but what I think of rational choice theory or instrumentality within the broader possibilities for reinvigorating democratic public life.

CT: Do you accept the postmodern criticism that the philosophical perspective dominated by values like rationality, autonomy, and progress will be abandoned over time?

HG: I have always been skeptical of the way in which the debate around postmodernism has been framed. There is a tendency to either dismiss postmodernism because it is seen as apolitical or ahistorical, or to suggest that it falsely posits a break with modernism, and, as such, is antimodern. I think there are a number of theorists who politicize postmodernism, and here I am thinking of feminists such as Nancy Fraser and Chantal Mouffe, on the one hand, and social theorists such as Stanley Aronowitz and Doug Kellner, on the other. None of these theorists posit a definitive split between postmodernism and modernism. In fact, most of them subscribe to a distinction between postmodern conditions and new forms of cultural criticism that have emerged in the last twenty years. Within social criticism there has been a revolution of sorts in the fields of linguistics, psychology, media studies, and postcolonial studies, all of which can be linked to the changing conditions of modernism and to the decline of the old narratives endemic to a highly Eurocentric, linear, homogenous model of culture and progress. For me, these conditions do not suggest the rejection of modernism, nor do they suggest a definitive split historically. They suggest the emergence of new economic and cultural conditions that demand that we re-evaluate the central tenets of modernism and appropriate critically what is needed in light of such changes. I am not willing to give up on the political legacy of modernism with its emphasis on social justice, liberty, freedom, and equality.

But I am willing to argue that the social and aesthetic legacy of modernism has to be rethought in light of changing postmodern conditions. Certainly, in addition to the dwindling influence of the nation-state, and the emergence of new information technologies that shape the relationship between knowledge and authority in vastly different ways, there has also been the emergence of a kind of contingency, a hybridity across international boundaries that refigures the question of identity in ways that no longer link it to the autonomous notion of the liberal self. And we can go on and on. What many people are now asking is, "How might postmodern criticism help to interrogate and expand the democratic possibilities of modernism?" That is the issue that should be at the heart of the debate around the relationship between modernism and postmodernism and the issue of rationality.

Obviously, rationality cannot be eschewed. That makes no sense to me whatsoever. But rationality, especially instrumental rationality, in light of the Holocaust, Gulag, Hiroshima, and Abu Ghraib needs to be refigured in terms that take it out of the modernist infatuation with technology, efficiency, and progress. We need to understand the limits of modernist conceptions of rationality in light of these horrors and their legitimating discourses about history, progress, technology, and science. What are the limits of rationality when it makes an appeal to an enlightenment notion of progress that falls within a universalizing discourse and master narrative that is almost never suspicious of its own politics?

For me, the emergence of postmodernism, in all of its varieties, has been very stimulating intellectually and theoretically. It has brought with it a heated debate within a number of disciplines and around a diverse theoretical considerations. I see something very exciting emerging that can't be dismissed on the grounds that the only entry into such a debate is to call oneself either a postmodernist or a modernist. This type of binarism is very unproductive and doesn't get us very far. It is simply a canceling-out process or a strategy of reversals, with one category invoked in order to cancel out the other. I think that what this debate has done at its best is to draw attention to a world in which the old arguments don't work anymore. A new language needs to be formulated. For the Left, this suggests that the central elements of a nineteenth-century Marxism, whether they be around agency, domination, identity, ideology, theology, media politics, etc., have to be rethought in light of the changing historical and economic conditions we find ourselves in. This is not a rejection of Marxism—it is an attempt to appropriate its most useful theoretical insights while rejecting those that are no longer applicable or worth bothering with.

CT: What do you see as the consequences of the logic of the New Right and the new Republican majority in Congress for education?

HG: The rise of the New Right or, to be more specific, the market fundamentalists, the neoconservatives, and the evangelical Christians is tantamount to an attack on the very notion of public life and the democratic possibilities of difference. Any institution that can't be controlled through the logic of the market, subordinated to the ideology of the Religious Right, or privatized is seen as a threat to the new world order inaugurated during the Reagan-Bush revolution and in full bloom under the George W. Bush presidency. I see the new fundamentalism in the Republican Party waging a war on four fronts. First, there is the war against labor. Labor represents, to the Right, a real threat in light of its increasing drive to cater to the interest of the corporations and to reduce the logic of ethics to the dynamics of the marketplace. Second, there's a war against children. I mean, there's a racial and class war going on in this country in which it seems unfeasible, if not downright unproductive, to invest in children, particularly those who are black, Hispanic, and poor. Children have become the enemy, and in a society that values money more than its children, kids become an easy scapegoat for the country's social, economic, and political problems. Third, there's a war against any public institution that defines itself through democratic values. Any public institution that takes seriously the imperatives of social responsibility, ethical accountability, compassion, and civic courage is seen as a threat to the new world order. Fourth, there is an enormous threat against any cultural institution in which the conditions exist for intellectuals to develop who might offer an alternative critical perspective on what the world might be. This is what the antipolitical correctness movement is about. It sees social criticism as undermining rather than furthering democracy. Social criticism is seen as an excess of democracy, something that is not healthy to the ideology of right-wing Republicans, who see difference and dialogue as problems rather than resources to be used to nourish public life. Why the attack on public broadcasting, funding for the arts, and public schools? These are dangerous places that are not under the strict control of the private sector and the religious fundamentalists. And slowly we are losing these public spheres, and if the Right comes to power in the next election, we will have a real crisis in this country regarding what it means to live in and sustain a democratic society. This is truly about a crisis in democracy itself. One of the most serious issues is the way in which higher education is being turned into a site of training, being vocationalized if you will. This represents both an attack on critical intellectuals and an attempt to bring the university more in line with the logic of the corporations. Any pedagogical site that might be able to produce critical intellectuals is under siege in this country. While I don't want to sound harsh or overly deterministic, we are living in dangerous times, and I hope the American people can rise to the occasion to stave off this challenge to democracy.

CT: As a writer, you certainly have a particular method. What would that be?

HG: I do a lot of reading and I try to see relationships among ideas, gestate new ideas, and try to figure out how what I read will lead me to challenge my initial concerns or lead me in a new direction. I cut and paste everything I read. I figure out the ideas that matter the most, I take them out of an article, paste them up, and the go back and read them in their most forceful and condensed form. As I read, for example an article, I make insertions in the margins around ideas that I think are crucial to the article. These "organizing ideas" really represent the shorthand for gaining access quickly to the most important aspects of the article as I interpret them. I then duplicate sections of an article that contain the organizing ideas I have marked. Once I do that, I read the condensed version of the article again, take notes, and create a cover sheet. This provides me with a very quick way of reviewing a piece. It allows me to see relationships that ordinarily would be difficult to recognize. The most difficult part of writing for me is not the lack of ideas to write about, but rather figuring out how to develop a problematic in which to explore an idea and then how to sequence it. That is a real challenge in my own writing and one I take quite seriously. I can't write anything until I have figured out where I am going with a project, how I am going to develop it, and where it is going to end up.

When you have a lot of information at your disposal and you feel passionate about what you are saying, I think it becomes clear that the body is also a site of conflict and a terrain of struggle. How one links passion and information in this culture is a very political act. The body cannot escape its class, race, and gendered markings. For instance, a lot of people seem to dislike academics who are animated, use their bodies as they talk, raise their voices, gesture, and so on. I have often interpreted the call to be mild-mannered, to lower one's voice, not to be passionate about what one believes in as symptomatic of a dying colonial class, a middle class without life, passion, or desire. I often think that the people who invoke that criticism, unconsciously at times, are really celebrating a form of cultural capital that is institutionalized within the university, and that it's part of a colonial legacy. It is based on the assumption of class hatred, class divisiveness, and an unwillingness, in many ways, to recognize that different cultural capitals are affirmed in different settings. So, when people come to me and say, "I like what you said but I don't like the way you said it," I often say, "Look, this is not about aesthetics. This is about the question of class, the question of cultural capital. In your culture it may be a mark of privilege and acceptance to lower one's voice, appear entirely unanimated, etc., but in my upbringing it was a sign of affirmation to be passionate, to raise one's voice, to dance with an ideology." Paulo Freire used his hands and spoke with great passion—that's not about having an unacceptable form of demeanor. It is really about a cultural capital that is specific to his biography as a working-class boy growing up in Brazil and a revolutionary, and about the power of conviction in a person who doesn't separate his mind from his body. It's part of being alive.

CT: What is the role of your students in this process? How do you envision working with your graduate students in particular?

HG: My students have been for the entirety of my career, without any question whatsoever, the life-sustaining force that kept me going. I love my students, especially their energy, critical openness, and their ability to move in and out of different theoretical terrains. They have always provided for me an inspiration, and model of hope and learning. Students represent not just people you work with, they also represent a vision for the future. I am never concerned about the particularities of their politics as much as I am about their ability to think critically, to defend their positions, to be sensitive to what it means to address a certain degree of social and political responsibility for what they say and do. My own teaching is rooted in doing all I can to provide the pedagogical conditions that enable them to become agents, capable of governing and not just being governed, being able to take control of their own lives and how they mediate it with the larger society. If they adopt a left, progressive position, that would be great. But if they become critical agents in ways that question the pedagogy of their own self-formation, and link that with the ethical imperative to be able to define their lives in relation to others outside of merely instrumental criteria, I am satisfied. I plant seeds. And I hope that the planting of seeds will flower in ways that will eventually pay off for the students that I have and work with. It's not a giant dream; it's a dream in moderation. It's a dream with constraints.

8

Challenging Neoliberalism's New World Order

The Promise of Critical Pedagogy*

Introduction

Although critical pedagogy has a long and diverse tradition in the United States, its innumerable variations reflect both a shared belief in education as a moral and political practice and a recognition that its value should be judged in terms of how it prepares students to engage in a common struggle for deepening the possibilities of autonomy, critical thought, and a substantive democracy. We believe that critical pedagogy at the current historical moment faces a crisis of enormous proportions. It is a crisis grounded in the now common sense belief that education should be divorced from politics and that politics should be removed from the imperatives of democracy. At the center of this crisis is a tension between democratic values and market values, between dialogic engagement and rigid authoritarianism. Faith in social amelioration and a sustainable future appears to be in short supply as neoliberal capitalism performs the dual task of using education to train workers for service sector jobs and to produce life-long consumers. At the same time, neoliberalism feeds a growing authoritarianism steeped in religious fundamentalism and jingoistic patriotism encouraging intolerance and hate as it punishes critical thought, especially if it is at odds with the reactionary religious and political agenda being pushed by the Bush administration. Increasingly, education appears useful to those who hold power, and issues regarding how public and higher education might contribute to the quality

---

*Susan Searls Giroux co-author.

of democratic public life are either ignored or dismissed. Moral outrage and creative energy seem utterly limited in the political sphere, just as any collective struggle to preserve education as a basis for creating critical citizens is rendered defunct within the corporate drive for efficiency, a logic that has inspired bankrupt reform initiatives such as standardization, high-stakes testing, rigid accountability schemes, and privatization. Cornel West has argued recently that we need to analyze those dark forces shutting down democracy but "we also need to be very clear about the vision that lures us toward hope and the sources of that vision."[1] In what follows, we want to recapture the vital role that critical pedagogy might play as both a language of critique and possibility by addressing the growing threat of free market fundamentalism and rigid authoritarianism. At the same time, we want to explore what role critical pedagogy can take on in opposing these escalating anti-democratic tendencies and what it might mean to once again connect critical pedagogy to the more prophetic visions of a radical democracy.

Neoliberalism has become one of the most pervasive and dangerous ideologies of the twenty-first century. Its pervasiveness is evident not only by its unparalleled influence on the global economy, but also by its power to redefine the very nature of politics and sociality. Free market fundamentalism rather than democratic idealism is now the driving force of economics and politics in most of the world. Its logic, moreover, has insinuated itself into every social relationship, such that the specificity of relations between parents and children, doctors and patients, teachers and students has been reduced to that of supplier and customer. It is a market ideology driven not just by profits but by an ability to reproduce itself with such success, that to paraphrase Fred Jameson, it is easier to imagine the end of the world than the end of neoliberal capitalism. Wedded to the belief that the market should be the organizing principle for all political, social, and economic decisions, neoliberalism wages an incessant attack on democracy, public goods, the welfare state, and non-commodified values. Under neoliberalism everything either is for sale or is plundered for profit: public lands are looted by logging companies and corporate ranchers; politicians willingly hand the public's airwaves over to powerful broadcasters and large corporate interests without a dime going into the public trust; the environment is polluted and despoiled in the name of profit-making just as the government passes legislation to make it easier for corporations to do so; what public services have survived the Reagan-Bush era are gutted in order to lower the taxes of major corporations (or line their pockets through no-bid contracts, as in the infamous case of Halliburton); schools more closely resemble either jails or high-end shopping malls, depending on their clientele, and teachers are forced to get revenue for their school by hawking everything from hamburgers to pizza parties.

Under neoliberalism, the state now makes a grim alignment with corporate capital and transnational corporations. Gone are the days when the state "assumed responsibility for a range of social needs."[2] Instead, agencies of government now pursue a wide range of "'deregulations,' privatizations, and abdications of responsibility to the market and private philanthropy."[3] Deregulation, in turn, promotes "widespread, systematic disinvestment in the nation's basic productive capacity."[4] As the search for ever greater profits leads to outsourcing which accentuates the flight of capital and jobs abroad, flexible production encourages wage slavery for many formerly of the middle class and mass incarceration for those disposable populations (i.e. neither good producers nor consumers) at home. Even among the traditionally pro-union, pro-environment, pro-welfare state democratic party, few seem moved to challenge the prevailing neoliberal economic doctrine which, according to Stanley Aronowitz, proclaims "the superiority of free markets over public ownership, or even public regulation of private economic activities, [and] has become the conventional wisdom, not only among conservatives but among social progressives."[5]

Tragically, the ideology and power of neoliberalism is not confined to U.S. borders. Throughout the globe, the forces of neoliberalism are on the march, dismantling the historically guaranteed social provisions provided by the welfare state, defining profit-making as the essence of democracy, suppressing the wages of labor, and equating freedom with the unrestricted ability of markets to "govern economic relations free of government regulation."[6] Transnational in scope, neoliberalism now imposes its economic regime and market values on developing and weaker nations through structural adjustment policies enforced by powerful financial institutions such as the World Bank, the International Monetary Fund (IMF), and the World Trade Organization (WTO). The impact on schools in post-colonial nations is particularly bleak, as policy reforms financially starve institutions of higher learning as they standardize—with the usual emphasis on skills and drills over critical thinking or critical content—the curricula of primary schools.

Secure in its dystopian vision that there are no alternatives, as England's former Prime Minister Margaret Thatcher once put it, neoliberalism obviates issues of contingency, struggle, and social agency by celebrating the inevitability of economic laws in which the ethical ideal of intervening in the world gives way to the idea that we "have no choice but to adapt both our hopes and our abilities to the new global market."[7] Situated within a culture of fear and risk, market freedoms seem securely grounded in a defense of national security, capital, and property rights. When coupled with a media driven culture of panic and the everyday reality of insecurity, surviving public spaces have become increasingly monitored and militarized. Recently, events in New York, New Jersey, and Washington, D.C. provide an interesting case in point. When the media alerted the nation's citizenry to new terrorist threats specific to these areas, CNN ran a lead story on its impact on tourism—specifically on the enthusiastic clamor over a new kind of souvenir as families scrambled to get their pictures taken among U.S. paramilitary units now lining city streets, fully flanked with their imposing tanks and massive machine guns. The accouterments of a police state now vie with high-end shopping and museum visits for the public's attention, all amid a thunderous absence of protest. But the investment in surveillance and containment is hardly new. Since the early 1990s, state governments have invested more in prison construction than in education; prison guards and security personnel in public schools are two of the fastest growing professions. Such revolutionary changes in the global body politic demand that we ask what citizens are learning from this not so hidden curriculum organized around markets and militarization. As that syllabus is written, we must ponder the social costs of breakneck corporatization bolstered by an authoritarianism that links dissent with abetting terrorism.

In its capacity to dehistoricize and naturalize such sweeping social change, as well as in its aggressive attempts to destroy all of the public spheres necessary for the defense of a genuine democracy, neoliberalism reproduces the conditions for unleashing the most brutalizing forces of capitalism. Social Darwinism has risen like a phoenix from the ashes of the nineteenth-century and can now be seen in full display on most reality TV programs, and in the unfettered self-interest that now drives popular culture. As social bonds are replaced by unadulterated materialism and narcissism, public concerns are now understood and experienced as utterly private miseries, except when offered up on *Jerry Springer* as fodder for entertainment. Where public space—or its mass mediated simulacrum—does exist it is mainly used as a highly orchestrated and sensational confessional for private woes, a cut throat game of winner-take-all replacing more traditional forms of courtship, as in *Who Wants to Marry a Millionaire*, or as advertisement for crass consumerism, like MTV's *Cribs*.

As neoliberal policies dominate politics and social life, the breathless rhetoric of the global victory of free market rationality is invoked to cut public expenditures and undermine those non-commodified public spheres that serve as the repository for critical education, language, and public intervention. Spewed forth by the mass media, right-wing intellectuals, religious fanatics, and politicians, neoliberal ideology, with its merciless emphasis on deregulation and privatization, has found its material expression in an all-out attack on democratic values and social relations—particularly those spheres where such values are learned and take root. Public services such as health care, child care, public assistance, education, and transportation are now subject to the rules of the market. Forsaking the public good for the private good, while proclaiming the needs of the corporate and private sector as the only source of sound investment, neoliberal ideology produces, legitimates, and exacerbates the existence of persistent poverty, inadequate health care, racial apartheid in the inner cities, and the growing inequalities between the rich and the poor.[8]

As Stanley Aronowitz points out, the Bush administration has made neoliberal ideology the cornerstone of its domestic program and has been in the forefront in actively supporting and implementing the following policies:

> deregulation of business at all levels of enterprises and trade; tax reduction for wealthy individuals and corporations; the revival of the near-dormant nuclear energy industry; limitations and abrogation of labor's right to organize and bargain collectively; a land

policy favoring commercial and industrial development at the expense of conservation and other proenvironment policies; elimination of income support to the chronically unemployed; reduced federal aid to education and health; privatization of the main federal pension programs, Social Security; limitation on the right of aggrieved individuals to sue employers and corporations who provide services; in addition, as social programs are reduced, [Republicans] are joined by the Democrats in favoring increases in the repressive functions of the state, expressed in the dubious drug wars in the name of fighting crime, more funds for surveillance of ordinary citizens, and the expansion of the federal and local police forces.[9]

Central to neoliberal ideology and its implementation by the Bush administration is the ongoing attempts by right-wing politicians to view government as the enemy of freedom (except when it aids big business) and discount it as a guardian of the public interest. The call to eliminate big government is neoliberalism's grand unifying idea and has broad popular appeal in the United States because it is a principle deeply embedded in the country's history and tangled up with its notion of political freedom— not to mention the endless appeal of its clarion call to cut taxes. And yet, the right-wing appropriation of this tradition is wracked with contradictions, as they outspend their democratic rivals, drive up deficits, and expand—not shrink—the largely repressive arm of big government's counter-terrorism-military-surveillance-intelligence complex.

Indeed neoliberals have attacked what they call big government when it has provided crucial safety nets for the poor and dispossessed, but they have no qualms about using the government to bail out the airline industry after the economic nosedive that followed the 2000 election of George W. Bush and the events of September 11, 2001. Nor are there any expressions of outrage from free market cheerleaders when the state engages in promoting various forms of corporate welfare by providing billions of dollars in direct and indirect subsidies to multinational corporations. In short, the current government responds not to citizens, but to citizens with money, bearing no obligation for the swelling ranks of the poor or for the collective future of young people.

The liberal democratic lexicon of rights, entitlements, social provisions, community, social responsibility, living wage, job security, equality, and justice seem oddly out of place in a country where the promise of democracy—and the institutions necessary for its survival over generations—have been gutted, replaced by casino capitalism, a winner-take-all philosophy suited to lottery players and day traders alike. As corporate culture extends even deeper into the basic institutions of civil and political society, buttressed daily by a culture industry in the hands of a few media giants, free market ideology is reinforced even further by the pervasive fear and insecurity of the public, who have little accessibility to countervailing ideas and believe that the future holds nothing beyond a watered down version of the present. As the prevailing discourse of neoliberalism seizes the public imagination, there is no vocabulary for progressive social change, democratically inspired visions, critical notions of social agency, or the kinds of institutions that expand the meaning and purpose of democratic public life. In the vacuum left by diminishing democracy, a new kind of authoritarianism steeped in religious zealotry, cultural chauvinism, xenophobia, and racism has furnished the dominant tropes of neoconservatives and other extremist groups eager to take advantage of the growing insecurity, fear, and anxiety that result from increased joblessness, the war on terror, and the unravelling of communities.

As a result of the consolidated corporate attack on public life, the maintenance of democratic public spheres from which to launch a moral vision or to engage in a viable struggle over institutions and political vision loses all credibility—as well as monetary support. As the alleged wisdom and common sense of neoliberal ideology remains largely unchallenged within dominant pseudo-public spheres, individual critique and collective political struggles become more difficult.[10] Dominated by extremists, the Bush administration is driven by an arrogance of power and an inflated sense of moral righteousness mediated largely by a false sense of certitude and never ending posture of triumphalism. As George Soros points out, this rigid ideology and inflexible sense of mission allows the Bush administration to believe that "because we are stronger than others, we must know better and we must have right on our side. This is where religious fundamentalism comes together with market fundamentalism to form the ideology of supremacy."[11]

II

As public space is increasingly commodified and the state becomes more closely aligned with capital, politics is defined largely by its policing functions rather than an agency for peace and social reform. As the state abandons its social investments in health, education, and the public welfare, it increasingly takes on the functions of an enhanced security or police state, the signs of which are most visible in the increasing use of the state apparatus to spy on and arrest its subjects, the incarceration of individuals considered disposable (primarily people of color), and the ongoing criminalization of social policies. Nowhere is this more visible than in the nation's schools. Part of the reason for this continuous crisis in U.S. public schooling lies in federal cuts in education, ongoing since the Reagan administration. The stated rationale for such a shift in national priorities is that U.S. public schools are bureaucratic, wasteful, and altogether ineffectual—the result of a "big government" monopoly on education. As a result of such inefficiency, the public school system poses a threat to national security and U.S. economic dominance in the world market. To be sure, some public schools are really ailing, but the reasons for this, according to David Berliner and Bruce Biddle, authors of *The Manufactured Crisis*, have to do with the grossly unequal funding of public education, residential segregation, the astonishingly high poverty rates of U.S. school children relative to most other industrialized nations, coupled with inadequate health care and social services. Preferring the former diagnosis of general ineptitude, the current administration insists that throwing money at schools will not cure public school ills and will no longer be tolerated.

Rather than address the complexity of educational inequalities disproportionately impacting poor and minority students, the George W. Bush administration sought solutions to troubled public schools in the much-touted No Child Left Behind (NCLB) legislation, which afforded certain key advantages to constituencies in favor of privatization, all the while appearing sympathetic to the plight of poor and minority youth. Not only do they maintain the advantages accorded white students who per-form better on average than black and Latino students on standardized tests, but the proposed school reforms were also very business friendly. Renamed No Child Left Untested by critics, the reform places high priority on accountability, tying what little federal monies schools receive to improve test performance. For additional financial support, public schools are left no other meaningful option than engaging in public/private partnerships, like the highly-publicized deals cut with soft drink giants providing schools with needed revenue in exchange for soda machines in cafeterias. And, clearly, media giants who own the major publishing houses will benefit from the 52 million strong market of public school students now required to take tests every year from the third grade on. The impact of NCLB also proved highly televisable, visibility now being a key factor in the art of persuading a public weaned from political debate in favor of the spectacle. Thus, the media provides routine reportage of school districts' grade cards, public—often monetary—rewards given to those schools that score high marks on achievement tests, liquidization of those that do not. Media preoccupation with school safety issues, moreover, ensured highly publicized expulsion, sometimes felony incarceration, of troublemakers, typically students of color. In short, accountability for teachers and administrators and zero tolerance for students who commit even the most minor infractions are the new educational imperatives. All of which demonstrates that the federal government is "doing something" to assuage public fears about the nation's schools that it largely created through financial deprivation and policies favoring resegregation. As a result, in accordance with NCLB, financially strapped schools spend precious resources on either testing, prep materials, or new safety measures, such as metal detectors, armed guards, security cameras, fencing. In addition to draining public schools financially, both high stakes testing and zero tolerance policies have served to push out or kick out black and Latino youth in disproportionate numbers, as has been extensively documented by Henry Giroux in *The Abandoned Generation*, William Ayers et al. in *Zero Tolerance*, and Gary Orfield and Mindy Kornhaber in *Raising Standards or Raising Barriers?* As democracy becomes a burden under the reign of neoliberalism, civic discourse disappears and the reign of a growing authoritarianism in which politics is translated into unquestioning allegiance to authority and secular education is dis-dained as a violation of God's law.

Market fundamentalism increasingly appears at odds with any viable notion of critical education, and appears even more ominous as it aligns itself with the ideologies of militarism and religious fundamentalism. The democratic character of critical pedagogy is defined largely through a set of basic assumptions, which holds that knowledge, power, values, and institutions must be made available to critical scrutiny, be understood as a product of human labor (as opposed to God-given), and evaluated in terms of how they might open up or close down democratic practices and experiences. Yet, critical pedagogy is about more than simply holding authority accountable through the close reading of texts, the creation of radical classroom practices, or the promotion of critical literacy. It is also about linking learning to social change, education to democracy, and knowledge to acts of intervention in public life. Critical pedagogy encourages students to learn to register dissent, as well as to take risks in creating the conditions for forms of individual and social agency that are conducive to a substantive democracy. Part of the challenge of any critical pedagogy is making schools and other sites of pedagogy safe from the baneful influence of market logics—ranging from the discourses of privatization and consumerism, the methodologies of standardization and accountability, and new disciplinary techniques of surveillance, expulsion and incarceration aimed at the throwaways of global capital, principally poor youth and youth of color. Taking up such a radical challenge to democratic principles and practices means that educators need to rethink the important presupposition that public education cannot be separated from the imperatives of a nonrepressive and inclusive democratic order and that the crisis of public education must be understood as part of the wider crisis of politics, power, and culture. Recognizing the inextricable link between education and politics is central to reclaiming the sanctity of public education as a democratic public sphere, necessarily free of the slick come-ons of corporate advertisers or for that matter, JROTC. Central, too, is the recognition that politics cannot be separated from the pedagogical force of culture. Pedagogy should provide the theoretical tools and resources necessary for understanding how culture works as an educational force, how public education connects to other sites of pedagogy, and how identity, citizenship, and agency are organized through pedagogical relations and practices. Rather than viewed as a technical method, pedagogy must be understood as a moral and political practice that always presupposes particular renditions of what constitutes legitimate knowledge, values, citizenship, modes of understanding, and views of the future.

Moreover, pedagogy as a critical practice should provide the classroom conditions that offer the knowledge, skills, and culture of questioning necessary for students to engage in critical dialogue with the past, question authority and its effects, struggle with ongoing relations of power, and prepare themselves for what it means to be critically active citizens in the interrelated local, national, and global public spheres. Of course, acknowledging that pedagogy is political because it is always tangled up with power, ideologies, and the acquisition of agency does not mean that it is by default propagandistic, closed, dogmatic, or uncritical of its own authority. Most importantly, any viable notion of critical pedagogy must demonstrate there is a difference between critical pedagogical practices and propagandizing, critical teaching and demagoguery. Such a pedagogy should be open and discerning, fused with a spirit of inquiry that fosters rather than mandates critical modes of individual and social agency.

We believe that if public education is a crucial sphere for creating citizens equipped to exercise their freedoms and competent to question the basic assumptions that govern democratic political life, teachers in both public schools and higher education will have to assume their responsibility as citizen-scholars by taking critical positions, relating their work to larger social issues, offering students knowledge, debate and dialogue about pressing social problems, and providing the conditions for students to have hope and to believe that civic life matters, that they *can* make a difference in shaping it so as to expand its democratic possibilities for all groups. It means taking positions and engaging in practices currently at odds with both religious fundamentalism and neoliberal ideology. Educators now face the daunting challenge of creating new discourses, pedagogies, and collective strategies that will offer students the hope and tools necessary to revive the culture of politics as an ethical response to the demise of democratic public life. Such a challenge suggests struggling to keep alive those institutional spaces, forums, and public spheres that support and defend critical education, help students come to terms with their own power as individual and social agents to exercise civic courage, and to engage in community projects and research that are socially responsible, while refusing to surrender knowledge and skills to the highest bidder. In part, this requires pedagogical practices that connect the space of language, culture, and identity to their deployment in larger physical and social spaces. Such a pedagogy is based on the presupposition that it is not enough to teach students to break with accepted ideas. Students must also learn to directly confront the threat from fundamentalisms of all varieties that seek to turn democracy into a mall, a sectarian church, or a wing of the coming carceral state, a set of options that must be understood as an assault on democracy.

There are those critics who in tough economic times insist that providing students with anything other than work skills threatens their future viability in the job market. While we believe that public education should equip students with skills to enter the workplace, it should also educate them to contest workplace inequalities, imagine democratically organized forms of work, and identify and challenge those injustices that contradict and undercut the most fundamental principles of freedom, equality, and respect for all people who constitute the global public sphere. Public education is about more than job preparation or even critical consciousness raising; it is also about imagining different futures and politics as a form of intervention into public life. In contrast to the cynicism and political withdrawal that media culture fosters, a critical education demands that its citizens be able to translate the interface of private considerations and public issues, be able to recognize those anti-democratic forces that deny social, economic, and political justice, and be willing to give some thought to their experiences as a matter of anticipating and struggling for a better world. In short, democratic rather than commercial values should be the primary concerns of both public education and the university.

If right-wing reforms in public education continue unchallenged, the consequences will reflect a society in which a highly-trained, largely white elite will command the techno-information revolution while a vast, low-skilled majority of poor and minority workers will be relegated to filling the McJobs proliferating in the service sector. In contrast to this vision, we strongly believe that genuine, critical education cannot be confused with job training. If educators and others are to prevent this distinction from becoming blurred, it is crucial to challenge the ongoing corporatization of public schools while upholding the promise of the modern social contract in which all youth, guaranteed the necessary protections and opportunities, were a primary source of economic and moral investment, symbolizing the hope for a democratic future. In short, we need to recapture our commitment to future generations by taking seriously the Protestant theologian Dietrich Bonhoeffer's belief that the ultimate test of morality for any democratic society resides in the condition of its children. If public education is to honor this ethical commitment, it will have to not only re-establish its obligation to young people, but reclaim its role as a democratic public sphere.

Our insistence on the promise of critical pedagogy is not a call for any one ideology on the political spectrum to determine the future direction of public and university education. But at the same time, it reflects a particular vision of the purpose and meaning of public and higher education and the crucial role of pedagogy in educating students to participate in an inclusive democracy. Critical pedagogy is an ethical referent and a call to action for educators, parents, students, and others to reclaim public education as a democratic public sphere, a place where teaching is *not* reduced to either learning how to master tests or to acquire low-level jobs skills, but a safe space where reason, understanding, dialogue, and critical engagement are available to all faculty and students. Public education, in this reading, becomes a site of ongoing struggle to preserve and extend the conditions in which autonomy of judgment and freedom of action are informed by the democratic imperatives of equality, liberty, and justice. Public education has always, though within damaged traditions and burdened forms, served as a symbolic and concrete reminder that the struggle for democracy is, in part, an attempt to liberate humanity from the blind obedience to authority and that individual and social agency gain meaning primarily through the freedoms guaranteed by the public sphere, where the autonomy of individuals only becomes meaningful under those conditions that guarantee the workings of an autonomous society. Critical pedagogy is a reminder that the educational conditions that make democratic identities, values, and politics possible and effective have to be fought for more urgently at a time when democratic public spheres, public goods, and public spaces are under attack by market and other ideological fundamentalists who either believe that powerful corporations can solve all human problems or that dissent is comparable to aiding terrorists—positions that share the common denominator of disabling a substantive notion of ethics, politics, and democracy.

We live in very dark times, yet as educators, parents, activists, and workers, we can address the current assault on democracy by building local and global alliances and engaging in struggles that acknowledge and transcend national boundaries, while demonstrating how these intersect with people's everyday lives. Democratic struggles cannot underemphasize the special responsibility of intellectuals to shatter the conventional wisdom and myths of neoliberalism with its stunted definition of freedom and its depoliticized and dehistoricized definition of its own alleged inevitability. As the late Pierre Bourdieu argued, any viable politics that challenges neoliberalism must refigure the role of the state in limiting the excesses of capital and providing important social provisions.[12] In particular, social movements must address the crucial issue of education as it develops both formally and informally throughout the cultural sphere because the "power of the dominant order is not just economic, but intellectual—lying in the realm of beliefs," and it is precisely within the domain of ideas that a sense of utopian possibility can be restored to the public realm.[13] Pedagogy in this instance is not simply about critical thinking but also about social engagement, a crucial element of not just learning and social engagement but politics itself. Most specifically, democracy necessitates forms of education and critical pedagogical practices that provide a new ethic of freedom and a reassertion of collective identity as central preoccupations of a vibrant democratic culture and society. Such a task, in part, suggests that intellectuals, artists, unions, and other progressive individuals and movements create teach-ins all over the country in order to name, critique, and connect the forces of market fundamentalism to the war at home and abroad, the shameful tax cuts for the rich, the dismantling of the welfare state, the attack on unions, the erosion of civil liberties, the incarceration of a generation of young black and brown men and women, the attack on public schools, and the growing militarization of public life. As the Bush administration spreads its legacy of war, destruction, poverty, and violence across the globe, the time has come to link matters of economics with the crisis of political culture, and to connect the latter to the crisis of democracy itself. We need a new language for politics in the global public sphere; we need a new understanding for analyzing what agents can bring it into being and where such struggles can take place. Most significantly, we need a new understanding of what it means to mobilize various alliances to reclaim hope in dark times. We need a language in which, as Zygmunt Bauman points out, we recognize that the real pessimism is quietism—falsely believing in not doing anything because nothing can be changed and that we become part of a just society when we recognize that not only is a moral person someone who does not think he or she is moral enough, but that a just society is one that believes "that there is not enough justice in our society."[14]

Notes

1. Cornel West, "Finding Hope in Dark Times," *Tikkun* 19:4 (2004), 18.

2. George Steinmetz, The State of Emergency and the Revival of American Imperialism; Toward an Authoritarian Post-Fordism, *Public Culture* 15:2 (Spring 2003), 337.

3. Ibid., 337.

4. Barry Bluestone and Bennett Harrison, *The Deindustrialization of America: Plant Closings, Community Abandonment and the Dismantling of Basic Industry* (New York: Basic Books, 1982), 6

5. Stanley Aronowitz, *How Class Works* (New Haven: Yale University Press, 2003), 21.

6. Ibid., 101.

7. Stanley Aronowitz, "Introduction," in Paulo Freire, *Pedagogy of Freedom* (Lanham: Rowman and Littlefield, 1998), 7.

8. Doug Henwood, *After the New Economy* (New York: The New Press, 2003); Kevin Phillips, *Wealth and Democracy: A Political History of the American Rich* (New York: Broadway, 2003); Paul Krugman, *The Great Unraveling: Losing Our Way in the New Century* (New York: W.W. Norton, 2003).

9. Stanley Aronowitz, *How Class Works*, 102.

10. Of course, there is widespread resistance to neoliberalism and its institutional enforcers such as the WTO and IMF among many intellectuals, students, and global justice movements, but this resistance rarely gets aired in the dominant media and if it does it is often dismissed as irrelevant or tainted by Marxist ideology.

11. George Soros, "The US is Now in the Hands of a Group of Extremists," *The Guardian/UK* (January 26, 2004). Available online: http://www.commondreams.org/views04/0126-01.htm

12. Pierre Bourdieu, *Acts of Resistance: Against the Tyranny of the Market* (New York: The New Press, 1998).

13. Pierre Bourdieu and Gunter Grass, "The 'Progressive' Restoration: A Franco-German Dialogue," *New Left Review* 14 (March–April, 2003), 66.

14. Madeleine Bunting, "Zygmunt Bauman: Passion and Pessimism," *The Guardian* (April 5, 2003), 3. Available online: http://books.guardian.co.uk/print/0,3858,4640858-11-738,00.html.

9

Education after Abu Ghraib

Revisiting Adorno's Politics of Education[1]

Every image of the past that is not recognized by the present as one of its own concerns threatens to disappear irretrievably.

Walter Benjamin

Warring Images

Visual representations of the war in Iraq have played a prominent role in shaping public perceptions of the United States' invasion and occupation. The initial, much celebrated image that was widely used to represent the war, captured the toppling of the statue of Saddam Hussein in Baghdad soon after the invasion. The second image, also one of high drama and spectacle, portrayed President Bush in full flight gear after landing on the deck of the USS *Abraham Lincoln.* The scripted photo-op included a banner behind the President proclaiming "Mission Accomplished."

The mainstream media gladly seized upon the first image since it reinforced the presuppositions that the invasion was a justified response to the hyped-up threat Saddam's regime posed to the United States and that his fall was the outcome of an extension of American democracy and an affirmation of its role as a beneficent empire, animated by "the use of military power to shape the world according to American interests and values."[2] The second image fed into the scripted representations of Bush as a "tough," even virile leader who had taken on the garb of a Hollywood warrior determined in his efforts to protect the United States from terrorists and to bring the war in Iraq to a quick and successful conclusion.[3] The narrow ideological field that framed these images in the American media proved impervious to dissenting views, exhibiting a deep disregard for either accurate or critical reporting as well as an indifference to fulfilling its traditional role as a fourth estate, as guardians of democracy and defenders of the public interest. Slavishly reporting the war as if they were on the Pentagon payroll, the dominant media rarely called into question either the Bush administration's reasons for going to war or the impact the war was to have on both the Iraqi people and U.S. domestic and foreign policy.

In the spring of 2004, a new set of images challenged the mythic representations of the Iraqi invasion with the release of hundreds of gruesome photographs and videos documenting the torture of Iraqi prisoners by American soldiers at Abu Ghraib. They were first broadcast on the television series, *60 Minutes II*, and later leaked to the press, becoming something of a nightly feature in the weeks and months that ensued. Abu Ghraib prison was one of the most notorious sites used by the deposed Hussein regime to inflict unspeakable horrors on those Iraqis considered disposable for various political reasons. Ironically, the photos reinforced the growing perception in the Arab world that one tyrant simply had replaced another. In sharp contrast to the all-too-familiar and officially sanctioned images of good-hearted and stalwart U. S. soldiers patrolling dangerous Iraqi neighborhoods, caring for wounded soldiers, or passing out candy to young Iraqi children, the newly discovered photos depicted Iraqi detainees being humiliated and tortured. The face of the U.S. invasion was soon recast by a number of sadistic images, including now infamous photos depicting the insipid, grinning faces of Specialist Charles A. Graner and Pfc. Lynndie R. England flashing a thumbs-up behind a pyramid of seven naked detainees, a kneeling inmate posing as if he is performing oral sex on another hooded male detainee, a terrified male Iraqi inmate trying to ward off an attack dog being handled by U.S. soldiers, and a U.S. soldier grinning next to the body of a dead inmate packed in ice. Two of the most haunting images depicted a hooded man standing on a box, with his arms outstretched in Christ-like fashion, electric wires attached to his hands and penis. Another image revealed a smiling England holding a leash attached to a naked Iraqi man lying on the floor of the prison. Like Oscar Wilde's infamous picture of Dorian Gray, the portrait of American democracy was irrevocably transformed into its opposite. The fight for Iraqi hearts and minds was now irreparably damaged as the war on terror appeared to reproduce only more terror, mimicking the very crimes it claimed to have eliminated.

As Susan Sontag points out, the leaked photographs include both the victims and their gloating assailants. For Sontag, the images from Abu Ghraib are not only "representative of the fundamental corruptions of any foreign occupation and its distinctive policies which serve as a perfect recipe for the cruelties and crimes in American run prisons . . . [but are also] like lynching pictures and are treated as souvenirs of a collective action."[4] Reminiscent of photos taken by whites who lynched blacks after Reconstruction, the images were circulated as trophy shots in order to be passed around and sent out to friends. For Sontag and others, Abu Ghraib could not be understood outside of the racism and brutality that accompanied the exercise of nearly unchecked, unaccountable, absolute power both at home and abroad. Similarly, Sidney Blumenthal argues that Abu Ghraib was a predictable consequence of the Bush administration to fight terrorism by creating a system "beyond law to defend the rule of law against terrorism." One consequence of such obscenely ironic posturing, as he points out, is a Gulag:

> that stretches from prisons in Afghanistan to Iraq, from Guantanamo to secret CIA prisons around the world. There are perhaps 10,000 people being held in Iraq, 1,000 in Afghanistan and almost 700 in Guantanamo, but no one knows the exact numbers. The law as it applies to them is whatever the executive deems necessary. There has been nothing like this system since the fall of the Soviet Union.[5]

As time passed, it became clear that the instances of abuse and torture that took place at Abu Ghraib were extensive, systemic, and part of a larger pattern of criminal behavior that had taken place in other prisons in both Iraq and Afghanistan—not to mention the prisons on the homefront.[6] Patterns of mistreatment by U.S. soldiers had also taken place in Camp Bucca, a U.S. run detention center in southern Iraq as well as in an overseas CIA interrogation center at the Bagram airbase in Afghanistan, where the deaths of three detainees were labeled as homicide by U.S. military doctors.[7]

The most compelling evidence refuting the argument that what happened at Abu Ghraib was the result of the actions of a few isolated individuals who strayed from protocol is spelled out by Seymour Hersh in his May 10 *New Yorker* article in which he analyzes the fifty-eight-page classified report by Major General Antonio Taguba who investigated the abuses at Abu Ghraib. In the report, Taguba insisted that "a huge leadership failure"[8] at Abu Ghraib was responsible for what he described as "sadistic, blatant, and wanton criminal abuses."[9] Taguba not only documented examples of torture and sexual humiliation, he also elaborated on the range of indignities, which included:

> Breaking chemical lights and pouring the phosphoric liquid on detainees; pouring cold water on naked detainees; beating detainees with a broom handle and a chair; threatening male detainees with rape; allowing a military police guard to stitch the wound of a detainee who was injured after being slammed against the wall in his cell; sodomizing a detainee with a chemical light and perhaps a broomstick, and using military working dogs to frighten and intimidate detainees with threats of attack, and in one instance actually biting a detainee.[10]

Not only does Taguba's report reveal scenes of abuse more systemic than aberrant, but also tragically familiar to communities of color on the domestic front long subjected to profiling, harassment, intimidation, and brutality by law and order professionals.

The Politics of Delay and Outrage

Responses from around the world exhibited outrage and disgust over the U.S. actions at Abu Ghraib. The rhetoric of American democracy was denounced all over the globe as hypocritical and utterly propagandistic, especially in light of President Bush's April 30th remarks claiming that with the removal of Saddam Hussein, "there are no longer torture chambers or mass graves or rape rooms in Iraq."[11] The protracted release of new sets of pictures of U.S. soldiers grinning as they tortured and sexually humiliated Iraqi prisoners at Abu Ghraib further undermined the moral and political credibility of the United States both in the Arab world and around the globe. Restoring one of Saddam Hussein's most infamous torture chambers to its original use reinforced the image of the United States as a dangerous, rogue state with despicable imperial ambitions. As columnist Katha Pollitt puts it,

> The pictures and stories [from Abu Ghraib] have naturally caused a furor around the world. Not only are they grotesque in themselves, they reinforce the pre-existing impression of Americans as racist, cruel and frivolous. They are bound to alienate—further alienate—Iraqis who hoped that the invasion would lead to secular democracy and a normal life and who fear Islamic rule. Abroad, if not here at home, they underscore how stupid and wrong the invasion of Iraq was in the first place, how predictably the "war of choice" that was going to be a cakewalk has become a brutal and corrupt occupation, justified by a doctrine of American exceptionalism that nobody but Americans believes.[12]

But Abu Ghraib did more than inspire moral revulsion, it also became a rallying cry for recruiting radical extremists as well as producing legitimate opposition to the American occupation. At one level, the image of the faceless, hooded detainee, arms outstretched and wired, conjured up images of the Spanish Inquisition, the French brutalization of Algerians, and the slaughter of innocent people at My Lai during the Vietnam War. The heavily damaged rhetoric of American democracy now gave way to the more realistic discourse of empire, colonization, and militarization. At another level, the images shed critical light on the often ignored connection between U.S. domination abroad, often aimed at the poor and dispossessed, and at home, particularly against people of color, including the lynching of American blacks in the first half of the twentieth century and the increasingly brutalizing incarceration of large numbers of youth of color that continues into the new millennium. Patricia Williams links the criminal abuse of Iraqi detainees at Abu Ghraib prison to a web of secrecy, violation of civil rights, and racist violence that have become commonplace on the domestic front. She writes:

> [I]t's awfully hard not to look at those hoods and think Inquisition; or the piles of naked and sodomized men and think Abner Louima; or the battered corpses and think of Emmett Till . . . This mess is the predictable byproduct of any authority that starts "sweep-

ing" up "bad guys" and holding them without charge, in solitary and in secret, and presuming them guilty. It flourished beyond the reach of any formal oversight by Congress, by lawyers or by the judiciary, a condition vaguely rationalized as "consistent with" if not "precisely" pursuant to the Geneva Conventions. Bloodied prisoners were moved around to avoid oversight by international observers, a rather too disciplined bit of sanitizing.[13]

Outrage abroad was matched by often low-keyed, if not crude, responses by those implicated whether in military barracks or Washington offices. For the high priests of "personal responsibility," it was a study in passing the buck. President Bush responded by claiming that what happened at Abu Ghraib was nothing more than "disgraceful conduct by a few American troops."[14] General Richard Myers, chairman of the Joint Chiefs of Staff, suggested it was the work of a "handful" of enlisted individuals.[15] But the claim that the Pentagon was unaware that the abuses committed at Abu Ghraib were at odds with International Red Cross reports which regularly notified the Pentagon of such crimes. It was further contradicted by both the Taguba report as well as by a series of memos leaked to the press indicating that the White House, Pentagon, and Justice Department had attempted to justify interrogation practices that violated the federal anti-torture statute two years prior to the invasion.

One such memo was written in August 2002, authored by Assistant Attorney General Jay S. Bybee, head of the Justice Department's Office of Legal Counsel. In it, he argued that in a post 9/11 world any attempt to apply the criminal laws against torture under the Geneva Convention Against Torture undermined Presidential power and should be considered unconstitutional. More specifically, the Bybee memo argued "on behalf of the Justice Department that the President could order the use of torture."[16] Alberto Gonzales, a high-ranking government lawyer, argued in a draft memo to President Bush on January 25, 2002 that the Geneva Conventions are "quaint," if not "obsolete," and that certain forms of traditionally unauthorized methods of inflicting physical and psychological pain might be justified under the aegis of fighting the war on terrorism.[17] Anthony Lewis in commenting on the memo states, "Does he believe that any treaty can be dismissed when it is inconvenient to an American government?"[18] In fact, a series of confidential legal memoranda produced by the Justice Department flatly stated that the "administration is not bound by prohibitions against torture."[19] A Defense Department memo echoed the same line in a calculated attempt to incorporate torture as part of normal interrogating procedures in defiance of international protocols. The *Wall Street Journal* reported on 7 June 2004 that these memos "sought to assign the President virtually unlimited authority on matters of torture."[20] Exercising a degree of rhetorical licence in defining torture in narrow terms, they ended up legitimizing interrogation practices at odds with both the Geneva Convention Against Torture and the Army's own Field Manual for intelligence, which prohibits "The use of force, mental torture, threats, insults or exposure to unpleasant and inhumane treatment of any kind."[21] In reviewing the government's case for torture, Anthony Lewis writes:

The memos read like the advice of a mob lawyer to a mafia don on how to skirt the law and stay out of prison. Avoiding prosecution is literally a theme of the memoranda . . . Another theme in the memoranda, an even more deeply disturbing one, is that the President can order the torture of prisoners even though it is forbidden by a federal statute and by the International Convention Against Torture, to which the United States is a party . . . the issues raised by the Bush administration's legal assertions in its "war on terror" are so numerous and so troubling that one hardly knows where to begin discussing them. The torture and death of prisoners, the end result of cool legal abstractions, have a powerful claim on our national conscience. . . . But equally disturbing, in its way, is the administration's constitutional argument that presidential power is unconstrained by law.[22]

Both John Ashcroft and Secretary of Defense Donald Rumsfeld denied any involvement by the Bush administration either in providing the legal sanctions for torture or for creating the conditions that made the abuses at Abu Ghraib possible. Ashcroft refused the Senate Judiciary Committee's request to make public a 2002 Justice Department memo sanctioning high-risk interrogation tactics that may violate the federal anti-torture statute while repeatedly insisting that the Bush administration does not sanction torture. When the Abu Ghraib scandal first broke in the press and reporters started asking him about the Taguba report, Rumsfeld claimed that he had not read it.

When reporters raised questions about Seymour Hersh's charge that Rumsfeld had personally approved a clandestine program known as SAP "that encouraged physical coercion and sexual humiliation of Iraqi prisoners in an effort to generate more intelligence about the growing insurgency in Iraq," Pentagon spokesman Lawrence Di Rita responded by calling Hersh's article, "outlandish, conspiratorial, and filled with error and anonymous conjecture."[23] At the same time, Di Rita did not directly rebut any of Hersh's claims. When confronted directly about the charge that he authorized a secret program that was given the blanket approval to kill, torture, and interrogate high-value targets, Rumsfeld performed a semantic tap dance that would have made Bill Clinton blush. He told reporters: "My impression is that what has been charged thus far is abuse, which I believe technically is different from torture . . . I don't know if . . . it is correct to say what you just said, that torture has taken place, or that there's been a conviction for torture. And therefore I am not going to address the torture word."[24] But Rumsfeld's contempt for the Geneva Conventions and established military protocol was made public soon after the war on terror was launched in 2001. Disdaining a military machine shaped by the "old rules," he believed they prevented the military and its leadership from taking "greater risks."[25] In 2002, he went so far as to claim that "complaints about America's treatment of prisoners . . . amounted to 'isolated pockets of international hyperventilation.'"[26] It was later reported by a range of news sources, including the *Wall Street Journal* and *Newsweek*, that Rumsfeld had indeed supported interrogation techniques against the Taliban and Iraqi prisoners that violated the Geneva Conventions. As the facts surrounding the abuses emerged belatedly in the dominant media, he admitted he was responsible for the hiding of "Ghost detainees" from the Red Cross and asserted before a Senate Committee that he would assume the blame for Abu Ghraib, but also refused to resign.

What became clear soon after the scandal of Abu Ghraib went public was that it could not be reduced to the "failure of character" of a few soldiers, as George W. Bush insisted. In June 2004, both the *New York Times* and the *Washington Post* broke even more stories documenting the use of torture-like practices by U.S. soldiers who subjected prisoners to unmuzzled military dogs as part of a contest waged to see how many detainees they could make involuntarily urinate out of fear of the dogs[27] and forced detainees to stand on boxes and sing "the Star Spangled Banner" in the nude. Both tactics took place long before the famous photographs were taken at Abu Ghraib.[28] Far from the "frat boy pranks" apologists compared the torture to, these acts were designed to inflict maximal damage—performed on detainees whose culture views nudity as a violation of religious principles and associates public nudity with shame and guilt. Equally disturbing is the International Committee of the Red Cross estimate that 70 to 90 percent of the detainees arrested by Coalition troops "had been arrested by mistake" and had nothing to do with terrorism.[29] It gets worse. Since the release of the initial photos, a new round of fresh photographs and film footage of torture from Abu Ghraib and other prisons in Iraq "include details of the rape and . . . abuse of some of the Iraqi women and the hundred or so children—some as young as 10 years old."[30] One account provided by U.S. Army Sergeant Samuel Provance, who was stationed in the Abu Ghraib prison, recalls, "how interrogators soaked a 16-year-old, covered him in mud, and then used his suffering to break the youth's father, also a prisoner, during interrogation."[31] An Army investigation also revealed that unmuzzled military police dogs were employed at Abu Ghraib prison as part of a sadistic game used to "make juveniles—as young as 15 years old—urinate on themselves as part of a competition."[32]

The wanton abuse of Iraqi detainees, including children, the ongoing efforts at the highest levels of the Bush administration to establish new legal ground for torture, and the use of private contractors to perform the dirty work of interrogating detainees in order to skirt what is clearly an abdication of civil and military law is evidence of a systemic, widespread collusion with crimes against humanity. In spite of claims by the Bush administration that such abuses are the work of a few rogue soldiers, a number of inquiries by high-level outside panels, especially the four-member Schlesinger panel, have concluded that the Abu Ghraib abuses point to leadership failures at the "highest levels of the Pentagon, Joint Chiefs of Staff and military command in Iraq."[33] Such reports and the increasing revelations of the extent of the abuse and torture perpetuated in Iraq, Afghanistan, and American prisons do more than promote moral outrage at the growing injustices practiced by the U.S. government, it also positions the United States as one more rogue regime sharing, as an editorial in the *Washington Post* pointed out, the company of former military juntas "in Argentina and Chile . . . that claim[ed] torture is justified when used to combat terrorism."[34]

In spite of the extensive photographic proof, international and internal reports, and journalistic accounts revealing egregious brutality, racism, and inhumanity by American soldiers against Arab detainees, conservative pundits took their cue from the White House, attempting to justify such detestable acts and defend the Bush administration's usurpation of presidential power. Powerful right-wing ideologues such as Rush Limbaugh and Cal Thomas defended such actions as simply a way for young men (sic) to "blow off some steam," engage in forms of harmless frat hazing, or give Muslim prisoners what they deserve. More offensive than the blasé attitudes of talking-heads was the mantle of moral authority and outrage of politicians who took umbrage with those who dared criticize Bush or his army at a time of war. Former Speaker of the House Newt Gingrich and Republican Senator James Inhofe insisted that calling attention to such crimes not only undermined troop morale in Iraq, but was also deeply unpatriotic. Inhofe actually stated publicly at a Senate Armed Services Committee hearing that he was outraged by the "outrage everyone seems to have about the treatment of these prisoners . . . I am also outraged by the press and the politicians and the political agendas that are being served by this. . . . I am also outraged that we have so many humanitarian do-gooders right now crawling all over these prisons looking for human rights violations while our troops, our heroes, are fighting and dying."[35] That many of these prisoners were innocent civilians picked up in indiscriminate sweeps by the U.S. military or that U.S. troops were operating a chamber of horrors at Abu Ghraib was simply irrelevant, providing fodder for silencing criticism by labeling it unpatriotic, or scapegoating the "liberal" media for reporting such injustices. Inhofe provides a prime example of how politics is corrupted by a dangerous ethos of divine right informed by the mythos of American exceptionalism and a patriotic fervor that disdains reasonable dissent and moral critique. Inhofe's arrogant puffery must be challenged both for shutting down dialogue but also brought to task for the egregious way in which it invites Americans to identify with the violence of the perpetrators.

Other conservatives such as Watergate-felon-turned-preacher, Charles Colson, Robert Knight of the Culture and Family Institute, and Rebecca Hagelin, the vice president of the Heritage Foundation, assumed the moral high ground, blaming what happened at Abu Ghraib on the debauchery of popular culture. Invoking the tired language of the culture wars, Colson argued that "the prison guards had been corrupted by a 'steady diet of MTV and pornography.'" Knight argued that the depravity exhibited at Abu Ghraib was modeled after gay porn which gave military personnel "the idea to engage in sadomasochistic activity and to videotape in voyeuristic fashion." Rebecca Hagelin viewed the prison scandal as the outcome of a general moral laxity in which "our country permits Hollywood to put almost anything in a movie and still call it PG-13."[36] For those hard-wired Bush supporters who wanted to do more than blame Hollywood porn, MTV, prime time television, and (not least) gay culture, the scandalous images themselves were seen as the source of the problem because of the offensive nature of their representations and the controversy they generated.

Despite the colossal (and it seems deliberate) misrepresentations of the facts lead-ing to the war with Iraq along with the neoconservative and Christian fundamental-ism driving the Bush presidency and its disastrous policies at home and abroad, Bush's credibility remains intact for many conservatives. Consequently, they ignore the under-lying conditions that gave rise to the horrific abuses at Abu Ghraib, removing them from the inventory of unethical and damaging practices associated with American exceptionalism and triumphalism. Thus, they ignore Bush's disastrous, open-ended war on terrorism and how it has failed to protect the American populace at home while sanctioning wars abroad that have been used as recruiting tools for Islamic terror-ists; Bush's doctrine of secrecy[37] and unaccountability; Bush's suspension of basic civil liberties under the USA Patriot Act and his willingness to include some named terror-ists under the designation of enemy combatants so as to remove them from the protec-tion of the law; and, the Bush administration's all-out assault on the social contract and the welfare state.[38] Treating the Bush presidency as sacrosanct—and so unaccount-able and beyond public engagement—enables conservatives to conveniently overlook their own complicity in furthering those existing relations of power and politics that make the dehumanizing events of Abu Ghraib possible. Within this apologetic dis-course, matters of individual and collective responsibility disappear in a welter of hypo-critical and strategic diversions. As *New York Times* columnist Frank Rich puts it,

> the point of these scolds' political strategy—and it is a political strategy, despite some of
> its adherents' quasireligiosity—is clear enough. It is not merely to demonize gays and the
> usual rogue's gallery of secularist bogeymen for any American ill but to clear the Bush
> administration of any culpability for Abu Ghraib, the disaster that may have destroyed
> its mission in Iraq. If porn or MTV or Howard Stern can be said to have induced a "few
> bad apples" in one prison to misbehave, then everyone else in the chain of command,
> from the commander-in-chief down, is off the hook. If the culture war can be cross-
> wired with the actual war, then the buck will stop not at the Pentagon or the White
> House but at the Paris Hilton video, or *Mean Girls*, or maybe *Queer Eye for the Straight
> Guy*.[39]

When it comes to reconciling barbarous acts of torture and humiliation with the disingenuous rhetoric of democracy so popular among conservatives, the issue of blame can assume a brutalizing character. For instance, a number of conservatives (as well as those responsible for the 11 September, 2004 report by the Army's Inspector General) place the causes for abuse at Abu Ghraib at the doorstep of low-ranking personnel who, once considered disposable fodder for the war effort, now provide equally tal-ented scapegoats. Powerless to defend themselves against the implied accusation that their working-class and rural backgrounds produced the propensity for sexual deviancy and cruelty in the grand style of the film *Deliverance*, they merely claimed to be follow-ing orders. But class hatred proved a serviceable means to deflect attention from the Bush administration. How else to explain Republican senator Ben Campbell's comment,

"I don't know how these people got into our army"?[40] But class antagonism was not the only weapon in right-wing arsenals. Even more desperate, Ann Coulter blames Abu Ghraib on the allegedly aberrant nature of woman, particularly evident in her assertion that "This is yet another lesson in why women shouldn't be in the military . . . Women are more vicious than men."[41] All of these arguments, as Rich points out, share in an effort to divert attention from matters of politics and history in order to clear the Bush administration of any wrongdoing.[42] Of course, I am not suggesting that Lynndie England, Sabrina Harman, Jeremy Sivits, Charles Graner Jr., and others should not be held responsible for their actions; rather my claim is that responsibility for Abu Ghraib does not lie with them alone.

Susan Sontag has argued that photographs lay down the "tracks for how important conflicts are judged and remembered."[43] But at the same time, she makes it very clear that all photographs cannot be understood through one language recognized by all. Photographs are never transparent, existing outside of the "taint of artistry or ideology."[44] Understood as social and historical constructs, photographic images entail acts of translation necessary to mobilize compassion instead of indifference, witnessing rather than consuming, and critical engagement rather than *aesthetic appreciation or crude repudiation*. Put differently, photographs such as those that revealed the horrors that took place at Abu Ghraib prison have no guaranteed meaning, but rather exist within a complex of shifting mediations that are material, historical, social, ideological, and psychological in nature.[45]

Abu Ghraib Photographs and the Politics of Public Pedagogy

Hence, the photographic images from Abu Ghraib prison cannot be taken up outside of history, politics, or ideology. This is not to suggest that photographs do not record some element of reality as much as to insist that what they capture can only be understood as part of a broader engagement over cultural politics and its intersection with various dynamics of power, all of which inform the conditions for reading photographs as both a pedagogical intervention and a form of cultural production.[46] Photographic images do not reside in the unique vision of their producer or the reality they attempt to capture. Representations privilege those who have some control over self-representation, and they are largely framed within dominant modes of intelligibility.

The Abu Ghraib photographs are constitutive of both diverse sites and technologies of pedagogy and as such represent political and ethical forms of address that make moral demands and claims upon their viewers. Questions of power and meaning are always central to any discussion of photographic images as forms of public pedagogy. Such images not only register the traces of cultural mythologies which must be critically mediated, they also represent ideological modes of address tied to the limits of human discourse and intelligibility and function as pedagogical practices regarding how agency should be organized and represented. The pictures of abuse at Abu Ghraib prison gain their status as a form of public pedagogy by virtue of the spaces they create between the sites in which they become public and the forms of pedagogical address that both frame and mediate their meaning. As they circulate through various sites including talk radio, computer screens, television, newspapers, the Internet, and alternative media, they initiate different forms of address, mobilize different cultural meanings, and offer up different sites of learning. The meanings that frame the images from Abu Ghraib prison are "contingent upon the pedagogical sites in which they are considered"[47] and their ability to limit or rule out certain questions, historical inquiries, and explanations. For example, news programs on the Fox Television Network systematically occlude any criticism of the images of abuse at Abu Ghraib that would call into question the American presence in Iraq. If such issues are raised, they are quickly dismissed as unpatriotic.

Attempts to defuse or rewrite images that treat people as things, as less than human, have a long history. Commentators have invoked comparisons to the images of lynchings of black men and women in the American South and Jews in Nazi death camps. John Louis Lucaites and James P. McDaniel have documented how *Life Magazine* during the World War II put a photograph on its cover of a woman gazing pensively at the skull of a Japanese solider sent to her by her boyfriend serving in the Pacific, a lieutenant who when he left to fight in the war "promised her a Jap."[48] Far from reminding its readers of the barbarity of war, the magazine invoked the patriotic gaze in order to frame the barbaric image as part of a public ritual of mortification and a visual marker of humiliation.

As forms of public pedagogy, photographic images must be engaged ethically as well as socio-politically because they are implicated in history and they often work to suppress the very conditions that produce them. Often framed within dominant forms of circulation and meaning, such images generally work to legitimate particular forms of recognition and meaning marked by disturbing forms of diversion and evasion. This position is evident in those politicians who believe that the photographs from Abu Ghraib are the real problem not the conditions that produced them. Or in the endless commentaries that view the abuses at Abu Ghraib as caused by a few "bad apples." Subjecting such public pronouncements to critical inquiry can only emerge within those pedagogical sites and practices in which matters of critique and a culture of questioning are requisite to a vibrant and functioning democracy. But public pedagogy at its best offers more than forms of reading that are critical and that relate cultural texts, such as photographs, to the larger world. Public pedagogy not only defines the cultural objects of interpretation, it also offers the possibility for engaging modes of literacy that are not just about competency but also about the possibility of interpretation as an intervention in the world. While it is true as Arthur C. Danto insists that images such as those associated with Abu Ghraib "tell us something worth knowing about where we are as a culture,"[49] meaning does not rest with the images alone, but with the ways in which such images are aligned and shaped by larger institutional and cultural discourses and how they call into play the condemnation of torture (or its celebration), how it came about, and what it means to prevent it from happening again. This is not merely a political issue but also a pedagogical one. Making the political more pedagogical in this instance connects what we know to the conditions that make learning possible in the first place. It creates opportunities to be critical, but also as Susan Sontag notes, to "take stock of our world, and [participate] in its social transformation in such a way that non-violent, cooperative, egalitarian international relations remain the guiding ideal."[50] While Sontag is quite perceptive in pointing to the political nature of reading images, a politics concerned with matters of translation and meaning, she does not engage such reading as a pedagogical issue.

As part of a politics of representation, photographic images necessitate both the ability to read critically and to utilize particular analytical skills that enable viewers to study the relations between images, discourses, everyday life, and broader structures of power. As both the subject and object of public pedagogy, photographs both deploy power and are deployed by power and register the conditions under which people learn how to read texts and the world. Photographs demand an ability to read within and against the representations they present and to raise fundamental questions about how they work to secure particular meanings, desires, and investments. As a form of public pedagogy, photographic images have the potential, though by no means guaranteed, to call forth from readers modes of witnessing that connect meaning with compassion, a concern for others, and a broader understanding of the historical and contemporary contexts and relations that frame meaning in particular ways. Critical reading demands pedagogical practices that short-circuit common sense, resist easy assumptions, bracket how images are framed, engage meaning as a struggle over power and politics, and as such refuse to posit reading (especially images) exclusively as an aesthetic exercise but also view it as a political and moral practice.

What is often ignored in the debates about Abu Ghraib, both in terms of its causes and what can be done about it, are questions that foreground the relevance of critical education to the debate. Such questions would clearly focus, at the very least, on what pedagogical conditions need to be in place to enable people to view the images of abuse at Abu Ghraib prison not as part of a voyeuristic, even pornographic, reception but through a variety of discourses that enable them to ask critical and probing questions that get at the heart of how people learn to participate in sadistic acts of abuse and torture, internalize racist assumptions that make it easier to dehumanize people different from themselves, accept commands that violate basic human rights, become indifferent to the suffering and hardships of others, and view dissent as basically unpatriotic. What pedagogical practices might enable the public to foreground the codes and structures which give photographs their meaning while also connecting the productive operations of photography with broader discourses? For example, how might the images from Abu Ghraib prison be understood as part of a broader debate about dominant infor-

mation networks that not only condone torture, but also play a powerful role in organizing society around shared fears rather than shared responsibilities? Photographs
demand more than a response to the specificity of an image; they also raise fundamentally crucial questions about the sites of pedagogy and technologies that produce, dis-
tribute, and frame them in particular ways and what these operations mean in terms
of how they resonate with historical and established relations of power and the identities
and modes of agency that enable such relations to be reproduced rather than resisted
and challenged. Engaging the photographs from Abu Ghraib and the events that produced them would point to the pedagogical practice of foregrounding "the cultures of
circulation and transfiguration within which those texts, events, and practices become
palpable and are recognized as such."[51] For instance, how do we understand the Abu
Ghraib images and the pedagogical conditions that produced them without engaging
the discourses of privatization, particularly the contracting of military labor, the intersection of militarism and the crisis of masculinity, and the war on terrorism and the
racism that makes it so despicable? How might one explain the ongoing evaporation
of political dissent and opposing viewpoints in the United States that proceeded the
events at Abu Ghraib without engaging the pedagogical campaign of fear mongering
adorned with the appropriate patriotic rhetoric waged by the Bush administration?
How might we provide a historical context for linking Abu Ghraib to its legacy of
racial abuse?

I have spent some time on suggesting that there is a link between how we translate
images and pedagogy because I am concerned about what the events of Abu Ghraib
prison might suggest about education as both the subject and object of a democratic
society and how we might engage it differently. What kind of education connects pedagogy and its diverse sites to the formation of a critical citizenry capable of challenging
the ongoing quasi-militarization of everyday life, the growing assault on secular democracy, the collapse of politics into a permanent war against terrorism, and the growing culture of fear that increasingly is used by political extremists to sanction the
unaccountable exercise of presidential power? What kinds of educational practices can
provide the conditions for a culture of questioning and engaged civic action? What
might it mean to rethink the educational foundation of politics so as to reclaim not
only the crucial traditions of dialogue and dissent but also critical modes of agency
and those public spaces that enable collectively engaged struggle? How might education
be understood as a task of translation but also as a foundation for enabling civic engagement? What new forms of education might be called forth to resist the conditions
and complicities that have allowed most people to submit "so willingly to a new political
order organized around fear?"[52] What does it mean to imagine a future beyond "permanent war," a culture of fear, and the triumphalism that promotes the sordid demands
of empire? How might education be used to question the common sense of the war on
terrorism or to rouse citizens to challenge the social, political, and cultural conditions
that lead to the horrible events of Abu Ghraib? Just as crucially, we must ponder the

limits of education. Is there a point where extreme conditions short-circuit our moral instincts and ability to think and act rationally? If this is the case, what responsibility do we have to challenge the reckless violence-as-first-resort-ethos of the Bush administration?

Such questions extend beyond the events of Abu Ghraib, but, at the same time, Abu Ghraib provides an opportunity to connect the sadistic treatment of Iraqi prisoners to the task of redefining pedagogy as an ethical practice, the sites in which pedagogy takes place, and the consequences of pedagogy for rethinking the meaning of politics in the twenty-first century. In order to confront the pedagogical and political challenges arising from the reality of Abu Ghraib, I want to revisit a classic essay by Theodor Adorno in which he tries to grapple with the relationship between education and morality in light of the horrors of Auschwitz. While I am certainly not equating the genocidal acts that took place at Auschwitz with the abuses at Abu Ghraib, a completely untenable analogy, I do believe that Adorno's essay offers some important theoretical insights about how to think about the larger meaning and purpose of education as a form of public pedagogy in light of the Abu Ghraib prison scandal. Adorno's essay raises fundamental questions about how acts of inhumanity are inextricably connected to the pedagogical practices that shape the conditions that bring them into being. Adorno insists that crimes against humanity cannot be simply reduced to the behavior of a few individuals but often speak in profound ways to the role of the state in propagating such abuses, the mechanisms employed in the realm of culture that silence the public in the face of horrible acts, and the pedagogical challenge that would name such acts as a moral crime against humankind and translate that moral authority into effective pedagogical practices throughout society so that such events never happen again. Of course, the significance of Adorno's comments extends far beyond matters of responsibility for what happened at Abu Ghraib prison. Adorno's plea for education as a moral and political force against human injustice is just as relevant today as it was following the revelations about Auschwitz after World War II. As Roger W. Smith points out, while genocidal acts have claimed the lives of over 60 million people in the twentieth century, 16 million of them have taken place since 1945.[53] The political and economic forces fueling such crimes against humanity—whether they are unlawful wars, systemic torture, practiced indifference to chronic starvation and disease, or genocidal acts—are always mediated by educational forces just as the resistance to such acts cannot take place without a degree of knowledge and self-reflection about how to name these acts and to transform moral outrage into concrete attempts to prevent such human violations from occuring in the first place.

Education After Abu Ghraib

In 1967, Theodor Adorno published an essay titled "Education After Auschwitz." In it, he asserted that the demands and questions raised by Auschwitz had so barely penetrated the consciousness of people's minds that the conditions that made it possible contin-ued, as he put it, "largely unchanged."[54] Mindful that the societal pressures that pro-duced the Holocaust had far from receded in post-war Germany and that under such circumstances this act of barbarism could easily be repeated in the future, Adorno argued that "the mechanisms that render people capable of such deeds"[55] must be made visible. For Adorno, the need to come to grips with the challenges arising from the reality of Auschwitz was both a political question and a crucial educational consider-ation. Adorno recognized that education had to be an important part of any politics that took seriously the premise that Auschwitz should never happen again. As he put it:

> All political instruction finally should be centered upon the idea that Auschwitz should never happen again. This would be possible only when it devotes itself openly, without fear of offending any authorities, to this most important of problems. To do this educa-tion must transform itself into sociology, that is, it must teach about the societal play of forces that operates beneath the surface of political forms.[56]

Implicit in Adorno's argument is the recognition that education as a critical practice could provide the means for disconnecting common sense learning from the narrowly ideological impact of mass media, the regressive tendencies associated with hyper-masculinity, the rituals of everyday violence, the inability to identify with others, as well as from the pervasive ideologies of state repression and its illusions of empire. Adorno's response to retrograde ideologies and practices was to emphasize the role of autonomous individuals and the force of self-determination which he saw as the out-come of a moral and political project that rescued education from the narrow language of skills, unproblematized authority, and the seduction of common sense. Self-reflection, the ability to call things into question, and the willingness to resist the material and symbolic forces of domination were central to an education that refused to repeat the horrors of the past and engaged the possibilities of the future. Adorno urged educators to teach students how to be critical, to learn how to resist those ideologies, needs, social relations, and discourses that lead back to a politics where authority is simply obeyed and the totally administered society reproduces itself through a mixture of state force and often orchestrated consensus. Freedom in this instance meant being able to think critically and act courageously, even when confronted with the limits of one's knowledge. Without such thinking, critical debate and dialogue degenerate into slogans; and politics, disassociated from the search for justice, becomes a power grab. Within the realm of education, Adorno glimpsed the possibility of knowledge for self and social formation as well as the importance of pedagogical practices capable of "influencing the next generation of Germans so that they would not repeat what their parents or grandparents had done."[57]

Adorno realized that education played a crucial role in creating the psychological, intellectual, and social conditions that made the Holocaust possible, yet he refused to dismiss education as an institution and set of social practices exclusively associated with domination. He argued that those theorists who viewed education simply as a tool for social reproduction had succumbed to the premier supposition of any oppressive hegemonic ideology: Nothing can change. To dismiss the political and critical force of pedagogy, according to Adorno, was to fall prey to both a disastrous determinism and a complicitous cynicism. He argues:

> For this disastrous state of conscious and unconscious thought includes the erroneous idea that one's own particular way of being—that one is just so and not otherwise—is nature, an unalterable given, and not a historical evolution. I mentioned the concept of reified consciousness. Above all this is a consciousness blinded to all historical past, all insight into one's own conditionedness, and posits as absolute what exists contingently. If this coercive mechanism were once ruptured, then, I think, something would indeed be gained.[58]

Realizing that education in Germany before and after Auschwitz was separated by an unbridgeable chasm, Adorno wanted to invoke the promise of education through the moral and political imperative of never allowing the genocide witnessed at Auschwitz to happen again. For such a goal to become meaningful and realizable, Adorno contended that education had to be addressed as both a promise and a project in order to reveal not only the conditions that laid the psychological and ideological groundwork for Auschwitz but also to defeat the "potential for its recurrence as far as peoples' conscious and unconscious are concerned."[59]

Investigating the powerful role that education played to promote consensus among the public along with the conscious and unconscious elements of fascism, he understood education as more than social engineering and argued that it also had to be imagined as a democratic public sphere. In this context, education would take on a liberating and empowering function, refusing to substitute critical learning for mind-deadening training.[60] At its best, such an education would create the pedagogical conditions in which individuals would function as autonomous subjects capable of refusing to participate in unspeakable injustices while actively working to eliminate the conditions that make such injustices possible. Human autonomy through self-reflection and social critique became for Adorno the basis for developing forms of critical agency as a means of resisting and overcoming both fascist ideology and identification with what he calls the fascist collective. According to Adorno, fascism as a form of barbarism defies all educational attempts at self-formation, engaged critique, self-determination, and transformative engagement. He writes: "The only true force against the principle of Auschwitz would be human autonomy . . . that is, the force of reflection and of self-determination, the will to refuse participation."[61] While there is a deep-seated tension in Adorno's belief in the increasing power of the totally administered society and his call for modes of education that produce critical, engaging, and free minds, he still believed that without critical education it was impossible to think about politics and agency, especially in light of the new technologies and material processes of social integration. Similarly, Adorno did not believe that education as an act of self-reflection alone could defeat the institutional forces and relations of power that existed outside of both institutionalised education and other powerful sites of pedagogy in the larger culture, though he rightly acknowledged that changing such a powerful complex of economic and social forces begins with the educational task of recognizing that such changes were necessary and could actually be carried out through individual and collective forms of resistance. What Adorno brilliantly understood—though in a somewhat limited way given his tendency, in the end, toward pessimism—was the necessity to link politics to matters of individual and social agency.[62] Engaging this relationship, in part, meant theorizing what it meant to make the political more pedagogical; that is, how the very processes of learning constitute the political mechanisms through which identities—both individual and collective—are shaped, desired, mobilized, and experienced, and take on form and meaning within those social formations that provide the educational foundation for constituting the realm of the social.

While it would be presumptuous to suggest that Adorno's writings on education, autonomy, and Auschwitz can be directly applied to theorizing the events at Abu Ghraib prison, his work offers some important theoretical insights for addressing how education might help to rethink the project of politics that made Abu Ghraib possible as well as how violence and torture become normalized as part of the war on terrorism and those others considered marginal to American culture and life.

Recognizing how crucial education was in shaping everyday life and the conditions that made critique both possible and necessary, Adorno insisted that the desire for freedom and liberation was a function of pedagogy and could not be assumed a priori. At the same time, Adorno was acutely aware that education took place both in schools and in larger public spheres, especially in the realm of media. Democratic debate and the conditions for autonomy grounded in a critical notion of individual and social agency could only take place if the schools addressed their critical role in a democracy. Hence, Adorno argued that the critical education of teachers played a crucial role in preventing dominant power from eliminating the possibility of reflective thought and engaged social action. Such an insight appears particularly important at a time when public education is being utterly privatized, commercialized, and test-driven, or, if it serves underprivileged students of color, turned into disciplinary apparatuses that resemble prisons.[63] Public schools are under attack precisely because they have the potential to become democratic public spheres instilling in students the skills, knowledge, and values necessary for them to be critical citizens capable of making power accountable and knowledge an intense object of dialogue and engagement. Of course, the attack on public education is increasingly taking place along with an attack on higher education, particularly the humanities.[64] Everything from affirmative action to academic freedom is up for grabs as neoconservatives, religious fundamentalists, and hard-core right-wing ideologues (such as David Horowitz) have organized to impose political quotas by making conservative ideology a basis for faculty hires,[65] have introduced "ideological diversity" legislation that would cut federal funding for colleges and universities harboring faculty and students who criticize Israel,[66] and have incessantly attacked curricula and faculty for being too liberal. If Adorno is right about educating teachers to neither forget nor allow horrors such as Auschwitz from happening again, the struggle over public and higher education as a democratic public sphere must be defended against base right-wing attacks.

At the same time, how we educate teachers for all levels of schooling must be viewed as more than a technical or credentialized task—it must be seen as a pedagogical practice of both learning and unlearning. Drawing upon Freudian psychology, Adorno believed that educators had to be educated to think critically and to avoid becoming the mediators and perpetrators of social violence. This meant addressing their psychological deformations by making clear the ideological, social, and material mechanisms that encourage people to participate or fail to intervene in such deeds. Pedagogy, in this instance, was not simply concerned with learning particular modes of knowledge, skills, and self-reflection, but also with addressing those dominant sedimented needs and desires that allowed teachers to blindly identify with repressive collectives and to unreflectingly mimic their values while venting acts of hate and aggression.[67] If *unlearning* as a pedagogical practice meant resisting those social deformations that shaped everyday needs and desires, critical learning meant making visible those social practices and mechanisms that represented the opposite of self-formation and autonomous thinking so as to resist such forces and prevent them from exercising such power and influence.

Adorno realized far more so than Freud that the range and scope, not to mention the impact of education, had far exceeded the boundaries of public and higher education. Adorno increasingly believed that the media as a force for learning constituted a mode of public pedagogy that had to be criticized for discouraging critical reflection and reclaimed as a crucial force in providing the "intellectual, cultural, and social climate in which a recurrence [such as Auschwitz] would no longer be possible, a climate, therefore in which the motives that led to the horror would become relatively conscious."[68] Adorno rightly understood and critically engaged the media as a mode of public pedagogy, arguing that they contributed greatly to particular forms of barbarization that necessitated that educators and others "consider the impact of modern mass media on a state of consciousness."[69] If we are to take Adorno seriously, the role of the media in inspiring a fear and hatred of Muslims and Arabs, and suppressing dissent regarding the U.S. invasion and occupation of Iraq, and their determining influence in legitimating a number of myths and lies by the Bush administration must be addressed as part of the larger set of concerns leading to the horror of Abu Ghraib. The media have consistently refused, for example, to comment critically on the ways in which the United

States, in its flaunting of the Geneva Conventions regarding torture, was breaking international law, favoring instead the discourse of national security provided by the Bush administration. The media has also put into place forms of jingoism, patriotic correctness, narrow-minded chauvinism, and a celebration of militarization that rendered dissent as treason and the tortures at Abu Ghraib outside of the discourses of ethics, compassion, human rights, and social justice.

Adorno also insisted that the global evolution of the media, and new technologies that shrank distances as it eroded face-to-face contact (and hence the ability to disregard the consequences of one's actions), had created a climate in which rituals of violence had become so entrenched in the culture that "aggression, brutality, and sadism" had become a normalized and unquestioned part of everyday life. The result was a twisted and pathological relationship with the body that not only tends toward violence, but also promotes what Adorno called the ideology of hardness. Hardness, in this instance, referred to a notion of masculinity based on an idea of toughness in which:

> virility consists in the maximum degree of endurance [that] aligns itself all too easily with sadism . . . [and inflicts] physical pain—often unbearable pain—upon a person as the price that must be paid in order to consider oneself a member, one of the collective . . . Being hard, the vaunted quality education should inculcate, means absolute indifference toward pain as such. In this the distinction between one's pain and that of another is not so stringently maintained. Whoever is hard with himself earns the right to be hard with others as well and avenges himself for those manifestations he was not allowed to show and had to repress.[70]

The rituals of popular culture, especially reality television programs like *Survivor, The Apprentice, Fear Factor,* and the new vogue of extreme sports, either condense pain, humiliation, and abuse into digestible spectacles of violence[71] or serve up an endless celebration of retrograde competitiveness, the compulsion to "go it alone," the ideology of hardness, and power over others as the central features of masculinity. Masculinity in this context treats lies, manipulation, and violence as a sport, a crucial component that lets men connect with each other at some primal level in which the pleasure of the body, pain, and competitive advantage are maximized while coming dangerously close to giving violence a glamorous and fascist edge.

The celebration of both violence and hardness (witness the fanfare over Donald Trump's tag-line "you're fired!") can also be seen in those ongoing representations and images that accompany the simultaneous erosion of security (around health care, work, education) and the militarization of everyday life. The United States has more police, prisons, spies, weapons, and soldiers than at any time in its history—coupled with a growing "army" of the unemployed and incarcerated. Yet, its military is enormously popular, as its underlying values, social relations, and patriotic, hyper-masculine aesthetic spread out into other aspects of American culture. The ideology of hardness, toughness, and hyper-masculinity are constantly being disseminated through a militarized culture that functions as a mode of public pedagogy, instilling the values and the aesthetic of militarization through a wide variety of pedagogical sites and cultural venues.

The ideology of hardness and hyper-masculinity in its present form also speak to a discontinuity with the era in which the crimes of Auschwitz were committed. As Zygmunt Bauman has pointed out to me in a private correspondence, Auschwitz was a closely guarded secret for which even the Nazis were ashamed. Such a secret could not be defended in light of bourgeois morality (even as it made Auschwitz possible); but in the current morality of downsizing, punishment, violence, and kicking the excluded, the infliction of humiliation, pain, and abuse on those considered weak or less clever is not only celebrated but also served up as a daily ritual of cultural life. Such practices, especially through the proliferation of "Reality TV," have become so familiar that the challenge for any kind of critical education is to recognize that the conduct of those involved in the abuse at Abu Ghraib was neither shocking, alienating, nor unique. Hence, the ideology of hardness is far more pervasive today and poses much more difficult challenges educationally and politically.[72]

Flags increasingly appear on storefront windows, lapels, cars, houses, SUVs, and everywhere else as a show of support for the expanding interests of empire abroad. Public schools not only have more military recruiters; they also have more military personnel teaching in the classrooms. JROTC programs are increasingly becoming a conventional part of the school day. Humvee ads offer up the fantasy of military glamour and modes of masculinity, marketed to suggest that ownership of these military vehicles guarantees virility for its owner and promotes a mixture of fear and admiration from everyone else. The military industrial complex now joins hands with the entertainment industry in producing everything from children's toys to video games that both construct a particular form of masculinity and also serve as an enticement for enlistment. In fact, over 10 million people have downloaded *American Army,* a video game the Army uses as recruitment tool. From video games to Hollywood films to children's toys, popular culture is increasingly bombarded with militarized values, symbols, and images. Such representations of masculinity and violence mimic fascism's militarization of the public sphere where physical aggression is a crucial element of male bonding and violence is the ultimate language, referent, and currency through which to understand how, as Susan Sontag has suggested in another context, politics "dissolves . . . into pathology."[73]

Such militarized pedagogies play a powerful role in producing identities and modes of agency completely at odds with those elements of autonomy, critical reflection, and social justice that Adorno privileged in his essay. Adorno's ideology of hardness, when coupled with neoliberal values that aggressively promote a Hobbesian world based on fear, the narrow pursuit of individual interests, and an embrace of commodified relations, profoundly influence individuals who seem increasingly indifferent towards the pain of others, pit their own ambitions against those of everyone else, and assimilate themselves to things, numb to those moral principles that hail us as moral witnesses and call for us to do something about human suffering. Adorno goes so far as to suggest that the inability to identify with others was one of the root causes of Auschwitz:

> The inability to identify with others was unquestionably the most important psycho-logical condition for the fact that something like Auschwitz could have occurred in the midst of more or less civilised and innocent people. What is called fellow travelling was primarily business interest: one pursues one's own advantage before all else, and simply not to endanger oneself, does not talk too much. That is a general law of the status quo. The silence under the terror was only its consequence. The coldness of the societal monad, the isolated competitor, was the precondition, as indifference to the fate of others, for the fact that only very few people reacted. The torturers know this, and they put it to test ever anew.[74]

Adorno's prescient analysis of the role of education after Auschwitz is particularly important in examining those values, ideologies, and pedagogical forces at work in American culture that suggest that Abu Ghraib is not an aberration as much as an outgrowth of those dehumanizing and demonizing ideologies, values, and social relations characteristic of an expanding market fundamentalism, militarism, and national-ism. While these are not the only forces that contributed to the abuses and human rights violations that took place at Abu Ghraib, they do point to how particular mani-festations of hyper-masculinity, violence, militarization, and a jingoistic patriotism are elaborated through forms of public pedagogy that produce identities, social relations, and values conducive to both the ambitions of empire and the cruel, inhuman, and degrading treatment of those others who are its victims. What ultimately drives the ideological vision behind these practices, what provides a stimulus for abuse and sanc-tioned brutality, is the presupposition that a particular society and its citizens are above the law, either indebted only to God, as John Ashcroft has insisted, or rightfully scornful of those individuals and cultures who do not deserve to be accorded human rights because they are labeled as part of an evil empire or dismissed as terrorists.[75] The educa-tional force of these ideological practices allows state power to be held unaccountable while legitimizing an "indifference to the concerns and the suffering of people in places remote from our Western metropolitan sites of self-interest."[76]

Adorno believed that the authoritarian tendencies in capitalism were creating individuals who make a cult out of efficiency, suffer from emotional callousness, have a tendency to treat other human beings as things, and reproduce the ultimate expres-sions of reification under capitalism. The grip that these pathogenic traits had on the German populace then and have on the American public today can, in part, be ex-plained, through the inability of people to recognize that such traits are conditioned rather than determined. In keeping with Adorno's reasoning, such traits even when seen as an intolerable given are often posited as an absolute, "something that blinds itself toward any process of having come into being, toward any insight into our own conditionality."[77] Adorno's insights regarding the educational force of late capitalism to construct individuals who were cold through and through and incapable of empathizing with the plight of others are theoretically useful in illuminating some of the conditions that contributed to the abuses, murders, and acts of torture that took place at Abu Ghraib. Adorno was particularly prescient in forecasting the connection among the subjective mechanisms that produced political indifference and racialized intolerance, the all-encompassing market fundamentalism of neoliberal ideology, and a virulent nationalism that fed on the pieties of theocratic pretentiousness and their relationship to an escalating authoritarianism. What is remarkable about his analysis is that it appears to apply equally well to the United States.

The signals are everywhere. Under the reign of market fundamentalism, capital and wealth have been largely distributed upward while civic virtue has been undermined by a slavish celebration of the free market as the model for organizing all facets of everyday life. Financial investments, market identities, and commercial values take precedence over human needs, public responsibilities, and democratic relations. With its debased beliefs that profit-making is the essence of democracy and that citizenship should be defined as an energized plunge into consumerism, market fundamentalism eliminates government regulation of big business, celebrates a ruthless competitive individualism, and places the commanding political, cultural, and economic institutions of society in the hands of powerful corporate interests, the privileged, and unrepentant religious bigots. Under such circumstances, individuals are viewed as privatized consumers rather than public citizens. As the Bush administration rolls American society back to the Victorian capitalism of the Robber Barons, social welfare is viewed as a drain on corporate profits that should be eliminated, while at the same time the development of the economy is left to the wisdom of the market. Market fundamentalism destroys politics by commercializing public spheres and rendering politics corrupt and cynical.[78]

The impoverishment of public life is increasingly matched by the impoverishment of thought itself, particularly as the media substitute patriotic cheerleading for real journalism.[79] The cloak of patriotism is now cast over retrograde social policies as well as a coercive unilateralism in which military force has replaced democratic idealism, and war has become the organizing principle of society—a source of pride—rather than a source of alarm. In the face of massive corruption, the erosion of civil liberties, and a spreading culture of fear, the defining feature of politics is its insignificance, as it is reduced to an ideology and practice that celebrate passivity and cynicism while promoting conformity and collective impotence.[80] For many, the collapse of democratic life and politics is paid for in the hard currency of isolation, poverty, inadequate health care, impoverished schools, and the loss of decent employment.[81] Within this regime of symbolic and material capital, the other—figured as a social drain on the individual and corporate accumulation of wealth—is either feared, exploited, reified, or considered disposable, but rarely is the relationship between the self and the other mediated by compassion and empathy.[82]

But market fundamentalism does more than destroy the subjective political and ethical conditions for autonomous political agency and concern for fellow citizens; it also shreds the social order as it threatens destruction abroad. As Cornel West points out,

> Free market fundamentalism—the basic dogma across the globe—is producing obscene levels of wealth and inequality around the world. Market as idol. Corporation as fetish. Acting as if workers are just appendages or some kind of market calculation. Outsourcing here, outsourcing there. Ascribing magical powers to the market and thinking it can solve all problems. When free market fundamentalism is tied to escalating authoritarianism, it results in increasing surveillance of citizens and monitoring of classes at universities and colleges. When it is tied to aggressive militarism, we get not just invasion of those countries perceived to be threats, but a military presence in 132 countries, a ship in every ocean.[83]

We also get the privatized armies of mercenaries that take over traditional military functions extending from cooking meals to interrogating prisoners. In Iraq, it has been estimated that "for every ten troops on the ground . . . there is one contract employee. That translates to 10,000 to 15,000 contract workers, making them the second-largest contingent (between America and Britain) of the 'coalition of the willing.'"[84] Firms such as Erinys and CACI International provide rental Rambos, some of whom have notorious backgrounds as mercenaries-for-hire. One widely reported incident involved two civilian contractors blown-up by a suicide bomber in Baghdad in the winter of 2003. Both were South Africans who belonged to a terrorist organization infamous for killing blacks, terrorizing anti-apartheid activists, and paying a bounty on the bodies of black activists.[85] In Iraq, Steve Stefanowicz, a civilian interrogator employed by CACI International was cited in the Taguba report as having "'allowed and/or instructed' MPs to abuse and humiliate Iraqi prisoners and as giving orders that he knew 'equated to physical abuse.'"[86] While the Justice Department has opened up a criminal investigation on an unnamed civilian contractor in Iraq, CACI has refused to take action against Stefanowicz, making clear the charge that private contractors are not monitored as closely as military personnel and are not subject to the same Congressional and public oversights and scrutiny. The lack of democratic accountability results in more than bungled services and price gouging by Halliburton, Bechtel, Northrop Grumman, and other corporations that have become familiar news. It also results in human rights abuses organized under the logic of rationalizing and market efficiency. Journalist Tim Shorrock claims, "The military's abuse of Iraqi prisoners is bad enough, but the privatization of such practices is simply intolerable."[87]

The pedagogical implications of Adorno's analysis of the relationship between authoritarianism and capitalism suggest that any viable educational project would have to recognize how market fundamentalism has not only damaged democratic institutions but also the ability of people to identify with democratic social formations and invest in crucial public goods, let alone reinvigorate the very concept of compassion as an antidote to the commodity-driven view of human relationships. Adorno understood that critical knowledge alone could not adequately address the deformations of mind and character put into place by the subjective mechanisms of capitalism. Instead, he argued that critical knowledge had to be reproduced and democratic social experiences put into place through shared values, beliefs, and practices that created inclusive and compassionate communities which make democratic politics possible and safeguard the autonomous subject through the creation of emancipatory needs. Within the boundaries of critical education, students have to learn the skills and knowledge to narrate their own stories, resist the fragmentation and seductions of market ideologies, and create shared pedagogical sites that extend the range of democratic politics. Ideas gain relevance in terms of whether and how they enable students to participate in both the worldly sphere of self-criticism and the publicness of everyday life. Theory and knowledge, in other words, become a force for autonomy and self-determination within the space of public engagement, and their significance is based less on a self-proclaimed activism than on their ability to make critical and thoughtful connections "beyond theory, within the space of politics itself."[88] Adorno's educational project for autonomy recognizes the necessity of a worldly space in which freedom is allowed to make its appearance, a space that is both the condition and the object of struggle for any viable form of critical pedagogy. Such a project also understands the necessity of compassion to remind people of the full humanity and suffering of others, as well as "the importance of compassion in shaping the civic imagination."[89] If Adorno is correct and I think he is, his call to refashion education in order to prevent inhuman acts has to take as one of its founding tasks today the necessity to understand how free market ideology, privatization, outsourcing, and the relentless drive for commodified public space radically diminish those political and pedagogical sites crucial for sustaining democratic identities, values, and practices.

Adorno's critique of nationalism appears as useful today as it did when it appeared in the late 1960s. He believed that those forces pushing an aggressive nationalism harbored a distinct rage against divergent groups who stood at odds with such imperial ambitions. Intolerance and militarism, according to Adorno, fueled a nationalism that became "pernicious because in the age of international communication and supranational blocks it cannot completely believe in itself anymore and has to exaggerate boundlessly in order to convince itself and others that it is still substantial. . . . [Moreover] movements of national renewal in an age when nationalism is outdated, seem to be especially susceptible to sadistic practices."[90] Surely, such a diagnosis would fit the imperial ambitions of Richard Cheney, Richard Perle, Donald Rumsfeld, Paul Wolfowitz, and other neoconservatives whose dreams of empire are entirely at odds with either a desire to preserve human dignity or respect for international law. Convinced that the

United States should not only maintain political and military dominance in the post-cold war world, but also prevent any nation or alliance from challenging its superiority, nationalists across the ideological spectrum advocate a discourse of exceptionalism that calls for a dangerous unity at home and reckless imperial ambitions abroad. Belief in empire has come to mean that the United States would now shape rather than react to world events and act decisively in using "its overwhelming military and economic might to create conditions conducive to American values and interests."[91] American unilateralism buttressed by the dangerous doctrine of preemption has replaced multi-lateral diplomacy; religious fundamentalism has found its counterpart in the ideological messianism of neoconservative designs on the rest of the globe; and a reckless moralism that divides the world into good and evil has replaced the possibility of dialogue and debate. Within such a climate, blind authority demands as it rewards authoritarian behavior so as to make power and domination appear beyond the pale of criticism or change, providing the political and educational conditions for eliminating self-reflection and compassion even in the face of the most sadistic practices and imperial ambitions.

American support for the invasions of Iraq and the Apartheid wall in Israel as well as targeted assassinations and torture are now defended in the name of righteous causes even by liberals such as Niall Ferguson, Paul Berman, and Michael Ignatieff, who, like their neoconservative counterparts, swoon in the illusion that American power can be used as a force for progress, in spite of the official terror and reckless suffering it imposes on much of the world.[92] National justification for the most messianic militar-istic policies, as indicated by the war in Iraq, is wrapped up in the discourse of democ-racy and divine mission, an updated version of American exceptionalism, in spite of the toll the war takes on Iraqi lives—mostly children—and young U.S. soldiers. Then there is the wasted $141 billion being spent on the war that could be used to support life-giving social programs at home. Even moderately liberal democrats now appeal to an uncritical chauvinism with a fervor that is equally matched by its ability to cheapen the most basic tenets of democracy and deaden in some of its citizens the obligation to be responsible to the suffering and hardships of those others who exist outside of its national borders. Barack Obama, a rising star in the Democratic Party and a keynote speaker at the 2004 Democratic convention insisted we are "One America," a moniker that does more to hide contradictions and injustices than to invoke their continuing presence and the necessity to overcome them. Equally important, "One America" when appealed to outside of a critical examination of the damaging chauvinism that informs such a call ends up reproducing a more liberal, though equally privileged, notion of America's role in the world, a role that seems to have little understanding of what the limits might be or the legacy of human suffering it has produced historically and con-tinues to produce.

The aggressive nationalism that Adorno viewed as fundamental to the conditions that produced Auschwitz has not been laid to rest. Echoes of such jingoistic rhetoric can be heard from neoconservatives who want to wage a holy war against the non-

Western hordes that threaten all things Christian, European, and civilized. This virulent nationalism can be heard in the semantic contortions justifying hard and soft versions of empire, often produced by conservative think-tanks and Ivy League intellectuals acting as modern day missionaries for their corporate sponsors. It can be heard in the fundamentalist rhetoric of religious bigots such as Jerry Falwell and Pat Robertson who are fanatically pro-Israel and are waging an incessant propaganda war for Palestinian land in the name of Christian ideals. The discourse of empire finds a more tangible expression in the presence of 725 U.S. military bases in 138 foreign countries that circle the globe.[93]

The discourse of empire must be deconstructed and replaced in our schools and other sites of pedagogy with new global models of democracy, models grounded in an ethics and morality in which the relationship between the self and others extends beyond the chauvinism of national boundaries and embraces a new and critical understanding of the interdependencies of the world and their implications for citizenship in global democracy. Memory must serve as a bulwark against the discourse of empire, which is often built on the erasure of historical struggles and conflicts. Memory in this instance is more than counter-knowledge; it is a form of resistance, a resource through which to wage pedagogical and political struggles to recover those narratives, traditions, and values that remind students and others of the graphic nature of suffering that unfolded in the aftermath of America's claims for a permanent war on terrorism. Appeals to American exceptionalism and the obligations of empire building sound hollow in the face of the monstrosities they produce, even as such appeals also legitimize a process of othering, demonizing those who are not included by appeals to human dignity, human rights, and international law.

At the heart of Adorno's concern with education was the call to create pedagogical practices in which we supplement knowledge with self-criticism. Self- and social criticism was for Adorno a crucial element of autonomy, but criticism was not enough. Agency as a political force mattered in that it was not only capable of saying no to abusive power, but also because it could imagine itself as a mechanism for changing the world. As a condition of politics and collective struggle, agency requires being able to engage democratic values, principles, and practices as a force for resistance and hope in order to challenge unquestioned modes of authority while also enabling individuals to connect such principles and values to "the world in which they lived as citizens."[94] Adorno's plea for education rests on the assumption that human beings make both knowledge and history, rather than both simply washing over them. For Adorno, critical reflection was the essence of all genuine education as well as politics. Ongoing reflection provided the basis for individuals to become autonomous by revealing the human origins of institutions and as such the recognition that society could be open to critique and change. Politics is thus theorized as a practical effort to link freedom to agency in the service of extending the promise of democratic institutions, values, and social relations. The capacity for self-knowledge, self-critique, and autonomy becomes more powerful when it is nourished within pedagogical spaces and sites that refuse to be parochial, that embrace difference over bigotry, global democracy over chauvinism, peace over militarism, and secularism over religious fundamentalism. The urgency of such a call can be heard in William Greider's plea for critical education to bring the presidency of George W. Bush to an end:

> The only way out of this fog of pretension is painful self-examination by Americans— cutting our fears down to more plausible terms and facing the complicated realities of our role in the world. The spirited opposition that arose to Bush's war in Iraq is a good starting place, because citizens raised real questions that were brushed aside. I don't think that most Americans are interested in imperial rule, but they were grossly misled by patriotic rhetoric. Now is the time for sober, serious teach-ins that lay out the real history of U.S. power in the world, and that also explain the positive and progressive future that is possible. Once citizens have constructed a clear-eyed, dissenting version of our situation, perhaps politicians can also be liberated from exaggerated fear. The self-imposed destruction that has flowed from Bush's logic cannot be stopped until a new cast of leaders steps forward to guide the country.[95]

Teach-ins, reading groups, public debates, and film screenings should take place in a variety of sites and spaces for dialogue and learning, and they should focus not simply on the imperial ambitions of the United States but also on the dehumanizing practices informed by a political culture in which human life that does not align itself with official power and corporate ideology becomes disposable. The connection between Auschwitz and Abu Ghraib can also be traced in the educational force of popular culture in which pedagogy is disassociated from justice, citizenship is restricted to the obligations of consumerism, and compassion is dissolved in the mechanics of social Darwinism. As mentioned previously, Abu Ghraib cannot be equated with the genocidal intent of Auschwitz, but the conditions that allowed Americans to commit such abuses on Iraqi detainees harbor the possibilities for atrocious acts of inhumanity, only this time they are dressed up in the rhetoric of advancing the democratic principles of freedom and justice. Adorno believed that education as a democratic force could play a central role in altering the rising tide of authoritarianism on both a national and global level. His call to rethink the value and importance of education as a central element of politics offers an opportunity, especially for educators and other cultural workers, to learn not only from the horrors of Abu Ghraib but also to rethink the value of critical education and public pedagogy as an all-important part of politics, the future of public institutions, and global democracy itself. In addition, Adorno brilliantly understood that it was not enough to turn the tools of social critique simply upon the government or other apparatuses of domination. Critique also had to come to grips with the affective investments that tied individuals, including critics, to ideologies and practices of domination, and how analyses of the deep structures of domination might help to provide a more powerful critique and healthy suspicion of various appeals to community, the public, and the social. Clearly, while it is imperative to reclaim the discourse of community, the commons, and public good as part of a broader discourse of democracy, such terms need to be embraced critically in light of the ways in which they have often served the instruments of dominant power.

Adorno was insistent that education was crucial as a point of departure for imagining autonomy, recognizing the interdependency of human life, and stopping cycles of violence. Education can help us to imagine a world in which violence can be minimized as well as to reject the disparagement, exclusion, and abuse of those deemed others in a social order in which one's worth is often measured through the privileged categories of gender, class, race, citizenship, and language. Education can also seek to identify and destroy the conditions that provide an outlet for murderous rage, hatred, fear, and violence. This requires a pedagogical commitment, in Judith Butler's eloquent words,

> to return us to the human where we do not expect to find it, in its frailty and at the limits of its capacity to make sense. We would have to interrogate the emergence and vanishing of the human at the limits of what we can know, what we can hear, what we can see, what we can sense. This might prompt us, affectively to reinvigorate the intellectual projects of critique of questioning, of coming to understand the difficulties and demands of cultural translation and dissent, and to create a sense of the public in which oppositional voices are not feared, degraded or dismissed, but valued for the instigation to a sensate democracy they occasionally perform.[96]

But under certain circumstances, the limits of education have to be understood. What is difficult to grasp is that simply because one learns to be nonviolent as part of a respect for humanity, a visceral repulsion for the suffering of others, or an ethical conception of mutual obligation, outbursts of violence cannot be entirely contained within such a rationality or mode of understanding. Under certain enormously stressful conditions, violence merges with circumstances of extreme social and bodily vulnerability and may appear to be one of the few options available for dealing with those already dismissed as inhuman or disposable.[97] Even more horrible is the possibility that inhuman acts of abuse under incredibly nerve-wracking conditions represent one of the few outlets for pleasure. Is it conceivable that under certain conditions of violence and stress only the unthinkable is imaginable, that the only avenue for the release of pleasure can be attained by extending the logic of violence to those deemed as the other, those undeserving of narration, agency, and power? Under certain modes of domination with all of its stress-inducing consequences, those who exercise a wanton and dehumanizing power often feel that everything is permissible because all of the rules appear to have broken down. The stress soldiers sometimes experience under such circumstances is often satisfied through the raw feel and exercise of power. Abu Ghraib remains, tragically, a terrible site of violence, a site in which an ethics of nonviolence seems almost incomprehensible given the tension, anxiety, and daily violence that framed both what happened in the prison and in daily life in Iraq. Under these conditions, neither education nor ethics of peace may be enough to prevent "fear and anxiety from turning into murderous action."[98] Under extreme conditions in which abuse, loss, hardship, and dehumanization shape the consciousness and daily routines of one's existence, whether it be for U.S. soldiers working in Abu Ghraib or Israeli soldiers occupying Hebron, violence can undercut the appeal to ethics, critical reflection, and all educated sensibilities.[99] This is not to suggest that education does not matter much in light of such conditions as much as to suggest, following Adorno's insight, that education that particularly matters must address what it means to prevent the conditions in which violence takes root and develops a life of its own.

As a political and moral practice, education must be engaged not only as one of the primary conditions for constructing political and moral agents, but also as a public pedagogy—produced in a range of sites and public spheres—that constitutes cultural practice as a defining feature of any viable notion of politics. Education after Abu Ghraib must imagine a future in which learning is inextricably connected to social change, the obligations of civic justice, and a notion of democracy in which peace, equality, compassion, and freedom are not limited to the nation-state but extend to the international community. Education after Abu Ghraib must take seriously what it might mean to strive for the autonomy and dignity of a global citizenry and peace as its fundamental precondition.

Notes

1. I want to thank Susan Giroux for her generous support and wonderful insights while I was researching and writing this chapter.
2. Ronald Steel, "Fight Fire With Fire," *New York Times Book Review* (July 25, 2004), 12–13.
3. For an interesting comment on how the Bush media team attempted to enhance presidential persona through the iconography of conservative, hyped-up, macho-phallic masculinity, see Richard Goldstein, "Bush's Basket," *Village Voice* (May 21–27, 2003). Available online: http://www.villagevoice.com/issues/0321/goldstein.php.
4. Susan Sontag, "Regarding the Torture of Others: notes on what has been done—and why—to prisoners, by Americans," *New York Times Sunday Magazine* (May 23, 2004), 26–27.
5. Sidney Blumenthal, "This is the New Gulag," *The Guardian* (May 6, 2004). Available online: http://www.guardian.co.uk/print/0,38584917539-103677,00.html.
6. While I can't name all of the relevant sources theorizing the ethical nature of torture or its use by the American military, some important recent contributions include: Seymour M. Hersh, "Torture at Abu Ghraib," *The New Yorker* (May 10, 2004), 42–47; Mark Danner, "Torture and Truth," *The New York Review of Books* (May 27, 2004), 46–50; Mark Danner, "The Logic of Torture," *The New York Review of Books* (June 24, 2004), 70–74; Anthony Lewis, The US Case for Torture," *The New York Review of Books* (July 15, 2004), 4–8.
7. See Edward T. Pound and Kit R. Roane, "Hell on Earth," *U.S. News and World Report* (July 19, 2004). Available online: http://www.usnews.com/usnews/issue/040719/usnews/19prison.htm. Also see Editorial, "The Horror of Abu Ghraib," *The Nation* (May 24, 2004),

3. Degrading prisoners at Abu Ghraib had become so pervasive that forced nudity was seen as a commonplace phenomenon by both military personnel and detainees. See Kate Zernike and David Rohde, "Forced Nudity of Iraqi Prisoners is Seen as a Pervasive Pattern, Not Isolated Incidents," *New York Times* (June 8, 2004), A11.

8. Cited in Seymour Hersh, "Chain of Command," *The New Yorker* (May 17, 2004), 40.

9. Cited in Edward T. Pound and Kit R. Roane, "Hell on Earth," *U.S. News and World Report* (July 19, 2004). Available online: http://www.usnews.com/usnews/issue/040719/usnews/19prison.htm.

10. Section of Taguba's report cited in Seymour M. Hersh, "Torture at Abu Ghraib," *The New Yorker* (May 10, 2004), 43.

11. Bush cited in Lisa Hajjar, "Torture and the Politics of Denial," *In These Times* (June 21, 2004), 12.

12. Katha Pollitt, "Show and Tell in Abu Ghraib," *The Nation* (May 24, 2004), 9.

13. Patricia J. Williams, "In Kind," *The Nation* (May 31, 2004), 10.

14. George Bush, "President Outlines Steps to Help Iraq Achieve Democracy and Freedom," Office of the White House Press Secretary (May 24, 2004). Available online: http://www.whitehouse.gov/news/releases/2004/05/20040524-10.html.

15. General Myers' remarks are cited in Dave Moniz and Tom Squitieri, "Lawyers Raised Questions and Concerns on Interrogations," *USA Today* (June 10, 2004), 13A.

16. Anthony Lewis, "Making Torture Legal," *The New York Review of Books* (July 15, 2004), 8.

17. The memo can be found online: http://www.cooperativeresearch.org/entity.jsp?entity=draft_memo_to_the_president_from_alberto_gonzales,_january_25,_2004.

18. Lewis, "Making Torture Legal," 6.

19. Neil A. Lewis, "Bush Didn't Order any Breach of Torture Laws, Ashcroft Says," *New York Times* (June 9, 2004). Available on line: http://www.nytimes.com/2004/06/09/politics/html.

20. Jess Bravin, "Pentagon Report Set Framework for Use of Torture," *Wall Street Journal* (June 7, 2004). Available online: http://www.commondreams.org/cgi-bin/print.cgi?file=/headlines04/0607-01.htm.

21. See chapter one of the manual, "Interrogation and the Interrogator." Available online: http://www.globalsecurity.org/intell/library/policy/army/fm/fm34-52/chapter1.htm.

22. Lewis, "Making Torture Legal," 4, 6.

23. Associated Press, "DOD Denies Report's Claims," *Military.Com* (May 16, 2004). Available online: http://www.military.com/NewsContent/0,13319,FL_rumsfeld_051604,00.html.

24. Cited in David Folkenflik, "Dodging Using Words Like 'Torture,'" *BaltimoreSun.Com* (May 26, 2004). Available online: http://www.baltimoresun.com/entertainment/tv/bal-to.media26may26,0,7304614.column?coll=bal-artslife-tv.

25. Cited in Seymour Hersh, "Chain of Command," *The New Yorker* (May 17, 2004), 41.

26. Ibid.

27. Josh White and Scott Higham, "Use of Dogs to Scare Prisoners Was Authorized," *Washington Post* (June 11, 2004), A01.

28. Kate Zernike and David Rohde, "Forced Nudity of Iraqi Prisoners Is Seen as a Pervasive Pattern, Not Isolated Incidents," *New York Times* (June 8, 2004), A11.

29. Bob Drogin, "Most 'Arrested by Mistake,'" *Los Angeles Times* (May 11, 2004). Available online: http://www.commondreams.org/cgi-bin/print.cgi?file=headlines04/0511-04.htm.

30. Ray McGovern, "Not Scared Yet? Try Connecting These Dots," *Common Dreams* (August 11, 2004). Available online: http://www.commondreams.org/views04/0809-11.htm.

31. Ibid.

32. Josh White and Thomas E. Ricks, "Iraqi Teens Abused at Abu Ghraib, Report Finds," *Washington Post* (August 24, 2004), A01.

33. Eric Schmitt, "Defense Leaders Faulted by Panel in Prison Abuse," *New York Times* (August 24, 2004), 1.

34. Editorial, "Legalizing Torture," *Washington Post* (June 9, 2004), A20.
35. Norman Solomon, "The Coming Backlash Against Outrage," *Common Dreams* (May 12, 2004). Available online: http://www.commondreams.org/cgi-bin/print.cgi?file=views04/0512-05.htm.
36. All of these examples are cited in Frank Rich, "It Was Porn That Made Them Do It," *New York Times* (May 30, 2004), AR1.
37. The level of secrecy employed by the Bush administration is both dangerous and absurd. For example, some individuals were shocked to learn that if they wanted to attend a rally hosted by Vice President Dick Cheney at Rio Rancho Mid-High School in New Mexico the weekend of July 30, 2004, they could not get tickets to the rally unless they signed an endorsement pledging allegiance to President George W. Bush. See Jeff Jones, *Albuquerque Journal* (July 30, 2004), 1.
38. I take up many of these issues in greater detail in Henry A. Giroux, *The Terror of Neoliberalism: The New Authoritarianism and the Eclipse of Democracy* (Denver, CO: Paradigm Press, 2004).
39. Rich, "It Was Porn That Made Them Do It," AR1, AR16.
40. Cited in Gary Younge, "Blame the White Trash," *Guardian*/UK (May 17, 2004). Available online: http://www.commondreams.org/cgi-bin/pring.cgi?file=/views04/0517-03.htm.
41. Ibid.
42. Rich, "It was Porn That Made Them do It," AR1
43. Sontag, "Regarding the Torture of Others: notes on what has been done—and why—to prisoners, by Americans," 25.
44. Susan Sontag, *Regarding the Pain of Others* (New York: Farrar, Straus and Giroux, 2003), 26.
45. For an excellent discussion of this issue, see John Louis Lucaites and James P. McDaniel, "Telescopic Mourning/Warring in the Global Village: Decomposing (Japanese) Authority Figures," *Communication and Critical/Cultural Studies* 1:1 (March 2004), 1–28.
46. This issue is taken up brilliantly in Abigail Solomon-Godeau, *Photography At The Dock* (Minnesota: University of Minnesota Press, 1994).
47. Jeffrey R. DiLeo, Walter Jacobs, and Amy Lee, "The Sites of Pedagogy," *Symploke* 10: 1–2, 9.
48. John Louis Lucaites and James P. McDaniel, "Telescopic Mourning/Warring in the Global village: Decomposing (Japanese) Authority Figures," 7.
49. Arthur C. Danto, "American Self-Consciousness in Politics and Art," *Artforum* (September 2004). Available online: http://www.artforum.com/inprint/id=7391/html.
50. Judith Butler, "Explanation and Exoneration, or What We Can Hear," *Theory & Event* 5:4 (2002), 19.
51. Dilip Parameshwar Gaonkar and Elizabeth A. Povinelli, "Technologies of Public Forms: Circulation, Transfiguration, Recognition," *Public Culture* 15:3 (2003), 386.
52. William Greider, "Under the Banner of the 'War' on Terror," *The Nation* (June 21, 2004), 14.
53. Roger W. Smith, "American Self-Interest and the Response to Genocide," *The Chronicle Review* (July 30, 2004). Available online: http://chronicle.com/cgi2-bin/printible.cgi?article=http://chronicle.co.
54. This was first presented as a radio lecture on April 18, 1966, under the title "Padagogik nack Auschwitz." The first published version appeared in 1967. The English translation appears in Theodor Adorno, "Education after Auschwitz," *Critical Models: Interventions and Catchwords* (New York: Columbia University Press, 1998), 191.
55. Ibid., 192.
56. Ibid., 203.
57. Peter Hohendahl, "Education After the Holocaust," *Prismatic Thought: Theodor Adorno* (Lincoln: University of Nebraska Press, 1995), 51.
58. Adorno, "Education after Auschwitz," 200.

59. Ibid, 191.
60. See for instance, Theodor W. Adorno, "Philosophy and Teachers," *Critical Models: Interventions and Catchwords* (New York: Columbia University Press, 1998), 19–36.
61. Hohendahl, *Prismatic Thought: Theodor Adorno,* 58.
62. Some might argue that I am putting forward a view of Adorno that is a bit too optimistic. But I think that Adorno's political pessimism, which given his own experience of fascism, seems entirely justified to me, should not be confused with his pedagogical optimism which provides some insight into why he could write the Auschwitz essay in the first place. Even Adorno's ambivalence about what education could actually accomplish does not amount to an unadulterated pessimism as much as a caution about recognizing the limits of education as an emancipatory politics. Adorno wanted to make sure that individuals recognized those larger structures of power outside of traditional appeals to education while clinging to critical thought as the precondition but not absolute condition of individual and social agency. I want to thank Larry Grossberg for this distinction. I also want to thank Roger Simon and Imre Szeman for their insightful comments on Adorno's politics and pessimism.
63. On the relationship between prisons and schools, see Henry A. Giroux, *The Terror of Neoliberalism: The New Authoritarianism and the Eclipse of Democracy.*
64. Henry A. Giroux and Susan Searls Giroux, *Take Back Higher Education* (New York: Palgrave, 2004).
65. On the intellectual diversity issue, see Donald Lazere, "The Contradictions of Cultural Conservatism in the Assault on American Colleges," *Chronicle of Higher Education* (July 2, 2004), B15–B16.
66. Michael Collins Piper, "Schools Not Teaching Pro-Israel Views to Lose Funding: Congress to Pass 'Ideological Diversity' Legislation," *American Free Press* (April 22, 2003). Available online: http://www.picosearch.com/cgi-bin/ts.pl.
67. Adorno, "Education After Auschwitz," 192.
68. Ibid., 194
69. Ibid., 196
70. Ibid., 197–198.
71. George Smith refers to one program in which a woman was tied up in a clear box while some eager males "dumped a few hundred tarantulas onto her . . . you can hear the screaming and crying from her and the witnesses. Some guy is vomiting. This is critical, because emptying the contents of the stomach is great TV. Everyone else is laughing and smirking, just like our good old boys and girls at Abu Ghraib." George Smith, "That's Entrail-Tainment!" *Village Voice* (August 3, 2004). Available online: http://www.villagevoice.com/isues/0431/essay.php/html.
72. This paragraphs draws almost directly from a correspondence with Zygmunt Bauman, dated August 31, 2004.
73. Cited in Carol Becker, "The Art of Testimony," *Sculpture* (March 1997), 28.
74. Adorno, "Education After Auschwitz," 201.
75. This issue is taken up with great insight and compassion in Robert Jay Lifton, *Super Power Syndrome: America's Apocalyptic Confrontation with the World* (New York: Thunder Mouth Press, 2003).
76. Akeel Bilgrami, "Forward," in Edward Said, *Humanism and Democratic Criticism* (New York: Columbia, 2004),. x.
77. Theodor Adorno, "Education After Auschwitz," transcript of radio version (April 1966). Available online: http://www.chemtrailcentral.com/ubb/Forum6/HTML/001718.
78. I take up this issue in great detail in Henry A. Giroux, *Public Spaces, Private Lives: Democracy Beyond 9/11* (Lanham, MD: Rowman and Littlefield, 2003).

79. One of the best books examining this issue is Robert W. McChesney, *Rich Media, Poor Democracy* (New York: The New Press, 1999).

80. Zygmunt Bauman, *In Search of Politics* (Stanford, CA: Stanford University Press, 1999).

81. See Kevin Phillips, *Wealth and Democracy* (New York: Broadway Books, 2003).

82. Constructions of the impoverished other have a long history in American society, including more recent manifestations that extend from the internment of Japanese Americans during World War II to the increasing incarceration of young black and brown men in 2004. Of course, they cannot be explained entirely within the discourse of capitalist relations. The fatal combination of chauvinism, militarism, and racism has produced an extensive history of photographic images in which depraved representations such as blacks hanging from trees or skulls of "Japanese soldiers jammed onto a tank exhaust pipe as a trophy" depict a xenophobia far removed from the dictates of objectified consumerism. See John Louis Lucaites & James P. McDaniel, "Telescopic Mourning/Warring in the Global Village: Decomposing (Japanese) Authority Figures," 4. Also, see Zygmunt Bauman, *Wasted Lives* (Cambridge, England: Polity Press, 2004).

83. Cornel West, "Finding Hope in Dark Times," *Tikkun* 19:4 (2004), 19–20.

84. William D. Hartung, "Outsourcing is Hell," *The Nation* (June 7, 2004), 5.

85. Louis Navaer, "Terrorist Mercenaries on U.S. Payroll in Iraq War," *Pacific News Service* (May 4, 2004). Available online: http://www.mindfully.org/Reform/2004/Terrorist-Mercenaries-US4may04.htm.

86. Tim Shorrok, "CACI and Its Friends," *The Nation* (June 21, 2004), 22.

87. Ibid., 22.

88. Nick Couldry, "In the Place of a Common Culture, What?" *The Review of Education, Pedagogy, and Cultural Studies* 26:1 (January–March, 2004), 15.

89. Martha C. Nussbaum, "Compassion and Terror," *Daedalus* (Winter 2003), 11.

90. Adorno, "Education after Auschwitz," 203.

91. Janadas Devan, "The Rise of the Neo Conservatives," *The Straits Times* (March 30, 2004). Available online: http://www.straitstimes.asia1.com.sg/columnist/0,1886,145-18017100.html.

92. See for instance, Niall Ferguson, *Colossus: The Price of America's Empire* (New York: The Penguin Press, 2004); Michael Ignatieff, *The Lesser Evil: Political Ethics in An Age of Terror* (Princeton, NJ: Princeton University Press, 2004).

93. See Marc Cooper, "Dissing the Republic to Save It: A Conversation with Chalmers Johnson," *LA Weekly* (July 2-8, 2004). Available online: http://www.commondreams.org/views04/0701-2htm.

94. Edward Said, *Humanism and Democratic Criticism* (New York: Columbia University Press, 2004), 6.

95. Greider, "Under the Banner of the 'War' on Terror," 18.

96. Judith Butler, *Precarious Life: The Powers of Mourning and Violence* (London: Verso, 2004), 151.

97. This issue is taken up brilliantly in Zygmunt Bauman, *Wasted Lives: Modernity and Its Outcasts*.

98. Butler, *Precarious Life: The Powers of Mourning and Violence*, xviii.

99. I want to illustrate this point with a comment taken from an Israeli soldier about his experience in Hebron:

> I was ashamed of myself the day I realized that I simply enjoy the feeling of power. I don't believe in it: I think this is not the way to do anything to anyone, surely not to someone who has done nothing to you, but you can't help but enjoy it. People do what you tell them. You know it's because you carry a weapon. Knowing that if you didn't have it, and if your fellow soldiers weren't

beside you, they would jump on you, beat the shit out of you, and stab you to death—you begin to enjoy it. Not merely enjoy it, you need it. And then, when someone suddenly says "No" to you, "what do you mean no? Where do you draw the chutzpah from, to say no to me?" . . . I remember a very specific situation: I was at a checkpoint, a temporary one, a so-called strangulation checkpoint, it was a very small checkpoint, very intimate, four soldiers, no commanding officer, no protection worthy of the name, a true moonlighting job, blocking the entrance to a village. From one side a line of cars wanting to get out, and from the other side a line of cars wanting to pass, a huge line, and suddenly you have a mighty force at the tip of your fingers, as if playing a computer game. I stand there like this, pointing at someone, gesturing to you to do this or that, and you do this or that, the car starts, moves toward me, halts beside me. The next car follows, you signal, it stops. You start playing with them, like a computer game. You come here, you go there, like this. You barely move, you make them obey the tip of your finger. It's a might feeling. It's something you don't experience elsewhere. You know it's because you have a weapon, you know it's because you are a soldier, you know all this, but it's addictive. When I realized this . . . I checked in with myself to see what had happened to me. That's it. And it was a big bubble that burst. I thought I was immune, that is, how can someone like me, a thinking, articulate, ethical, moral man—things I can attest to about myself as such. Suddenly, I notice that I am getting addicted to controlling people.

I want to thank Roger Simon for this insight and for his making available to me the transcript from which this quote is taken. See "Soldiers Speak Out About Their Service in Hebron." Available online: www.shovrimshtika.org.

Index

A

Abu Ghraib prison, 221–249
  class, 229–230
  conservatives, 228–229
  mistreatment by U.S. soldiers, 222–249
  personal responsibility, 225
  politics of delay, 224–230
  politics of outrage, 224–230
  rhetoric of democracy, 229–230
Abuse, 222–249
Adorno, Theodor, 234–248
Aesthetic modernism, 36–38
  feminism, 38
  postmodernism, 38
Aesthetic standards, cultural studies, 140–141
Afro-American feminists, 97
  Afro-American identity, 100–102
  discourse of difference, 98–99
  discourse of possibility, 98–106
  discourse of solidarity, 98–99
  politics of difference, 98–99, 103–104
Agency, 131–133, 246
  modernism, 66
Aid to Families with Dependent Children, 138
American power restructured, 3
American public education, crisis, 137–138
American state, nature, 4
Antiracism
  difference, 100
  ethnicity, 100
Antiracist pedagogy
  basic elements, 108–111

cultural production, 112
  politics of difference, 103
  power, 112
Appropriated, 201
Aronowitz, Stanley, 191
Articulation, 166
Auschwitz, 234–248
Authoritarianism, 4
  capitalism, 243–244
Authority, 131–133
  border pedagogy, 21
  crises, 11, 31
  white dominant culture, 111
Autonomy, postmodernism, 203–204

B

Binary oppositions, 15–17
  educational writers, 16–17
  Eurocentrism, 16
  logic, 15
  postcolonial theory, 13
  radical educational feminists, 16
Bloom, Allan, 127
Border crossing, 1–2
  concept, 6
Borderless world, 2
Border pedagogy, 20–21
  authority, 21
  characterized, 20
  critical democracy, 24
  demystification, 22
  difference, 25, 147–153
  discourse of teacher location, 26–27
  examples, 22–23

Border pedagogy (*continued*)
  knowledge, 21
  liberatory theory, 147–153
  politics of community, 24–26
  politics of identity, 24–26
  postmodern resistance, 108–111
  power, 21
  practice of representation, 21
  race, 110–111
  radical educational theory, 20
  representation of practice, 21–24
  struggle, 106–114
  transformation, 106–114
  uses, 20–21
  voice, 25
Borders, 1–2, 6
  concept, 2
  proliferation of policed, 2
Boston University, 188–190
Bush administration, 219
  crimes against humanity, 227–228
  education, 215
  neoliberalism, 212–213
  torture, 221–249
Bybee memo, 225–226

C
Capitalism
  authoritarianism, 241–242, 243–244
  neoliberalism, 212
Carnegie Mellon University, 188
Censorship, 188–190
Certainty, modernism, 32
Clarity
  language, 198–200
  universal standard, 17
  vs. complexity binarism, 17
Class, 196–197
  Abu Ghraib, 229–230
  language, 199–200
Class exploitation, 147–148
Cold war ideology, 138–139
Collective action, 222–223
Collective struggle, 201
Colonial binarisms, reversals, 16
Colonialism
  oppression, 11–12
  politics of difference, 19
  privilege, 11–12
Colonizing language reversals, politics of
      reversals, 15–17
Common culture, higher education, 129
Common governance, moral commitment, 123

Communicative rationality, modernity, 40–41
Community, culture, 145–146
Consent
  dialectic of ideology and pleasure, 169–174
  popular culture, 164, 169–174
Conservatives
  Abu Ghraib, 228–229
  mass culture, 162
  popular culture, 162
Contingency, neoliberalism, 211–212
Corporate public pedagogy, 4–5
Corporate sovereignty, 3
Corporations, neoliberalism, 210–211
Corporeality, 167–169
Crimes against humanity, Bush
      administration, 227–228
Critical democracy, border pedagogy, 24
Critical education, market fundamentalism,
      216
Critical pedagogy, 66–67, 195–196
  cultural power, 123–135
  cultural studies, 137–153, 140–142
  cultural workers, 71–72
  disciplinary boundaries, 69–70
  educators, 71–72
  ethics, 67–68
  history of, 123–124
  inequality, 68–69
  justice, 68–69
  lack of adequate conception, 158–180
  language, 68–69
  master narrative, 68–69
  new forms of knowledge, 69–70
  politics of voice, 73–74
  popular culture, 178–180
  postmodern feminism, 70–71
  power, 68–69, 124
  promise, 218
  resisting difference, 137–153
  sense of alternatives, 70–71
  struggle, 68–69
Critical reason, modernism, 66
Cultural demographics, 83
Cultural languages, postmodernism, 48
Cultural politics
  binary oppositions, 13
  organization, 134–135
  schooling, 128–131
  student experience, 157
Cultural power, critical pedagogy, 123–135
Cultural production
  antiracist pedagogy, 112
  minority cultures, 93

pedagogy, 142
power, 112
Cultural studies, 193
  aesthetic standards, 140–141
  critical pedagogy, 140–142
  difference, 141–142
  domination, 141, 193
  education, 139–142
  new forms of knowledge, 140
  as pedagogical practice, 139–142
  role of teachers as intellectuals, 194
Cultural turn, 1
Cultural workers, 12, 123
  critical pedagogy, 71–72
  postcolonial theory, 13
Culture, 24
  community, 145–146
  knowledge, 13
  language, 13
  pedagogy, 145–146
  politics of identity, 145–146
  postmodern feminism, 56
  power, 13
  power relations, 166–169
  site of struggle, 166–169
Culture of the Other, neocolonial modernism,
     49–52
Curricular democracy, 133–134

D
Death of the subject
  human agency, 19–20
  postcolonial discourse, 19–20
Democracy
  Eastern Europe, 65
  ethics, 65
  higher education, 129
  knowledge, 13
  language, 13
  neoliberalism, 213
  organization, 134–135
  politics, 65
  power, 13
  schooling, 128–131
  United States, 65–66
Demystification, border pedagogy, 22
Deregulation, 211, 212–213
Dialectic of ideology and pleasure
  consent, 169–174
  popular culture, 169–174
Difference
  antiracism, 100
  border pedagogy, 25, 147–153

class exploitation, 147–148
cultural studies, 141–142
ethnicity, 100
between groups, 148–149
identities, 148
infantilization, 99
patriarchy, 147–148
politics of resistance, 102
politics of voice, 144–147
racism, 147–148
radical notion, 148–151
retheorizing relationship with postmodern
     discourse, 52–53
retheorizing relationship with power, 52–53
silencing, 99
solidarity, 102
subjectivity, 148
subjugation, 99
theories, 144–145
voice, 102
Dirty Dancing, 174–178
Disciplinary boundaries, critical pedagogy,
     69–70
Discourse of difference, Afro-American
     feminists, 98–99
Discourse of empire, 246
Discourse of possibility, Afro-American
     feminists, 98–106
Discourse of solidarity, Afro-American
     feminists, 98–99
Discourse of teacher location, border
     pedagogy, 26–27
Discursive terminology, 124–125
Domestic intelligence, 4
Dominant ideology, 163–166
Domination, cultural studies, 141, 193
Dropout rate, 83–84

E
Eastern Europe, 32–34
  democracy, 65
  liberal ideology, 33–34
Economic power, 3
Education
  after Abu Ghraib, 234–249
  Bush administration, 215
  cultural politics, 128–131
  cultural studies, 139–142
  democracy, 128–131
  fascism, 236–237
  federal cuts, 214
  Holocaust, 234–248
  impact, 238–239

Education (*continued*)
  limits, 248–249
  politics of language, 142–144
  as popular struggle, 126–127
  range and scope, 238–239
  right-wing reforms, 216–218
  social reproduction, 189
  struggle over public schools, 137–138
Educational policy, instrumental rationality, 202–203
Educational theory
  ethnicity, 89–90
  race, 89–90
Educational writers, binary oppositions, 16–17
Electronic medium, postmodernism, 48
Elite culture, postmodernism, 51–52
Epistemological essentialism, modernism, 32
Equality, modernism, 32
Equal opportunity, schools, 142–143
Ethics
  crisis, 31
  critical pedagogy, 67–68
  democracy, 65
  postmodern feminism, 54–56
Ethnicity
  antiracism, 100
  difference, 100
  educational theory, 89–90
  liberal ideology, 89–90
  Otherness, 89–90
  radical essentialism, 89–90
  redefining boundaries, 83–114
Eurocentrism
  binary oppositions, 16
  radical educational feminists, 16
Eurocentric radical discourses
  modernity, 88–89
  racism, 88–89
Eurocentric writing, 12
Evangelical Christians, 204–205

F
Fascism, education, 236–237
Fear, 3
  spreading culture, 3–4
Feminism, 197, *see also* Postmodern feminism
  aesthetic modernism, 38
  oppositional and transformative politics, 14
  postmodernism, 31–32
  radical educational feminists
    binary oppositions, 16
    Eurocentrism, 16
  radical politics of democracy, 34

subject position, 14
Feminist theory, 54–64
  assumptions, 54–56
  personal is political, 57
  racism, 98–103
Formalism, 167
Foundationalism
  modernism, 32
  postmodern feminism, 56
Frankfurt School, 39, 189, 192
  reason, 161
Freedom, modernism, 32
Freire, Paulo, 191, 195–196

G
Gender, construction, 58
Gender relations, dialectical significance, 58
Geneva Conventions, 225, 226
Globalization, 2
Government, neoliberalism, 210–211, 213
Graduate students, writing, 207
Gramsci, Antonio, 163

H
Habermas, Jürgen, modernism, 39–42
Hardness, 239–240
Hegemony, pedagogical process, 163–166
Heterogeneity, 16, 87
Higher education
  common culture, 129
  democracy, 129
  personal biography, 200–202
History
  end of, 64
  postmodernism, 93–95
Holocaust, education, 234–248
Human agency
  death of the subject, 19–20
  postcolonial discourse, 19–20
Human suffering, modernism, 66
Hyper-masculinity, 240

I
Identity
  crisis, 31
  difference, 148
  individual, 48
  linguistic, 144–147
Identity politics, 149
Ideology, Culture and the Process of Schooling, 189–190
Imperialist master narrative, postmodernism, 49–52

Individual identities, postmodernism, 48
Inequality, critical pedagogy, 68–69
Infantilization, difference, 99
Instrumental rationality
  educational policy, 202–203
  modernity, 40–41
Integrity, 201

J
Judeo-Christian racist logic, 86
Justice
  critical pedagogy, 68–69
  modernism, 32

K
Knowledge
  border pedagogy, 21
  cultural studies, 140
  culture, 13
  democracy, 13
  new forms, 140
  pedagogy, 13
  producing, 125–128

L
Language, 124–125
  as central, 11
  clarity, 198–200
  class, 199–200
  critical pedagogy, 68–69
  culture, 13
  democracy, 13
  elements, 143
  negation of humanist subject, 52–54
  pedagogy, 13
  postmodern feminism, 56
  postmodernism, 52–54
  totalizing, 143–144
  unitary, 143–144
Language of difference, 12–13
Language of possibility, 144
Liberal ideology
  Eastern Europe, 33–34
  ethnicity, 89–90
  race, 87–88, 89–90
Linguistic identity, 144–147

M
Marginality, everyday experience, 110–111
Market fundamentalism, 205, 241, 242–243
  critical education, 216
  militarism, 216
  religious fundamentalism, 216

Marxist theory, popular culture, 160–161
Mass culture
  conservatives, 162
  popular culture, 160–161
Master narrative, 15–17, 92
  critical pedagogy, 68–69
  postmodernism, 49–52
Meaning, crises in, 11
Media
  global evolution, 239
  war in Iraq, 221
Mercenaries, 243
Miami University, 190–191
Militarism, 2, 240, 241
  market fundamentalism, 216
  mistreatment by U.S. soldiers, 222–249
Militarized pedagogies, 240
Minority cultures, cultural production, 93
Modernism
  agency, 66
  assumptions, 54–56
  certainty, 32
  characterized, 35
  communicative rationality, 40–41
  counter-discourse, 87
  critical reason, 66
  epistemological essentialism, 32
  equality, 32
  Eurocentric radical discourses, 88–89
  foundationalism, 32
  freedom, 32
  human suffering, 66
  instrumental rationality, 40–41
  Jürgen Habermas, 39–42
  justice, 32
  mapping the politics of, 35–39
  oppositional and transformative politics, 14
  postmodernism
    epistemological shifts, 91–92
    political shifts, 91–92
  race, refiguring boundaries, 85–89
  radical politics of democracy, 34
  subject position, 14
  vocabularies, 33–34

N
Narrative forms, 103–106
Nationalism, 241
  critique, 243–245
Negation of border cultures, postmodernism, 47–52
Negation of foundationalism, postmodernism, 44–47

Negation of humanist subject
  language, 52–54
  postmodernism, 52–54
Negation of reason, postmodernism, 44–47
Negation of totality, postmodernism, 44–47
Neocolonial modernism, culture of the Other,
    49–52
Neoconservative public philosophy, 138–139
Neoconservatives, 205–206
Neoliberalism, 5–6
  Bush administration, 212–213
  capitalism, 212
  contingency, 211–212
  corporations, 210–211
  democracy, 213
  government, 210–211, 213
  international, 211
  New World Order, 209–219
  pervasiveness, 210
  postcolonial nations, 211
  social agency, 211–212
  Social Darwinism, 212
  struggle, 211–212
  transnational corporations, 210–211
New Right, 205–206
New World Order, neoliberalism, 209–219
No Child Left Behind (NCLB) legislation, 215

O
Oppression, colonialism, 11–12
Otherness
  ethnicity, 89–90
  postmodernism, shifting boundaries, 91–97
  race, 89–90

P
Patriarchy
  crisis, 31
  difference, 147–148
Patriot Act, 4
Pedagogy
  cultural production, 142
  culture, 145–146
  importance, 194
  knowledge, 13
  language, 13
  nature, 1
  pedagogical process, hegemony, 163–166
  power, 13
  scholarship, 66–67
Penn State, 191
Personal biography
  higher education, 200–202

  power, 200–202
Personal-political relationship, 58
Personal responsibility, Abu Ghraib, 225
Photographic images, public pedagogy, 230–234
Plurality, 87
Political modernism, 38–39
Political practice, postmodern feminism, 54–56
Politics
  defined, 214
  democracy, 65
  meaning, 2
  nature, 1
Politics of agency
  postcolonial discourse, 18–20
  postmodern feminism, 61–64
Politics of community, border pedagogy, 24–
    26
Politics of delay, Abu Ghraib, 224–230
Politics of difference, 6
  Afro-American feminists, 98–99, 103–104
  antiracist pedagogy, 103
  colonialism, 19
  postmodern feminism, 61–64
Politics of identity
  border pedagogy, 24–26
  culture, 145–146
Politics of language, schooling, 142–144
Politics of location, postcolonial discourse,
    18–20
Politics of outrage, Abu Ghraib, 224–230
Politics of public pedagogy, Abu Ghraib
    photographs, 230–234
Politics of radical pedagogy, 187–207
Politics of reason, postmodern feminism, 59–
    61
Politics of representation, 194
Politics of resistance, difference, 102
Politics of reversals, colonizing language
    reversals, 15–17
Politics of struggle, postcolonial discourse, 18–
    20
Politics of totality, postmodern feminism, 59–
    61
Politics of voice
  critical pedagogy, 73–74
  difference, 144–147
Popular culture, 158–180, 194
  consent, 164, 169–174
  conservative approaches, 160–163
  critical pedagogy, 178–180
  dialectic of ideology and pleasure, 169–174
  dominant Left views, 162–163
  importance, 158

lack of adequate conception, 158–180
Marxist theory, 160–161
mass culture, 160–161
postmodernism, 51–52, 93
production of meaning, 159–160
racism, 111–112
radical approaches, 160–163
rituals, 239
theoretical concepts, 166–167
Postcolonial discourse, 11–28
death of the subject, 19–20
dislocating discourse, 12
human agency, 19–20
politics of agency, 18–20
politics of location, 18–20
politics of struggle, 18–20
relationship between margin and center, 19
Postcolonial imperialism, postmodernism, 50
Postcolonialism
oppositional and transformative politics, 14
subject position, 14
Postcolonial nations, neoliberalism, 211
Postcolonial theory
binary oppositions, 13
central theoretical assumptions, 14–15
cultural workers, 13
Post-democratic society, 3
Postmodern discourse
difference, 52–53
power, 52–53
Postmodern feminism
critical pedagogy, 70–71
culture, 56
ethical practice, 54–56
foundationalism, 56
language, 56
political practice, 54–56
politics of agency, 61–64
politics of difference, 61–64
politics of reason, 59–61
politics of totality, 59–61
power, 59
primacy of the political, 57–59
subjectivity, 56
totality, 56
Postmodernism, 31, 192–193
aesthetic modernism, 38
antagonism, 92
assumptions, 54–56
autonomy, 203–204
challenge to cultural politics of modernism,
47–52
cultural languages, 48

electronic medium, 48
elite culture, 51–52
feminism, 31–32
history, 93–95
imperialist master narrative, 49–52
individual identities, 48
language, 52–54
modernism
epistemological shifts, 91–92
political shifts, 91–92
popular culture, 51–52
postcolonial imperialism, 50
radical politics of democracy, 34
reason, 44–47
retheorizing of subjectivity, 53–54
social formations, 48
subject position, 14
totality, 44–47
universality, 44–47
uses, 43–44
using term, 43
negation of border cultures, 47–52
negation of foundationalism, 44–47
negation of humanist subject, 52–54
negation of reason, 44–47
negation of totality, 44–47
oppositional and transformative politics, 14
Otherness, shifting boundaries, 91–97
popular culture, 93
progress, 203–204
rationality, 203–204
unified, rational subject, 95
Postmodern pedagogy, 64–74
Poverty, 138
Power, 223
antiracist pedagogy, 112
border pedagogy, 21
crisis, 31
critical pedagogy, 68–69, 124
cultural production, 112
culture, 13
democracy, 13
difference, 52–53
pedagogy, 13
personal biography, 200–202
postmodern discourse, 52–53
postmodern feminism, 59
producing, 125–128
Power relations, culture, 166–169
Practice of representation, border pedagogy, 21
Primacy of the political, postmodern
feminism, 57–59
Privilege, colonialism, 11–12

Production of meaning, popular culture, 159–160
Progress, postmodernism, 203–204
Public culture of dissent, 25–26
Public good, 138–139
Public intellectuals, teachers, 133–134
Public life, impoverishment, 242–243
Public pedagogy, 4
    defined, 4
    photographic images, 230–234
    sites, 5
    uses, 5
Public schools
    American public education crisis, 137–138
    equal opportunity, 142–143
    struggle over, 137–138

Q
Quietism, 219–220

R
Race
    border pedagogy, 110–111
    educational theory, 89–90
    liberal ideology, 87–88, 89–90
    modernism, refiguring boundaries, 85–89
    Otherness, 89–90
    radical essentialism, 89–90
    redefining boundaries, 83–114
Racial slurs, 84
Racism
    difference, 147–148
    Eurocentric radical discourses, 88–89
    feminist theories, 98–103
    popular culture, 111–112
    teachers, 112–114
Radical democracy, development, 106–107
Radical educational feminists
    binary oppositions, 16
    Eurocentrism, 16
Radical educational theory, border pedagogy, 20
Radical essentialism
    ethnicity, 89–90
    race, 89–90
Radical politics of democracy
    feminism, 34
    modernism, 34
    postmodernism, 34
Rationality, postmodernism, 203–204
Reagan, Ronald, 138
Reagan revolution, 126–127
Reason, 70
    Frankfurt School, 161

postmodernism, 44–47
Relationship between personal and political, 58
Religious fundamentalism, market fundamentalism, 216
Representation of politics, 194
Representation of practice, border pedagogy, 21–24
Reproduction vs. resistance paradigm, 192
Resistance, 192, 200–201
Retheorizing of subjectivity, postmodernism, 53–54
Reversals, colonial binarisms, 16
Rhetoric of democracy, Abu Ghraib, 229–230

S
Scholarship, pedagogy, 66–67
Schools
    American public education crisis, 137–138
    equal opportunity, 142–143
    struggle over, 137–138
Self-criticism, 246
September 11th, 3, 4
Silber, John, 189–190
Silencing, difference, 99
Social agency, neoliberalism, 211–212
Social amelioration, 209
Social contract, 3
Social Darwinism, neoliberalism, 212
Social formations, postmodernism, 48
Social modernity, 36, 37–38
Social programs, 126
Social reproduction, 125
    schooling, 189
Solidarity, difference, 102
Stories, 103–106
Struggle
    border pedagogy, 106–114
    critical pedagogy, 68–69
    neoliberalism, 211–212
Student experience
    cultural politics, 157
    theory of schooling, 157
    work skills, 217
Subjectivity
    difference, 148
    postmodern feminism, 56
Subjugation, difference, 99

T
Teachers
    critical pedagogy, 71–72
    discourse of various others, 26–27
    education of, 238

public intellectuals, 133–134
  racism, 112–114
  voice, 146–147
Theory of schooling, 157
Torture, 221–249
  Bush administration, 221–249
  justification of interrogation practices, 225
  war on terror, 225–226
Totalitarianism, 64–65, 84
Totality
  postmodern feminism, 56
  postmodernism, 44–47
Transformation, border pedagogy, 106–114
Transnational corporations, neoliberalism,
    210–211
Trilateral Commission Study of 1965, 127

U
United States
  American power restructured, 3
  American public education crisis, 137–138
  democracy, 65–66
  mistreatment by U.S. soldiers, 222–249
  nature of American state, 4
Universality, postmodernism, 44–47
Universal reason, 92

Universal standard
  clarity, 17
  literacy, 17
Urban context, 190

V
Violence, 84–85, 239–240
Voice
  border pedagogy, 25
  difference, 102
  teachers, 146–147

W
War in Iraq
  media, 221
  visual representations, 221–222, 230–234
War on terrorism, 4
  torture, 225–226
Wealth, concentrated, 3
White dominant culture, authority, 111
White supremacists, 86–87
Work skills, students, 217
Writing
  graduate students, 206–207
  method, 206–207
  role of students, 207